Communications in Computer and Information Science 457

T0215201

More information about this series at http://www.springer.com/series/7899

José Cordeiro · Marten van Sinderen (Eds.)

Software Technologies

8th International Joint Conference,
ICSOFT 2013
Reykjavik, Iceland, July 29–31, 2013
Revised Selected Papers

 Springer

Editors
José Cordeiro
Polytechnic Institute of Setúbal
Setúbal
Portugal

Marten van Sinderen
Centre for Telematics and Information
  Technology
University of Twente
Enschede
The Netherlands

ISSN 1865-0929   ISSN 1865-0937   (electronic)
ISBN 978-3-662-44919-6   ISBN 978-3-662-44920-2   (eBook)
DOI 10.1007/978-3-662-44920-2

Library of Congress Control Number: 2014950815

Springer Heidelberg New York Dordrecht London

Printed on acid-free paper

Springer is part of Springer Science+Business Media (www.springer.com)

Preface

The present book includes extended and revised versions of a set of selected papers from the 8th International Joint Conference on Software Technologies (ICSOFT 2013), which was co-organized by the Reykjavik University (RU) and sponsored by the Institute for Systems and Technologies of Information, Control and Communication (INSTICC).

The purpose of ICSOFT – since 2013 designated as the International Joint Conference on Software Technologies – is to bring together researchers, engineers, and practitioners working in areas that are related to software engineering and applications. ICSOFT is composed of two co-located conferences, namely ICSOFT-PT, which specializes in new software paradigm trends, and ICSOFT-EA, which specializes in mainstream software engineering and applications.

ICSOFT 2013 received 121 paper submissions from 42 countries. To evaluate each submission, a double-blind paper evaluation method was used: each paper was reviewed by at least two internationally known experts from the ICSOFT Program Committee. In total 75 papers are published in these proceedings and presented at the conference. Of these, 9 papers were selected to be published as full papers and 66 papers were selected as short papers. The full paper acceptance ratio was 7 %, and the short paper acceptance ratio was 55 %.

The quality of the papers herewith presented stems directly from the dedicated effort of the Steering and Scientific Committees and the INSTICC team responsible for handling all secretariat and logistics' details. We are further indebted to the conference keynote speakers, who presented their valuable insights and visions regarding areas of interest to the conference. Finally, we like to thank all authors and attendants for their contribution to the conference and the scientific community.

We hope that you will find these papers interesting and consider them a helpful reference in the future when addressing any of the research areas mentioned above.

December 2013

José Cordeiro
Marten van Sinderen

Organization

Conference Chair

José Cordeiro   Polytechnic Institute of Setúbal/INSTICC, Portugal

Program Co-chairs

ICSOFT-EA

David Marca   University of Phoenix, USA

ICSOFT-PT

Marten van Sinderen   University of Twente, The Netherlands

Organizing Committee

Marina Carvalho	INSTICC, Portugal
Helder Coelhas	INSTICC, Portugal
Bruno Encarnação	INSTICC, Portugal
Ana Guerreiro	INSTICC, Portugal
André Lista	INSTICC, Portugal
Filipe Mariano	INSTICC, Portugal
Andreia Moita	INSTICC, Portugal
Raquel Pedrosa	INSTICC, Portugal
Vitor Pedrosa	INSTICC, Portugal
Cláudia Pinto	INSTICC, Portugal
Cátia Pires	INSTICC, Portugal
Susana Ribeiro	INSTICC, Portugal
Rui Rodrigues	INSTICC, Portugal
Sara Santiago	INSTICC, Portugal
André Santos	INSTICC, Portugal
Fábio Santos	INSTICC, Portugal
Mara Silva	INSTICC, Portugal
José Varela	INSTICC, Portugal
Pedro Varela	INSTICC, Portugal

ICSOFT-EA Program Committee

Hamideh Afsarmanesh, The Netherlands
Waleed Alsabhan, UAE
Kenneth Anderson, USA
Toshiaki Aoki, Japan
Gabriela Noemí Aranda, Argentina
Farhad Arbab, The Netherlands
Cyrille Artho, Japan
Bernhard Bauer, Germany
Jorge Bernardino, Portugal
Marko Boškovic, Austria
Mark van den Brand, The Netherlands
Lisa Brownsword, USA
Manfred Broy, Germany
Dumitru Burdescu, Romania
Antoni Lluís Mesquida Calafat, Spain
Gerardo Canfora, Italy
Krzysztof Cetnarowicz, Poland
Kung Chen, Taiwan
Marta Cimitile, Italy
Peter Clarke, USA
Rem Collier, Ireland
Sergiu Dascalu, USA
Steven Demurjian, USA
Juan C. Dueñas, Spain
Philippe Dugerdil, Switzerland
Fikret Ercal, USA
Maria Jose Escalona, Spain
João Faria, Portugal
Dror Feitelson, Israel
Rita Francese, Italy
Nikolaos Georgantas, France
Paola Giannini, Italy
J. Paul Gibson, France
Athula Ginige, Australia
Slimane Hammoudi, France
Markus Helfert, Ireland
Brian Henderson-Sellers, Australia
Jose Luis Arciniegas Herrera, Colombia
Jose R. Hilera, Spain
Jang-eui Hong, Korea
Milan Ignjatovic, Switzerland
Ivan Ivanov, USA
Sanpawat Kantabutra, Thailand

Dimitris Karagiannis, Austria
Foutse Khomh, Canada
Roger (Buzz) King, USA
Mieczyslaw Kokar, USA
Dimitri Konstantas, Switzerland
Martin Kropp, Switzerland
Konstantin Läufer, USA
Hua Liu, USA
Ricardo J. Machado, Portugal
Leszek Maciaszek, Poland/Australia
Ahmad Kamran Malik, Pakistan
David Marca, USA
Eda Marchetti, Italy
Katsuhisa Maruyama, Japan
Stephen Mellor, UK
Marian Cristian Mihaescu, Romania
Dimitris Mitrakos, Greece
Valérie Monfort, Tunisia
Mattia Monga, Italy
José Arturo Mora-Soto, Spain
Paolo Nesi, Italy
Jianwei Niu, USA
Rory O'Connor, Ireland
Pasi Ojala, Finland
Flavio Oquendo, France
Marcos Palacios, Spain
Vincenzo Pallotta, Switzerland
Patrizio Pelliccione, Italy
Massimiliano Di Penta, Italy
Andreas Polze, Germany
Yu Qi, USA
Anders Ravn, Denmark
Werner Retschitzegger, Austria
Claudio de la Riva, Spain
Colette Rolland, France
Gustavo Rossi, Argentina
Krzysztof Sacha, Poland
Francesca Saglietti, Germany
Sreedevi Sampath, USA
Maria-Isabel Sanchez-Segura, Spain
Luis Fernandez Sanz, Spain
Beijun Shen, China
Istvan Siket, Hungary

Harvey Siy, USA
Yeong-tae Song, USA
Cosmin Stoica Spahiu, Romania
Davide Tosi, Italy
László Vidács, Hungary
Sergiy Vilkomir, USA
Gianluigi Viscusi, Italy

Christiane Gresse von Wangenheim, Brazil
Martijn Warnier, The Netherlands
Dietmar Wikarski, Germany
Jongwook Woo, USA
Hong Zhu, UK
Elena Zucca, Italy

ICSOFT-EA Auxiliary Reviewers

Alberto De La Rosa Algarin, USA
Ana Almeida, Portugal
Dragan Bosnacki, The Netherlands
Kassidy Clark, The Netherlands
Joost Gabriels, The Netherlands
José García-Fanjul, Spain
Thibaut Le Gully, Denmark

Joseph Kaylor, USA
Fuensanta Medina-Dominguez, Spain
Deolinda Rasteiro, Portugal
Pedro Ribeiro, Portugal
Yaira Rivera, USA
Serguei Roubtsov, The Netherlands
Alexander Serebrenik, The Netherlands

ICSOFT-PT Program Committee

Markus Aleksy, Germany
Kenneth Anderson, USA
Farhad Arbab, The Netherlands
Cyrille Artho, Japan
Colin Atkinson, Germany
Fevzi Belli, Germany
Jorge Bernardino, Portugal
Marko Boškovic, Austria
Mark van den Brand, The Netherlands
Dumitru Burdescu, Romania
Fergal Mc Caffery, Ireland
Olivier Camp, Vietnam
Gerardo Canfora, Italy
Mauro Caporuscio, Italy
Krzysztof Cetnarowicz, Poland
Kung Chen, Taiwan
Marta Cimitile, Italy
Peter Clarke, USA
Sergiu Dascalu, USA
Steven Demurjian, USA

Juan C. Dueñas, Spain
Jürgen Ebert, Germany
Fikret Ercal, USA
Maria Jose Escalona, Spain
João Faria, Portugal
Cléver Ricardo Guareis de Farias, Brazil
Jose M. Garrido, USA
Paola Giannini, Italy
J. Paul Gibson, France
Athula Ginige, Australia
Cesar Gonzalez-Perez, Spain
Gregor Grambow, Germany
Slimane Hammoudi, France
Christian Heinlein, Germany
Markus Helfert, Ireland
Brian Henderson-Sellers, Australia
Jose Luis Arciniegas Herrera, Colombia
Jose R. Hilera, Spain
Jang-eui Hong, Korea
Milan Ignjatovic, Switzerland

Ivan Ivanov, USA
Edson A. Oliveira Junior, Brazil
Sanpawat Kantabutra, Thailand
Bill Karakostas, UK
Mieczyslaw Kokar, USA
Martin Kropp, Switzerland
Konstantin Läufer, USA
Bernardi Mario Luca, Italy
Ricardo J. Machado, Portugal
Leszek Maciaszek, Poland/Australia
Ahmad Kamran Malik, Pakistan
David Marca, USA
Eda Marchetti, Italy
Tommaso Mazza, Italy
Stephen Mellor, UK
Marian Cristian Mihaescu, Romania
Dimitris Mitrakos, Greece
Valérie Monfort, Tunisia
Mattia Monga, Italy
José Arturo Mora-Soto, Spain
Paolo Nesi, Italy
Jianwei Niu, USA
Rory O'Connor, Ireland
Pasi Ojala, Finland

Marcos Palacios, Spain
Patrizio Pelliccione, Italy
Massimiliano Di Penta, Italy
Andreas Polze, Germany
Anders Ravn, Denmark
Werner Retschitzegger, Austria
Claudio de la Riva, Spain
Colette Rolland, France
Gustavo Rossi, Argentina
Gunter Saake, Germany
Krzysztof Sacha, Poland
Francesca Saglietti, Germany
Harvey Siy, USA
Yeong-tae Song, USA
Cosmin Stoica Spahiu, Romania
Davide Tosi, Italy
Gianluigi Viscusi, Italy
Christiane Gresse von Wangenheim, Brazil
Martijn Warnier, The Netherlands
Jongwook Woo, USA
Haiping Xu, USA
Jinhui Yao, Australia
Hong Zhu, UK
Elena Zucca, Italy

ICSOFT-PT Auxiliary Reviewers

Dragan Bosnacki, The Netherlands
Alexandre Braganca, Portugal
Joost Gabriels, The Netherlands
Thibaut Le Gully, Denmark

Rishi Kanth, USA
Ramtin Khosravi, Iran
Michel Oey, The Netherlands
Alexander Serebrenik, The Netherlands

Invited Speakers

François E. Cellier
Alexander Smirnov
Armin Größlinger
Claes Wohlin

ETH Zürich, Switzerland
SPIIRAS, Russian Academy of Sciences, Russia
University of Passau, Germany
Blekinge Institute of Technology, Sweden

Contents

Software Paradigm Trends

Software Engineering and Applications

Strategies for Scheduling Risk Mitigation in Software Project Management

Peng Zhou[1] and Hareton K.N. Leung[2(✉)]

[1] School of Computer, Dongguan University of Technology, Dongguan, China
[2] Department of Computing, The Hong Kong Polytechnic University,
Hung Hom, Hong Kong
hareton.leung@polyu.edu.hk

Abstract. The adoption of risk management practices can help to increase the success rate of software project. As an essential process of risk management, risk mitigation aims to reduce or eliminate risks. To make the best use of resources, a scheduling strategy for risk mitigation is needed to determine the risks to be mitigated and when to mitigate them. Both PMI risk management framework and IEEE standard for software project risk management point out that time elements should be considered in risk mitigation. However, the traditionally used strategy for scheduling risk mitigation does not consider time elements. In this paper, we formally define scheduling strategy for risk mitigation, identify new scheduling strategies with due consideration of time elements, and compare their performance by applying stochastic simulation.

Keywords: Scheduling strategy · Risk mitigation · Time element · Risk management · Software project management

1 Introduction

Taking careful measures to manage the risks involved in projects is a key contributor to the success of these projects [9]. The positive correlation between effective risk management and project success was emphasized in [5, 13, 17]. The adoption of risk management practices can help to increase the success rate of project and then enhance the competitiveness of organizations.

Risk mitigation is essential for risk management because it aims to reduce or eliminate risks. To make the best use of resources, a scheduling strategy for risk mitigation is needed to determine the risks to be mitigated and when to mitigate them. The generally used strategy for scheduling risk mitigation is "risk value first strategy". That is, risks are prioritized for response action based on their risk values. For example, we can first use Risk Exposure (RE) [2] to compute the risk value. $RE = P \times I$, where P is the probability of risk occurrence and I is the impact of the risk if it occurs. Then risks are scheduled for mitigation according to their risk values so that risks with higher risk values will be treated earlier. However this strategy does not consider time elements of risk. Managing time elements of risk is necessary for an effective risk management. Both Project Management Institute (PMI) risk management framework [14]

© Springer-Verlag Berlin Heidelberg 2014
J. Cordeiro and M. van Sinderen (Eds.): ICSOFT 2013, CCIS 457, pp. 3–23, 2014.
DOI: 10.1007/978-3-662-44920-2_1

and the IEEE standard for software project risk management [7] point out that time elements should be considered in risk mitigation.

A simple example shown in Fig. 1 illustrates the necessity of considering time elements in risk mitigation. In Fig. 1, $R_i(P_i, I_i)$ represents risk R_i with probability P_i and impact I_i. In this example, we suppose that: (1) There are three risks which would occur during design, coding and testing phase of a hypothetical software development project respectively. (2) We can only treat one risk at a time and it takes the same amount of time to mitigate each risk. (3) The mitigation of each risk eliminates the risk at the end of the mitigation.

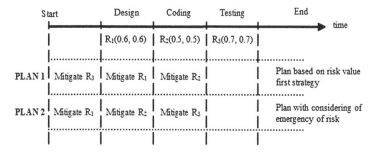

Fig. 1. An example showing the necessity of managing time elements.

PLAN 1 applies the risk value first strategy to schedule the risk mitigation. Since R_3 has the highest risk value and R_2 has the lowest risk value, R_3 is treated first and R_2 is treated at last. Then, R_3 will never occur (risk mitigation eliminates R_3 before it would occur) while R_1 and R_2 would occur during the time period of their risk mitigation. PLAN 2 considers the emergency of risk that is ignored by PLAN 1. All risks will be eliminated before they would occur according to PLAN 2. Thus, it is better than PLAN 1.

Although the PMI framework and the IEEE standard point out the necessity of managing time elements in risk mitigation, there is a lack of principles and guidelines on how to schedule risk mitigation with due consideration of time elements.

This paper aims to formally define scheduling strategy for risk mitigation, identify new scheduling, and focus on following research questions:

1. Is the traditionally used strategy, risk value first strategy, a good choice for scheduling risk mitigation?
2. Is there a best scheduling strategy for most projects?
3. Is there a worst scheduling strategy for most projects?

According to [19], stochastic simulation is a better choice than other methods to compare the performance of different scheduling strategies. A stochastic simulation model (SMRMP) [21] with due consideration of time elements of risk will be used in our study to obtain meaningful results.

The paper is organized as follows. We briefly review the risk management process and the stochastic simulation model in Sect. 2. In Sect. 3, we formally define scheduling strategy for risk mitigation and identify new scheduling strategies. Section 4 presents the methodology of our paper. We compare the performance of identified strategies and answer the research questions in Sect. 5. At last, we conclude our study and outline the future work in Sect. 6.

2 Literature Review

2.1 Project Risk

Risk is a potential event that would impact the project. It has two basic attributes, risk probability (P) and risk impact (I). Accordingly, risk is a function of P and I [6]. We use Risk Value (RV) to represent the measurement of risk. So

$$RV = f(P, I) \tag{1}$$

For a given project, the project risk set and its risks are defined as follows.

Definition 1. Given a project Z, it includes a set of identified n risks at time t, $RS(Z, t) = \{R_1, R_2, \dots R_n\}$.

The size of $RS(Z, t)$, $|RS(Z, t)|$ may change as time elapses since new risks may be identified and added into $RS(Z, t)$ and expired risks will be eliminated from $RS(Z, t)$.

Definition 2. For any $R_i \in RS(Z, t)$, and $1 \le i \le |RS(Z, t)|$, $R_i(P_i, I_i)$ represents risk R_i with probability P_i and impact I_i.

2.2 Risk Management Process

Risk management aims to identify risks and take actions to reduce or eliminate their probability and/or impact so that the project is kept from being damaged by risks. There are many paradigms, models and standards to guide the risk management practice, such as risk management paradigm developed by Software Engineering Institute [18], PMI framework [14], IEEE Std 1540 [7], AS NZS 4360 [1] and ISO 31000 [8]. Although these models and standards address the risk management processes in different manners, they can be mapped to each other to a large extent. Generally, these paradigms, models and standards follow the cyclic process shown in Fig. 2.

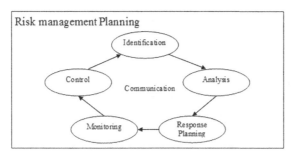

Fig. 2. Cyclic process of risk management.

Risk Management Planning defines how to conduct risk management practices throughout the project. It is important to provide adequate resources and time and establish both internal and external context of risk management.

Risk identification aims to identify risks that would affect the project objectives and document their characteristics. Current risk identification methods include examining the major areas of the project, collecting information from personnel, learning from past and applying analytical tools [10, 14, 16]. Among these proposed approaches, the taxonomy developed by [4] is more popular than others.

The risk analysis aims to understand the identified risks and provide data to assist in managing them. Generally, risk analysis includes: (1) estimate the probability, impact, and the expected timing of the risk [7]; (2) analyze risks and prioritize them. Recently, risk analysis is expanded with the consideration of risk dependency [11].

There are four different options that can be used to treat a risk. They are avoid, transfer, mitigate and accept [1, 14]. Risk response planning aims to identifying possible options to reduce or eliminate risks, assessing these options and making a plan to implement risk mitigation activities. To make the best use of resources, a scheduling strategy is used to determine the risks to be mitigated and when to mitigate them. The generally used strategy for scheduling risk mitigation is "risk value first strategy".

Risk monitoring and control aims to tracking the change of all identified risks and identifying new risks, monitoring residual risks, and evaluating risk response effectiveness and performance of risk management [14].

2.3   Time Elements in Risk Management

In risk management, time elements exist at both the project level and risk level. Time elements of risk management (project-level) are different times that directly associate with the process of risk management. Time elements of risk (risk-level) are different times that directly associate with the risk from its first identification to its expiration.

All well accepted risk management paradigms, frameworks and standards clearly define the lifecycle of risk management. In practice, for each project, we can clearly define the time duration for all five risk management processes and the time for periodical risk review. However, there is no explicit model for many time elements of individual risk.

"IEEE Standard for Software Life Cycle Processes - Risk Management" [7] points out that practitioners should estimate the expected timing of the risk and document it. Then, practitioners need to schedule the treatment of each risk accordingly. PMI risk management model [14] also points out that the risk mitigation should be scheduled with due consideration of the expected occurrence time of the risk. However, both the PMI framework and the IEEE standard lack principles and guidelines on how to schedule risk mitigation with due consideration of many key times of risk. Consequently, these time elements are rarely used in practice. This may lead to improper risk mitigation activities and an ineffective risk management.

Very few studies have explicitly modeled the time elements of risk. Leung proposed variants of risk, presented a model of risk lifecycle, and gave the relationship between the risk variants by explicit consideration of the occurrence time of risk [12].

Zhou and Leung identified two key time periods of individual risk for an effective risk management [20]. These two time periods are time period of risk occurrence and risk mitigation. The time period of occurrence is the duration that a risk would occur. The time period of mitigation is the duration for executing planned mitigation activity of a risk.

Zhou and Leung also proposed a stochastic simulation model of risk management process with due consideration of time elements of risks [21]. This simulation model can be used for many risk management issues, such as understanding of risk management process, predicting risk management outcome, and making informed risk management decision. This model will be presented in next section.

2.4   A Stochastic Simulation Model

Figure 3 shows the "Simulation Model of Risk Management Process" (SMRMP) proposed in [21].

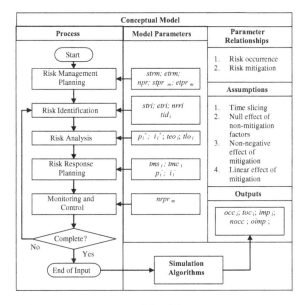

Fig. 3. Conceptual model for risk management process.

Based on a two levels approach, the inputs and outputs of the model have been identified [21]. The first level is the risk level which focuses on a single risk. The second level is the project level which considers all risks of the whole project. Some natural relationships between the parameters are identified. Algorithms are also developed to compute output of the simulation from the input parameters. Besides that, the model has four assumptions. This model was evaluated to be valid [21] by applying the paradigm proposed by Sargent [15].

Tables 1 and 2 summarize the input parameters and outputs of SMRMP respectively.

The model assumptions are listed as follows.

1. Time slicing. For a given project Z, the time period of its risk management is equally divided into L time intervals with a set of L + 1 time points, $TP(Z) = \{0, 1, 2, \ldots L\}$. All management activities start at one of these time points and take integral multiple of intervals.
2. Null effect of non-mitigation factors. The factors not related to risk mitigation,
3. such as change of external and internal risk management environments, will not change the probability and impact of a risk.
4. Non-negative effect of mitigation. Risk mitigation will not increase the probability and impact of a risk. It is reasonable since risk mitigation should not increase the risk and is often effective in reducing the risk.
5. Linear effect of mitigation. The probability and impact of a risk will linearly decrease during its mitigation period from p_i^+ to p_i^- and from i_i^+ to i_i^- respectively.

Model users should go through the whole process of risk management to determine the values of model parameters based on the parameter relationships and model assumptions. After inputting all model parameters, users can run the simulation for each risk, and get outputs which can help to predict the expected impact on projects.

Table 1. Parameters of SMRMP [21].

No	Notation	Value	Level	Description
1	$strm$	0^{*1}	Project-level	Start time of risk management
2	$etrm$	L^{*1}	Project-level	End time of risk management
3	$stri$	>0	Project-level	Start time of the risk identification
4	$etri$	$> stri > 0$	Project-level	End time of the risk identification
5	$nrri$	≥ 0	Project-level	Number of risks identified in risk identification
6	npr	>0	Project-level	Number of periodical reviews
7	$stpr_m$	>0	Project-level	Start time of the mth periodical review
8	$etpr_m$	$>stpr_m$	Project-level	End time of the mth periodical review
9	$nrpr_m$	≥ 0	Project-level	Number of risks identified in the mth periodical review
10	tid_i	>0	Risk-level	The time that R_i is identified
11	teo_i	>0	Risk-level	Earliest time of occurrence of R_i
12	tlo_i	$>teo_i > 0$	Risk-level	Latest time of occurrence of R_i
13	p_i^+	$\in (0, 1)$	Risk-level	Probability of R_i when it is first identified
14	i_i^+	$\in (0, 1]$	Risk-level	Impact of R_i when it is first identified
15	tms_i	$\geq tid_i > 0$	Risk-level	Mitigation start time of R_i
16	tmc_i	$\in (tms_i, tlo_i]$	Risk-level	Mitigation close time of R_i
17	p_i^-	$\in [0, 1)$	Risk-level	Expected probability of R_i after the mitigation
18	i_i^-	$\in [0,1]$	Risk-level	Expected impact of R_i after the mitigation

*1 suppose the risk management starts at time 0 and ends at time L

Table 2. Outputs of SMRMP [21].

No	Notation	Value	Level	Description
1	occ_i	Yes/No	Risk-level	Represent whether R_i occurs or not
2	toc_i	$\in (teo_i, tlo_i]$	Risk-level	Occurrence time of R_i if it occurs
3	imp_i	>0	Risk-level	Impact of R_i if it occurs at toc_i
4	$nocc$	≥ 0	Project-level	Number of all occurred risks
5	$oimp$	≥ 0	Project-level	Overall impact of all risks

Since the probability and impact of a risk may change with time, EOR and EAI are introduced to measure the expected occurrence rate and expected impact during $(teo_i, tlo_i]$ [21]. Since a risk cannot be repeated in real-life projects, IIR is introduced to facilitate the computation of EOR and EAI [21].

Definition 3. Independent and Identical Risks (IIR): If R_1 and R_2 are independent risks and have the exactly same values in all risk-level parameters, then they are independent and identical risks (IIR).

Definition 4. Suppose there are N IIRs, if M risks occurred among all N risks when N is sufficiently large, then EOR = M/N.

Definition 5. Expected Actual Impact (EAI): Suppose there are N IIRs, if M risks occurred among all N risks when N is sufficiently large, then $EAI = \sum_M imp_i/N$, where $\sum_M imp_i$ the total impact of M occurred risks.

3   Scheduling Strategy for Risk Mitigation

3.1   Definition of Scheduling Strategy

To facilitate the definition of scheduling strategy for risk mitigation, we first define the set of risks need to be treated at time t and the resource assigned for risk mitigation.

Definition 6. Given a risk set $TRS(Z, t)$ and $TRS(Z, t) \subseteq RS(Z, t)$, $\forall R_j \in TRS(Z, t)$, R_j is a risk which does not have a mitigation plan and waiting for treatment, and $\forall R_k \in RS(Z, t)$ - $TRS(Z, t)$, R_k is a risk which is acceptable and need not to be treated or has been scheduled for mitigation.

We abstract the human resource for risk mitigation as a set of processors which have different capabilities to mitigate risk.

Definition 7. For a given project Z, a set of k processors at time t, $ProS(Z, t) = \{processor_i \mid 0 < i \leq k\}$, are available for risk mitigation. $\forall processor_i \in ProS(Z,t)$, CAP $(processor_i) = c_i$, where $CAP(processor_i)$ is the capability of $processor_i$ for risk treatment and c_i is a real number greater than 0.

The capability of a processor can be considered as 1 if it represents the capability of a team member that has normal capability for risk mitigation. Then the capabilities of all processors can be estimated according to capabilities of different team members.

For R_i assigned to *processor$_j$* $(0 < j \leq k)$,

$$tmc_i - tms_i = Effort_i/c_j \tag{2}$$

where *Effort$_i$* is the estimated effort for the treatment of R_i.

Note that the processor is assumed to process one risk at a time. However, it is possible that a team member may treat two (or more) different risks at the same time in practice. In this case, this team member can be abstracted as two (or more) processors with capability equal to the capability of the team member. From this point of view, we can consider each processor can process one risk at a time.

For convenient sake, in this study, we assume all processors in *ProS(Z, t)* have the same capability equal to 1, and each processor processes one risk at a time. Then the effort of mitigating a risk can be estimated according to the capability of the processor and the time needed to mitigate the risk. Note that the time unit should be consistent with the time unit adopted in the simulation model.

The mitigation scheduling of a project Z aims to allocate a set of m risks ($|TRS(Z, t)| = m$) to a set of k processors ($|ProS(Z, t)| = k$), to minimize the expected impact on Z. Suppose there is only one processor ($k = 1$), then there are $m!$ different sequences to allocate risks to this single processor. We can choose the schedule with the minimal expected impact among all $m!$ different sequences. However, this approach is unreasonable in practice because the time for finding the best option from $m!$ options is non-polynomial. The situation become more complicated when there are more processors ($k > 1$). Thus there is a need to develop scheduling strategies to determine the order for treating the risks in *TRS(Z, t)*.

Based on *TRS(Z, t)* and *ProS(Z, t)*, we define scheduling strategy for risk mitigation as follows.

Definition 8. Scheduling strategy for risk mitigation is an algorithm that takes *TRS(Z, t)* and *ProS(Z, t)* as input and generates a scheduled risk mitigation plan as its output. For each $R_i \in TRS(Z, t)$, it decides whether R_i is to be mitigated, and then chooses *processor$_j$* $\in ProS(Z, t)$ to mitigate R_i during a selected time period.

Since risk mitigation aims to prevent the project from impacted by the risks, the performance of a scheduling strategy S can be measured by the expected impact of all risks in *TRS(Z, t)*, *EAI(S/TRS(Z,t))*, after S has been applied to *TRS(Z, t)*. *EAI(S/TRS(Z,t))* is defined as

Definition 9. Let *EAI(S/TRS(Z,t))* be the expected impact of all risks in *TRS(**Z**, t)* after a scheduling strategy S has been applied to *TRS(**Z**, t)*.

$$EAI(S|TRS(Z,t)) = \sum_{R \in TRS(Z,t)} EAI(R_i) \tag{3}$$

where *EAI(R$_i$)* is EAI of R$_i$. *EAI(S|TRS(Z,t))* ranges in $(0, |TRS(Z, t)|)$ because EAI ranges in $(0, 1)$.

A higher value of $EAI(S/TRS(Z,t))$ means a higher expected impact on the project and indicates a lower performance of S. Thus we define the performance of a scheduling strategy as follows.

Definition 10. Let $Perf(S)$ represents the performance of a scheduling strategy S applied to the risk set $TRS(Z, t)$. For two scheduling strategies S_i and S_j,

$$Perf(S_i) > Perf(S_j) \text{ when } EAI(S_i|TRS(Z,t)) < EAI(S_j|TRS(Z,t));$$
$$Perf(S_i) = Perf(S_j) \text{ when } EAI(S_i|TRS(Z,t)) = EAI(S_j|TRS(Z,t));$$
$$Perf(S_i) < Perf(S_j) \text{ when } EAI(S_i|TRS(Z,t)) > EAI(S_j|TRS(Z,t)).$$

3.2   New Scheduling Strategies

Traditionally, risk value first strategy (V strategy) is used in practice. However, it does not consider the time elements of risk. Besides the V strategy, we propose several new strategies.

1. Emergency first strategy (E strategy). Emergency first strategy first orders all risks according to their T_{eo}, then risks with an earlier T_{eo} will be treated earlier. For example, suppose $teo_i = 30$ and $teo_j = 50$ are earliest occurrence time of R_i and R_j respectively, then R_i will be mitigated first. The principle behind this strategy is that we should mitigate the risk before it would occur. The best case of applying this strategy is all risks are mitigated before they would occur. No risk will occur if all mitigations are successful in eliminating the risks. The example shown in Fig. 1 is a good example of applying this strategy.
2. Lowest effort first strategy (L strategy). Lowest effort first strategy first orders all risks according to the efforts needed for mitigating the risk, then risks requiring a lower effort will be treated earlier. For example, suppose 40 Man-hour and 80 Man-hour are needed effort to mitigate R_i and R_j respectively, then R_i will be mitigated first. The principle behind this strategy is that we can mitigate more risks within the same time period because mitigating a risk with lower effort will use less time. Consequently, we may prevent more risks from occurring and this leads to a low overall impact of the project.
3. Combined strategies. We consider applying combination of V, E and L strategies at the same time by constructing some combined strategies. For example, we can combine the risk value first strategy and emergency first strategy together. The resulting strategy first prioritizes all risks based on their risk value and T_{eo} respectively, producing two risk lists. For risk R_i, a score is calculated by combining its priority values from these two risk lists. Using the calculated scores, all risks can be finally prioritized and then scheduled so that a risk with a higher priority will be treated earlier.

As there are three basic strategies, V strategy, E strategy and L strategy, we can create four combined strategies, VE strategy (combined V with E), VL strategy (combined V with L), EL strategy (combined E with L) and VEL strategy (combined all three basic strategies). We assign weights, w_1, w_2 and w_3, to the priority according to the three basic strategies. In this study, we apply equal weights to these three strategies as there are no prior studies showing that one basic strategy is better than another. The combined strategy is equivalent to VE Strategy when $w_1 = w_2$ and $w_3 = 0$, VL Strategy when $w_1 = w_3$ and $w_2 = 0$, EL Strategy when $w_2 = w_3$ and $w_1 = 0$ and VEL Strategy when $w_1 = w_2 = w_3$. We can create more combined strategies by using unequal weights in the future.

Table 3 shows examples of applying different strategies to schedule risk mitigation. The number shown under basic strategies is the priority that the risk is scheduled (a lower value indicates a higher priority). For example, R_1 is scheduled first, and then followed by R_2, R_3 and R_4 when applying V strategy. The score value under combined strategies is calculated by adding the priority of corresponding basic strategies. For example, for VE strategy, the score of the 5th column is the result of adding the priority in V strategy (the 2nd column) and that in E strategy (the 3rd column). Then all risks are prioritized based on their scores. Note that if two or more risks have the same score, then they can be prioritized in any order. Since we have to choose one order to mitigate the risks, in our study, the risk with a smaller index will get a higher priority when several risks have the same score. For example, R_2 and R_3 have the same score of 4 under VL strategy. Then R_2 is assigned a higher priority than R_3 and will be mitigated earlier than R_3.

Table 3. Examples of mitigation strategies.

Risk	Basic strategy			Combined strategy							
	V	E	L	VE		VL		EL		VEL	
	Pri	Pri	Pri	Sco	Pri	Sco	Pri	Sco	Pri	Sco	Pri
R_1	1	2	4	3	1	5	3	6	3	7	2
R_2	2	3	2	5	3	4	1	5	2	7	3
R_3	3	1	1	4	2	4	2	2	1	5	1
R_4	4	4	3	8	4	7	4	7	4	11	4

We next formally define above scheduling strategies. Suppose $TRS(Z,t) = \{R_1, R_2, \dots R_n\}$. Let $Rank(R_i/RL)$ be the rank of R_i in the prioritized risk list (RL) of n risks, with rank of 1 indicating the first risk of RL and rank of n indicating the last risk of RL. That is a lower rank value indicates a higher priority.

Recall that RV_i, teo_i and $Effort_i$ ($1 \leq i \leq N$) represent the risk value, earliest time of occurrence and estimated mitigation effort of R_i respectively. Algorithms 1, 2 and 3 shows three different ways to prioritize $TRS(Z, t)$.

Algorithm 1 produces a risk list such that a risk with a higher risk value will have a higher priority.

Algorithm 1. Prioritization_RV($TRS(Z, t)$)

1. Prioritize risks in $TRS(Z, t)$ to get a risk list RL
   such that for any R_i and R_j ($1 \bullet i < j \bullet N$) $\in$ $TRS(Z, t)$,
   IF $RV_i \bullet RVj$ **THEN** $Rank(R_i|RL) < Rank(R_j|RL)$;
   IF $RV_i < RV_j$ **THEN** $Rank(R_i|RL) > Rank(R_j|RL)$;
2. **Return** RL.

As mentioned earlier, two risks with the same score will be prioritized according to their risk indexes. Thus, in Algorithm 1, R_i has a higher priority than R_j when $RV_i = RV_j$ and $1 \le i < j \le N$. Similarly, in Algorithms 2, 3, and 9, if two risks have the same T_{eo}, estimated mitigation effort, and computed score respectively, then they will be prioritized according to their risk indexes too.

Algorithm 2 produces a risk list such that a risk with an earlier T_{eo} will have a higher priority.

Algorithm 2. Prioritization_TEO($TRS(Z, t)$)

1. Prioritize risks in $TRS(Z, t)$ to get a risk list RL
   such that for any R_i and R_j ($1 \bullet i < j \bullet N$) $\in$ $TRS(Z, t)$,
   IF $teo_i \bullet teo_j$ **THEN** $Rank(R_i|RL) < Rank(R_j|RL)$;
   IF $teo_i > teo_j$ **THEN** $Rank(R_i|RL) > Rank(R_j|RL)$;
2. **Return** RL.

Algorithm 3 produces a risk list such that a risk with a smaller mitigation effort will have a higher priority.

Algorithm 3. Prioritization_EFFORT($TRS(Z, t)$)

1. Prioritize risks in $TRS(Z, t)$ to get a risk list RL
   such that for any R_i and R_j ($1 \bullet i < j \bullet N$) $\in$ $TRS(Z, t)$,
   IF $Effort_i \bullet Effort_j$ **THEN** $Rank(R_i|RL) < Rank(R_j|RL)$;
   IF $Effort_i > Effort_j$ **THEN** $Rank(R_i|RL) > Rank(R_j|RL)$;
2. **Return** RL.

V strategy is defined as Algorithm 4.

Algorithm 4. V strategy($TRS(Z, t)$, $ProS(Z, t)$)

1. RL = Prioritization_RV($TRS(Z, t)$).
2. Allocation(RL, $ProS(Z, t)$).

Allocation(RL, $ProS(Z, t)$) is shown as Algorithm 5, which allocates the prioritized risks to the processors in $ProS(Z, t)$ such that the risk with a higher priority will be allocated first.

Algorithm 5. Allocation(RL, $ProS$(Z, t))

1. Get the first risk R_i in the prioritized risk list RL.
2. Find a set of processors, $ProS_i \subseteq ProS$(Z, t), which can process R_i.
3. **IF** $ProS_i$ is not empty, **THEN** select a *processor$_j$* which is the first one that completes its currently assigned work in $ProS_i$, and assign R_i to *processor$_j$*.
4. Remove R_i from RL.
5. **IF** RL is not empty, **THEN** go to step 1.

Note that a processor is not able to process risk R_i if it cannot complete the mitigation of R_i before its latest time of occurrence. For example, suppose a processor completes its currently assigned work at $t = 50$. If $tlo_i = 40$, then the processor is not able to process R_i since the mitigation after the latest time of occurrence does not make sense. Another example is that suppose $tlo_i = 60$ and the time length for mitigating R_i is 20. In this case, if the mitigation is started at $t = 50$, the processor cannot complete the mitigation before tlo_i (actually it completes the mitigation at $t = 50 + 20 = 70$).

There may exist more than one processor that can process risk R_i at the same time. Then, we should select the first processor that completes its work because the risk in RL should be treated as early as possible. For example, assume some risks have been assigned to *processor$_1$* and *processor$_2$*, *processor$_1$* will complete its currently assigned works at $t = 20$ and *processor$_2$* will complete its currently assigned works at $t = 40$. Suppose teo_i, tlo_i and $Effort_i$ are 40, 60 and 10 respectively. Then, both *processor$_1$* and *processor$_2$* can process R_i because they can complete the mitigation of R_i (at t = 30 and t = 50 respectively) before $tlo_i = 60$. In this case, we should select *processor$_1$* to mitigate R_i because it completes its currently assigned work earlier (at $t = 20$) and consequently the mitigation of R_i can be started earlier if it is assigned to *processor$_1$*.

Also, there may not exist any processors that can process risk R_i if they are all busy. In this case, R_i is removed from RL directly.

E strategy and L strategy are defined as Algorithms 6 and 7 respectively.

Algorithm 6. E strategy(TRS(Z, t), $ProS$(Z, t))

1. RL = Prioritization_TEO(TRS(Z, t)).
2. Allocation(RL, $ProS$(Z, t)).

Algorithm 7. L strategy(TRS(Z, t), $ProS$(Z, t))

1. RL = Prioritization_EFFORT(TRS(Z, t)).
2. Allocation(RL, $ProS$(Z, t)).

Algorithm 8 defines VE strategy.

Algorithm 8. VE strategy(TRS(Z, t), $ProS$(Z, t))

1. RL_1 = Prioritization_RV(TRS(Z, t)).
2. RL_2 = Prioritization_TEO(TRS(Z, t)).
3. RL= CombinedRL(RL_1, RL_2).
4. Allocation(RL, $ProS$(Z, t)).

CombinedRL(RL_1, RL_2,…, RL_l) is shown as Algorithm 9, which produces a risk list such that the risk with a lower score (which is computed by its rank from input risk lists, RL_1, RL_2,…, RL_l) will have a higher priority.

Algorithm 9. CombinedRL(RL_1, RL_2,…, RL_l)

1. Prioritize risks in $TRS(Z, t)$ to get a risk list RL such that for any R_i and R_j ($1 \bullet i<j \bullet N) \in TRS(Z, t)$,
   IF $Rank(R_i/RL_1) + Rank(R_i/RL_2) +…+ Rank(R_i/RL_l) \bullet$ $Rank(R_j/RL_1) + Rank(R_j/RL_2) +…+ Rank(R_j/RL_l)$
   THEN $Rank(R_i/RL) < Rank(R_j/RL)$;
   IF $Rank(R_i/RL_1) + Rank(R_i/RL_2) +…+ Rank(R_i/RL_l) >$ $Rank(R_j/RL_1) + Rank(R_j/RL_2) +…+ Rank(R_j/RL_l)$
   THEN $Rank(R_i/RL) > Rank(R_j/RL)$;
2. **Return** RL.

VL, EL and VEL strategies can be implemented similarly to Algorithm 8.

4 Methodology

4.1 Simulation and SMRMP

To compare the performance of different scheduling strategies on a specific project, we apply stochastic simulation to obtain meaningful results.

The reasons for applying stochastic simulation in our study are: (1) We can obtain enough data for analysis at the project level. There is no public data available for use. Since current risk management practices do not consider many time elements of risk, we cannot get the relevant data from past projects. (2) We can do comparison study easily. Even if we have enough time and resource to collect data from real projects, it would be hard to do comparison study. To compare two different approaches, we should apply them in the same context. However, we cannot apply two incompatible risk management practices in the same project as each real project is a one-time process that cannot be repeated. Also, it is difficult to find two similar projects with similar risk sets and are managed by risk management teams with similar experience. So, it is difficult to perform comparison study and analyze the performance of different risk management practices using real projects. However, we can easily run any number of simulations on the same project, and compare the results of applying different risk management practices. (3) We can get more meaningful results. Since projects are not repeatable and risks involve uncertainties, we cannot draw a conclusion that one practice is better than another based on a small number of cases. For example, the result of performing Practice-A is better than Practice-B when we apply them to two similar projects. However, it does not mean that Practice-A is better than Practice-B since we may be "lucky" (risks did not occur even if they have a high chance to occur) when we perform Practice-A, while we are "unlucky" (risks occurred even if they have a low chance to occur) when we perform Practice-B. We cannot eliminate this uncertainty factor when we cannot repeat a project many times. On the contrary, we can run many different simulations of the same project and use the average result for the comparison of different practices, giving a more meaningful result.

Given above advantages of simulation, we use a stochastic simulation model to analyze the influences of introduced time elements on risk management practices. In particular, we use SMRMP in our study to compare the performance of applying different scheduling strategies.

4.2   Measurement of Strategy Performance

Let $imp(R)$ denotes the impact of a given risk R in one simulation. $\sum_{i=1}^{N} imp(R)_i/N$ is the average impact of R in N simulations, where $imp(R)_i$ is the impact of R in the ith simulation $(1 < i \leq N)$. According to [21], if N is sufficiently large, then $\sum_{i=1}^{N} imp(R)_i/N$ follows a normal distribution with mean EAI(R). That is $\sum_{i=1}^{N} imp(R)_i/N$ can be used to approximate EAI(R) when N is sufficiently large. Let $imp(S|TRS(Z,t))$ denotes the total impact of all risks of $TRS(Z,t)$ in one simulation with strategy S. Then, $\sum_{i=1}^{N} imp(S|TRS(Z,t))_i/N$ can be used to approximate $EAI(S|TRS(Z, t))$ when N is sufficiently large. $imp(S|TRS(Z,t))_i$ is the total impact of all risks of $TRS(Z, t)$ in the ith simulation $(1 < i \leq N)$. For example, after applying V strategy to $TRS(Z,t)$ and running simulation for 1000 times, the average $imp(V|TRS(Z,t))$ from these simulations can be used to measure the performance of V strategy.

Definition 11. Let average overall impact, AVEOI(S) denotes the average $imp(S/TRS(Z,t))$ of running a large number (N) of simulations on $TRS(Z,t)$ with strategy S. AVEOI(S) is computed as

$$AVEOI(S) = \sum_{i-1}^{N} imp(S|TRS(Z,t))_i/N \qquad (4)$$

If all risks of project Z need to be scheduled for mitigation, then $imp(S/TRS(Z,t))$ can be replaced by **oimp** of SMRMP because **oimp** is the total impact of the project.

Since AVEOI(S) is an approximation of $EAI(S/TRS(Z,t))$, it can be used to measure the performance of S. That is a lower AVEOI(S) indicates S has a higher performance and a higher AVEOI(S) indicates S has a lower performance.

We are also interested in the difference in performance of two strategies when they are applied to the same project.

Definition 12. Suppose S_i and S_j are two scheduling strategies that are applied to project Z, with AVEOI(S_i) $\geq$ AVEOI(S_j). PIP (Percentage of Improved Performance) is defined as

$$PIP(S_i, S_j) = (AVEOI(S_i)) - (AVEOI(S_j))/(AVEOI(S_i)) \qquad (5)$$

PIP(S_i,S_j) measures the relative improvement of impact of S_j over that of S_i. PIP(S_i,S_j) ranges in [0, 1]. PIP(S_i,S_j) equals 0 when AVEOI(S_i) = AVEOI(S_j), indicating that S_i and S_j have the same performance. It equals 1 when AVEOI(S_j) = 0. The higher the value of PIP(S_i,S_j), the larger the improvement of S_j over S_i.

4.3   Cases for Simulation

In this section, we identify the cases used for comparing performance of different scheduling strategies. Risk mitigation can be viewed as using a set of processors to mitigate a given set of risks. The processor takes risks as input and mitigates them. So, the risk set is the input to the risk mitigation. For output, we are most interested in the effectiveness of risk mitigation. Next, we identify different cases from these two aspects of input and output of risk mitigation.

The input to risk mitigation is a set of risks $TRS(Z, t)$. The external context of these risks is a project Z of a certain project type (Cadle and Yeates, 2008) [3], size and application domain. The basic internal attributes of risk are probability and impact. First, we explore the external context and internal attributes of risk to identify key parameters for simulation.

After identifying the response option of mitigating a risk, the next issue is to determine when and which processor should work on mitigating the risk. Thus, the scheduling problem can be formulated as how to order the mitigation of a set of risks given a set of processors. Consequently, the type of project, (i.e. software development project, system enhancement project and so on), and the domain of the project (i.e. banking, medical, telecommunication and so on) are not important in the context of our study.

A large project having a large number of risks and a large mitigation team is similar to a small project having a small number of risks and a small mitigation team when scheduling risk mitigation. For example, suppose a large project has 100 risks and 100 processors, and another project have 20 risks and 20 processors. In both cases, each risk can be allocated to a unique processor and all risks can be treated at the same time. Therefore, compared with the ratio of the number of risks to the number of processors, the project size is less important for scheduling risk mitigation because it may indicate the number of risks only and cannot represent the size of mitigation team.

Definition 13. RRP (Ratio of Risks to Processors) is defined as

$$RRP = |TRS(Z, t)| / |ProS(Z, t)| \tag{6}$$

where $TRS(Z, t)$ and $ProS(Z, t)$ are the set of risks waiting for mitigation and the set of processors respectively.

RRP is more meaningful than the number of risks for scheduling risk mitigation because it integrates both the number of risks and number of processors. RRP is a better parameter for the simulation when compared to the number of risks.

It is meaningful that we use different RRP values obtained from different contexts to represent different cases. We obtain RRP values from different combinations of project sizes and mitigation team (processor) sizes. We assume the number of risks is related to the project size so that larger projects will have more risks. In this study, we consider two categories of project size, large project and small project, and consider three categories of team size, large team, medium team and small team. We will consider more categories of project size and team size in future study. Note that we will not consider following two combinations: (1) small project and a large mitigation team, leading to a very small RRP and (2) large project and a small mitigation team, leading to a very large RRP, because effective risk mitigation is hard to be achieved in this case. Thus we consider four most common cases: 1. small project (with a small number of risks) and a small mitigation team, 2. small project and a medium mitigation team, 3. large project (with a large number of risks) and a medium mitigation team and 4. large project and a large mitigation team. We choose following values for RRP for the simulations.

1. $|TRS(Z, t)| = 20$, $|ProS(Z, t)| = 2$, with RRP = 10
2. $|TRS(Z, t)| = 20$, $|ProS(Z, t)| = 4$ with RRP = 5
3. $|TRS(Z, t)| = 60$, $|ProS(Z, t)| = 4$, with RRP = 15
4. $|TRS(Z, t)| = 60$, $|ProS(Z, t)| = 15$, with RRP = 4

Larger projects usually require a longer development lifecycle. So, projects of different sizes would have different time periods of risk management. However, the time unit used in SMRMP is a relative time scale. Hence, different time periods can be normalized into 100 time units. Consequently, we can consider that **strm** = 0 and **etrm** = 100.

For the internal attributes of risk, we consider the distribution (DoP) of the probability and the distribution (DoI) of impact of risks. To be meaningful, we consider four different distributions which represent majority of risks having large RV, medium RV, small RV and randomly distributed RV respectively. (1) Both P and I follow the distribution shown in Fig. 4-I. It implies that most risks have medium P and I. (2) Both P and I follow the distribution shown in Fig. 4-II. It implies that most risks have high P and I. (3) Both P and I follow the distribution shown in Fig. 4-III. It implies that most risks have low P and I. (4) Both P and I follow the distribution shown in Fig. 4-IV.

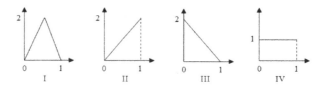

Fig. 4. Different distributions of P and I.

Note that the distribution of probability and the distribution of impact need not be the same. In our study, the probability and impact of a risk are independent even if they follow the same distribution. In future study, we will consider more cases with different distributions of probability and distributions of impact. The other attributes of risk, such as the time period of occurrence and efforts to mitigate a risk are randomly generated (details will be provided in Sect. 4.4).

To model the effectiveness of risk mitigation, we consider two cases: (1) Full reduction. Each processor can eliminate the assigned risks. (2) Random reduction. Each processor randomly reduces the probability and impact of assigned risks. That is each processor reduces the probability and impact of R_i from p_i^+ and i_i^+ to $p_i^- = r_1 \times p_i^+$ and $i_i^- = r_2 \times i_i^+$ respectively, where r_1 and r_2 are random numbers in $[0, 1]$.

Note that we will not consider the case of Zero reduction that a processor does not reduce the probability and impact of assigned risks because this case is same as no mitigation. Naturally all scheduling strategies give the same performance for this case.

In summary, with due consideration of different inputs (external context and internal attributes of *TRS(Z, t)*), and outputs (effectiveness of mitigation) of processor, we obtain totally $4 \times 4 \times 2 = 32$ different cases.

4.4   Parameters of SMRMP

To simulate different cases, we first identify the values of parameters of SMRMP. Based on settings discussed in last section, we select values or probability distributions for the parameters of SMRMP (see Table 1). For each case, we set the parameters of SMRMP as follows.

- Parameters of SMRMP at project-level. (1) **strm** $= 0$ and **etrm** $= 100$. (2) we consider that all risks are identified in the first risk identification and no new risks are identified in periodical reviews. The reason is in comparing performance of different scheduling strategies, it is not important to consider the effect of the periodical reviews, since we can apply scheduling strategies to the risk set *TRS(Z, t)* at any time. At the beginning of the project, we can select a scheduling strategy based on risks identified in risk identification to generate a schedule for risk mitigation. Then we can repeat the strategy selection at the end of each periodical review if new risks have been identified. Consequently, we just assume all risks are identified at the beginning of risk management. For convenient sake, we set the start time of risk identification to 0 (**stri** $= 0$) and the end time of risk identification to 1 (**etri** $= 1$) respectively.

- Parameters of SMRMP at risk-level. (1) **tid**$_i$ of any risk R_i is 1 since **etri** $= 1$. (2) p_i^+ and i_i^+ of risk R_i are generated according to the distribution of the case. (3) p_i^- and i_i^- of risk R_i are generated according to mitigation effectiveness of the case. (4) the time period of occurrence of all risks is randomly generated within the lifecycle of risk management, because risks can occur at any phase of the project. Suppose we identify risk R_i before it would occur, then [**teo**$_i$, **tlo**$_i$] should be in the range [1, 100] since **tid**$_i = 1$ and **etrm** $= 100$. (5) the effort of mitigating a risk is randomly generated within the available time for its mitigation. Since the effort for mitigating a randomly generated risk is unpredictable, we consider that a randomly generated mitigation effort is a good choice. According to the effort, the scheduling strategy is applied to determine whether R_i can be mitigated by a specific processor and the time to mitigate it. Thus, the time period of risk mitigation will be determined according to the selected scheduling strategy.

5   Performance of Scheduling Strategies

5.1   Results of Simulation

We generate 1000 projects for each case and apply all 7 scheduling strategies to each project. Therefore there are 7000 combinations of projects and scheduling strategies for each case. We run 1000 simulations for each combination to compare the performance of different scheduling strategies.

We run simulations on all 32 cases. Table 4 summarizes the chance of different strategies to be the best/worst strategy among 32 cases. For example, the chance for V strategy to be the best strategy in 32 different cases ranges in [0.1 %, 66 %]. V strategy has 21 % chance to be the best strategy on average (that is, it is the best strategy for 21 % of all 32000 sample projects).

Table 4. Summary of strategies to be the best/worst.

	(%)	V	E	L	VE	VL	EL	VEL
Chance to be	Range	0.1–66	0–5	0–17	0.3–36	4–65	0–13	2–34
the best	Ave	21	0.8	4	14	32	4	24
Cases to be the best		8	0	0	3	18	0	3
Chance to be	Range	0–17	45–99	0–45	0–14	0–16	0–4	0–43
the worst	Ave	5	68	15	4	1	6	0.8
Cases to be the worst		0	32	0	0	0	0	0

Table 5 shows average AVEOI of 7 identified strategies from all 32 cases. From Table 5, we find that *Perf(VL) > Perf(VEL) > Perf(V) > Perf(VE) > Perf(L) > Perf (EL) > Perf(E)* for all sample projects.

Table 5. Average AVEOI of all cases.

	V	E	L	VE	VL	EL	VEL
AVEOI	5.8815	7.0276	6.1485	5.9916	5.5475	6.1607	5.6132

Table 6 shows the average PIP between the best strategy and the worst strategy and other 7 identified strategies. From Table 6, we find that: On average, always applying the best strategy can improve the performance by 10 % over the traditional V strategy, by 31 % over the worst strategy, and by at least 8 % over other strategies.

Table 6. Average AVEOI of all cases.

B-W	B-V	B-E	B-L	B-VE	B-VL	B-EL	B-VEL
0.31	0.10	0.28	0.19	0.13	0.08	0.19	0.09

5.2 Answers to the Research Questions

Next we answer the research questions listed at the beginning of the paper.

1. Is the traditionally used strategy, risk value first strategy (V), a good choice for scheduling risk mitigation?

From the Table 4, we find that V strategy is the best strategy for only 21 % of all 32000 sample projects, and has a lower chance to be the best strategy than VL and VEL strategy. It also has a higher chance to be the worst strategy than three other strategies (VE, VL and VEL). From Table 6, we find that the best strategy can improve the performance by 10 % over V strategy on average. That is, applying the best strategy for each project will improve the performance of always applying the V strategy by 10 %. Moreover, V strategy has a lower performance than VL and VEL strategy on average. *Thus, V strategy is not a good choice for scheduling risk mitigation.*

2. Is there a best scheduling strategy for most projects?

From simulation results, we find that none of the 7 strategies can be a "dominate strategy" for projects of a certain case. The dominate strategy of a case is the strategy that is the best strategy for most projects (i.e. more than 70 % projects) of the case. From Table 4, we find that VL strategy has the highest chance to be the best strategy for all sample projects and in 18 cases out of 32 cases. It is the best strategy for 32 % projects of all 32000 sample projects. It has only 1 % chance to be the worst strategy. This performance is similar to that of VEL strategy (0.8 %) and is lower than that of the other 5 strategies. However, VL strategy is the best strategy for less than half of projects (only 32 % projects) from all cases. *In summary, there is no strategy that can be the best strategy for most projects of all cases or for most projects of a certain case.*

3. Is there a worst scheduling strategy for most projects?

From Table 4, we find that E strategy has the highest chance to be the worst strategy in all 32 cases. It has at least 45 % chance and 68 % chance on average to be the worst strategy for all cases. Moreover, it has a lower performance than all other strategies. So, it is the least preferred strategy for scheduling risk mitigation. However, it can be the best strategy for some projects. Among 32000 sample projects, it is the best strategy for 0.8 % projects.

6   Conclusion

In this paper, we formally define the scheduling strategy for risk mitigation, identify some new scheduling strategies with due consideration of key time elements of risk, and compare their performance by applying a stochastic simulation model.

From the simulation results, we find that, for all tested cases: (1) The traditionally strategy, V strategy, is not a good choice for scheduling risk mitigation. The best strategy can improve the performance of V strategy by 10 % on average. That means we should not always use V strategy. (2) There is no strategy that can be the best strategy for most projects or for most projects of a certain case. This indicates we should not always apply the same strategy to all projects or to the projects of a certain case. (3) For scheduling risk mitigation, E Strategy is the least preferred strategy among 7 identified strategies. According to above findings, we do not recommend the user to always apply the same strategy to all projects. We suggest the user find the best strategy for each project by running simulation.

Our study has some limitations: (1) The "*Null effect of non-mitigation factors*" assumption and "*Linear effect of mitigation*" assumption are a bit strong for real projects. (2) Compared to the variety of real-life projects, we only run simulation for 32 different cases covering a total of 32000 projects.

In the future, we shall: (1) Expand our study by running more simulation with due consideration of effects of non-mitigation factors and some non-linear risk reduction models. (2) Identify new mitigation scheduling strategies. We will try to identify better strategies. (3) Apply the proposed methods to real-life projects including some large-scale applications to confirm their value.

Acknowledgements. This research is partly supported by Hong Kong Polytechnic University grant G-YK27.

References

1. AS/NZS 2004. AS/NZS 4360: Risk Management. Standards Australia International Ltd
2. Boehm, B.W.: Software Risk Management. IEEE Computer Society Press, New York (1989)
3. Cadle, J., Yeates, D.: Project Management for Information Systems. Harlow, Prentice Hall (2008)
4. Carr, M.J., Konda, S.L., Monarch, I., Ulrich, C., Walker, C.F.: Taxonomy-Based Risk Identification. Software Engineering Institute, Pittsburgh (1993)
5. Heemstra, F.J., Kusters, R.J.: Dealing with risk: a practical approach. J. Inf. Technol. **11**, 333–346 (1996)
6. Holton, G.A.: Defining risk. Financ. Anal. J. **60**, 12–25 (2004)
7. IEEE 2001. IEEE Std 1540-2001: IEEE Standard for Software Life Cycle Processes—Risk Management. IEEE SA, New York
8. ISO 2009. ISO 31000: Risk Management - Principle and Guidelines. International Standard Organization, Switzerland
9. Keil, M., Cule, P.E., Lyytinen, K., Schmidt, R.C.: A framework for identifying software project risks. Commun. ACM **41**(11), 76–83 (1998)
10. Kwan, T.W.: A Risk Management Methodology with Risk Dependencies. Doctor of Philosophy, The Hong Kong Polytechnic University (2009)
11. Kwan, T.W., Leung, H.K.N.: A risk management methodology for project risk dependencies. IEEE Trans. Softw. Eng. **37**, 635–648 (2011)
12. Leung, H.K.N.: Variants of risk and opportunity. In: 17th Asia Pacific Software Engineering Conference, Sydney, Australia (2010)
13. Lister, T.: Risk management is project management for adults. IEEE Softw. **14**(3), 20 (1997)
14. PMI 2008. A Guide to the Project Management Body of Knowledge. Project management Institute, Newtown, PA
15. Sargent, R.G.: Verification and validation of simulation models. In: Proceedings of the 2010 Winter Simulation Conference (2010)
16. Sei 2006. CMMI® for Development Version 1.2. Software Engineering Institute, Pittsburgh, PA
17. Sherer, S.A.: Managing risk beyond the control of is managers: the role of business management. In: Proceedings of 37th Hawaii International Conference on System Sciences, Hawaii (2004)

18. Williams, R.C., Pandelios, G.J., Behrens, S.G.: Software Risk Evaluation (SRE) Method Description (version 2.0). Software Engineering Institute, Pittsburgh, PA (1999)
19. Zhou, P.: Managing Time Elements of Risk. Doctor of Philosophy, The Hong Kong Polytechnic University (2012)
20. Zhou, P., Leung, H.K.N.: Improving risk management with modeling time element. In: 15th IASTED International Conference on Software Engineering and Applications, Dallas, USA (2011)
21. Zhou, P., Leung, H.K.N.: A stochastic simulation model for risk management process. In: 19th Asia-Pacific Software Engineering Conference (APSEC 2012), Hong Kong (2012)

Real-Time Reconfigurable Scheduling of Sporadic Tasks

Hamza Gharsellaoui[1,2]([⊠]) and Samir Ben Ahmed[3]

[1] Higher School of Technology and Computer Science,
University of Carthage, Carthage, Tunisia
[2] Al-Jouf College of Technology, Technical and Vocational Training Corporation,
Al-Jouf, Kingdom of Saudi Arabia
gharsellaoui.hamza@gmail.com
[3] Faculty of Mathematical, Physical and Natural Sciences of Tunis, FST,
University of Tunis El Manar, Tunis, Tunisia
Samir.benahmed@fst.rnu.tn

Abstract. This book chapter deals with the problem of scheduling multiprocessor real-time tasks by an optimal EDF-based scheduling algorithm. Two forms of automatic reconfigurations which are assumed to be applied at run-time: Addition-Removal of tasks or just modifications of their temporal parameters: WCET and/or deadlines. Nevertheless, when such a scenario is applied to save the system at the occurrence of hardware-software faults, or to improve its performance, some real-time properties can be violated at run-time. We define an Intelligent Agent that automatically checks the system's feasibility after any reconfiguration scenario was applied on a multiprocessor embedded system. Indeed, if the system is unfeasible, then the Intelligent Agent dynamically provides precious technical solutions for users to send sporadic tasks to idle times, by modifying the deadlines of tasks, the worst case execution times (WCETs), the activation time, by tolerating some non critical tasks, by sending some tasks from their current processors to be scheduled in other processors, or in the worst case by removing some soft tasks according to predefined heuristic. We implement the agent to support these services.

Keywords: Real-time reconfigurable sporadic tasks · Intelligent agent · Multiprocessor systems automatic reconfigurations · EDF-based scheduling algorithm

1 Introduction

Nowadays, the new generations of embedded control systems are addressing new criteria such as flexibility and agility [1]. For these reasons, there is a need to develop tools, methodologies in embedded software engineering and dynamic reconfigurable embedded control systems as an independent discipline. Each system is a subset of tasks. Each task is characterized by its worst case execution times (WCETs) C_i^{p,ψ_h}, an offset (release time) a_i^{p,ψ_h}, a period T_i^{p,ψ_h} and a deadline D_i^{p,ψ_h} for each reconfiguration scenario ψ_h, (h ∈ 1..M, we assume that we

© Springer-Verlag Berlin Heidelberg 2014
J. Cordeiro and M. van Sinderen (Eds.): ICSOFT 2013, CCIS 457, pp. 24–39, 2014.
DOI: 10.1007/978-3-662-44920-2_2

have M reconfiguration scenarios) and on each processor p, (p $\in$ 1..K, we assume that we have K identical processors numbered from 1 to K), and n real-time tasks numbered from 1 to n that composed a feasible subset of tasks entitled ξ_{old}. The general goal of this work is to be reassured that any reconfiguration scenario ψ_h changing the implementation of the embedded system does not violate real-time constraints: i.e. the system is feasible and meets real-time constraints even if we change its implementation and to correctly allow the minimization of the response time of this system after any reconfiguration scenario [1]. To obtain this optimization (minimization of response time), we propose an intelligent agent-based architecture in which a software agent is deployed to dynamically adapt the system to its environment by applying reconfiguration scenarios. A reconfiguration scenario ψ_h means the addition, removal or update of tasks in order to save the whole system on the occurrence of hardware/software faults, or also to improve its performance when random disturbances happen at run-time. Sporadic task is described by minimum interarrival time P_i^{p,ψ_h} which is assumed to be equal to its relative deadline D_i^{p,ψ_h}, and a worst-case execution time (WCET) C_i^{p,ψ_h} for each reconfiguration scenario ψ_h and on each processor p. A random disturbance is defined in the current work as any random internal or external event allowing the addition of tasks that we assume sporadic or removal of sporadic/periodic tasks to adapt the system's behavior. Indeed, a hard real-time system typically has a mixture of off-line and on-line workloads and assumed to be feasible before any reconfiguration scenario ψ_h. The off-line requests support the normal functions of the system while the on-line requests are sporadic tasks to handle external events such as operator commands and recovery actions which are usually unpredictable. For this reason and in this original work, we propose a new optimal scheduling algorithm based on the dynamic priorities scheduling Earliest Deadline First (EDF) algorithm principles on each processor p and for each dynamic reconfiguration scenario ψ_h in order to obtain the feasibility of the system at run-time, meeting real-time constraints and for the optimization of the response time of this system. Indeed, for independent, preemptable tasks, on a uni-processor, EDF is optimal in the sense that if any algorithm can find a schedule where all tasks meet their deadlines, then EDF can meet the deadlines [2].

According to [3], a hyperperiod is defined as $HP = [\zeta, 2 * LCM + \zeta]$, where LCM is the well-known Least Common Multiple of the tasks periods and ζ is the largest task offset. This algorithm, in our original work assumes that sporadic tasks span no more than one hyperperiod of the periodic tasks $HP^{(p,\psi_h)} = [\zeta^{(p,\psi_h)}, 2 * \mathrm{LCM} + \zeta^{(p,\psi_h)}]$, where LCM^{p,ψ_h} is the well-known Least Common Multiple of tasks periods and (ζ^{p,ψ_h}) is the largest task offset of all tasks τ_k^{p,ψ_h} for each reconfiguration scenario ψ_h on each processor p. The problem is to find which solution proposed by the agent that reduces the response time. To obtain these results, the intelligent agent calculates the residual time R_i^{p,ψ_h} before and after each addition scenario and calculates the minimum of those proposed solutions in order to obtain $Resp_k^{p,\psi_h}$ optimal noted $Resp_k^{p,\psi_h\,opt}$.

Where $Resp_k^{p,\psi_h^{opt}}$ is the minimum of the response time of the current system under study calculated by the intelligent agent.

To calculate this previous value $Resp_k^{p,\psi_h^{opt}}$, we proposed a new theoretical concepts R_i^{p,ψ_h}, S_i^{p,ψ_h}, s_i^{p,ψ_h}, f_i^{p,ψ_h} and L_i^{p,ψ_h} for the case of real-time sporadic operating system (OS) tasks. Where R_i^{p,ψ_h} is the residual time of task σ_i^{p,ψ_h}, S_i^{p,ψ_h} denotes the first release time of task σ_i^{p,ψ_h}, s_i^{p,ψ_h} is the last release time of task σ_i^{p,ψ_h}, f_i^{p,ψ_h} denotes the estimated finishing time of task σ_i^{p,ψ_h}, and L_i^{p,ψ_h} denotes the laxity of task σ_i^{p,ψ_h} for each reconfiguration scenario ψ_h and on each processor p.

The organization of this work is as follows. Section 2 introduces the related work of the proposed approach and gives the basic guarantee algorithm. In Sect. 3, we present the new approach with deadline tolerance for optimal scheduling theory. Section 4 presents the performance study, showing how this work is a significant extension to the state of the art of EDF scheduling and discusses experimental results of the proposed approach research. Section 5 summarizes the main results and presents the conclusion of the proposed approach and describes the intended future works.

2   Background

We present related works dealing with reconfigurations and real-time scheduling of embedded systems. Today, real-time embedded systems are found in many diverse application areas including; automotive electronics, avionics, telecommunications, space systems, medical imaging, and consumer electronics. In all of these areas, there is rapid technological progress. Companies building embedded real-time systems are driven by a profit motive. To succeed, they aim to meet the needs and desires of their customers by providing systems that are more capable, more flexible, and more effective than their competition, and by bringing these systems to market earlier. This desire for technological progress has resulted in a rapid increase in both software complexity and the processing demands placed on the underlying hardware [3].

To address demands for increasing processor performance, silicon vendors no longer concentrate wholly on the miniaturisation needed to increase processor clock speeds, as this approach has led to problems with both high power consumption and excessive heat dissipation. Instead, there is now an increasing trend towards using multiprocessor platforms for high-end real-time applications [3].

For these reasons, we will use in our work the case of real-time scheduling on homogeneous multiprocessor platforms. Before presenting our original contribution, we will present some definitions below. According to [1], each periodic task is described by an initial offset a_i (activation time), a worst-case execution time (WCET) C_i, a relative deadline D_i and a period T_i.

According to [4], each sporadic task is described by minimum interarrival time P_i which is assumed to be equal to its relative deadline D_i, and a worst-case execution time (WCET) C_i. Hence, a sporadic task set will be denoted as follows:

$Sys_2 = \{\sigma_i(C_i, D_i)\}$, i = 1 to m. Reconfiguration policies in the current paper are classically distinguished into two strategies: static and dynamic reconfigurations. Static reconfigurations are applied off-line to modify the assumed system before any system cold start, whereas dynamic reconfigurations are dynamically applied at run-time, which can be further divided into two cases: manual reconfigurations applied by users and automatic reconfigurations applied by intelligent agents [1,5]. This book chapter work focuses on the dynamic reconfigurations of assumed mixture of off-line and on-line workloads that should meet deadlines defined according to user requirements. The extension of the proposed algorithm should be straightforward, when this assumption does not hold and its running time is O(n + m) [6].

2.1   State of the Art

Nowadays, several interesting studies have been published to develop reconfigurable embedded control systems. In [7] Marian et al. propose a static reconfiguration technique for the reuse of tasks that implement a broad range of systems. The work in [11] proposes a methodology based on the human intervention to dynamically reconfigure tasks of considered systems. In [10], an ontology-based agent is proposed by Vyatkin et al. to perform system reconfigurations according to user requirements and also the environment evolution. Window-constrained scheduling is proposed in [8], which is based on an algorithm named dynamic window-constrained scheduling (DWCS). The research work in [9] provides a window-constrained-based method to determine how much a task can increase its computation time, without missing its deadline under EDF scheduling. In [9], a window-constrained execution time can be assumed for reconfigurable tasks in n among m windows of jobs. In the current paper, a window constrained schedule is used to separate old and new tasks that assumed sporadic on each processor p and after each reconfiguration scenario ψ_h. Old and new tasks are located in different windows to schedule the system with a minimum response time. In [5], a window constrained schedule is used to schedule the system with a low power consumption.

In the following, we only consider periodic and sporadic tasks. Few results have been proposed to deal with deadline assignment problem. Baruah, Buttazo and Gorinsky in [1] propose to modify the deadlines of a task set to minimize the output, seen as secondary criteria of this work. So, we note that the optimal scheduling algorithm based on the EDF principles and on the dynamic reconfiguration scenario ψ_h is that we propose in the current original work in which we give solutions computed and presented by the intelligent agent for users to respond to their requirements.

2.2   Formalization

To illustrate the key point of the proposed dynamically approach, we assume that there are K identical processors numbered from 1 to K, and n real-time tasks numbered from 1 to n that composed a feasible subset of tasks entitled ξ_{old} and need to be scheduled. At time t and before the application of the reconfiguration scenario ψ_h, each one of the tasks of ξ_{old} is feasible, e.g. the execution of each instance in each processor is finished before the corresponding deadline and the tasks are not assumed to be arranged in any specific order.

Every processor p assigns a set of periodic tasks $TS^p = \{\tau_1^p, \tau_2^p, ..., \tau_n^p\}$. This allocation is made with an allowance algorithm at the time of the design, for example by using one of the well known techniques: first-fit (FF), next-fit (NF), best-fit (BF), worst-fit (WF). These tasks are independent and can be interrupted at any time. Every task τ_i^p has an execution time (Worst Case Execution Time) C_i^p, one period T_i^p, a deadline D_i^p which is assumed to be less than or equal to its period, e.g. $D_i^p \leq T_i^p$. Every task instance k has to respect its absolute deadline, namely the kth authority of the task τ_i^p, named $\tau_{i,k}^p$ must be completed before time $D_{i,k}^p = (k-1)T_i^p + D_i^p$. These tasks are handled by a global scheduler (GS), which assigns them to processors by using the state informations of the local schedulers. Moreover, under EDF scheduling, a task will fit on a processor as long as the total utilization of all tasks assigned to that processor does not exceed unity (the total utilization factor $= 1$). Finally, for reasons of simplicity, we assume that the migration cost of the tasks are equal to zero.

We assume now the arrival at run-time of a second subset ξ_{new} which is composed of m real-time tasks at time t_1 ($t_1 = t + \Delta t$). We have a system $Current_{Sys}(t_1)$ composed of $n+m$ tasks. In this case a reconfiguration scenario ψ_h is applied. The reconfiguration of the system Sys^{ψ_h} means the modification of its implementation that will be as follows at time t_1:

$$\xi^{\psi_h} = Current_{Sys}^{\psi_h}(t_1) = \xi_{old} \cup \xi_{new}^{\psi_h}$$

where ξ_{old} is a subset of old tasks which are not affected by the reconfiguration scenario ψ_h (e.g. they implement the system before the time t_1), and $\xi_{new}^{\psi_h}$ a subset of new tasks in the system. We assume that an updated task is considered as a new one at time t_1. When the reconfiguration scenario ψ_h is applied at time t_1, two cases exist:

- If tasks of $\xi^{\psi_h} = \xi_{old} \cup \xi_{new}^{\psi_h}$ are feasible, then no reaction should be done by the agent,
- otherwise, the agent should provide different solutions for users in order to re-obtain the system's feasibility.

Running Example

In this section, we demonstrate the performance of our proposed approach for both periodic synchronous and asynchronous, and sporadic tasks. The simulation runs on our tool RT-Reconfiguration and proved by the real-time simulator Cheddar [12] with a task set composed of old tasks (ξ_{old}) and new tasks (ξ_{new}^{p,ψ_h}) on the processor p for each reconfiguration scenario ψ_h. We illustrate with a simplified example to ease the understanding of our approach. The task set considered for this example is given in Table 1 and is composed of 10 tasks. The sum of utilization of all tasks is given in Table 1 and is equal to 426.1%.

Table 1. Task parameters of running example.

Tasks	C_i	D_i	$T_i = P_i$
τ_1	2	9	7
τ_2	3	21	20
τ_3	2	9	9
τ_4	2	13	10
τ_5	3	15	9
τ_6	14	21	19
τ_7	10	24	16
τ_8	8	18	18
τ_9	13	16	17
τ_{10}	5	11	12

We have 3 identical processors in our system to schedule these tasks. In this case, we assume that each task's deadline is less than or equal to its period. The worst case execution times, deadlines, and the time periods of all tasks are generated randomly. In this experiment, the system runs for time units equal to hyper-period of periodic tasks.

In this experiment, our task set example is initially implemented by 5 characterized old tasks ($\xi_{old} = \{\tau_1; \tau_2; \tau_3; \tau_4; \tau_5\}$). These tasks are feasible because the processor utilization factor U $= 1.19 \leq 3$. These tasks should meet all required deadlines defined in user requirements and we have $Feasibility(Current_{\xi_{old}}(t)) \equiv True$.

Firstly, tasks are partitioned; task τ_1 is partioned on first processor, τ_2 and τ_3 are partitioned on processor 2 while task τ_4 and τ_5 are partitioned on processor 3. We have three sets of local tasks. As there is only one task on first processor then task τ_1 utilization factor is the same as the first processor 1 utilization factor ($u^{1,0} = 0.285 \leq 1$) while utilization factors of processor 2 and processor 3 are calculated as follows:

$$U^{2,0} = \sum_{i=1}^{(2)^2} \frac{C_i^2}{T_i^2} = 0.372 < 1,$$

$$U^{3,0} = \sum_{i=1}^{(2)^3} \frac{C_i^3}{T_i^3} = 0.533 < 1.$$

We suppose that a first reconfiguration scenario ψ_1 (h $= 1$) is applied at time t_1 to add 5 new tasks $\xi_{new}^{\psi_1} = \{\tau_6; \tau_7; \tau_8; \tau_9; \tau_{10}\}$. The new processor utilization becomes $U^{\psi_1} = 4.261 > 3$ time units. Therefore the system is unfeasible. $Feasibility(Current_{\xi}^{\psi_1}(t1)) \equiv False$. Indeed, if the number of tasks increases, then the overload of the system increases too. Our optimal earliest deadline first (OEDF) algorithm is based on the Guarantee Algorithm presented by Buttazo and Stankovic in [4]. Indeed, OEDF algorithm is an extended and ameliorate version of Guarantee Algorithm that usually guarantee the system's feasibility.

3   New Approach with Deadline Tolerance

In this section we will present some preliminaries concepts and we will describe our contribution after.

In [4], Buttazo and Stankovic present the Guarantie Algorithm without the notion of deadline tolerance, and then we will extend the algorithm in our new proposed approach by including tolerance indicator and task rejection policy. For this reason, and in order to more explain these notions we will present some preliminaries.

3.1   Preliminaries

ξ denotes a set of active sporadic tasks σ_i ordered by increasing deadline in a linked list, σ_1 being the task with the shortest absolute deadline.

a_i denotes the arrival time of task σ_i, i.e., the time at which the task is activated and becomes ready to execute.

C_i denotes the maximum computation time of task σ_i, i.e., the worst case execution time (WCET) needed for the processor to execute task $\sigma_{i,k}$ without interruption.

c_i denotes the dynamic computation time of task σ_i, i.e., the remaining worst case execution time needed for the processor, at the current time, to complete task $\sigma_{i,k}$ without interruption.

d_i denotes the absolute deadline of task τ_i, i.e., the time before which the task should complete its execution, without causing any damage to the system.

D_i denotes the relative deadline of task σ_i, i.e., the time interval between the arrival time and the absolute deadline. S_i denotes the first start time of task σ_i, i.e., the time at which task σ_i gains the processor for the first time. s_i denotes the last start time of task σ_i, i.e., the last time, before the current time, at which task σ_i gained the processor.

f_i denotes the estimated finishing time of task σ_i, i.e., the time according to the current schedule at which task σ_i should complete its execution and leave the system.

L_i denotes the laxity of task σ_i, i.e., the maximum time task σ_i can be delayed before its execution begins.

R_i denotes the residual time of task σ_i, i.e., the length of time between the finishing time of σ_i and its absolute deadline. Baruah et al. [13] present a necessary and sufficient feasibility test for synchronous systems with pseudo-polynomial complexity. The other known method is to use response time analysis, which consists of computing the worst-case response time (WCRT) of all tasks in a system and ensuring that each task WCRT is less than its relative deadline. To avoid these problems, and to have a feasible system in this paper, our proposed tool RT-Reconfiguration can be used. For this reason, we present the following relationships among the parameters defined above:

$$d_i = a_i + D_i \tag{1}$$
$$L_i = d_i - a_i - C_i \tag{2}$$
$$R_i = d_i - f_i \tag{3}$$
$$f_1 = t + c_1; \quad f_i = f_{i-1} + c_i \; \forall \; i > 1 \tag{4}$$

The basic properties stated by the following lemmas and theorems are used to derive an efficient $O(n+m)$ algorithm for analyzing the schedulability of the sporadic task set whenever a new task arrives in the systems.

Lemma 1. Given a set $\xi = \{\sigma_1, \sigma_2, ..., \sigma_n\}$ of active sporadic tasks ordered by increasing deadline in a linked list, the residual time R_i of each task σ_i at time t can be computed by the following recursive formula:

$$R_1 = d_1 - t - c_1 \tag{5}$$

$$R_i = R_{i-1} + (d_i - d_{i-1}) - c_i. \tag{6}$$

Proof. By the residual time definition (Eq. 3) we have:

$$R_i = d_i - f_i.$$

By the assumption on set ξ, at time t, the task σ_1 in execution and cannot be preempted by other tasks in the set ξ, hence its estimated finishing time is given by the current time plus its remaining execution time:

$$f_1 = t + c_1$$

and, by Eq. 3, we have:

$$R_1 = d_1 - f_1 = d_1 - t - c_1.$$

For any other task σ_i, with $i > 1$, each task σ_i will start executing as soon as σ_{i-1} completes, hence we can write:

$$f_i = f_{i-1} + c_i \tag{7}$$

and, by Eq. 3, we have:

$$R_i = d_i - f_i = d_i - f_{i-1} - c_i =$$
$$d_i - (d_{i-1} - R_{i-1}) - c_i = R_{i-1} + (d_i - d_{i-1}) - c_i$$

and the lemma follows.

Lemma 2. A task σ_i is guaranteed to complete within its deadline if and only if $R_i \geq 0$ [4].

Theorem 3. A set $\xi = \{\sigma_i, i = 1 \text{ to m}\}$ of m active sporadic tasks ordered by increasing deadline is feasibly schedulable if and only if $R_i \geq 0$ for all $\sigma_i \in \xi$, [4].

3.2 Feasibility Analysis for Tasks

By considering real-time tasks and as we mentioned before, the schedulability analysis should be done in the hyperperiod $HP^{(p,\psi_h)} = [\zeta^{(p,\psi_h)}, 2^* \text{LCM} + \zeta^{(p,\psi_h)}]$, where LCM^{p,ψ_h} is the well-known Least Common Multiple of tasks periods and (ζ^{p,ψ_h}) is the largest task offset of all tasks τ_k^{p,ψ_h} for each reconfiguration scenario ψ_h on each processor p.

Let $n + m$ be the number of tasks respectively in ξ_{old} and $\xi_{new}^{\psi_h}$. By assuming unfeasible system at time t_1, and every processor p will execute its tasks in local by using EDF, the following formula is satisfied:

$$\sum_{i=1}^{n+m} \frac{C_i^{\psi_h}}{T_i^{\psi_h}} > K, \text{where K is the number of identical processors.}$$

Our proposed algorithm provides guarantees to both old and new tasks in each processor p if and only if,

$$\sum_{i=1}^{n-j} \frac{C_i^{p,\psi_h}}{T_i^{p,\psi_h}} + \sum_{i=n-j+1}^{n+m} \frac{C_i^{p,\psi_h}}{T_i^{p,\psi_h}} \leq 1$$

where $\sum_{i=1}^{n-j} \frac{C_i^{p,\psi_h}}{T_i^{p,\psi_h}}$ denotes sum of utilization factor of n old tasks in processor p for each reconfiguration scenario ψ_h and, $\sum_{i=n-j+1}^{n+m} \frac{C_i^{p,\psi_h}}{T_i^{p,\psi_h}}$ denotes sum of utilization factor of new arrival m tasks to the processor p for each reconfiguration scenario ψ_h.

We propose, for each reconfiguration scenario ψ_h, to add the tasks of ξ_{old} to a linked list $L_{old}^{\psi_h}$ that we sort on the increasing order of their utilization factor values.

3.3 Contribution: An Algorithm for Feasibility Testing with Respect to Sporadic Task Systems

In the current book chapter, we suppose that on each processor p, each system $\xi^{(p)}$ can be automatically and repeatedly reconfigured at each reconfiguration scenario ψ_h. $\xi^{(p)}$ is initially considered as $\xi^{(p,0)}$ and after the h_{th} reconfiguration $\xi^{(p)}$ turns into $\xi^{(p,\psi_h)}$, where $h \in 1..M$. We define VP_1^{p,ψ_h} and VP_2^{p,ψ_h} two virtual processors to virtually execute old and new sporadic tasks, implementing the system after the h_{th} reconfiguration scenario for each processor p. In $\xi^{(p,\psi_h)}$, all old tasks from $\xi^{(p,\psi_{h-1})}$ are executed by the newly updated $VP_1^{(p,\psi_h)}$ and the added sporadic tasks are executed by $VP_2^{(p,\psi_h)}$. The proposed intelligent agent is trying to minimize the response time $Resp_k^{p,\psi_h^{opt}}$ of $\xi^{(\psi_h)}$ after each reconfiguration scenario ψ_h and for each processor p.

For example, after the first addition scenario, $\xi^{(p,0)}$ turns into $\xi^{(p,1)}$. $\xi^{(p,1)}$ is automatically decomposed into $VP_1^{(p,1)}$ and $VP_2^{(p,1)}$ for old and new tasks with the processor utilization factors $UVP_1^{(p,1)}$ and $UVP_2^{(p,1)}$ respectively on each processor p.

After each addition scenario, the proposed intelligent agent proposes to modify the virtual processors, to modify the deadlines of old and new tasks, the WCETs and the activation time of some tasks, to send some tasks from processor i to another processor j, or to remove some soft tasks as following:

- **Solution 1:** Moving some arrival tasks to be scheduled in idle times for each reconfiguration scenario ψ_h and on each processor p. (idle times are caused when some tasks complete before its worst case execution time)   (S1)
- **Solution 2:** maximize the d_i^{p,ψ_h} for each reconfiguration scenario ψ_h and on each processor p   (S2)

By applying Eq. 3 that notices:
$R_i = d_i - f_i$, we have:

$$R_i^{p,\psi_h} = d_i^{p,\psi_h} - \mathrm{t} - C_i^{p,\psi_h}.$$

Or, to obtain a feasible system after a reconfiguration scenario $^{\psi_h}$, the following formula must be enforced:

$$R_i^{p,\psi_h} \geq 0 \text{ on each processor p.}$$

By this result we can write: $d_{inew}^{p,\psi_h} - \mathrm{t} - C_i^{p,\psi_h} \geq 0$, where $d_{inew}^{p,\psi_h} = d_i^{p,\psi_h} + \theta_i^{p,\psi_h}$.
So, $d_i^{p,\psi_h} + \theta_i^{p,\psi_h} - \mathrm{t} - C_i^{p,\psi_h} \geq 0 \Rightarrow$

$$\theta_i^{p,\psi_h} \geq \mathrm{t} + C_i^{p,\psi_h} - d_i^{p,\psi_h}.$$

- **Solution 3:** minimize the c_i for each reconfiguration scenario ψ_h and on each processor p   (S3)

By applying Eq. 3 that notices:
$R_i = d_i - f_i$, we have:

$$R_i^{p,\psi_h} = d_i^{p,\psi_h} - \mathrm{t} - C_i^{p,\psi_h}.$$

Or, to obtain a feasible system after a reconfiguration scenario, the following formula must be enforced:
$$R_i^{p,\psi_h} \geq 0.$$

By this result we can write: $d_i^{p,\psi_h} - \mathrm{t} - C_{inew}^{p,\psi_h} \geq 0$, where $C_{inew}^{p,\psi_h} = C_i^{p,\psi_h} + \beta_i^{p,\psi_h}$.
So, $d_i^{p,\psi_h} - \mathrm{t} - C_i^{p,\psi_h} - \beta_i^{p,\psi_h} \geq 0 \Rightarrow d_i^{p,\psi_h} - \mathrm{t} - C_i^{p,\psi_h} \geq \beta_i^{p,\psi_h}$

$$\Rightarrow \beta_i^{p,\psi_h} \leq d_i^{p,\psi_h} - \mathrm{t} - C_i^{p,\psi_h}$$

- **Solution 4.** Enforcing the release time to come back: $a_i^{p,\psi_h} \rightarrow a_{inew}^{p,\psi_h} \rightarrow$ $(a_{inew}^{p,\psi_h} = a_i^{p,\psi_h} + \Delta^{p,\psi_h}t)$ for each reconfiguration scenario ψ_h and on each processor p   (S4)

By applying Eq. 1 that notices:
$d_i = a_i + D_i$, we have:

$$R_i^{p,\psi_h} = a_i^{p,\psi_h} + D_i^{p,\psi_h} - t - C_i^{p,\psi_h}.$$

Or, to obtain a feasible system after a reconfiguration scenario, the following formula must be enforced:

$$R_i^{p,\psi_h} \geq 0 \Rightarrow a_i^{p,\psi_h} + D_i^{p,\psi_h} - t - C_i^{p,\psi_h} \geq 0.$$

By this result we can write:

$$a_{inew}^{p,\psi_h} + D_i^{p,\psi_h} - t - C_i^{p,\psi_h} \geq 0, \text{ where } a_{inew}^{p,\psi_h} = a_i^{p,\psi_h} + \Delta^{p,\psi_h}t.$$

So, we obtain: $a_i^{p,\psi_h} + \Delta^{p,\psi_h}t + D_i^{p,\psi_h} - t - C_i^{p,\psi_h} \geq 0.$

$$\Rightarrow \Delta^{p,\psi_h}t \geq t + C_i^{p,\psi_h} - a_i^{p,\psi_h} - D_i^{p,\psi_h}.$$

- **Solution 5:** Tolerate some non critical Tasks m_1^p among $(n+m)^p$ (according to the (m, n) firm model), on each processor p for a reasonable cost, and for each reconfiguration scenario ψ_h (S5)

$$\xi^p = \{\tau_i^p(C_i^p, D_i^p, m_i^p, I_i^p), i = 1 \, to \, n^p\}.$$

$m_i^p = 1$, it tolerates missing deadline,
$m_i^p = 0$, it doesn't tolerate missing deadline,
$I_i^p = H$, Hard task,
$I_i^p = S$, Soft task.
- **Solution 6:** Migration of some tasks from a processor source i in order to be scheduled on another processor destination j for each reconfiguration scenario ψ_h (S6)

The agent proceeds now as a sixth solution to migrate some tasks of ξ_{new}^{p,ψ_h} and ξ_{old}^p on the processor p for each reconfiguration scenario ψ_h. Indeed, the agent is responsible for allocating the tasks to the K computing processors in an optimal way (Fig. 1).

Run-time task migration can be defined as the relocation of an executing task from its current location, the source processor i, to a new location, the destination processor j (i $\neq$ j; i, j = 1..K) that must belong to the inclusion set. We need by inclusion set in paper, the set of processors in which tasks can be scheduled after any reconfiguration scenario ψ_h when a migration request has done and in this case all the relevant state information of that migration is transferred to the new processor. Otherwise, it is called exclusion set.

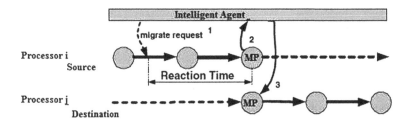

Task migration sequence.

Fig. 1. The task migration sequence.

This allows the OS to e.g., minimize energy savings and response time of the whole system. It also enables processors management by moving tasks away from processors with a high amount of workload or which have their utilization factors >1. The architectural differences between the source processor i and destination source processor j are masked by capturing and transferring the logical task state, shown by Fig. 2. In order to relocate a task, the intelligent agent notifies the task by means of a migration request signal[1]. Whenever that signaled task reaches a migration point (MP), it checks if there is a pending migration request or the destination processor j belongs to the exclusion group of the current migrated task for each reconfiguration scenario ψ_h. In such case of these two reasons, all the relevant state information of that migration point is transferred to the intelligent agent[2]. Consequently, the intelligent agent will instantiate the same task on a different processor. The new task instantiation will be initialized using the state information previously captured by the intelligent agent[3]. Finally, the task resumes execution at the corresponding migration point (MP).

- **Solution 7:** Removal of some non critical tasks (to be rejected) for each reconfiguration scenario ψ_h and on each processor p   (S7)

$$\xi^p = \{\tau_i^p(C_i^p, D_i^p, m_i^p, I_i^p), \ i = 1 \text{ to } n^p\}.$$

$m_i^{p,\psi_h} = 1$, it tolerates missing deadline,
$m_i^{p,\psi_h} = 0$, it doesn't tolerate missing deadline,
$I_i^{p,\psi_h} = \text{H}$, Hard task,
$m_i^{p,\psi_h} = \text{S}$, Soft task.

For every solution the corresponding response time is:
$Resp_{k,1}^{p,\psi_h} = $ the response time calculated by the first solution,
$Resp_{k,2}^{p,\psi_h} = $ the response time calculated by the second solution,
$Resp_{k,3}^{p,\psi_h} = $ the response time calculated by the third solution,
$Resp_{k,4}^{p,\psi_h} = $ the response time calculated by the fourth solution,

$Resp_{k,5}^{p,\psi_h}$ = the response time calculated by the fifth solution,

$Resp_{k,6}^{p,\psi_h}$ = the response time calculated by the sixth solution,

$Resp_{k,7}^{p,\psi_h}$ = the response time calculated by the seventh solution.

We define now, $Resp_k^{p,\psi_h}$ optimal noted $Resp_k^{p,\psi_h}{}^{opt}$ according to the previous seven solutions calculated by the intelligent Agent (Solution 1, Solution 2, Solution 3, Solution 4, Solution 5, Solution 6 and Solution 7) by the following expression: $Resp_k^{p,\psi_h}{}^{opt} = \min(Resp_{k,1}^{p,\psi_h}, Resp_{k,2}^{p,\psi_h}, Resp_{k,3}^{p,\psi_h}, Resp_{k,4}^{p,\psi_h},$ $Resp_{k,5}^{p,\psi_h}, Resp_{k,6}^{p,\psi_h}$ and $Resp_{k,7}^{p,\psi_h})$ (the minimum of the seven values). So, the calculation of $Resp_k^{p,\psi_h}{}^{opt}$ allows us to obtain and to calculate the minimizations of response times values and to get the optimum of these values. In conclusion, we can deduce that by arrival of $\xi_{new}^{\psi_h}$ tasks at run-time and the whole system become unfeasible, the following formula is satisfied for each reconfiguration scenario ψ_h:

$$\sum_{i=1}^{(n+m)^{\psi_h}} \frac{C_i^{\psi_h}}{T_i^{\psi_h}} > K, \text{where K is the number of identical processors.}$$

Then, after the reconfiguration scenario ψ_h was applied at run-time to the whole system by the intelligent agent, our proposed algorithm provides guarantees to both old and new tasks if and only if, we have in each processor p for each reconfiguration scenario ψ_h:

$$\sum_{i=1}^{(n+m)^{(p,\psi_h)}} \frac{C_i^{(p,\psi_h)}}{T_i^{(p,\psi_h)}} \leq 1, \text{in each processor p for each reconfiguration scenario } \psi_h.$$

Moreover, we have calculated $R_k^{(p,\psi_h)}{}^{opt} = \min(R_{k,1}^{(p,\psi_h)}, \ R_{k,2}^{(p,\psi_h)}, \ R_{k,3}^{(p,\psi_h)},$ $R_{k,4}^{(p,\psi_h)}, R_{k,5}^{(p,\psi_h)}, R_{k,6}^{(p,\psi_h)}$ and $R_{k,7}^{(p,\psi_h)}$); so we obtain also:

$$\sum_{i=1}^{(n+m)^{(p,\psi_h)}} \frac{C_i^{(p,\psi_h)}}{T_i^{(p,\psi_h)}} < 1, \begin{array}{l} \text{in each processor p for each reconfiguration scenario } \psi_h \\ \text{with } 1 \leq p \leq K, 1 \leq h \leq M. \end{array}$$

We can observe that all tasks meet their deadlines after a reconfiguration scenario ψ_h was applied at run-time. We can also observe that our proposed algorithm outperforms other scheduling multiprocessor algorithms and a number of scheduling events are much lower than appearing in others.

3.4   The General OEDF Scheduling Strategy

When dealing with the deadline tolerance factor m_i, each task has to be computed with respect to the deadline tolerance factor m_i.

Algorithm GUARANTEE(ξ; σ_a)
For each h in [1..M] **Do**
begin t = get current time();
$R_0^{p,\psi_h} = 0$;
$d_0^{p,\psi_h} = $ t;
Insert σ_a in the ordered task list;
ξ^{p,ψ_h} ` $= \xi^{p,\psi_h} \bigcup \sigma_a$;
k = position of σ_a in the task set ξ^{p,ψ_h} `;
for each task σ_i^{p,ψ_h} ` such that i $\geq$ k do
{
$R_i^{p,\psi_h} = R_{i-1}^{p,\psi_h} + (d_i^{p,\psi_h} - d_{i-1}^{p,\psi_h}) - c_i^{p,\psi_h}$;
if ($R_i^{p,\psi_h} \geq 0$) then
{
return ("Guaranteed");
}

else **return**
("You can try by using solution 1, or,
You can try by using solution 2, or,
You can try by using solution 3, or,
You can try by using solution 4, or,
You can try by using solution 5, or,
You can try by using solution 6, or,
You can try by using solution 7 !");
}

- Compute($Resp_{k,1}^{p,\psi_h}$);
- Compute($Resp_{k,2}^{p,\psi_h}$);
- Compute($Resp_{k,3}^{p,\psi_h}$);
- Compute($Resp_{k,4}^{p,\psi_h}$);
- Compute($Resp_{k,5}^{p,\psi_h}$);
- Compute($Resp_{k,6}^{p,\psi_h}$);
- Compute($Resp_{k,7}^{p,\psi_h}$);
- Generate($Resp_k^{p,\psi_h\,opt}$);

end

We show the results of our optimal proposed algorithm by means of experimental result's evaluation.

4   Experimental Results

In order to evaluate our optimal OEDF algorithm, we consider the following experiments applied to our running example.

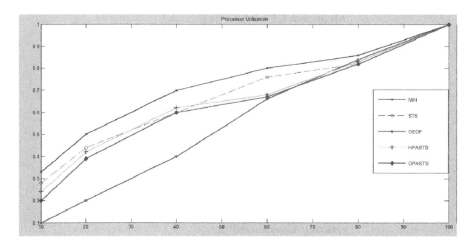

Fig. 2. Processor utilization.

4.1 Simulations

To quantify the benefits of the proposed approach (OEDF algorithm) over
the predictive system shutdown (PSS) approach, over the MIN algorithm, the
OPASTS algorithm and over the HPASTS algorithm. We performed a number
of simulations to compare the response time and the utilization processor under
the four strategies. The PSS technique assumes the complete knowledge of the
idle periods while the MIN algorithm assumes the complete knowledge of the
arrivals of sporadic tasks. For more details about both four techniques, you can
see [14]. The OEDF scheduling result is shown in figure (Fig. 2).

4.2 Discussion

We observe that our approach, by the solutions of the OEDF algorithm gives us
the minimum bound for response time and utilization factor. This observation
was proven by the results given by OEDF algorithm which are lower (better) than
these of the solutions given by the predictive system shutdown approach, the
MIN algorithm, the OPASTS algorithm and the HPASTS algorithm. Also, we
observe that, when we have no knowledge of the arrival of sporadic tasks, our
proposed algorithm is optimal and gives better results than others for a big
number of arrival sporadic tasks and in overload conditions, but in a small
number of tasks or light workload, OEDF algorithm is optimal but not strictly
since it gives results close to that of the solutions of MIN, OPASTS and HPASTS
algorithms, but it is efficient and effective.

5 Conclusions

This book chapter deals with reconfigurable homogeneous multiprocessor systems to be implemented by hybrid systems composed of a mixture of periodic

and sporadic tasks that should meet real-time constraints. In this work, we propose an optimal scheduling algorithm based on the EDF principles and on the dynamic reconfiguration for the minimization of the response time of sporadic and periodic constrained deadline real-time tasks on multiprocessor systems and proven it correct.

References

1. Gharsellaoui, H., Khalgui, M., BenAhmed, S.: Feasible Automatic Reconfigurations of Real-Time OS Tasks. IGI-Global Knowledge, London (2012)
2. Dertouzos, M.: Control robotics: the procedural control of physical processes. In: Proceedings of the IFIP Congress (1974)
3. Balbastre, P., Ballester, R., Brocal V., Ripoll, L.: Task period selection to minimize hyperperiod, emerging technologies and factory automation. In: 16th IEEE International Conference on Emerging Technologies and Factory Automation (ETFA), pp. 1–4. IEEE Press, Toulouse, France (2011)
4. Buttazzo, G., Stankovic, J.: RED: robust earliest deadline scheduling. In: 3rd International Workshop On Responsive Computing Systems, Austin (1993)
5. Wang, X., Khalgui, M., Li, Z.W.: Dynamic low power reconfigurations of real-time embedded systems. In: 16th IEEE International Conference on Emerging Technologies and Factory Automation (ETFA), pp. 1–4. IEEE Press, Toulouse, France (2011)
6. Tia, T., Liu, J.W.-S., Sun, J., Ha, R.: A linear-time optimal acceptance test for scheduling of hard real-time tasks, Technical report. Department of Computer Science, University of illinois at Urbana-Champaign, Urbana-Champaign (1994)
7. Marian, N., Angelov, C., Sierszecki, K.: Design models for reusable and reconfigurable state machines. In: Yang, L.T., et al. (eds.) Proceedings of Embedded Ubiquitous Computing (2005)
8. Schwan, K., West, R.: Dynamic window-constrained scheduling for multimedia applications. In: 6th IEEE International Conference on Multimedia Computing and Systems (1999)
9. Balbastre, P., Ripoll, I., Crespo, A.: Schedulability analysis of window-constrained execution time tasks for real-time control. In: 14th IEEE International Conference on Euromicro Conference Real-Time Systems (ECRTS) (2002)
10. Al-Safi, Y., Vyatkin, V.: An ontology-based reconfiguration agent for intelligent mechatronic systems. In: Mařík, V., Vyatkin, V., Colombo, A.W. (eds.) HoloMAS 2007. LNCS (LNAI), vol. 4659, pp. 114–126. Springer, Heidelberg (2007)
11. Rooker, M.N., Subder, C., Strasser, T., Zoitl, A., Hummer, O., Ebenhofer, G.: Zero downtime reconfiguration of distributed automation systems: the CEDAC approach. In: 3rd IEEE International Conference on Industrial Applications of Holonic and Multi-Agent Systems, Regensburg (2007)
12. Legrand, J., Singhoff, L.M.F.: Cheddar : a flexible real time scheduling framework. In: ACM SIGAda Ada Letters, vol. 24, no 4, pp. 1–8. ACM Press, ISSN:1094–3641 (2004)
13. Baruah, S., Koren, G., Mishra, B., Raghunathan, A., Rosier, L., Shasha, D.: On-line scheduling in the presence of overload. In: IEEE Symposium on Foundations of Computer Science, San Juan, Puerto Rico (1991)
14. Hong, I., Potkonjak, M., Srivastava, B.M.: On-line scheduling of hard real-time tasks on variable voltage processor. In: 8th International Conference on Computer-Aided Design, San Jose, California, USA (1998)

Applying a Knowledge Management Technique to Improve Risk Assessment and Effort Estimation of Healthcare Software Projects

Emilia Mendes[(⊠)]

Software Engineering Research Laboratory,
Blekinge Institute of Technology, Karlskrona, Sweden
emilia.mendes@bth.se

Abstract. One of the pillars for sound Software Project Management is reliable effort estimation. Therefore it is important to fully identify what are the fundamental factors that affect an effort estimate for a new project and how these factors are inter-related. This paper describes a case study where a Knowledge Management technique was employed to build an expert-based effort estimation model to estimate effort for healthcare software projects. This model was built with the participation of seven project managers, and was validated using data from 22 past finished projects. The model led to numerous changes in process and also in business. The company adapted their existing effort estimation process to be in line with the model that was created, and the use of a mathematically-based model also led to an increase in the number of projects being delegated to this company by other company branches worldwide.

Keywords: Software project management · Effort estimation · Decision support system · Bayesian networks · Uncertainty · Process improvement · Cost estimation · Web systems

1 Introduction

Effort estimation, the process by which effort is forecasted and used as basis to predict costs and to allocate resources effectively, is one of the main pillars of sound project management, given that its accuracy can affect significantly whether projects will be delivered on time and within budget [4]. However, because it is a complex domain where corresponding decisions and predictions require reasoning with uncertainty, there are countless examples of companies that underestimate effort. Jørgensen and Grimstad [7] reported that such estimation error can be of 30 %–40 % on average, thus leading to serious project management problems.

There is a large body of knowledge in software effort estimation [8], and Web-development effort estimation [1]. Most of those studies focused on solving companies' inaccurate effort predictions via investigating techniques that are used to build formal effort estimation models, in the hope that such formalization will improve the accuracy of estimates. They do so by assessing, and often also comparing, the prediction

© Springer-Verlag Berlin Heidelberg 2014
J. Cordeiro and M. van Sinderen (Eds.): ICSOFT 2013, CCIS 457, pp. 40–56, 2014.
DOI: 10.1007/978-3-662-44920-2_3

accuracy obtained from applying numerous statistical and artificial intelligence techniques to datasets of completed projects developed by industry, and sometimes also developed by students.

The variables characterizing such datasets are determined in different ways, such as via surveys [12], interviews with experts [21], expertise from companies [5], a combination of research findings [10], or even a researcher's own consulting experience [20]. In all of these instances, once variables are defined, a data gathering exercise takes place, obtaining data (ideally) from industrial projects volunteered by companies. However, in addition to eliciting the important effort predictors (and optionally also their relationships), such mechanism does not provide the means to also quantify the uncertainty associated with these relationships and to validate the knowledge obtained. Why should these be important?

Research on effort estimation models built using a technique that incorporates the uncertainty inherent in this domain has shown very promising results relating to improved decision making for project management. This technique is called Bayesian Networks (BNs), and has also been employed successfully in a wide range of other domains (e.g. Pollino et al. [17]; Korb and Nicholson [6]). Some of the models described in those studies were built automatically from existing datasets on software or Web-development projects (e.g. Nauman and Lali [14]; Mendes and Mosley [9]); however, some other models in that literature were built using a structured iterative process in which factors and relationships were identified, quantified and validated (e.g. Mendes et al. [13]) through a process of knowledge creation (Nonaka and Toyama [15]), where experts' tacit knowledge relating to effort estimation was explicitated (thus leading to models that mirror their mental models), and later internalized (tacit knowledge is modified due to the use of the models) by those employing these models for decision making, in order to obtain effort estimates for projects.

The goal of this paper, and hence its contribution, is to detail a case study in which the process of knowledge creation abovementioned was used to build an effort estimation BN model within a domain that had not been previously investigated in the software and Web-development literature (Jorgensen and Shepperd [8]; Azhar et al. [1]) – that of healthcare software project management. This model was built for one of the branches of a large Japanese healthcare software provider, with the participation of seven project managers.

Post-mortem interviews with the participating company showed that the understanding it gained by being actively engaged in building the models led to both improved estimates and project management decision making.

The remainder of this paper is structured as follows: Sect. 2 provides an overview of BNs, followed by the description, in Sect. 3, of the general process used to build and validate BNs. Section 4 details this process within the context of the model described herein, followed by a discussion of the results in Sect. 5, and finally conclusions in Sect. 6.

2   Introduction to Bayesian Networks

A Bayesian Network (BN) is a model that supports reasoning with uncertainty due to the way in which it incorporates existing knowledge of a complex domain [16].

This knowledge is represented using two parts. The first, the qualitative part, represents the structure of a BN as depicted by a directed acyclic graph (digraph) (see Fig. 1). The digraph's nodes represent the relevant variables (factors) in the domain being modeled, which can be of different types (e.g. observable or latent, categorical). The digraph's arcs represent the causal relationships between variables, where relationships are quantified probabilistically [16].

The second, the quantitative part, associates a conditional probability table (CPT) to each node, its probability distribution. A parent node's CPT describes the relative probability of each state (value) (Fig. 1, nodes 'Pages complexity' and 'Functionality complexity'); a child node's CPT describes the relative probability of each state conditional on every combination of states of its parents (Fig. 1, node 'Total Effort'). So, for example, the relative probability of 'Total Effort' being 'Low' conditional on 'Pages complexity' and 'Functionality complexity' being both 'Low' is 0.7. Each row in a CPT represents a conditional probability distribution and therefore its values sum up to 1 [16].

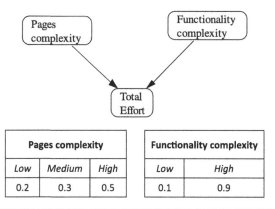

Pages complexity				Functionality complexity	
Low	Medium	High		Low	High
0.2	0.3	0.5		0.1	0.9

Total Effort (Low, Medium, High)				
Pages complexity	Functionality complexity	Low	Medium	High
Low	Low	0.7	0.2	0.1
Low	High	0.2	0.6	0.2
Medium	Low	0.1	0.7	0.2
Medium	High	0	0.5	0.5
High	Low	0.2	0.6	0.2
High	High	0	0.1	0.9

Fig. 1. Example of a BN and three CPTs.

Once a BN is specified, evidence (e.g. values) can be entered into any node, and probabilities for the remaining nodes automatically calculated using Bayes' rule [16]. Therefore BNs can be used for different types of reasoning, such as predictive, diagnostic, and "what-if" analyses to investigate the impact that changes on some nodes have on others.

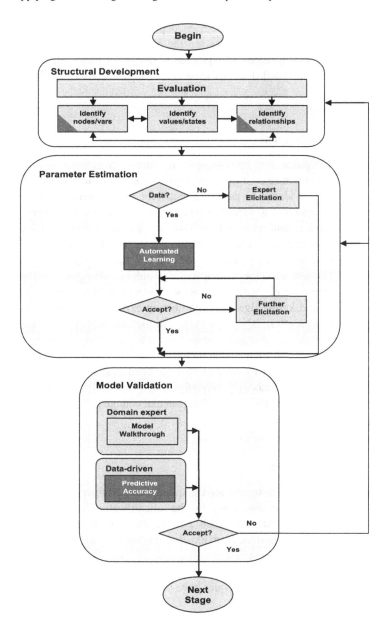

Fig. 2. Adapted KEBNs process [13].

3   Adapted Knowledge Engineering of Bayesian Networks Process

The BN model presented herein was built and validated using the adapted Knowledge Engineering of Bayesian Networks (KEBN) process [9] (see Fig. 2). In Fig. 2 arrows represent flows through the different processes, depicted by rectangles. The three main steps within the adapted KEBN process are the Structural Development, Parameter Estimation, and Model Validation. This process iterates over these steps until a complete BN is built and validated. Each of these three steps is detailed in the next Subsections.

3.1 Structural Development

The Structural Development step represents the qualitative component of a BN, which results in a graphical structure comprised of, in our case, the factors (nodes, variables) and causal relationships identified as fundamental for effort estimation of healthcare software projects. In addition to identifying variables, their types (e.g. query variable, evidence variable) and causal relationships, this step also comprises the identification of the states (values) that each variable should take. The BN's structure is refined through an iterative process. This structure construction process has been validated in previous studies [2] and uses the principles of problem solving employed in data modelling and software development [18]. As will be detailed later, existing literature in effort estimation, and knowledge from the domain experts were employed to elicit the Healthcare software effort BN's structure. Throughout this step the author also evaluated the BN's structure to check whether variables and their values have a clear meaning; all relevant variables have been included; variables are named conveniently; all states are appropriate (exhaustive and exclusive). The BN structure may also need to be optimised to reduce the number of probabilities that need to be elicited or learnt for the network. Whenever this is the case, techniques that change the causal structure (e.g. divorcing [3]) are employed.

3.2 Parameter Estimation

The Parameter estimation step represents the quantitative component of a BN, where conditional probabilities corresponding to the quantification of the relationships between variables [3] are obtained. Such probabilities can be attained via Expert Elicitation, automatically from data, from existing literature, or using a combination of these. When probabilities are elicited from scratch, or even if they only need to be revisited, this step can be very time consuming. In order to minimise the number of probabilities to be elicited some techniques have been proposed in the literature [2, 19].

3.3 Model Validation

The Model validation step validates the BN that results from the two previous steps, and determines whether it is necessary to re-visit any of those steps. Two different validation methods are generally used - Model Walkthrough and Predictive Accuracy.

Model walkthrough represents the use of real case scenarios that are prepared and used by domain experts to assess if the predictions provided by the BN model correspond to the predictions experts would have chosen based on their own expertise.

Success is measured as the frequency with which the BN's predicted value for a target variable (e.g. quality, effort) that has the highest probability corresponds to the experts' own assessment.

Predictive Accuracy uses past data (e.g. past project data), rather than scenarios, to obtain predictions. Data (evidence) is entered on the BN model, and success is measured as the frequency with which the BN's predicted value for a target variable (e.g. quality, effort) that has the highest probability corresponds to the actual past data.

4   Process Used to Build the BN Model

Here in we revisit the adapted KEBN process (see Fig. 2), detailing the tasks carried out for each of the three main steps, within the context of the effort estimation BN model for healthcare projects that is the focus of this paper. Before starting the elicitation of the model, the seven project managers participating in the model elicitation & validation were given an overview of BNs, and examples of "what-if" scenarios using a made-up BN. This, we believe, facilitated the entire process as the use of an example, and the brief explanation of each of the steps in the adapted KEBN process, provided a concrete understanding of what to expect. We also made it clear that the author was solely a facilitator of the process, and that the Healthcare company's commitment was paramount for the success of the process.

The entire process took 324 person hours to be completed, with seven projet managers participating at 12 3-hour slots, and two other project managers participating at other 12 3-hour slots.

The company for which the model was created, located in the Pacific Rim region, represents one of the several branches worldwide that are part of a larger Healthcare organization, which headquarters in Japan. The company had ∼ 100 employees. The project managers had each worked in Healthcare software development for more than 10 years. In addition, this company developed a wide range of Healthcare software applications, using different types of technology.

4.1   Detailed Structural Development & Parameter Estimation

In order to identify the fundamental factors that the project managers considered when preparing a project quote, and also taking into account that most of the projects managed were Web-development projects, we used, as suggested in [13], the set of variables from the Tukutuku dataset [12] as a starting point (see Table 1). We first sketched them out on a white board, each one inside an oval shape, and then explained what each one meant.

Once the Tukutuku variables had been sketched out and explained, the next step was to remove all variables that were not relevant for the project managers, followed by adding to the white board any additional variables (factors) suggested by them. We also documented descriptions for each of the factors suggested. Next, we identified the states that each factor would take. All states were discrete. Whenever a factor represented a measure of effort (e.g. Total effort), we also documented the effort range corresponding to each state, to avoid any future ambiguity. For example, 'very low' Total effort corresponded to 4+ to 10 person hours, etc. Once all states were identified and documented, it was time to elicit the cause and effect relationships. As a starting point to this task we used the same example used in [13] - a simple medical example from [3] (see Fig. 3).

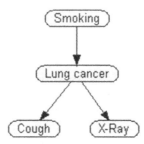

Fig. 3. A simple medical example from [3].

This example clearly introduces one of the most important points to consider when identifying cause and effect relationships – timeline of events. If smoking is to be a cause of lung cancer, it is important that the cause precedes the effect. This may sound

Table 1. The Tukutuku variables [12].

	Variable Name	Description
Project Data	TypeProj	Type of project (new or enhancement).
	nLang	Number of different development languages used
	DocProc	If project followed defined and documented process.
	ProImpr	If project team involved in a process improvement programme.
	Metrics	If project team part of a software metrics programme.
	DevTeam	Size of a project's development team.
	TeamExp	Average team experience with the development language(s) employed.
Web application	TotWP	Total number of Web pages (new and reused).
	NewWP	Total number of new Web pages.
	TotImg	Total number of images (new and reused).
	NewImg	Total number of new images created.
	Num_Fots	Number of features reused without any adaptation.
	HFotsA	Number of reused high-effort features/functions adapted.
	Hnew	Number of new high-effort features/functions.
	TotHigh	Total number of high-effort features/functions
	Num_FotsA	Number of reused low-effort features adapted.
	New	Number of new low-effort features/functions.
	TotNHigh	Total number of low-effort features/functions

obvious with regard to the example used; however, it is our view that the use of this simple example significantly helped the project managers understand the notion of cause and effect, and how this related to software effort estimation and the BN being elicited.

Table 2. Description of all the factors elicited from the Des.

Factor	Categories	Description, observation
Actual pre-sales effort	Low (0+ to 10 person-hours (prs)) Medium (10+ to 20 prs) High (20+ prs)	Contract signing (optional), requirements elicitation (prepared before preparation of quote) + quote preparation, user requirements specification (optional), programming specification (aka technical spec, functional spec)
Number of technologies	Small (1 technology) Medium (2 to 3 technologies) Large (4 and above)	Examples of internal technologies: Cobol, Web (ASP, .NET, C#), Windows, Lotus Notes, Oracle, SQL
Application testing effort	None Low (0+ to 10 prs) Medium (10+ to 30 prs) High (30+ to 150 prs) Very high (150+ prs)	Testing throughout the project, but only inside the company
Testing environment setup	Low (0+ to 1 prs) Medium (1+ to 4 prs) High (4+ prs)	Number of person hours to set up the testing environment
High risk programs effort	None Low (0+ to 5 prs) Medium (5+ to 10 prs) High (10+ to 20 prs) Very high (20+ prs)	Programs used by only a few customers, and difficult to test; programs that are historically difficult to manage or change (e.g. non-documented features, cobol legacy)
Estimated third party effort	None Low (0+ to 10 prs) Medium (10+ to 30 prs) High (30+ to 60 prs) Very high (60+ prs)	Estimated effort to third party-related issues (number and risk factor)
Effort adapting items	None Very low (0+ to 10 prs) Low (10+ to 20 prs) Medium (20+ to 40 prs) High (40+ to 80 prs) Very high (80+ prs)	Number of person hours adapting items

(Continued)

Table 2. *(Continued)*

Factor	Categories	Description, observation
Effort creating new items	None Low (0+ to 40 prs) Medium (40+ to 80 prs) High (80+ to 150 prs) Very high (150+ to 1000 prs) Extremely high (1000 + prs)	Number of person hours creating new items
Effort to create and package product	None Low (0+ to 1 prs) Medium (1+ to 4 prs) High (4+ prs)	Effort to create and package a product (includes paperwork, burning a CD, printing and binding the manuals, issuing the product (send the CD to the customer, or uploading into a FTP site)); also includes maintaining internal source code repository, and patches
Writing of user documentation effort	None Low (0+ to 10 prs) Medium (10+ to 50 prs) High (50+ to 200 prs) Very high (200+ prs)	Estimate of the number of hours writing the user documentation (aka product documentation, user manual)
Estimated testing effort	Low (0+ to 10 prs) Medium (10+ to 30 prs) High (30+ to 150 prs) Very high (150+ to 450 prs) Extremely high (450 + prs)	Total estimated testing effort from environment set up and application testing
Estimated development effort	None Very low (0+ to 20 prs) Low (20+ to 80 prs) Medium (80+ to 150 prs) High (150+ to 450 prs) Very high (450+ to 1000 prs) Extremely high (1000 + prs)	Total estimated dev effort from the items
Total product development effort	None Very low (0+ to 20 prs) Low (20+ to 80 prs) Medium (80+ to 150 prs) High (150+ to 450 prs) Very high (450+ to 2500 prs) Exceptionally high (2500 + prs)	

(Continued)

Table 2. *(Continued)*

Factor	Categories	Description, observation
Customer environment effort	Low (0+ to 1 prs) Medium (1+ to 5 prs) High (5+ prs)	Time zone, system access. These are tangible points
Customer risk factors effort (generally represented as an effort %)	None Low (0+ to 5 prs) Medium (5+ to 10 prs) High (10+ prs)	Personality, capabilities, expectations, involvement, track record, language barrier, language difficulties, size customer representation/team
Customer support effort	None Low (0+ to 8 prs) Medium (8+ to 40 prs) High (40+ prs)	Pre and post go live support
Customer training effort	None Low (0+ to 8 prs) Medium (8+ to 40 prs) High (40+ prs)	Amount of training (includes preparation)
Estimated customer effort	None Low (0+ to 20 prs) Medium (20+ to 85 prs) High (85+ prs)	Estimated effort for customer-related items (environment, support, training)
Involved in SPI (software process improvement)	Yes No	Part of the project management
Number of adapted high effort (20+) items off-the-shelf	None Small (1 item) Medium (2 items) High (3+ items)	Number of hours that represent high and low effort need to be defined (excludes testing). One adaptation can incur several changes. High effort here means the use of 20 + person/hours to adapt a single item
Number of adapted medium effort (5+ to 20) items off-the-shelf	None Small (1 item) Medium (2 to 4 items) High (5 + items)	Number of hours that represent high and low effort need to be defined (excludes testing). One adaptation can incur several changes. Medium effort here means the use of 5 + to 20 person/hours to adapt a single item
Number of adapted low effort (1->5) items off-the-shelf	None Small (1 to 3 items) Medium (4 to 6 items) High (7+ items)	(Excludes testing) One adaptation can incur several changes. Low effort here means the use of up to 5 person/hours to adapt a single item

(Continued)

Table 2. *(Continued)*

Factor	Categories	Description, observation
Number of new high effort (80+) items	None Small (1 item) Medium (2 to 4 items) High (5+ items)	(Excludes testing) High effort here means the use of 80 + person/hours to develop a single item
Number of new low effort items	None Small (1 item) Medium (2 to 4 items) High (5+ items)	(Excludes testing) Low effort here means the use of up to 20 person/hours to develop a single item
Number of new medium effort items	None Small (1 item) Medium (2 to 4 items) High (5+ items)	(Excludes testing) Medium effort here means the use of 20+ to 80 person/hours to develop a single item
Overall effort configuration items	None Very low (0+ to 1 prs) Low (1+ to 5 prs) Medium (5+ to 15 prs) High (15+ to 40 prs) Very high (40+ prs)	Effort to configure an installed system for use as per customer requirements
Overall effort installation items	None Low (0+ to 5 prs) Medium (5+ to 15 prs) High (15+ prs)	Items are interpreted as an area, program, or module. Items have hour figures next to them. (either it's only development, or pure training, cd sent to client for them to install)
Total implementation effort	None Very low (0+ to 2 prs) Low (2+ to 5 prs) Medium (5+ to 20 prs) High (20+ to 80 prs) Very high (80+ prs)	
Project management effort	None Low (15 % of estimated effort) Medium (20 to 30 % of estimated effort) High (30+ % of estimated effort)	Project management overhead, including status reports; communication; Implementation plan (more for large projects) which includes the tasks to be done and their estimated completion dates; risk analysis; data analysis; planning (project execution plan)
Size of project team	Small (2 to 5 people) Medium (6 to 8 people) Large (9+ people)	Only the team internally to the company
	None Low (0+ to 5 prs)	Requirements elicitation, user requirements specification,,

(Continued)

Table 2. *(Continued)*

Factor	Categories	Description, observation
Estimated analysis & design effort (post-sales)	Medium (5+ to 20 prs) High (20+ to 70 prs) Very high (70+ prs)	programming specification (aka technical spec, functional spec)
Specification effort	None Low (0+ to 3 prs) Medium (3+ to 10 prs) High (10+ prs)	Set-up plan, Cut-over plan (steps required to move changes into production), Customer test specification
Total analysis and specification effort	None Low (0+ to 8 prs) Medium (8+ to 30 prs) High (30+ to 80 prs) Very high (80+ prs)	
Team competency impact	Very low (0 % of the team have low competency) Low (0 %+ to 25 % of the team have low competency) Medium (25 %+ to 40 % of the team have low competency) High (40 %+ to 70 % of the team have low competency) Very high (70 %+ to 100 % of the team have low competency)	Definition/to be considered when rating: − years of experience with the domain (e.g. Hematology), − years of experience with programming language, technical skill − knowledge of the product, (Y/N) − training (not charged to the customer), − technology (development technology and target technology, e. g. virtual environment), − non SNZ team members (Y/N) − English as a second language (Y/N) − Software Development Lifecycle Role − proven past performance − customer/market knowledge (e.g. when writing specifications) − personality (e.g. attention to detail, easily distracted, note: this is often only known after the project) − experience in development and implementation of Beta products
Third party risk effort	None Low (0+ to 5 prs) Medium (5+ to 10 prs) High (10+ prs)	Not company's customers (for example, emailing third party, phone calls, finalising specs, reading their documentation, communication plan, messages)
Number of third parties	None Small (1 third party)	Number of external systems (sw, hw) or organisations (people)

Table 2. *(Continued)*

Factor	Categories	Description, observation
	Medium (2 to 3 third parties) High (4 or more third parties)	(third parties company has no control over)
Estimated effort	None Very Low (0+ to 15 prs) Low (15+ to 40 prs) Medium (40+ to 150 prs) High (150+ to 1000 prs) Very High (1000+ to 3000 prs) Exceptionally High (3000+ prs)	Estimated effort to develop a project, excluding project management
Total estimated effort	None Very Low (0+ to 15 prs) Low (15+ to 40 prs) Medium (40+ to 150 prs) High (150+ to 1500 prs) Very High (1500+ to 4000 prs) Exceptionally High (4000+ person-hours)	Total estimated effort to develop a project, including project management

Once the cause and effect relationships were identified the Healthcare software effort & risk BN's causal structure was as follows (see Fig. 4). Note that Fig. 4 is not a BN based directly on Table 1.

At this point the project managers seemed happy with the BN's causal structure and the work on eliciting the probabilities was initiated. All probabilities were created from scratch, and the probabilities elicitation took 72 h (one project manager and the author). The complete BN, including its probabilities, is shown in Fig. 5. Figure 5 shows the BN using belief bars rather than labelled factors, so readers can see the probabilities that were elicited (Table 2).

5 Discussion

In terms of the use of this BN model, it can also be employed for diagnostic reasoning, and to run numerous "what-if" scenarios. Figure 7 shows an example of a model being used for diagnostic reasoning, where the evidence was entered for Total Estimated Effort, and used to assess the highest probabilities for each of the other factors.

Six months after the completion of the BN model, the author participated in a post-mortem interview with the company's project managers. The changes that took place as the result of developing the BN model were as follows:

- The model was explained to the entire software development group and all the estimations provided by any team member (e.g. developers, managers) had to be based on the factors that were part of the BN model. This means that the entire team started to use the factors that have been elicited, as well as the BN model, as basis for decision making during their effort estimation sessions.
- Initially, project managers estimated effort using both subjective means and also the BN model. If there were differences between estimates, they would discuss and reach a consensus on which estimate to use. Later both estimates were compared to the actual effort once projects were completed. However, in less than 6 months from using the BN model, managers moved to using the model-based estimates only.

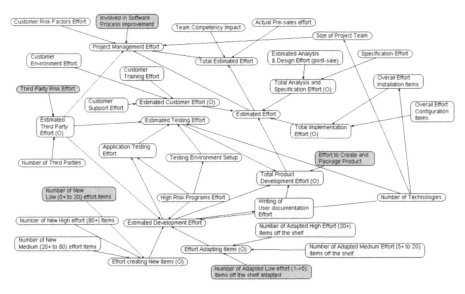

Fig. 4. BN model's causal structure.

Finally, as a consequence from using this model, this company branch started to increase the number of requests from other branches for software development projects. This occurred when one of the project managers presented the model at a meeting with other company branches, so to detail how their branch was estimating effort for their healthcare projects.

Overall, such change in approach provided extremely beneficial to the company (Fig. 6).

We believe that the successful development of this Effort estimation BN model was greatly influenced by a number of factors, such as:

- The company's commitment to providing their time and expertise.
- The use of a process where project managers' participation was fundamental. This approach was seen as extremely positive by the company as they could implicitly

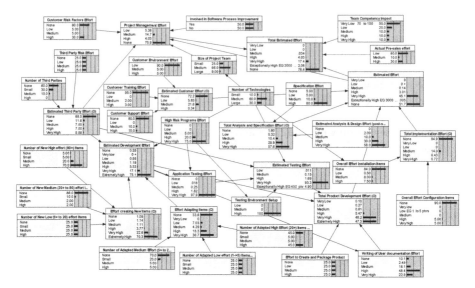

Fig. 5. Effort estimation BN model for healthcare software development.

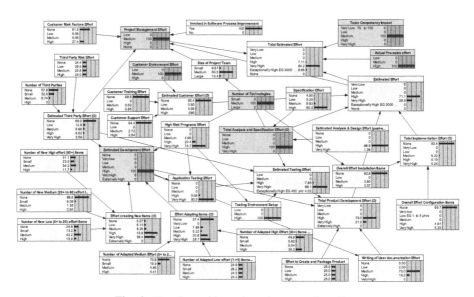

Fig. 6. Entering evidence in order to predict effort.

understand the value from building a model that was totally geared towards their needs.

– The project managers' excellent experience in managing healthcare software projects.

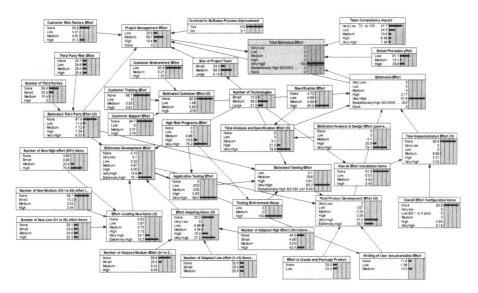

Fig. 7. Diagnostic reasoning.

6 Conclusions

This paper has presented a case study where a Bayesian Model for effort estimation of Healthcare projects was built using solely knowledge of seven Domain Experts from a well-established Healthcare company in the Pacific Rim. This model was developed using an adaptation of the knowledge engineering for Bayesian Networks process (see Fig. 2). Each session with the project managers lasted for no longer than 3 h. The final BN model was calibrated using data on 22 past projects. These projects represented typical projects developed by the company, and believed by the experts to provide enough data for model calibration.

Since the model's adoption, it has been successfully used to provide effort quotes for the new projects managed by the company.

The entire process used to build and validate the BN model took 324 person hours.

As part of our future work, we plan to compare our model to that from other related research using BNs within the context of software effort estimation.

Acknowledgements. We would like to thank the project managers who participated in the elicitation and validation of this model.

References

1. Azhar, D., Mendes, E., Riddle, P.: A systematic review of web resource estimation. In: Proceedings of Promise'12 (2012)
2. Druzdzel, M.J., van der Gaag, L.C.: Building probabilistic networks: where do the numbers come from? IEEE Trans. Knowl. Data Eng. **12**(4), 481–486 (2000)

3. Jensen, F.V.: An Introduction to Bayesian Networks. UCL Press, London (1996)
4. Fenton, N., Marsh, W., Neil, M., Cates, P., Forey, S., Tailor, M.: Making resource decisions for software projects. In: Proceedings of ICSE'04, pp. 397–406 (2004)
5. Ferrucci, F., Gravino, C., Di Martino, S.: A case study using web objects and COSMIC for effort estimation of web applications. In: EUROMICRO-SEAA, pp. 441–448 (2008)
6. Korb, K.B., Nicholson, A.E.: Bayesian Artificial Intelligence. CRC Press, Boca Raton (2004)
7. Jørgensen, M., Grimstad, S.: Software development effort estimation: demystifying and improving expert estimation (Chap. 26). In: Tveito, A., Bruaset, A.M., Lysne, O. (eds.) Simula Research Laboratory - by Thinking Constantly About it, pp. 381–404. Springer, Heidelberg (2010). ISBN 978-3642011559
8. Jorgensen, M., Shepperd, M.: A systematic review of software development cost estimation studies. IEEE Trans. Softw. Eng. **33**(1), 33–53 (2007)
9. Mendes, E., Mosley, N.: Bayesian network models for web effort prediction: a comparative study. Trans. Softw. Eng. **34**(6), 723–737 (2008)
10. Mendes, E., Mosley, N., Counsell, S.: Web metrics - metrics for estimating effort to design and author Web applications. IEEE MultiMed. **8**(1), 50–57 (2001)
11. Mendes, E., Mosley, N., Counsell, S.: The need for web engineering: an introduction. In: Mendes, E., Mosley, N. (eds.) web engineering, pp. 1–26. Springer, Heidelberg (2005). ISBN 3-540-281 96-7
12. Mendes, E., Mosley, N., Counsell, S.: Investigating web size metrics for early web cost estimation. J. Syst. Softw. **77**(2), 157–172 (2005)
13. Mendes, E., Polino, C., Mosley, N.: Building an expert-based web effort estimation model using Bayesian networks. In: 13th International Conference on Evaluation and Assessment in Software Engineering (2009)
14. Nauman, A.B., Lali, M.I.: Productivity inference with dynamic Bayesian models in software development projects. Int. J. Comput. Electron. **1**(2), 50–57 (2012)
15. Nonaka, I., Toyama, R.: The knowledge-creating theory revisited: knowledge creation as a synthesizing process. Knowl. Manag. Res. Pract. **1**, 2–10 (2003)
16. Pearl, J.: Probabilistic Reasoning in Intelligent Systems. Morgan Kaufmann, San Mateo (1988)
17. Pollino, C., White, A., Hart, B.T.: Development and application of a Bayesian decision support tool to assist in the management of an endangered species. Ecol. Model. **201**, 37–59 (2007)
18. Studer, R., Benjamins, V.R., Fensel, D.: Knowledge engineering: principles and methods. Data Knowl. Eng. **25**, 161–197 (1998)
19. Tang, Z., McCabe, B.: Developing complete conditional probability tables from fractional data for Bayesian Belief networks. J. Comput. Civ. Eng. **21**(4), 265–276 (2007)
20. Reifer, D.J.: Web development: estimating quick-to-market software. IEEE Softw. **17**(6), 57–64 (2000)
21. Ruhe, M., Jeffery, R., Wieczorek, I.: Cost estimation for web applications. In: Proceedings of ICSE 2003, pp. 285–294 (2003)
22. Woodberry, O., Nicholson, A., Korb, K., Pollino, C.: Parameterising Bayesian networks. In: Proceedings of the Australian Conference on Artificial Intelligence pp. 1101–1107 (2004)

A Scenario Analysis Method
with User Emotion and Its Context

Takako Nakatani[1]([✉]) and Keita Sato[2]

[1] Graduate School of Business Sciences, University of Tsukuba,
3-29-1, Otsuka, Bunkyo-ku, Tokyo 112-0012, Japan
`nakatani.takako.gf@u.tsukuba.ac.jp`
[2] DENSO CORPORATION, 1-1, Shouwacho, Kariya-shi, Aichi 448-8661, Japan

Abstract. Safe driving is mandatory for an Advanced Driver Assistance
System (ADAS). The adequacy and safety of an ADAS has to be evaluated not only by developers, but also by drivers. Evaluations by drivers
can be monitored by their positive and negative emotions, since for example, if they find a hazardous situation, they have a negative emotion,
"surprised" or "close call." An ADAS is considered "good", if it does not
cause driver emotions such as these, and hence, is viewed as adequate
and safety. In order to analyze the safety requirements of drivers for the
ADAS, we propose a multi-layered scenario analysis (MuLSA). MuLSA
is a kind of scenario analysis method consisting of a driver's journey,
his/her emotions, the mechanism of services, as well as the context of
the services. This paper shows the results of the observation of emotions
through a simulation, and we discuss the effectiveness of analyzing the
requirements of services with regard to the user's emotion.

Keywords: Requirements engineering · User's emotion · Scenario
analysis · Advanced driver assistance system

1 Introduction

In this paper, we introduce a method to analyze requirements on the adequacy
and safety of an Advanced Driver Assistance System (ADAS) based on evaluation of drivers. According to the SQuaRE (Software product Quality Requirements and Evaluation) [1], customer satisfaction is evaluated as, "the satisfaction
in the usability of services." The emotion of users should be taken into account
to introduce services into the competitive market. In general, when drivers con-
front a hazardous situation, they have a negative emotion, "surprised" or "close
call." Thus, the emotions of drivers tell us whether the service is comfortable or
dangerous for them. In order to analyze the satisfaction of the services of the
ADAS, we extend a scenario analysis method that includes driver emotions and
the related context.

When we analyze the requirements of a new system that extends an existing
system, we first extract problems from the existing system. The Cruise Control

© Springer-Verlag Berlin Heidelberg 2014
J. Cordeiro and M. van Sinderen (Eds.): ICSOFT 2013, CCIS 457, pp. 57–71, 2014.
DOI: 10.1007/978-3-662-44920-2_4

system (CC) of a car is one of the driver assistance systems (DAS), and is regarded as an existing system for the ADAS. CC only regulates the speed of a car, and furthermore, its structure is relatively simple. The requirements of CC can be analyzed with two layers: one is a service provider layer, while the other is a service receiver layer. The functions of CC are defined in the service provider layer. They are, "start" and "termination" of the service, and "maintenance of the speed." On the other hand, a driver is allocated within the layer of a service receiver. The driver initiates the services of CC and monitors the state and/or situation of his/her car. If we can observe the ups and downs of emotions of a driver when utilizing the CC, we can evaluate the customer satisfaction of the CC and find any problems within the CC.

The structure of the latest DAS is more complex than that of CC. The advanced cruise control system (ACC) regulates not only the speed of the car, but also the distance from the precedent car. The structure of the service of ACC consists of the precedent car, as well as the driver and the ACC. The lane departure warning system is another example of DAS. It helps the car navigate the traffic lane. In this case, the structure of the service analysis has to take into account the traffic lane. Some of these systems stop their services in heavy rain, since they cannot monitor the precedent car or the traffic lane under such bad weather conditions. Thus, the weather must also to be a consideration within the service structure.

The ADAS provides more complex services than the current DASs. It will be expected to monitor peripheral cars, load conditions, traffic lights, traffic signs, etc. and, make decisions in order to ensure the safety of the driver's journey. The purpose of this paper is to develop a scenario analysis method for the DAS in order to define problems and prioritize requirements of the ADAS. We refer to the method as multi-layered scenario analysis (MuLSA).

This paper is constructed as follows. In the next section, we introduce the related work. In Sect. 3, we describe the basic concept of MuLSA and an overview of MuLSA with its analysis structure and process. MuLSA is evaluated by applying it to a case. We describe the case and the results of the application in Sect. 4. In Sect. 5, we evaluate the result of the case based on the threats. In the final section, we discuss the strengths and weaknesses of MuLSA and conclude this paper.

2 Related Work

2.1 Emotion Analysis

Plutchik [2] introduces the three-dimensional circumplex model. In the model, every emotion composes a combination of the following eight basic ones: vigilance, rage, loathing, grief, amazement, terror, admiration, and ecstasy. We selected and categorized these emotions into positive and negative emotions. For example, ecstasy and admiration can be categorized into positive emotions. Thus, vigilance, rage, loathing, grief, amazement, as well as terror are categorized into negative emotions. The positive/negative emotions are reflections of the high/low quality of the service for the customer. For example, if the ADAS provides safe driving, the driver is satisfied with the services of the ADAS, and will accept the system. If the driver is fearful of the system, we regard the quality of the service as low, and needs to be improved.

There are several means to measure emotions [3]. Some researchers use questionnaires to assess emotions [4]. We developed a tool by which the emotions of a subject driver are recorded quantitatively from the inputs of keys that are assigned to the positive and negative emotions.

2.2   Scenario Analysis

J.M. Carroll [5] describes the strengths scenarios. Scenarios can explicitly envision and document typical and significant user activities. It also provides us reasoning with regard to the situation of use before we develop the system. Use case [6] and user story [7] are categorized into scenario analysis methods. Persona analysis is used to analyze a specific user's activities [8]. Even though a scenario reports a user's activities well, we need to analyze more than these reported activities. The problem with a simple scenario, such as a use case, is that it is constructed in a single-layered structure. In order to evaluate the quality of ADAS, we need a more complex analysis space.

In the service analysis, there are methods to analyzing the quality of services according to customer satisfaction. The concept of those methods is that, "the customer is satisfied with good service." For example, if the customer is unsatisfied with the service, it should be improved. A customer journey map (CJM) [9] is used to evaluate the customers' emotion while mapping them to their services. It is also a kind of scenario analysis method. Risdon [10] proposes a CJM to the analysis of the service of the Rail Europe. We can see a lot of examples of CJM on the Internet. CJM helps service marketing or business marketing improve their services or products. A scenario described in the CJM has a time line and a concrete story.

Though there is no standard notation for CJMs, most CJMs have a two-layered structure. In the first layer, services are shown as a user story with *touchpoints* at which the customer accesses the service. The story can be regarded as a customer's journey or their experiences in the forest of the services. In the second layer, the emotions or impressions of the customer are described according to the customer's journey. Richardson [11] shows an example of a journey into shopping. The scenario commences from a customer's awareness, to an out-of-box-experience. During the customer's activities, a CJM is used to evaluate motivations, questions and barriers. Our purpose is to analyze the quality and/or problems of the services provided by the DAS and prioritize the requirements of the ADAS. The analysis space of the ADAS should contain customer's activities, customer's emotions, environment of usage, as well as services. The method that we propose includes the structure of CJM and further layers.

A service blueprint (SB) applies a two-layered scenario: a "from stage" and a "back stage" [12]. A service is provided to a customer via a *front stage* of the service that is constructed in a *back stage*. In the front stage, direct communication between a customer and services is shown. In the back stage, there is indirect interaction between the customer and the underground mechanism that supports the services. These two stages represent how the services are implemented and serve the customer. However, it does not analyze the emotions of a customer, but simply designs the services. The method that we propose also includes the layer of the back stage of SB in order to analyze the mechanism of problems within the DAS.

Blueprint+ [13] is a multi-layered method that integrates emotional presentations and SB. The first layer is a system layer with a set of actors and a *touch-point* for each service. The second layer is a customer layer with the concerns of the customer including his/her emotions. The strength of our method is that it has a context layer to represent the environment of usage or services. It helps analysts analyze the context of the bad services.

There are various scenario analysis methods. We integrate and extend these methods in order to adopt them to the problem analysis of services of DAS and extract problems of the services.

3   MuLSA: Multi-layered Scenario Analysis

In this section, we describe the basic concept of MuLSA and give an overview of MuLSA as a method of analyzing customer satisfaction and the quality of the services of the current system.

3.1   Basic Concept

It becomes possible to drive the car automatically. For example, a driverless Audi TTS climbed up to the top of Pikes Peak in 2010 [14]. Google has also developed a google driverless car [15]. Though our focus is not on an automatic driving system, we do recognize that a car can be driven safely by computer; however, we do not think such an autonomous system will satisfy its human driver or passengers.

A car is on the road under various environmental conditions, and other cars may not behave in expected ways. We have to analyze the environmental and mechanical circumstances under which the services perform. Events and/or objects that are monitored by the ADAS are referred to as the environmental factors. Some of the environmental factors are called "hazards." When we elicit and analyze requirements of ADAS, we have to consider the possible hazard and keep the car and driver out of danger.

Drivers however, are the experts who detect hazards when they drive their car. When they detect a hazard, they become strained. If they feel they are free from the hazard, they must become relaxed. When they realize that they are not being cared for by the ADAS, they become scared and/or irritated. We can refer to these emotions, i.e. strained, surprised, scared, irritated, etc., as negative emotions. Furthermore, negative emotions may lead a driver to become dissatisfied with the system. Thus, we have to detect hazards by monitoring the emotions of drivers and define requirements for the future ADAS. We expect to elicit prioritized requirements by analyzing the emotions of real drivers.

Emotions, such as showing enjoyment, being relaxed, etc., are referred to as positive emotions. The mission of the ADAS is not only to keep a driver and fellow passengers safe, but also to give positive feelings to them, especially the drivers. In order to increase the satisfaction of drivers, we analyze the services that dissatisfy them, and clarify the reasons that drivers have negative emotions with regard to the services.

Companies that provide DAS sometimes research drivers' satisfaction through questionnaires. Some companies also survey drivers' satisfaction for each country the systems are operated in. However, the questionnaire survey is not adequate in detecting problematic services. In order to detect problematic services, we need to analyze the process of the service provision and the usage of the service. MuLSA has been developed to analyze the process and usage of the service of DAS.

3.2   Overview of MuLSA

MuLSA integrates CJM and SB through an extension, with environmental factors as the context of the services. The analysis structure of MuLSA is shown in Fig. 1. It has three layers.

– Customer layer
  In this layer, two kinds of information are presented. One is the customer's journey, and the other is the emotional line of the customer. In Fig. 1, this layer is shown at the top of the figure. The time line of a scenario is passed from left to right.
– Context layer
  The context of the service is shown in the context layer in the middle part of the figure. Every environmental factor that affects the service contents is identified and presented in one of the sublayers.
– Service Mechanism layer
  This layer is constructed with two sublayers that are a *front stage* and a *back stage*. The *front stage* is a communication facade between the customer and the system. The *back stage* represents major components of the system. This layer is shown at the bottom part of Fig. 1.

3.3   Measurement of Emotions

Psychologists have proposed methods to measure emotions [16]. For example, in the case of self-report questionnaires, it is the test subject who reports intuitively and/or subjectively their emotions as expressed through the use of various words, e.g. happiness, surprise, fear, anger, disgust, or sadness. Another way of measuring emotions with regard to vocabulary usage is by the application of a response scale, on which a test subject is observed so that their facial expressions

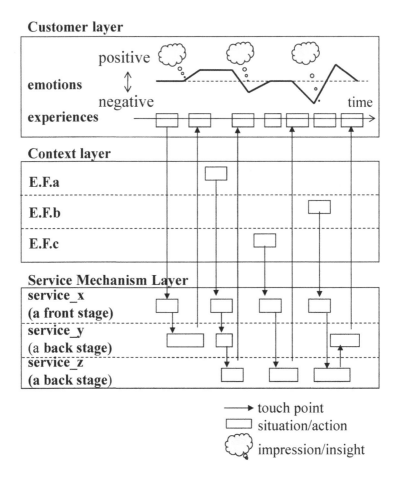

Fig. 1. The structure of MuLSA.

can be recorded. Our purpose in measuring emotions is to clarify any problem-atic behaviors with testing systems according to the subjective emotions of test subjects. Thus, we consider that, intuitive reporting is not only important, but if possible, we also expect a test subject to report their emotions consciously, because following the simulation or test, we may ask them what they felt and what they would require to the ADAS.

A tool to record their emotions is simple. A test subject only inputs keys according to their emotions. The positive and negative emotions are ranked into four levels. The highest emotions are assigned to key "a." Further rankings on our declining scale are, higher, high and rather positive, which are assigned to keys "s","d", and "f", respectively. Similarly, worst, worse, bad, rather negative are assigned to keys "l","k","j", and "h", respectively. Hence, the test subject can set their hands on a QWERTY keyboard and type the characters according to their emotions. The tool is simple enough, and needs little training. Moreover, the tool records the timing of the "key ins" and the key itself, and interprets input keys to the emotional scale described above, from −4 to +4.

3.4   The Requirements Analysis Process

With the three-layered scenario in MuLSA, we can extract the points of the emotional changes and analyze the state of the DAS and the environment. In order to develop the ADAS, we have to analyze problems within the existing DAS. The ADAS has to be able to analyze the circumstances and environment of the car through the use of numerous sensors. The requirements analysis process of MuLSA is shown below.

1. Identify subsystems and set them in the *back stage*.
   These subsystems represent the limitations of the current system. The sensors and controllers of the DAS can be detected. Define the functionalities and efficiency of those components according to the real components in the current system. In order to elicit requirements for the future system, we need to visualize the limitations of the current system.
2. Identify components in the *front stage*.
   A display is the most typical component in the *front stage*. Further, alarms, beeps, or announcements can be components as well.
3. Identify hazards as the environmental factors.
   In order to assess the quality of the services of the current system, listing hazards with regard to environmental factors as much as possible is done. Hazards will be the context of the scenario defined in the next step. Weather, road condition, peripheral vehicles, pedestrians and/or animals can be the hazards.
4. Construct a scenario as a customer's journey.
   The scenario is defined to analyze how much a given hazard affects a driver's emotions. If we can know how much the environmental factors affect the drivers' satisfaction, we can prioritize sensors that can detect and monitor the environmental factors. The best length of the scenario is still under consideration. The scenario of our first case is less than 30 seconds.
5. Develop simulation.
   The scenario is transformed into animation that is developed with PreScan [17]. PreScan is a development environment for DAS or intelligent vehicle systems. Two kinds of animation must be constructed as scenes seen through the windshield and a rearview mirror. Figure 2 represents the image of a tool with the movie being developed by PreScan.
6. Simulate the scenario with a test subject and get emotional data in the scenario. After the simulation, we map the emotional data in accordance with the simulation.
7. Analyze the emotional data and elicit requirements for the ADAS.

ACC is one of the current DASs. ACC safely controls the speed of the car, while establishing a safe distance from the precedent car. Sensors send signals to the ACC, which in turn sends other signals to the speed control unit and display.

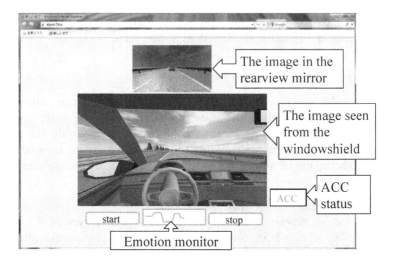

Fig. 2. The tool image of MuLSA

The ADAS will have more sensors and be able to establish the driving context with regard to the environmental factors.

4   Case Study

4.1   Overview

This section describes a case study by which we detect problems in the current ACC as an example of the DAS. We then analyze the problems in order to evaluate the effectiveness of MuLSA. There are various services with regard to ACCs. The ACC used in this case study provides the following services.

- The ACC starts when the driver turns on the ACC.
- The ACC is terminated when the driver turns off the ACC.
- The driver can set the speed for the ACC.
- The driver can increase or decrease the speed of the cruise within the permissible range.
- If there are no precedent vehicles or, there is enough distance from the precedent vehicle, the ACC maintains the set speed of the cruising car.
- If there is a precedent vehicle, the ACC keeps the adequate distance from the precedent vehicle by adjusting the cruising speed. The precedent vehicle is detected by a radar censor on-board.
- If the windshield wipers are used in strong mode, the ACC is automatically terminated, meaning that, the radar or laser cannot detect the precedent vehicle.
- If the precedent car goes out of its lane, the ACC gradually turns the speed back to the set speed.

– If the speed of the cruising car becomes slower than a certain speed, the ACC is automatically terminated.

The display in which the state of the ACC is shown is identified in the *front stage*, with the sensors, speed controller and ACC being defined in the *"back stage"*. In order to evaluate MuLSA, we made a simulation with PreScan [17]. We took various environmental factors into account within the simulation. They were, weather condition, a precedent vehicle, and another car that cuts in front of the cruising car.

4.2   The Scenario

The test scenario is as follows.

1. The driver increases the speed up to the desired speed and turns on the ACC.
2. The ACC comes into service state and starts to provide its services with the car cruising at the desired speed.
3. The driver releases the accelerator pedal.
4. A vehicle cuts in front of the car. Then, the sensor detects the vehicle and alarms the distance to the ACC.
5. The ACC decreases the speed of the car in order to keep an adequate distance from the precedent vehicle.
6. The driver feels the sudden gravity of reducing speed.
   Since the test subject only watched the simulation movie, the change in gravity was communicated to the test subject from the staff. The event of the "reduced speed" was caused by the precedent vehicle, which is one of the environmental factors, and which is dispatched via sensor and the ACC.
7. It starts to snow heavily.
8. The driver turns on the windshield wipers to the strong mode to keep visibility.
9. The ACC catches the event.
10. The ACC terminates its services to avoid sensor errors and notifies the driver of the termination via the display.
11. The speed of the car is reduced: the result of which sees the following vehicle increasing its approach.
    The simulation is made on the assumption that the driver can notice the termination of the ACC from the display. If the test subject does not notice the situation, the staff informs the test subject of the situation. The simulation is a movie, so the test subject is not actually operating the car.
12. The driver notices the termination of the ACC.
13. The driver puts their foot on the accelerator pedal and restarts the manual driving.

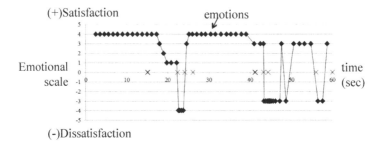

Fig. 3. The emotions monitored via key ins.

4.3 Data Collection

A test subject who is a driver accesses the simulation via a keyboard and display interface through a personal computer. Her insights were monitored by his/her utterances during the simulation. The emotions of the test subject were recorded via the keyboard.

Before the examination, we asked the test subject to practice typing the keys according to his/her emotions. As a result, we could establish an emotional evaluation of the test subject as shown in Fig. 3. After the examination, we interviewed with the test subject about the reasons for positive and negative emotions and utterances. In fact, the recorded utterances were not perfect. The subject provided us additional words to complement the sentences. After the interviews, we were able to map the events in scenarios and the changes in emotions. The results of application of MuLSA are presented in Fig. 4.

4.4 Results and Their Interpretation

In Fig. 4, the emotions of the test subject and their journey are shown in the customer layer. Their insights, recorded from their utterances, are shown in balloons. There were two kinds of environmental factors: other vehicles and weather. These factors are shown in the context layer.

MuLSA consists of three layers. Within MuLSA's layered structure, we can see the test subject's *touch-points* through the ACC, as well as when and how strong the test subject (driver) had positive or negative emotions toward the system (ACC). The negative/positive emotions of the test subject imply problematic and/or ideal behavior of the current ACC. In order to analyze in detail the emotion in and of each *touch-point*, we refer to the recorded utterances of the test subject. The first balloon (A) represents the feeling when the test subject displayed positive emotions. This is the effect of the service (2).

The purpose of our study is to analyze requirements of the ADAS. Hence, we focus on the negative emotions in Fig. 4 and refer to the causes of the test subject's negative emotions. The causes are the programmed behavior of the ACC, and the behavior was evaluated according to the context that is presented in the context of the scenario. If the context of the car is correctly detected

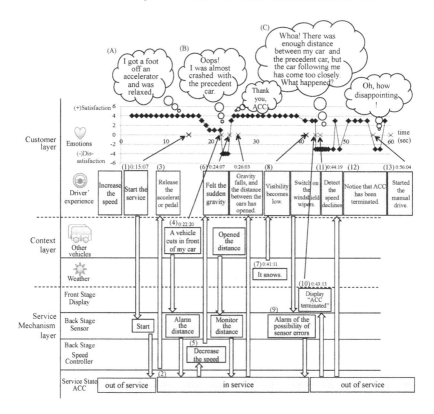

Fig. 4. The analysis with MuLSA

by the sensors of the ACC, the problem exists within the ACC software. If the context of the car is not correctly detected by the sensors, the addition of new sensors and expected behavior are required for the future ADAS. The priority of each sensor can be set in accordance to the level of the negative emotions.

The second balloon (B) represents the emotions of the test subject when he/she detected the sudden gravity change through the screen. Though he/she must have been surprised at the change in gravity, he/she thanked the ACC for avoiding danger, in this case, a car crash. The surprise is a kind of negative emotion, and it implies the dissatisfaction of the driver and a problem with the software of the ACC itself. The future ADAS is required to have smoother speed control, so that the driver does not feel fear or surprise by the sudden gravity changes.

The problems that we have to solve lay within balloon (C). The test subject did not realize the decline of speed. This situation can be interpreted to show that the ACC did not communicate its state securely to the driver. This problem implies that the problem occurred within the front stage of the ACC. If the test subject knows that the ACC may be stopped in the inevitability of low visibility, they could prepare for the termination and would not react with a negative emotion. We need to redesign the behavior of the communication in the *front stage.*

We have been able to elicit two new requirements for the future ADAS. One is the smooth speed control. If we analyzed the behavior of ACC only from the technical view, we may not be able to realize the problem of the sudden change unless the change has a physical impact on the body of the driver. The other is that of better communication support between the driver and the ADAS. Some kinds of announcements may annoy drivers. However, important messages, e.g. start, termination, etc., have to be securely communicated to the driver. This case also indicates that the technical analysis was not perfect for requirements analysis. Turning off the switch of the lamp of the "ACC" satisfies the requirement of "present the state of the ACC to the driver," but the simulation told us that it could not provide the information to the driver securely. When the car following behind runs into the subject car, the driver noticed the termination of the ADAS. This situation was not safe. The priority of this improvement of the notifier within the display must be high.

5   Threats to Validity

In order to validate the results of the case study, we apply three types of threats [18] to the case study. They are internal and external validity, and reliability.

5.1   Threats to Internal Validity

Internal validity refers to a risk that the investigated factor is affected by a third factor [18]. The data was collected from one scenario and one person. The emotions recorded in the study depend on personal characteristics of the test subject. If a driver believes in the DAS to avoid car accidents, his/her emotions may not change frequently. If a driver likes driving manually, all the services provided by ACC might cause negative emotions. In our study, we recorded utterances of the subject and interviewed with him/her. The results were shown in the balloons. According to the interview, he/she accepted the assistance of the ACC and did not believe the support provided by the ACC. In other words, when we apply the MuLSA to evaluate the services of the current system, we must concern ourselves with the affect of the personal characteristics of the subjects.

Another threat exists in the emotion capture system of the tool. The tool captures the emotions of the subjects via a keyboard. Therefore, we did not care about the use of recording his/her emotions through the keys input. The subject's familiarity with the keyboard affects the results of the study. If a subject could not operate the keys according to his/her emotions, we could neither capture his/her emotions properly. However, the subject of our study was familiar with the QWERTY keyboard, and thus, we could ignore the threat.

5.2 Threats to External Validity

External validity refers to the degree to which the results of a study can be generalized across population, time and setting [18]. In a real situation, there are infinite hazardous scenarios and engineers who are developing the ADAS who know that the current DAS cannot cope with most of the hazardous situations. The case study was carried out with only one scenario that included two hazardous situations: peripheral cars and snow. In order to evaluate the external validity of MuLSA for ADAS, more complex, long and frequent hazardous scenario settings have to be applied to the simulation. For example, long term simulation may strain the driver. Under such situations, a driver may not be able to concentrate their power on the driving with, for example, flattered emotions. The problems of the current DAS were elicited from negative emotions, and, we could not find problems from unexpressive emotions. However, even though the studied scenario was short and simple, the results gave us information showing that the emotions of a driver are a hopeful measurement to realize and gage problems within the existing system.

5.3 Reliability

Reliability is concerned with, to what extent the data and the analysis are dependent on the specific researchers of the study [18]. The analysis with MuLSA depends heavily on the emotions and/or insights of customers or users. In order to avoid the threat of reliability of the case study, we built a tool to capture emotions through the showing of a movie. Therefore, if and only if a researcher applies the tool in order to analyze problems in the scenario with DAS, the emotional data can be obtained properly, and measured.

6 Discussion and Conclusions

We are now developing other scenarios with more vehicles and various road conditions. The complex scenario may help us extract problems in visualizing the map of utterances, the scenario, and emotions. Hazardous scenarios can be collected through a driving recorder and provided by load service companies. However, MuLSA is not a method only for the ACC or ADAS. As Kimbell [19] described, one of the strengths of the user stories is that they proposes ideas for new service components and also entirely new services. MuLSA is also applicable to most software, when an analyst needs to elicit new requirements based on the current software. The strength of MuLSA is that it analyzes requirements through the utilization of its multiple-layered structure in which there are users, context of the usage, as well as the mechanism of services.

According to the result of the case study, MuLSA could be applied to analyze the problems of the existing system. The tool was developed as a prototype in order to evaluate the multi-layered structure of MuLSA for ADASs. In order to apply MuLSA into the development field of ADASs, we will develop a system by analyzing problems of the tool by applying MuLSA.

Researchers have proposed a lot of methods for requirements elicitation, such as goal oriented analysis methods [20,21] or use case analysis [6] focuses on initial requirements elicitation for new software. In contrast, MuLSA focuses on software that is developed as an innovation on the current existing software. This is one of the typical strength of MuLSA.

MuLSA is a kind of scenario analysis method. The scenario provides a real story within time. As Carroll mentioned [5], scenario is understandable for every user and gives a real experience to them. New requirements for innovations on current software are hard to elicit through interviews. We believe that most important requirements must be elicited from the users' real voice or emotions as a result of their experiences, rather than requirements analysis work on a table.

An analyst with MuLSA does not expect the users to propose problems or new requirements, but rather, their emotions and insights in their use of the current system is key. The effectiveness of MuLSA is to analyze the causes of the users' emotions. As a result, we can prioritize new requirements for the software of the next generation.

Acknowledgements. The authors thank Ms. Mineko Naoe and Mr. Kazuyuki Natsume for developing the tool of emotion monitoring.

References

1. ISO/IEC 25000:2005: Software engineering - Software product Quality Requirements and Evaluation (SQuaRE) - Guide to SQuaRE (2005)
2. Plutchik, R.: Emotion - A Psycho-Evolutionary Synthesis. Harpercollins College Div, New York (1980)
3. Iordache, O.: Methods. In: Iordache, O. (ed.) Polystochastic Models for Complexity, UCS, vol. 4, pp. 17–61. Springer, Heidelberg (2010)
4. Wallbott, H.G., Scherer, K.R.: Assessing emotion by questionnaire. In: Plutchik, R., Kellerman, H. (eds.) The Measurement of Emotions, vol. 4, pp. 55–82. Academic Press, San Diego (1989)
5. Carroll, J.M.: Five reasons for scenario-based design. In: The 32nd Hawaii International Conference on System Sciences (1999)
6. Jacobson, I., Christerson, M., Jonsson, P., Overgaard, G.: Object-Oriented Software Engineering. Addison-Wesley, Reading (1992)
7. Benyon, D., Macaulay, C.: A scenario-based design method for human-centered interaction design. In: Alexander, I., Maiden, N. (eds.) Scenarios, Stories, Use Cases Through the Systems Development Life-Cycle, pp. 211–235. Wiley, Chichester (2004)
8. Aoyama, M.: Persona-and-scenario based requirements engineering for software embedded in digital consumer products. In: IEEE International Conference on Requirements Engineering, pp. 85–94. IEEE Computer Society (2005)
9. Stickdorn, M., Schneider, J.: This is Service Design Thinking: Basics, Tools, Cases. Wiley, New Jersey (2012)
10. Risdon, C.: The anatomy of an experience map, Nov 2011. http://www.adaptivepath.com/ideas/the-anatomy-of-an-experience-map

11. Richardson, A.: Using customer journey maps to improve customer experience. Harvard Business Review, Blog Network (11 Nov. 15.2010). http://blogs.hbr.org/2010/11/using-customer-journey-maps-to/
12. Shostack, G.L.: Designing services that deliver. Harv. Bus. Rev. **62**(1), 133–139 (1984)
13. Polaine, A., Aebersold, R., Bossart, R., Mettler, A.: Blueprint+: Developint a tool for service design, (2009). http://www.slideshare.net/apolaine/blueprint-developing-a-tool-for-service-design
14. Kuchinskas, S.: Automatic auto: A car that drives itself, Aug 2010. http://www.scientificamerican.com/article.cfm?id=self-driving-audi-automobile
15. Markoff, J.: Google cars drive themselves, in traffic, Oct 2010. http://www.nytimes.com/2010/10/10/science/10google.html?pagewanted=all&_r=0
16. Russell, J.A.: Measures of emotion. In: Plutchik, R. (ed.) Emotion - Theory, Research, and Experience, vol. 4, pp. 83–111. Academic Press, San Diego (1989). The Measurement of Emotions
17. Advanced Simulation Technologies Ltd.: Prescan, Feb 2013. http://www.advancedsimtech.com/software/prescan/
18. Runeson, P., Höst, M.: Guidelines for conducting and reporting case study research in software engineering. Int. J. Empir. Softw. Eng. **14**(2), 131–164 (2009)
19. Kimbell, L.: From novelty to routine: Services in science and technology-based enterprises, pp. 105–111. In: Design for Services. Gower Publishing (2011)
20. Dardenne, A., van Lamsweerde, A., Fickas, S.: Goal-directed requirements acquisition. Sci. Comput. Program. **20**, 3–50 (1993)
21. Yu, E.S.K.: Towards modelling and reasoning support for early-phase requirements engineering. In: The 3rd International Symposium on Requirements Engineering (RE'97), pp. 226–235. IEEE (1997)

Assuring Dependability of Software Reuse:
An Industrial Standard

Fevzi Belli[1,2(✉)]

[1] Faculty of Computer Science, Electrical Engineering and Mathematics,
University of Paderborn, Paderborn, Germany
belli@upb.de
[2] Faculty of Engineering, Department of Computer Engineering,
Izmir Institute of Technology, Izmir, Turkey

Abstract. Whereas a software component may be perfectly suited to one application, it may prove to cause severe faults in other applications. The pre-standard IEC/PAS 62814 (*Dependability of Software Products Containing Reusable Components – Guidance for Functionality and Tests*), which has recently been released, addresses the functionality, testing, and dependability of software components to be reused and products that contain software to be used in more than one application; that is, reused by the same or by another development organization, regardless of whether it belongs to the same or another legal entity than the one that has developed this software. This paper introduces into this pre-standard and give hints how to use it. The author, who chaired its realization that started in 2006, briefly summarizes the difficult process to bring the industrial partners with controversial interests to a consensus.

Keywords: Software reuse · Dependability · Test · Industrial standardization

1 Introduction

Software reuse is the process of creating software systems from existing software rather than building software systems from scratch. The vision of software reuse is as old as software itself – it was introduced already in 1968, in the year as the term "Software Engineering" was coined during the constitutional NATO conference in Germany [9].

Many efforts to reuse software have succeeded; there is an increasingly overwhelming number of success stories available in literature. Almost all major companies and institutions that deal with information & communication technology practice software reuse and report about their success, e.g., Nippon Electronic Company, GTE Corporation, Raytheon, DEC, HP, NASA, and many more [6, 7, 10].

Nevertheless, the promises of decreased cost and increased dependability, and thus decreased risks, are not always realized. The frightening news about recent disasters definitely caused by careless soft-ware reuse are still being warningly associated with and attributed to all software reuse. The failure of Therac-25 system, in which a software component was carried over from a previous version of an X-ray system, caused the machine to malfunction, resulting in the loss of several lives in a terrible way; patients were actually burned [4].

© Springer-Verlag Berlin Heidelberg 2014
J. Cordeiro and M. van Sinderen (Eds.): ICSOFT 2013, CCIS 457, pp. 72–83, 2014.
DOI: 10.1007/978-3-662-44920-2_5

In the Ariane project, failure of a reused software component caused the loss of a rocket costing around half a billion dollars [5].

These recent disasters as a consequence of bad reuse on the one side and success stories as a consequence of good reuse on the other side are the key factors in deciding whether or not to enhance and sustain continued provision of reuse from a lucrative business perspective.

To sum up, before reusing a software component, the context and domain it was built for should be carefully compared with the context and domain it is intended to be built in, including the hardware and physical and organizational aspects [8]. Figure 1 depicts the elements of the reuse process which is the subject of this paper. It is evident that reusability is not a single feature of a components but a "bundle" of features (Fig. 2).

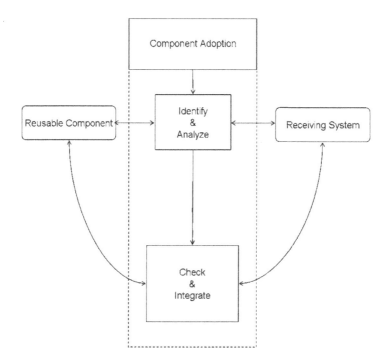

Fig. 1. Elements of the reuse process.

Standardization is the most efficient means to bring research, industrial, commercial, and consuming parties with different roles, but participating on the same objects and ethic objectives, e.g., to protect environment, to save resources, etc. Standardization helps with understanding and unifying the quality notion, also for reusing previously used products. Standardization helps also prevent legal problems that arise because reuse will be already practiced tentatively and insecurely.

This paper is on standardization of software reuse concerning its quality, test criteria etc., depending on the purpose of the software that will be reused.

The publicly available specification (PAS) *IEC/PAS 62814/Ed. 1: Dependability of Software Products Containing Reusable Components – Guidance for Functionality and Tests* is a pre-standard and addresses the functionality, testing, and dependability of software components to be reused and products that contain software to be used in more than one application; that is, reused by the same or by another development organization, regardless of whether it belongs to the same or another legal entity than the one that has developed this software. IEC is the acronym of "International Elect-rotechnical Commission" that is the world's leading organization that prepares and publishes International Standards for all electrical, electronic and related technologies.

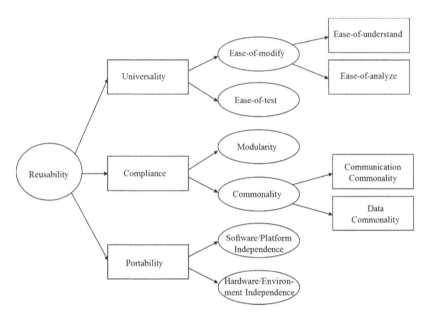

Fig. 2. Reusability characteristics.

The present paper gives an introduction into the PAS, which has been released in December 2012. The author chaired its realization that started in 2006 62814, and will give hint how to use it.

Next section clarifies terminology and discusses notions used in the practice. Section 3 introduces one of the most notable aspects of the PAS, that is, Reusability- & Dependability-Driven Software Development Technique. Recommended methods of validation, revalidation, and reliability of software reuse are summarizes in Sect. 4. Section 5 sketches the structure of the PAS, and explains and discusses its scope, objectives, and usage. Concluding remarks and future work are included in Sect. 6.

2 Notions and Practices of Reuse

Not each "copy and paste" action, which programmers do daily when they construct their programs, forms a software reuse that PAS 62814 has in mind. Also calling an internal or external function and even a remote-procedure call is not necessarily a reuse this PAS would regulate. All these examples suggest that the context and domain of the called software does not change. Therefore, there is no need for them to consider this PAS and, for example, perform pre-store and pre-use activities that are described in PAS 62814 in detail.

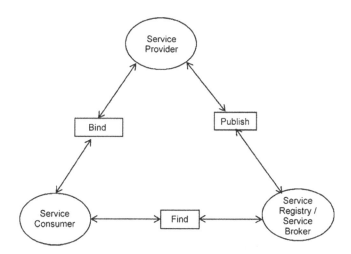

Fig. 3. Typical reuse by service-oriented architecture.

2.1   What Reuse Really Is

Using a service in a service-oriented (SO) landscape or in "Common Object Request Broker Architecture (CORBA)" is of more interest to this PAS because the context and domain of the software that delivers a service might change. Indeed, SO and CORBA are typical reuse constellations concerning constructing, offering, selecting, and validating services repeatedly. A service has to be registered and "published" before it will be offered. Infrastructural services are offered to realize a broker, etc. (Fig. 3) [1].

2.2   Where Reuse Will Be Practiced

Examples given above clarify that software reuse is not limited to the source or object code; it has, moreover, to consider all of the information that is related to the product generating processes, including also requirements, analysis, design, documents, and test cases apart from the code. Examples of well-known, widely accepted practices of software reuse are (Fig. 4) [11]:

- Component-based development (CBD): Building systems by integrating components that conform to system's specification.
- COTS integration: CBD using commercial components.
- Service-oriented systems: Building systems by linking shared services.
- Program generators: Embedding knowledge of a particular type of application to produce component(s) in that domain.

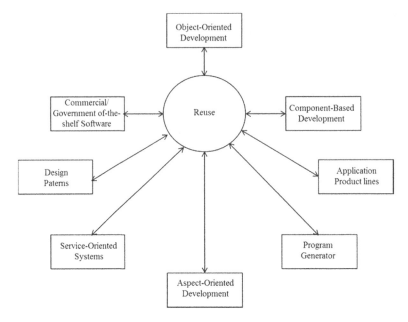

Fig. 4. Approaches to the reuse.

- Application product lines: Generalization of an application around a common architecture so that it can be used to produce different applications in different domains for different customers.
- Object-oriented programming: Implementing applications using "objects" that consist of data structures, methods (algorithms) and their interactions and computer programs
- Aspect-oriented software development: Weaving shared components into an application at different places when the program is compiled, if separation of concerns is feasible.

2.3   Software Reuse Has Many Faces

There is a great variety of reusing software, from ad hoc, unplanned to systematic. Following list attempts to structure this variety.

1. *Accidental* (ad hoc or *opportunistic*) reuse denotes reuse without strategy, typically reusing software components not designed for reuse.
2. *Systematic* (*planned*) reuse requires developing software components intended for reuse and/or building new applications from those reusable components, following a formal plan of product line.
3. *Adaptive* reuse uses previously developed software that is modified only for portability, e.g., a new application on a different operating system.
4. *Black-box* reuse uses unmodified software components, incorporating existing software components into a new application without modification.

5. *White-box* reuse modifies and integrates software (function) blocks into new applications.
6. *Vertical* reuse uses components in the same domain.
7. *Horizontal* reuse uses components in different domains.
8. *Internal* (*in-house*) reuse uses components developed within the company, or government unit.
9. *External* reuse uses components of another company, or government unit.

2.4   Software Reuse Has also Many Facets

The above discussion has identified practical and relevant kinds of reuse. A general taxonomy of software reuse is included in Table 1, which uses the following six aspects for a thorough, exemplary classification [2, 3]. Numbers in parentheses refer to the numbering used in the listing in Sect. 2.3.

- Reuse *assets* and *entities* can be product-oriented and, thus, concrete, such as components; they can also be ideal, such as concepts, ideas, algorithms, etc.
- *Domain scope* refers to application area (6 and 7).
- *Development scope* refers to origin of the component (8 and 9).
- Additional work required prior to reuse is referred to by *modification* (3, 4, and 5).
- Whether and which kind of work is to be done in performing reuse is a managerial aspect (1 and 2).
- Reuse *approach* is *compositional* if existing components are reused (such as the Unix^{TM} shell); *generative* reuse requires application or code generators (such as Refine and Meta tool).
- *Direct* reuse approach requires no "glue code" that intermediates between the reusable component and the receiving system, *indirect* reuse necessitates an intermediate entity (Fig. 5).

Table 1. Summary of reuse classification.

Reuse asset	Reuse entity	Domain scope	Development scope	Modification	Management	Approach
Ideas, concepts	Architectures	Vertical	Internal	Adaptive	Accidental	Compositional
Artefacts, components	Requirements	Horizontal	External	Black box	Systematic	Generative
Procedures, skills	Designs			White box		Indirect
	Specifications					Direct
	Source code					
	Object code					
	Test cases					

Note that Table 1 shows the summary of the classification. It is possible to add further issues, for example, the issue of "Information to Reuse." It means that reused-based software development can be required for the complete specification of the reusable component.

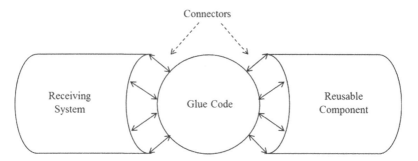

Fig. 5. Integration of reusable components.

3 Software Development Driven by Reusability and Dependability Aspects

Architecture is the key to software reuse. The architecture of a system commits its structure to combine the elements it is comprised of and their features, and relations among those elements.

Typical structures are hierarchical, centralized (star form), or decentralized (network form); relations are defined as consists-of or neighbored. Architectural elements can be event, state, or service-oriented.

It is important for reuse that the software architecture should allow a precise design and specification of interfaces and their dependability-critical features so that it enables evaluation, selection, acquisition, and integration of reusable components into the receiving system.

While planning substantial reuse of their software components, software engineers are often overly optimistic concerning how much reusable functionality can be achieved. Reuse is not a ultimate saver of costs, schedule, or dependability. Even COTS deployment often satisfies only less than 40 % of the functionality of an industrial application.

Also important is the addressing of the critical non-functional requirements, that is, dependability and quality, which certainly result in schedule and cost impacts, and, caused by poor dependability and reliability, maybe invoke severe safety and security risks.

Note that if the functional and interface requirements are not fulfilled, glue code and wrappers are to be planned, specified, designed, implemented, and carefully tested.

Dependability methodologies include application aspects and the organization of the reuse. Pre-store and pre-use characteristics should be met and the cases build-for reuse or build-by-reuse should be distinguished.

Another point covers validation and reliability aspects of the software. Also the assumptions and rules to improve software dependability are described and the hardware/software interaction is taken into account.

"Software-by-reuse" is the use of existing applications or their components to build new applications.

It is widely accepted and convenient to consider software reusability from the following viewpoints.

- Build-**for**-reuse enables planned production of reusable components.
- Build-**by**-reuse attempts planned production of systems using reusable components.

Both of these viewpoints focus on characteristics of reusability that are to be checked before storing the component and before reusing it in a new product.

Figure 7 depicts the coupling and orchestration of build-for and build-by aspects of reuse.

Following recommendations do not address only internal reuse; they can easily be adopted also for external reuse.

4 Validation, Revalidation, and Reliability of Software Reuse

Software reuse involves redesign, reimplementation, and re-testing. Redesign arises if the existing functionality does not fulfil the requirements of the new task because it requires reworking to realize the new function, and, prior to this, necessitates reverse engineering to understand its current functionality.

The design change leads to reimplementation. Exhaustive re-testing (as a kind of regression testing) is necessary to validate the functionality of the reused software in the new domain to determine whether or not redesign and reimplementation are needed.

Following undesirable events/situations, mostly caused by managerial misjudgment, negatively influence the dependability of software reuse:

- Failing to select the right component, or to favor the wrong selection criteria;
- Failing to justify and adjust the need for and/or extent of the modification of the selected component to fulfill operational or application requirements;
- Failing to justify and adjust the need for and/or extent of the maintenance of the selected component during operational stage.

To avoid such events/situations, redesign, re-implementation, and re-testing activities can be clustered in following groups:

- Redesign

  - Architectural design modification: Detection of architectural design part(s) to be modified, realization of the modification, re-validation of the entire architectural design;
  - Detailed redesign: Detection of design part(s) to be modified, realization of the modification, re-validation of the entire design;
  - Reverse engineering: Detection of the part(s) to be modified, which are not familiar to developers; understanding, modification, re-validation of the entire component;
  - Re-documentation: Detection of the part(s) to be modified, modification, re-validation of the entire document;
  - Re-implementation requires re-coding, code review, and unit testing (IEC 62628).

- Re-testing activities can be clustered in following groups:

  - Test re-planning
  - Test procedures to be altered
  - Re-integration testing
  - Re-release and re-acceptance testing
  - Test drivers/simulators to be altered
  - Test reports to be rewritten

Fundamental facts influence dependability, especially reliability when using commercially available components, e.g., COTS components for software development.

- Very often no source code is available, thus there is no way to correct a detected fault.
- This is a great restriction that prohibits application of the most widely used reliability models that require perfect correction of detected faults ("reliability growth models"; see, for example, AIAA R-013-1992, IEEE 1633-2008).
- If source code is available: Note that COTS software is no longer COTS after its source code is modified to correct a fault detected because the COTS supplier no longer maintains the documentation and source code (just as electronics equipment warranties are no longer valid after a seal is broken).
- Furthermore, the modifications can violate the original software design. From then on, modified COTS software is to be handled as an accidental reuse.

5 Structure of IEC/PAS 62814 and How to Use It

The international PAS 62814 introduces the concept of assuring reused components and their usage within new products. It provides information and criteria about the tests and analysis required for products containing such reused parts. The objective is to support the engineering requirements for functionality and tests of reusable software components and composite systems containing such components in evaluating and assuring reuse dependability (Figs. 6, 7).

Focus is on the dependability of software reuse and, thus, this document complements IEC 62309:2005-02 (Dependability of products containing reused parts – requirements for functionality and test), which exclusively considers hardware reuse. In addition to this previous, hardware-related IEC standard, the present PAS also crosses further, appropriate software-related standards to be applied in the development and qualification of software components that are intended to be reused and products that reuse existing components. In other words, this present standard encompasses the features of software components for reuse, their integration into the receiving system, and related tests. Their performance and qualification and the qualification of the receiving system is subject to existing standards, for example ISO/IEC 25000 and IEC 61508-3. The process framework of ISO/IEC 12207 on systems and software engineering and ISO/IEC 25000 on system aspects of dependability on software engineering apply to this present document.

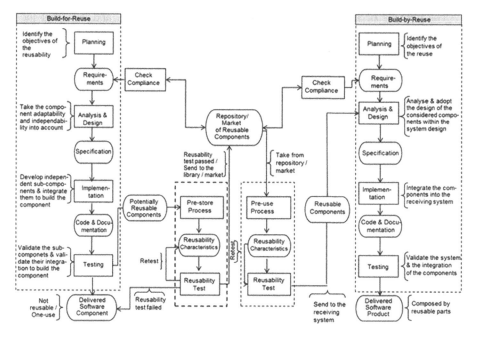

Fig. 6. Recommended framework of reuse.

NORMATIVE PART
1   Scope
2   Normative references
3   Terms and definitions and abbreviations
4   Dependability of software reuse methodology– reusability-driven software development
5   Software reuse dependability methodology applications
6   Software reuse assurance
7   Warranty and documentation

INFORMATIVE PART- ANNEXES
A General remarks on software reuse
B Qualification and integration of reusable software components
C Testing and integration of reusable software components – Issues for industrial best practice
D Example of software pre-use
E Influence of reused software to hardware components and products

Fig. 7. Structure of IEC/PAS 62814.

The purpose of IEC/PAS 62814 is to ensure through analysis and tests that the functionality, dependability and eco-friendliness of a new product containing reused software components is comparable to a product with only new components. This would justify the manufacturer providing the next customer with a warranty for the functionality and dependability of a product with reused components. As each set of hardware/software has a unique relationship and is governed by its operational scenario, the dependability determination has to consider the underlying operational background. Dependability also influences safety. Therefore, wherever it seems necessary, safety aspects have to be considered the way IEC 60300-1 addresses safety issues. This PAS can also be applied in producing product-specific standards by technical committees responsible for an application sector.

This paper could give only a brief introduction to the major aspects of IEC/PAS 62814. Due to lack of space nothing could be said about the informal part that comprehensively explains the methods and techniques for systematic reuse and its validation to assure dependability, and includes numerous examples from the practice and for the practice.

6 Concluding Remarks, Future Work

The most common form of reuse is using software developed for one-use in a new application, which is, accidental reuse. One of the major objectives of the present PAS 62814 is to warn the managers that this kind of unplanned reuse can be a potential minefield because it can cause the inheritance of all the problems of the pre-existing software in the reaping of only a few of its benefits. Many managers, while planning for software reuse, forget that both the reused component and composite system are to be tested in the new domain. Experience reports say that reusable software can cost 60 % more than one-use software, whereby a good portion of additional costs goes to testing.

This paper gave a brief introduction into IEC/PAS 62814 and which is a pre-standard, that is, it is not yet a standard. Further work and much energy are necessary to complete the work and produce a standard.

References

1. Belli, F., Linschulte, M.: Event-driven modeling and testing of real-time web services. J. Serv. Orient. Comput. Appl. **4**(1), 3–15. Springer, Heidelberg (2010)
2. Frakes, W. B., Terry, C.: Software reuse: metrics and models. ACM Comput. Surv. **28**(2), 415–435   (1996).   http://dl.acm.org/ft_gateway.cfm?id=234531&type=pdf&CFID=65178775&CFTOKEN=89447410
3. Frakes, W.B., Kang, K.: Software reuse research: status and future. IEEE Trans. Softw. Eng. **31**(7), 529–536 (2005). http://ieeexplore.ieee.org/stamp/stamp.jsp?tp=&arnumber=1492369
4. Leveson, N.: Medical devices: the Therac-25. In: Appendix A in Safeware: System Safety and Computers, pp. 1–49, Addison-Wesley, Boston (1995). http://citeseerx.ist.psu.edu/viewdoc/download;jsessionid=84A18B532CF53C4AEA6F64AA6038BFEF?doi=10.1.1.39.704&rep=rep1&type=pdf

5. Lions, J.L.: Ariane 5 Flight 501 Failure (1996). http://www.ima.umn.edu/ ∼ arnold/disasters/ariane5rep.html
6. Mathur, A.P.: Foundations of software Testing. Addison-Wesley Professional, Boston (2008)
7. Mohagheghi, P., Ict, S., Conradi, R.: An empirical investigation of software reuse benefits in a large telecom product. ACM Trans. Softw. Eng. Methodol. **17**(3), 13:1–13:31 (2008). http://dl.acm.org/ft_gateway.cfm?id=1363104&type=pdf&CFID=82907429&CFTOKEN=24134248
8. Mohammad, M., Alagar, V.: A component-based development process for trustworthy systems. J. Softw. Maint. Evol. Res. Pract. (2010) (Wiley InterScience, Published online), doi:10.1002/smr.472. http://onlinelibrary.wiley.com/doi/10.1002/smr.472/pdf
9. Naur, P., Randell, B. (eds.): Software Engineering, Report on a Conference Sponsored by the NATO Science Committee, Garmisch, Germany (1968). http://homepages.cs.ncl.ac.uk/brian.randell/NATO/nato1968.PDF
10. Orrego, A., Mundy, G.: SRAE: An integrated framework for aiding in the verification and validation of legacy artifacts in NASA flight control systems. In: Proceedings of the 31st Annual Intertnational Computer Software and Applications Conference. IEEE Computer. Press, New York (2007)
11. Sommerville, I.: Software Engineering. Addison Wesley Longman, Boston (2007)

Simultaneously Improving Quality and Time-to-Market in Agile Development

Pryscilla Marcilli Dóra[1,2], Ana Cristina Oliveira[1,3(✉)],
and J. Antão B. Moura[1]

[1] Systems and Computing Department,
Federal University of Campina Grande (UFCG), Campina Grande, Brazil
ana.oliveira@ifpb.edu.br, antao@dsc.ufcg.edu.br
[2] University Center of João Pessoa (UNIPÊ), João Pessoa, Paraíba, Brazil
pryscilla@copin.ufcg.edu.br
[3] Federal Institute of Paraíba (IFPB), Campina Grande, Paraíba, Brazil

Abstract. More recently, "post-agile" techniques seem to favor releasing early over quality. Pressure for low cost, rapid development and to code for new features leads to the allocation of resources to software development tasks preferably rather than to quality control. Such practices may put the responsibilities for development and test on the same team and even facilitate sloppy testing. Here, we present our experience in organizing an agile team that is divided into two independent cells, each one playing a different role: (i) software development, and (ii) testing exclusively. Results obtained by using a grid computing backup system as a case study point out to higher test efficiency and, surprisingly, possible shorter time-to-market simultaneously when the agile team is split into those two cells, and some complementary practices are adopted as well. These results may contribute to the on-going discussion on the role and impact of testing in agile development.

Keywords: Software quality · Independent testing · Agile process improvement

1 Introduction

"The quality of software is closely linked to the process used to develop it, and finding a process that fits exactly the specificities of the development environment is almost impossible" [12]. Hence, it may be better to adapt and adopt the process that most resembles the characteristics of the environment [8]. Some environmental features increase the complexity of that task, such as when you have a small team [5].

Agile methodologies, such as eXtreme Programming (XP) and Scrum, treat quality as a responsibility of the entire development team. However, in many situations, teams spend more time in production (coding) activities rather than activities related to quality, so the results still show unsatisfactory levels of quality and software discard remains high [4].

Mechanisms for quality control reduce the agility of a development team. In fact, if viewed in isolation, software testing activities require time, more physical resources,

© Springer-Verlag Berlin Heidelberg 2014
J. Cordeiro and M. van Sinderen (Eds.): ICSOFT 2013, CCIS 457, pp. 84–98, 2014.
DOI: 10.1007/978-3-662-44920-2_6

and properly trained personnel [17]. There is a growing debate in the industry about the need to stress delivery speed over testing in "post-agile" processes–see for instance [23]. For cost savings, there is a trend to (continue to) embed testers in product teams with the consequence of "the role of test and Quality Assurance (QA) management becoming unclear" [14]. Another trend indicates that testing activities are concentrating more on checking business alignment (uprooting idea bugs) rather than on code bug fixes [16] – i.e., post-agile practices seem to suggest end user testing after the product launch. Trends or practices that favor speed over testing may lead to defective software being released more often. Albeit in some scenarios–such as in testing by startups or in prototyping–this may be acceptable and even make sense to business, that is not the case of scenarios that include system software (e.g. a general purpose mobile operating system) or critical applications–for the banking or healthcare industries, say–which have stringent quality requirements.

Our own experience in developing system software, nevertheless, indicates that agile techniques can be improved with additional or adjusted practices that improve quality and speed simultaneously. That is surprising, since additional practices would tend to make the process slower. Here we present a case in such experience in the hope of contributing to the discussion about agile speed v. testing controversy.

The case study we consider is a backup utility (OurBackup [21]) from Our Grid project, an open source free-to-join peer-to-peer (P2P) grid that aggregates computational resources (grid machines) to support the execution of bag-of-tasks parallel applications on demand. The project was developed at the Distributed Systems Laboratory at the Federal University of Campina Grande (DSL/UFCG) in Brazil. Several strategies to mitigate the risks of low quality were adopted during the project, including the definition of a software development process originally named *OurProcess* (OP), an adaptation of the XP methodology for the development of distributed systems. Further (practice) additions to OP–including the adoption of an independent team for Quality Assurance–led to an agile, mainly quality-centered process named *OurQualityProcess* (OQP).

OQP's main characteristics and practices are briefly reviewed in Sect. 2. Section 3 compares results of OP's and OQP's application to the case study. Analysis of the results and recommendations are made in Sect. 4. Results from related work are compared to ours in Sect. 5. Conclusions, caveats and further work are presented in Sect. 6. The contents of the sections that follow are based on a previous work by the authors [9] but they have been expanded to provide more information on the complementary practices added to OQP's life cycle, on the adopted principles for the application of these practices, and on the organization and execution of the experiments and data collection & analysis in the case study.

2 OQP: Software Quality Control

XP was chosen as a starting point and base for QOP because the team at DSL/UFCG had familiarity with its concepts and usage.

The main goal of OQP is to maintain agility. But to also focus on producing clear requirements and automatic [3], reproducible tests, while being still minimally intrusive, additional practices were added to its XP base (or Our Process – OP, as we called it internally). OQP's additional practices and techniques focus on the number of defects identified before a new version is released. The main addition is the insertion of an external quality assurance (QA) team to focus exclusively on the quality of final products. (This does not eliminate the responsibility for quality of the development team which should cooperate with the inserted QA team).

Another adaptation of the base XP process entails validation of requirements, by analyzing and criticizing each specification sentence. While the development team writes software requirements and acceptance tests for the obvious cases, the QA team checks non-functional aspects, such as completeness, correctness and unambiguity. This practice minimizes problems of requirement writing and interpretation, leading to an executable documentation in the form of automatic, cohesive and correct tests that last the software "lifetime".

Yet another adjustment to OP to yield OQP is to halve the duration of XP's typical one-day long tasks. (This is because "software developers" at DSL/UFCG are usually students who need to take care of other daily duties–e.g., attending classes.)

During the implementation of the system functionalities, the practice of *Test-Driven-Development* (TDD) [2, 6] is also widely used by the development team, while the QA team identifies new test scenarios, sometimes by performing manual testing prior to automation. The practice of refactoring is also made to encompass both teams' codes, developers' as well as the QA team's.

One may question in which ways OQP differs from TDD. The former is based on principles of the latter, but it encompasses complementary practices. Additional practices include contract-driven development [20], execution of different test batteries (builds), constant revisions and synchronization between teams. With this incremented and adjusted set of practices, OQP's usage is carried out according to three basic principles as explained next.

2.1   OQP Principles

(i) **Gradual QA:** After the elaboration of basic acceptance tests (by the developers), a process called "explosion of test cases" begins with the purpose of stressing the code (when available). Each produced acceptance test leads to one or more tests, which are developed by the QA team.

Once the defects are fixed (by developers), the QA team runs the battery of (possibly manual) tests to validate the correction of defects and to identify new test cases. Testing stops when a set percentage of code coverage is reached. According to a survey of development practioners and managers that metric should be higher than 90 % [10].

(ii) **Validation of Requirements and Transformation into Verifiable Requirements:** The (XP) agile philosophy of "doing the simplest thing that could possibly work" [2] also suits well to software qualification. First, one should validate all the requirements through executable documentation in the form of automated tests that are cohesive and correct, which are valid for the entire software lifetime and can be rerun at a minimum cost.

After writing up the basic acceptance tests, the "test explosion phase" starts when tests are expanded. This phase aims to stress the code, where for each acceptance test produced by the developers, one or more additional tests, whenever possible, should be developed by the QA team. This practice identifies defects caused by programming vices and developers' errors of logic.

Then, the battery of manual tests is executed and the correction of defects is validated. It is important to notice that the stopping (terminate) condition for the test explosion phase is when coverage of at least 80 % is achieved for each feature, since it is almost impossible to cover 100 % of the code due to untestable classes and files, e.g. configuration files, code generated by automated tools, or classes related to graphical interface objects.

(iii) **Maintainability of Code Health:** Every new piece of code must go through a battery of automated tests to be integrated into the repository. At integration one can check the "health" of the code. Different batteries of tests are defined with different objectives. At first coding, a battery is still simple with only unit tests and mock tests [18, 19] related to the module under development. The battery of tests grows according to the evolution of the software being developed. A battery of integration tests is performed where the mock tests are replaced by integration tests, and every night the full battery of tests is performed creating a daily status of the "health" of the code.

Furthermore, the integration of a new developed test should occur as soon as possible so that all team members have access to the new test and thus increase the verification of newly developed code.

Note that *Development by Contract* (DBC) also contributes to code health by mapping the responsibilities of classes and objects, making the implementation more robust. Business rules are checked by logical assertions that verify whether the input and output data are correctly processed.

(iv) **Code Review:** It is enacted during pair programming or by a person who is not involved in the actual coding, preferably by the team leader, either of development or QA. The adoption of this principle reduces errors, misinterpretations, increases code legibility, reduces breaches of contracts, and improves design.

One may argue that code review and testing should be done by the developer that implemented that piece of code in order to improve his/her own skills, and thus be able to change roles in the future. Note that in our software qualification process: (i) code review may be done by another member of the same team, either development or QA, since it is valuable to have another person digging into the code to check whether it could be improved; and, (ii) tests are not exclusively developed by the QA team, because the members of the development team are responsible for implementing initial acceptance tests. We have not evaluated the impact of changing roles during development, but this might lead to an interesting future study. On the other hand, we believe the combination of this "code review principle" to the other two principles causes all developed code to be examined by at least two people in its life cycle.

2.2   Life Cycle

As in XP, integral development of the software occurs through a succession of coded and tested releases. The activities performed for a release are identified by the lines across Fig. 1 and are detailed in Table 1. Each release is divided into four phases: Requirements elicitation, Development, Alpha and Beta Testing. During these phases, the activities of the development and QA teams are performed in parallel.

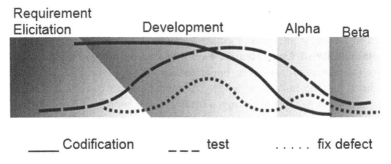

Fig. 1. OQP release life cycle.

Each of the four phases showed in Fig. 1 represents the state of the development over releases. Each release is represented by one different color, and the three lines represent the following activities: (a) coding, (b) testing and qualification, and (c) defect correction. Each phase has a well-defined goal as presented next.

Requirements Elicitation: All the features of a release are textually described to guide the development, providing an overview of the development needs. The role of the development team is, in conjunction with the customer and project coach, to formalize the requirements, while a member of the qualification team analyzes each requirement, suggests changes, new descriptions and turns the requirements into executable documentation, i.e. automated acceptance tests.

There is no milestone delimiting the *Requirements Elicitation* and the *Development* phases. The work of developers is not blocked while the QA team validates the requirements. The transition from one phase to the other is continuous and progressive, and it is finalized when all requirements are textually validated, and when the QA team has completed the set of acceptance tests (both manual and automatic) that map all the requirements of the release.

Development: This phase is based on the principles of XP. Before the implementation of any code unit, the development team creates tests (TDD). Therefore, the development is the conjunction of the preparation of the unit test and the coding of the unit in question. As a complement to the development phase, there is still one activity of analyzing/solving reported issues in tickets or requests - i.e., requests made by release stakeholders in the form of defect reports, requests for new features, requests for new tasks, new tests, and so forth.

Alongside the development of unit tests, the QA team plays the role of the development of tests within the same scenario, but in different situations. This is called explosion of test cases as commented briefly earlier. When a new defect is discovered, it is immediately reported by the qualifier or developer who found it. At this point, the person that registered the issue is also responsible for the validation analysis of the solution. She/he can accept the solution, reopen the issue, or even request new features.

Regarding the automated testing activity, the *Happy Day* acceptance tests (simplest tests) shall be prepared by the development team. From the Happy Day and according to the description of features, new test cases are carried out by the qualification team. The major effort by the qualification team should be towards the execution and development of automated tests.

Depending on the evolution of development, the QA team occupies itself with diversifying the test cases. The final stage of development yields the release of the software which should contain all of the implemented features or which are associated with at least one unit test implemented by the development team. At that moment, the development team freezes the implementation and formalizes the delivery of the release to the qualification team through the creation of a software *branch*.

Ideally the qualification team must also have developed most if not all of the automated tests. Otherwise, while the QA team finalizes the development of automated tests, the development team works on the *trunk* of the project with focus on correcting faults and/or elicitation of requirements for the next software release and/or on Happy Day acceptance tests.

At the end of the automation and explosion of test cases by the qualification team, the software versions should be synchronized in order to also synchronize the work of both teams in a consolidated version, the *Alpha release* for exploratory testing.

Exploratory (Alpha) Tests: The Exploratory Testing phase begins with the execution of a battery of manual tests (described in the test plan prepared by the development team) on the frozen version of the release (branch). Manual tests are performed by the qualification team to validate the cases where:

- Automation is not possible or
- The effort to automate is costlier than the effort to run the test manually.

Since the development environment is a university research lab, the exploration phase of the code includes a period of time when the students "become bug hunters". The best hunters are rewarded and the ranking of the best hunters is posted at the project's website. This promotes healthy competition and motivation to have the system being developed stressed up by "volunteer testers". Bugs (issues) are registered and corrected in anticipation of the launch of the Beta release.

The milestone between the *Exploratory* (Alpha) *Testing* and the *Beta Testing* phases is reached when the qualification team validates the solution of the issues. The goal is that all reported issues have a solution implemented by the development team.

Often an issue may become a new required functionality, or it may be impossible or even undesirable to have it corrected right then. Some defects found demand more time and cost to be corrected and do not justify the actual benefit that they will provide.

Therefore, after negotiating with the client, correcting such defects may be postponed, and a Beta release is launched.

Beta: It is the software release to the community, including project stakeholders, participants in the development and qualification, customers, members of other project teams, and guests. Complex situations are tested and (directed and undirected) exploratory tests are executed.

If any issue is registered while running the Beta release, then new meetings are held with the client to define what should be built, improved, corrected, removed, or refactored. The release is finalized and the client's evaluation may indicate new packages with changes and/or corrections that need be made.

To validate OQP we applied it to a pilot project and compared the results to OP's at DSL/UFCG.

Table 1. OQP activities and phases.

Teams	Requirement elicitation	Development	Alpha	Beta
Development	Write requirement	Code implementation	Correction of defects	Correction of defects
	Define design	Implementation of unit and integration test		
	Acceptance tests	Correction of defects		
QA	V&V requirements	Implementation of new cases of automated acceptance tests	Manual and exploratory testing	Validation of defect correction
	Acceptance tests			

3   Case Study

The proposed Our Quality Process (OQP) was applied to the OurBackup (OB) Home software [21], a backup system based on social networks. Initially, a set of six macro-features were defined and implemented under the OP process. These features enable the user to install the software, log onto the system, build his/her social network (by addition and/or acceptance of friends), and lastly, to perform and restore backups. Upon conclusion of the first version (V1), eight new features were added now under OQP, producing a "quality" version 2.

For the comparative study, three releases developed with OP (*OurBackup Release*)–OBRi, i = 1, 2 and 3; and, three releases developed with OQP (*OurBackup Quality Release*)–OBQRi, i = 1, 2 and 3–were considered.

Although every effort was directed to the production of automatic tests, some manual testing was needed. However, if a critical defect was discovered during manual testing, the manual procedure would be interrupted and a new test would be developed to detect the defect or to validate the correctness of the corresponding code.

The case study was carried based on six steps defined by the empirical methodology of Experimental Software Engineering [24, 25], namely: (i) Definition and Scope; (ii) Planning and Design; (iii) Preparation; (iv) Execution; (v) Analysis and Result Presentation; and, (vi) Packaging. The remainder of this section is devoted to describing each step in more detail.

3.1 Definition and Scope

We define and scope the experiment by means of the following terms:

- **Subject:** "Quality in Software Development Process";
- **Involved Areas:** "Software Engineering, Software Development Process";
- **Problem to be Addressed:** "Which development process results in products with higher quality";
- **Importance of the Problem:** "Improve the quality of developed products; increase the understanding of the products; and, improve the development process itself";
- The **Goal:** "Analyze two agile for software development processes, establish quality scores and, based on these scores, identify the process that yields products with higher level of quality";
- The **Null and Alternative Hypotheses:** "Processes generate products of similar quality" and "The processes do not generate similar quality products; one process is better than the other", respectively.

3.2 Planning and Design

- **Process used for Software Development and Quality Control:** *OurProcess* (**OP**) and *OurQualityProcess* (**OQP**)
- **Establishment of the Monitoring Phases:** Phase 01 - Automated Testing; Phase 02 - Verify Corrections; Phase 03 - Exploratory Testing; Phase 04 – Alpha Testing
- **Instrumentation and Data Collection:** to aid the setup of the experiment environment and to collect the metrics, some tools were used. The collected metrics are described below, and the tools are presented in Table 2.

  (a) **Percentage of Test Classes:** the percentage of the classes developed for test purposes among all the classes developed for the release under analysis;
  (b) **Percentage of Testing Methods:** the percentage of the methods developed for test purposes among all the methods developed for the release under analysis;
  (c) **Number of Cases of Manual Tests:** number of tests that were *manually* executed;
  (d) **Automatic Testing Coverage:** percentage of the features of the release that are covered by automatic tests, i.e. the percentage of the features that have their correctness verified by reproducible and automatic tests.

3.3 Preparation

Preparations are required before and during the execution of the experiment to:

- Provide appropriate training for team members to implement activities;
- Everyone involved in the work was trained on the new process (OQP) and on how to perform all activities in the process.
- Study tools, methods, techniques and practices;
- Everyone was made familiar with the tools, methods, techniques and practices in order to properly plan, instrument and execute the work.

Table 2. Tools used in the experimental process.

Metrics collected	Tool	Description
Classes of tests and testing methods	Metrics	A plug-in to Eclipse IDE that calculates several metrics, regarding the current development of a project, such as: number of methods, total lines of code, number of classes, number of test classes, instability, nested block depth, efferent coupling, and many more. It also performs analysis of dependency, definition of safe values for the metrics, the assignment of colors to different safety metrics values. All metrics may be exported to XML format
Manual tests	Wiki page	Since not all tests could be automated, due to high cost of implementation or to infeasibility caused by the complexity of the distributed environment, all manual tests' procedures were centralized in one Wiki page with read and write permissions for every member of the project
Automatic tests' code coverage	Clover	A plugin to Eclipse IDE that measures highly complex code, coverage lost due to recent changes, and precise per test coverage to ensure relevance of tests. It also addresses test optimization for Java by tracking code changes and test failures
Bugs' tracking	JIRA	It captures and organizes the issues into a repository. JIRA also has the functionality of assigning work to the members of team, and following up their activities
Version control	Subversion (SVN)	An open-source version control system
Test code	JUnit	Framework to write automated unit tests
Test code with Mock Objects	EasyMock	It provides Mock Objects, generating them on the fly, for interfaces, as well as objects through the class extension
Code Integration	Bamboo	This tool performs the building and testing processes, as well as connecting issues, commits, test results, and deployment. It was mostly used to perform continuing code integration

- Configure the environments;
- The environments where both development processes were to run was properly configured with the installation of tools in developers' and testers' machines. Server machines were also configured.
- Set up the case study scenarios;
- Use the same development and test teams.

3.4   Execution, Analysis and Result Presentation

Please consider Table 3. The increase in the amount of classes of tests by itself is not an indication that there has been an increase in the effort to produce automatic tests. Therefore, other data we recollected that indicated such an increase: column b in Table 3 shows the percentage of testing methods relatively to the total of developed methods.

Column c in Table 3 shows an increase in manual testing as one switches from OP to OQP to produce OBQR1 and OPQR2. But a consistent decrease from OBQR1 to OBQR3 and a lower amount of manual testing with OBQR3 relative to OBR3. This seems to indicate that OQP's sharper focus on testing tends to reduce manual testing which is tedious and error prone.

The relative larger number of manual tests for OQP can be attributed to this process' permanent availability of testers coupled with the functional code-breaking idiosyncrasies of OB's target distributed environment: different operating systems (OS) or different features across instances of a same OS (such as different versions, Network Address Translation, firewalls, antivirus software, and so forth). Environments such as OurBackup's tend to reduce the realistically possible amount of automatic testing (as a percentage of the entire code) to the range of 20–40 % [13].

It should be noted however, that the number of tests in a project is not the most appropriate metric to attest its quality, but it may suggest the amount of effort towards quality control. In the second column of Table 3 (percentage of testing methods), we note a gradual raise in the percentage of test classes as the OQP is adopted, achieving an increase of 50 % over OP's percentage (22 % over 14.8 %).

Table 3. Initial data comparison.

Version	(a) Classes of tests (%)	(b) Testing methods (%)	(c) # of Manual tests	(d) Automatic tests' code coverage (%)
OB R1	15.8	8.0	0	0
OB R2	14.4	11.0	74	21
OB R3	14.8	10.8	160	18
OBQ R1	13.5	13.4	275	34
OBQ R2	21.0	16.3	229	62
OBQ R3	22.2	17.7	143	91

Code coverage was measured in terms of lines, methods and classes covered by tests and it was collected using the Clover tool [7]. Column d brings these data and it shows a consistent increase in code coverage as OQP is continually employed to reach 91 % with $OBQR_3$ (meeting the quality baseline of over 90 % as indicated by 60 % of the respondents in the international survey in [10]). In contrast OP shows a somewhat haphazard behavior.

One may also note that, differently from OP, OQP meets baseline values for other metrics in this international survey: percentage of erroneous deadline and programmer-month effort estimations (within 5 to 15 % as indicated by 48 % of respondents) and percentage of defects discovered after release delivery (1 to 5 %).

Table 4. Lifetime of defects.

Software version	Minimum (days)	Maximum (days)	Average (days)	Median (days)
OB R1	–	–	–	–
OB R2	3	801	65	19
OB R3	1	328	168	221
OBQ R1	1	102	24	60
OBQ R2	0	29	9	13
OBQ R3	0	7	6	5

Regarding the lifetime of defects, or how fast the team is in resolving defects, a significant improvement with OQP was observed (please refer to Table 4). Again, Table 4 illustrates a gradual improvement in quality as OQP usage continues (by contrast, OP degrades on the average, while OQP's min, max, average and median times to fix defects improve).

3.5 Packaging

Both processes can be downloaded from the Distributed System Lab (LSD) website:

- **OurProcess:**
  http://twiki-public.lsd.ufcg.edu.br/twiki-public/bin/view/LSD/
  LSDProcessoDesenvolvimentoAntigo.
- **OurQualityProcess:**
  http://twiki-public.lsd.ufcg.edu.br/twiki-public/bin/view/LSD/
  LSDProcessoDesenvolvimento.

4   Evaluation and Lessons

We believe OQP's superiority over OP in the pilot project of *OurBackup* is due to:

Independence of Testers in the QA Team: there is a QA boss who is not the development leader. Testers are well regarded by the leader when they find critical defects and vulnerabilities in the software. Testers do not feel guilty when they reveal defects that they have not inserted themselves in the code.

Promoting Testing Competencies: testers should be trained to improve their skills in detecting failures and writing tests.

Sharper Focus on Quality: a tester is more productive than a developer that only tests his code in the remaining time of development. Moreover, an external tester, in general, is less likely to ignore errors caused by programming vices.

Also and contrary to agile processes that typically allow little emphasis on testing tasks initially [22], OQP recommends concentration on tests right from the onset of the project. This may not need to increase budgets by much. Test outsourcing may reduce the need for costly, in-house testing environments, thus easing the internal competition for resources between developers and testers. In turn, this should make it easier and cheaper to have a two-cell organization as advocated here.

5 Validation

We followed an experimental methodology for Software Engineering to evaluate our proposed development process with focus on the final quality of the software product. The results obtained by applying the *OurQualityProcess* approach validated our objectives to improve the quality of the software, besides reducing the time-to-market.

The experimental evaluation of the processes was done via a direct comparative analysis of software quality metrics. That type of comparison however, may not guarantee that the OQB process is always better than the OP. Further, regarding *validity of conclusion*, the experimental process may present threats to validity. Such is the case of the experience that the developers accumulated over time, as they migrated from OP to OQP. This may have affected OP more negatively than OQP.

However, the metrics collected show a significant improvement in quality when the OQP was applied.

6 Related Work

The debate on agile speed *v.* testing seems to have been kindled by the inability of agile practices of unit and acceptance tests to always meet the need for quality of delivered products [15]. Here it was indicated that testing and speed need not be traded off if practices that lead to development and independent testing activities are added to agile processes. The results presented here may have shed light on this debate, and may help practitioners' make informed decisions regarding quality management of software development projects.

One may contend at this point that the benefits of continuous, independent software testing activities having been established long ago, are undisputable and for that, need not be revisited. The on-going debate in the marketplace indicates otherwise: practices of yesteryears are criticized for being in want of reform to meet new challenges. Also and despite recent progress, most companies still present very low levels of testing maturity [11]. As stated in this last reference: "It is perhaps a damning indictment of the industry that after all these years we can consistently design and plan testing, but have no thought or regard for effectively measuring the success and efficiency of this activity (which, combined with the costs of rework, forms a significant proportion of project costs)". We hope to have offered some insight into measurements of test results.

State-of-the-practice requirements needed to measure (expected) software quality were elicited in an international survey of expert software development managers [10]. This survey yielded a software quality metrics baseline for the accuracy of project estimates, the detection of defects before product release, and the test coverage. This baseline was used for comparing results of the test-driven, adapted agile OQP process proposed here against those of its foundation XP process.

The authors of the work in [1] have proposed and studied a framework to scale up unit tests, and, as a result, they achieved test coverage of over 99 % with 36 % of the code dedicated to testing. In the case study worked out here, OQP achieved a test coverage of 91 %, with a total test code of 18 %. Although results of both works exceed the test coverage baseline of [10], OQP ended up having half of the test code percentage of total coding effort. One cannot vouch for OQP's superiority (or the framework in [1] for that matter), however, given environmental differences underlying both works. A more detailed scrutiny and comparison of both works could reveal interesting, complementary aspects that could be explored to support decisions concerning code coverage against test code amount trade-offs, which was not intentionally made here.

7 Conclusion and Outlook

This paper proposed complementing the basic aspects of Agile development processes with a few but significant techniques and practices that, taken together, have been shown effective in improving quality and defect-fixing-delays for the case of a backup utility in a large scale, open source free-to-join, peer-to-peer (P2P) grid computing environment.

The case studied compared results for two different versions of the backup utility. Although this may hinder the significance of conclusions and recommendations, it offered some evidence that investing in independent testing may indeed pay off not only in software quality but in development time as well.

Further work is needed to extricate and isolate cause-effect relationships (between added practices and the observed improvements), to establish the degree of significance of each cause to results, and to generalize conclusions. The early evidence presented here supports OQP's separation of testing from development. This separation may run against current industry trends but it may as well support agile practioners better, particularly those with responsibility for critical application development where a higher degree of compliance between requirements and implemented features is expected. We also consider that it might be relevant to further study and evaluate the impact of changing the roles played by the members of the teams during the development process.

Acknowledgements. The authors thank colleagues and anonymous reviewers whose comments clarified and enriched the work presented here.

References

1. Artho, C., Biere, A., Honiden, S., Schuppan, V., Eugster, P., Baur, M., Zweimüller, B., Farkas, P.: Advanced unit testing – how to scale up a unit test framework. In: AST 2006, Shanghai, China, May 2006
2. Beck, K., Beedle, M., Van Bennekum, A., Cockburn, A., Cunningham, W., Fowler, M., Grenning, J., Highsmith, J., Hunt, A., Jeffries, R., Kern, J., Marick, B., Martin, R.C., Mellor, S., Schwaber, K., Sutherland, J., Thomas, D.: Manifesto for agile software development (2001). http://www.agilemanifesto.org. Accessed 17 Dec 2008
3. Buglione, L., Hauck, J.C., Gresse Von Wangenheim, C., Mccaffery, F.: Hybriding CMMI and requirement engineering maturity and capability models. In: ICSOFT – 7th International Conference on Software Paradigm Trends, Italy (2012)
4. Chaos Report (2011). http://blog.standishgroup.com Accessed 18 Jun 2012
5. Crispin, L., Gregory. J.: Agile testing: practical guide for testers and agile teams. Addison-Wesley Signature Series (2009)
6. Crispin, L., House, T.: Testing extreme programming. XP Series (2002)
7. Clover (2012). http://www.atlassian.com
8. Dinakar, K.: Agile development: overcoming a short-term focus in implementing best practices. In: Conference on Object Oriented Programming Systems Languages and Applications (OOPSLA), Orlando, FL, pp. 579–588 (2009)
9. Dóra, P., Oliveira, A.C., Moura, J.A.B.: Improving quality in agile development processes. In: Proceedings of the 8th International Joint Conference on Software Technologies (ICSOFT-EA), pp. 411–416. July 29th to 31st, Reykjavíck, Iceland (2013). doi:10.5220/0004559704110416
10. Dóra, P., Oliveira, A.C., Moura, J.A.B.: A baseline for quality management in software projects. In: Proceedings of Informática 2013 – 15th International Convention and Fair, March 18th to 22nd, Havana, Cuba, ISBN 978-959-7213-02-4 (2013b)
11. Experimentus: Test Maturity Model Integrated (TMMi) – Survey Results, How Mature are Companies' Software Quality Management Processes in Today's Market? Update 2011, White paper, www.experimentus.com, 20 pp (2011)
12. Guerra, A., Santana, M.: Quality of software process or quality of software product?. In: International Conference on Software Quality, Canada (2002)
13. Harrison, J.A.: Cited in A debate on the merits of mobile software test automation. James A. Denman, Published 23 May 2013 (2013). http://searchsoftwarequality.techtarget.com/news
14. Heuser, M.: Exploring the shifting roles in test and QA management. http://searchsoftwarequality.techtarget.com. Accessed 12 Oct 2012
15. Hislop, W., Lutz, J., Naveda F., McCracken, M., Mead, R., Williams, L.A.: Integrating Agile Practices into Software Engineering Courses. In: 15th Conference on Software Engineering Education and Training (CSEET) (2002)
16. Lent, J.: Software Testing Trends 2012: Business Alignment, Not Bug Fixes. http://searchsoftwarequality.techtarget.com (2013). Accessed 28 Jan 2013
17. Lycett, M., Macredie, R.D., Patel, C., Paul, R.J.: Migrating agile methods to standardized development practice. Computer **36**(6), 79, 85 (2003)
18. Mackinnon, T., Freeman, S., Craig, P.: Endo-Testing: Unit Testing with Mock Objects. XP eXamined by Addison-Wesley, Reading (2000)

19. Meyer, B.: Object-Oriented Software Construction, 2nd edn. Prentice Hall, Upper Saddle River (1997)
20. Mitchell, R., McKim, J., Meyer, B.: Design By Contract, by example. Addison-Wesley Publishing Company, Redwood City (2001)
21. Oliveira, M., (2007). OurBackup: Uma Solução P2P de Backup Baseada em Redes Sociais. Master's Thesis, COPIN - UFCG, Campina Grande, PB, Brasil (In Portuguese)
22. Reichert, A.: How to focus an agile scrum team on quality and testing. http:// searchsoftwarequality.techtarget.com, first published in August 2012
23. Savoia, Al., (2011). Test is Dead. In: 6th Annual Google Test Automation Conference (GTAC). Uploaded on Oct 27, 2011
24. Travassos, G., Guroc, D. and Amaral, E.: Introdução à Engenharia de Software Experimental (Introduction to Experimental Software Engineering), Technical Report ES-590/02-Abr. Graduate Program in Systems Engineering and Computing, COPPE/UFRJ, Rio de Janeiro (2002) (In Portuguese)
25. Wohlin, C., Runeson, P., Höst, M., Ohlsson, M.C., Regnell, B., Wesslén, A.: Experimentation in Software Engineering: An Introduction. Kluwer Academic Publishers, Norwell, MA, USA (2000). ISBN 0-7923-8682-5

State of the Art of Dynamic Software Updating in Java

Allan Raundahl Gregersen[1], Michael Rasmussen[1],
and Bo Nørregaard Jørgensen[2(✉)]

[1] ZeroTurnaround, Tartu, Estonia
{allan.gregersen,michael.rasmussen}
@zeroturnaround.com
[2] The Maersk Mc-Kinney Moller Institute, University of Southern Denmark,
Odense, Denmark
bnj@mmmi.sdu.dk

Abstract. The dynamic software updating system JRebel from Zeroturnaround has proven to be an efficient mean to improve developer productivity, as it allows developers to change the code of their applications while developing and testing them. Hence, developers no longer have to go through the tedious cycle of serializing application state, halting execution, redeploy the binary, restarting, and de-serializing state before they can test the effect of a code change. However, the current version of JRebel has its limits, as it does not support all kinds of code changes. In this paper, we compare the three most comprehensive dynamic updating systems developed for Java to date. Together, these systems provide comprehensive support for changing class definitions of live objects, including adding, removing and moving fields, methods, classes and interfaces anywhere in the inheritance hierarchy. We then investigate the effects of dynamic updating by performing a dynamic updating experiment on five consecutive revisions of the classical arcade game Breakout using the dynamic updating system Gosh! (Prior to the acquisition by zeroturnaround.com known as Javeleon.). Based on the result of this experiment we show that dynamic updating of class definitions for live objects may under some circumstances result in different run-time behavior than would be observed after a cold restart of the upgraded application. Finally, we conclude by discussing the implication of integrating the dynamic updating model of Gosh! with JRebel. The successful integration of these two systems will set a new standard for dynamic software updating in Java.

1 Introduction

Software is subject to continuous change, not only as part of its development cycles, but also over time to stay useful to its users [1]. In most standard deployment environments this implies that use of the next software version typically requires halting the currently running version before deploying and starting the new version. Using a dynamic software-updating system (DSU) this is no longer necessary, as the DSU system will dynamically replace the running version with the new version. Depending on how advanced the DSU system is this may happen more or less transparent to end-users. We say that a DSU system is end-user transparent if it does not require any intervention of

© Springer-Verlag Berlin Heidelberg 2014
J. Cordeiro and M. van Sinderen (Eds.): ICSOFT 2013, CCIS 457, pp. 99–113, 2014.
DOI: 10.1007/978-3-662-44920-2_7

end-users during an update, and similarly we say it is developer transparent if it does not require developers to take specific precautions. Hence, the two forms of transparency is a key quality for any DSU system, since it strongly influences the degree to which it will be successful. The success of DSU systems is especially important as software systems tend to become more complex in terms of internal run-time state and interactions with external systems. This trend is for instance present in mission-critical systems such as surveillance and control of air traffic, ground transportation, oil and gas production, industrial process, power generation, and smart-grids. These application domains are all subject to safety, environmental and economical regulations and restrictions, which make system downtime due to maintenance tasks like software updates not only inconvenient but also very expensive.

Where past research has contributed significantly toward making DSU practical for systems written in C or C++, upgrading of server functionality [2–4], deploying security patches [5], and operating systems upgrades [6–11], there used to be a gap when it comes to systems written in managed languages, such as Java, Ruby, and C#. In the past DSU for managed languages was limited to HotSpot JVM [12] for Java. For some .NET languages [13] a similar limited support of on-the-fly updating of method bodies applies. However, this support is too restricting for all but the simplest updates. Limiting changes to method bodies would render the DSU system useless for updating most of the revision improvements reported for the Jetty webserver [14] in [15]. Academic approaches [16–19] offer more flexibility, but remain still to be proven on realistic development scenarios. Furthermore, these approaches employ designs for method and object indirection, which impose substantial space and time overheads on steady-state execution. The lack of approaches supporting managed languages had the potential to become a severe problem as an increasing number of enterprise systems and embedded systems are written in those languages. Fortunately, the research on DSU for managed languages has caught up and includes now multiple promising approaches. State-of-the-art approaches for Java includes; JRebel [20], an application-level system which is currently the de facto commercial tool for class reloading in Java; Dynamic Code Evolution VM [21], a VM-enhancement of the Java HotSwap[TM] VM [22]; JVolve [23], a VM approach based on the Jikes Research VM, and Gosh! [24], an application-level system.

In this paper, we first provide an overview of code changes supported by DSU systems targeting Java; we then give an introduction to the design and implementation of Gosh!, including some of the major challenges involved in creating a practical dynamic updating system, that supports the modern Java ecosystem with tons of different application servers and frameworks. This is followed by the latest development in the performance benchmarking of Gosh!. Then, we demonstrate the capabilities of Gosh! by applying it to a series of consecutive revisions of an in-house implementation of the classical arcade game Breakout. In Sect. 6, we report on the latest developments coming from the merger of the Gosh! dynamic updating model, formerly known as Javeleon, and the commercial tool JRebel, where the combined strengths will heavily advance the state-of-the-art in practical dynamic updating in Java. Finally, we discuss the result of this experiment and its implication for future research direction within dynamic software updating.

This paper is a revised and extended version that supersedes our paper from IC-SOFT 2013, [24]. In this paper we have incorporated many new insights primarily from experience gained through the efforts of merging the Gosh! with JRebel's large set plug-ins for handling changes to frameworks. In particular, in Sect. 3, a lot more details are found, not only for the model behind Gosh!, but also some of the practical implications that Gosh! has, that renders it not suitable for supporting modern development in Java. The reasoning behind this extension in Sect. 3 was to set the stage for why class reloading is not enough in itself, thus also why framework support is a prerequisite for supporting the Java ecosystem. Section 6, which is entirely new, contains many new insights in order to better understand some of the implications that a certain style of updating poses on the implementation requirements.

2   Comparison of Dynamic Software Updating Systems

A comparison of the code changes supported by DSU systems that are currently public available is given in Table 1. As the table shows, Gosh! is at the moment the DSU system with the most comprehensive support for redefinition of Java classes. The Issues symbol in Table 1 indicates that there are circumstances where the code change is not fully supported by the DSU system.

Table 1. DSU system comparison.

Code change	*Gosh!*	*JRebel*	*DCEVM*
Changes to method bodies	✓	✓	✓
Adding/removing fields	✓	✓	✓
Adding/removing methods	✓	✓	✓
Adding/removing constructors	✓	✓	✓
Adding/removing classes[i]	✓	✓	⚠
Replace superclass	✓	✗	✓
Adding/removing implemented interfaces	✓	✗	✓
Automatic new instance field initialization (developer-defined default value)[ii]	⚠	✗	✗
Automatic new static field initialization (developer-defined default value)[iii, iv]	⚠	⚠	✗
Move field to super class (preserving the state)[iv]	✓	✗	⚠
Move field to sub class (preserving the state)[iv]	✓	✗	⚠
Changing static field value[iii]	⚠	⚠	✗
Changing primitive static final field value[v]	✓	⚠	⚠
Adding/removing enum values[vi]	✓	⚠	✗

✓ Supported   ✗ Not supported   ⚠ Issues

i.   Only Gosh! and JRebel provide integration with custom class-loaders for adding new classes that is not present on the class path.
ii. Gosh! supports automatic field initialization without re-executing the constructor/static initializer. However, automatic initialization does currently not support branching (try/catch, ternary operator etc.)
iii. JRebel's support for changing static field values is based on re-executing the entire static initializer, which may lead to serious side-effects caused by repeated execution of code which should only execute once. Moreover, it will only happen if and only if a new static field besides the changed one is added to the class. Gosh! has built-in support for changing static final constants.
iv. Gosh! is currently the only DSU system cable of correctly transferring values of fields which have been moved up or down in the inheritance hierarchy. DCEVM copies field values to super/sub-classes even in situations where the field is also retained in the former class version.
v.   Only Gosh! fully supports changing primitive static final field values, as both JRebel and DCEVM gives wrong results for constant values accessed through reflection after updating.
vi. JRebel claims support. However, simple tests show that e.g. removing and adding enum values is not handled correctly in switch statements.

3 The Dynamic Updating System Gosh!

The core idea of the Gosh! updating model is to allow multiple versions of the same objects to co-exist in a running system. This is achieved by creating new class loaders for each new version, thus setting up distinct type namespaces. Since this approach imposes a version barrier [26] of incompatibility between differently versioned classes and objects, the updating model must maintain a versioned view of the involved objects and classes. Gosh! utilizes a novel concept of Dynamic Correspondence Proxification, a combination of the two mechanisms In-Place Proxification and Correspondence Mapping which transform live objects and classes of former versions into proxies that delegate to the most recent versions. In-Place Proxification enforces shared identity and state across the version barrier, while Correspondence Mapping handles type conversion for crossing the version barrier. Details on the Dynamic Correspondence Mapping used in Gosh! can be found in prior work [25]. While at first, such a versioned view controlled by proxies sounds expensive in terms of steady-state execution overhead, what makes the dynamic updating model of Gosh! fast is the novel usage of proxies that lifts the execution from updated methods into a new type namespace. Within this new type namespace the execution happens just as fast as before any updating took place (after the state has been lazily transferred from the former version to the current executing version). While delegating method execution to distinct typed classes (the updated classes) using some kind of reflective approach, as Gosh! does, will be inherently slow, not many such delegations ever take place when applying the In-Place Proxification model behind Gosh!. The reason is that when an entry method in an updated class is executed, it will by itself figure out (by injected bytecode in the beginning of the method) that it was updated, and therefore this method will delegate to the newly defined class in a completely new type namespace of the system. Once the execution continues within the parallel universe every single method that is executed in that universe will already be the updated one. Hence, the execution overhead will remain constant no matter how many subsequent dynamic updates are applied to the underlying application.

Clearly, making sure that methods delegates to a new type namespace for which updated code can execute is nowhere near enough to make practical updating of classes and objects in Java possible. There are numerous built-in language features and even certain assumptions within external frameworks that require additional handling to not confuse the runtime system (JVM). One area of particular interest is the reflection API, which is troubled by the fact that multiple versions of the "same" entity, that is a class or an object, can co-exist within the runtime. Imagine one example where before a dynamic updating operation, a reference to a reflective method object is stored e.g. in an instance field. Now, after applying a dynamic update to the class holding the method object reference, leaving the reflection API unhandled will yield IllegalArgumentException when trying to invoke that method through reflection using any object with a type defined in the new parallel universe. Therefore, all of the refection API must be made aware of the dynamic updating model behind Gosh! which is a substantial amount of bytecode patching. Moreover, any code that relies on cached class metadata, which is the case in any modern dependency injection framework will have outdated metadata that corresponds to the particular class version in use, when the class metadata scanner ran within the framework (in many cases during startup or deployment). Hence, when adding new properties to existing bean classes those new properties will not be injected as expected and therefore hard to track null-pointer-exceptions will often happen, which defeats the purpose of dynamically updating the application in the first place. In order to ensure reliable execution within the modern Java ecosystem a dynamic updating system for Java must provide a way to integrate with commonly used frameworks. What is truly challenging in this regard is the number of available frameworks in the wild. In this area there is only one current approach that has proper support for framework-related changes and that is JRebel. With JRebel's tailored plug-ins for numerous frameworks, integration with class loaders of almost all application servers and the ability to provide support for all major JVM vendors and versions, there are really no dynamic update approach within the academic world that could compete with JRebel when it comes to real world practical usage. With JRebel having shown the potential to support the Java ecosystem, and a couple of research dynamic updating systems having shown that it is possible to support changes to the type hierarchy of classes, including Gosh!, the ideal scenario would be to merge the two worlds together. This scenario is now one step closer to realization, since Zeroturnaround in early 2013 acquired rights to use the Gosh! dynamic updating model as well as hired the main research personal behind Gosh!. Section 6 will give a summary of current status of this merger.

An outline of the main components of the Gosh! dynamic updating system will be given below, whereas additional details on the architecture are provided in [27].

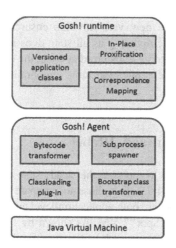

Fig. 1. Architectural overview of Gosh!

The architecture of Gosh!, shown in Fig. 1, features the following components:

- The *bootstrap-class-transformer* and *sub-process-spawner* components are responsible for statically transforming the JVM bootstrap-classes and to automatically spawn a new JVM process with the set of modified bootstrap-classes. This setup is necessary to make Gosh! transparent to the end-user, as the class instrumentation mechanism introduced in JDK 5.0 does not support instrumentation of bootstrap-classes on class loading.

- The *class-loading plug-in* component is used to integrate Gosh! with the class loading and resource management of different application frameworks. At present, Gosh! only provides an integration component for the NetBeans Platform, besides standard Java SE support. In general, the responsibility of these components is to deal with all the issues that cannot be handled simply by updating Java class files, i.e. reflecting changes made to application resources and configuration files.
- The *bytecode-transformer* component is responsible of instrumenting classes as they are loaded into the JVM. We distinguish between system classes that are made dynamic update-aware and application classes that are made dynamic update-enabled. Update-aware classes impose less run-time overhead than update-enabled classes. We make this distinction, because we consider it less likely that system classes are dynamically updated, as this would most likely include a dynamic update of the JVM. However, although system classes are not considered subject to dynamic updating they must be instrumented to accommodate changes to their possible subclasses.
- The *run-time* component implements the underlying dynamic updating model, which uses the In-Place-Proxification technique in combination with Correspondence Mapping to delegate requests to the most recent versions of updated classes. This component also ensures correct identity and equality preservation, handling of hashCode, thread synchronization, array-access handling for differently versioned objects etc. The core execution component is also responsible of transferring state from former versions to the new version. State is transferred using a thread-safe, non-blocking, lazy-state copying mechanism, which only transfers state when it is requested from within the new version. This ensures that the application stays responsive during dynamic updating as all state does not have to be transferred at once. In case all state had to be transferred at once, the end-user would experience a transition bump, where the application turns temporally inaccessible.

4   Benchmarking Gosh! and JRebel

We have used SPECjvm2008 to measure the steady-state performance overhead introduced by Gosh! and JRebel 4.5.2. We chose to compare Gosh! with JRebel and not DCEVM, as Gosh! and JRebel are both application-level approaches whereas DCEVM is based on a modified Java HotSpot^{TM} VM. As shown by Fig. 2, Gosh! and JRebel are comparable in performance, both approaches also show similar bottlenecks. The tests were performed so both Gosh! and JRebel identified the benchmark classes as update-enabled.

Since the SPECjvm2008 test only allowed us to measure the steady-state performance overhead before updating we also designed a number of micro benchmarks to measure the run-time overhead imposed by newly inserted code after updating. The result of our recursive Fibonacci number benchmarks is shown in Fig. 3. The dynamic update simply renames the recursive method, thus simulating the insertion of a new method. The benchmark results show that Gosh! is faster than JRebel both before and after an update. Furthermore, the results also show that the runtime overhead remains constant for Gosh! after updating whereas it increases drastically for JRebel. Hence, Gosh! demonstrates that it scales for supporting continues updating.

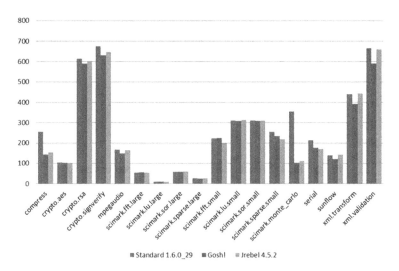

Fig. 2. Gosh! vs. JRebel 4.5.2 [operations/min.].

5 Experience

To evaluate practical application of Gosh!, we made four updates using five revisions of an in-house-developed version of the classical arcade game Breakout. The first version of the game contains 14 classes and 1.012 lines of code, which developed into 36 classes and 2.405 lines of code in the final version. The five revisions of the game contain many non-trivial code changes. A total of 120 code changes were found by manual inspection. Each code change has been classified according to the classification developed in [15]. Table 2 summarizes the code changes found for successive revisions. The ID numbering of the code changes is not consecutive, as we have only listed the code changes that took place between successive revisions. A blank field in the table indicates that no occurrences of the code change were found. The last column in the table summarizes the frequency of each code change for all revisions. We included this column to show how often a particular code change occurs during development of the game.

The experiment showed that the Breakout game could be successfully updated from one revision to the next, however, under some circumstances the applied updating sequence resulted in a run-time behavior that was quite different from that of a cold restart of the game. Updates that resulted in different behavior did so, because they introduced code changes that caused run-time phenomena. A classification of run-time phenomena in dynamic software updating was first introduced in [28]. The code changes listed in Table 3 were herein identified as the cause of these phenomena. It is important to note that these code changes may cause run-time phenomena, but that it is not always the case. Whether run-time phenomena do occur is very dependent on the application's design and the time of updating.

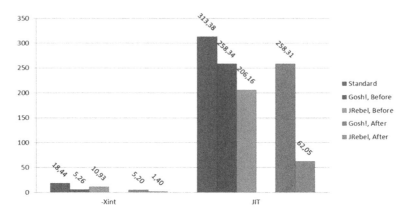

Fig. 3. Recursive Fibonacci Benchmark [operations/min.].

Table 2. Code change analysis of Breakout.

ID	Code change description	R1-R2	R2-R3	R3-R4	R4-R5	%
6	Class added	2	9	3	3	14
30	Constructor implementation changed in class		1	1		2
33	Instance method added to class	3	11	2	8	20
34	Instance method removed from class	2				2
35	Instance method renamed in class	4				3
37	Instance method return type changed in class	4				3
38	Instance method implementation changed in class	12	11	3	10	30
44	Static method implementation changed in class	4				3
68	Instance field added to class		2		2	3
84	Interface added			1		1
120	Resource added[a]	8	1	4	8	18
121	Resource removed[a]				1	1

5.1 Phantom Objects

Phantom Objects are live objects whose classes have been removed by a dynamic update. Whilst phantom objects will continue to exist in the system, their existence in the updated application will be void. Hence, if such objects are part of the existing application state, the updated application may try to reference them indirectly through, for instance, an array or a collection. Although removing classes is typically discouraged, there are situations where classes are either in-lined or renamed due to refactoring. For the DSU systems discussed in this paper, in-lining and class renaming corresponds to class-removed and class-added operations. Likewise, the use of dayfly

Table 3. Runtime Phenomena.

ID	Code change description	Possible run-time phenomenon
7	Class removed	Phantom objects
8	Class renamed	Phantom objects/Lost State
16	Modifier abstract added to class	Phantom objects
6	Class added	Absent state
22	Super class of class changed	Absent state
68/71	Instance/static field added to class	Absent state
21	Modifier static removed from inner class	Absent state
70/73	Instance/static field type changed in class	Lost state
65	Static initialization impl. changed in class	Oblivious update
30	Constructor impl. changed in class	Oblivious update
114	Static field value changed	Broken assumption
38/44	Instance/static method impl. changed (e.g., conditional statement, method split/merged)	Broken assumption/ Transient inconsistency

classes [29] is another example of class removals. Dayfly classes are classes that are typically created for evaluating a new idea and then removed shortly thereafter.

5.2 Absent State

Absent State refers to the situation where objects created in a former version lack state defined by the updated versions of their classes. Such state would typically have been created during a cold restart by an extra argument in a modified constructor.

5.3 Lost State

Lost State happens when an updated class makes binary incompatible changes to the type of a member field. E.g. change the field 'name' of type String to type Name. Given that it is not possible for the automatic state-transfer mechanism of Gosh! to automatically deduct how a changed type relates to a previously declared type, the run-time effect of changing the field type is that the field value for all existing objects of that class is lost and the new value is set to the default value.

5.4 Oblivious Update

Oblivious Update refers to the situation where some or all features introduced in the new revision are missing after updating. That is, the run-time behavior of the updated application is different from that of a cold restart. Changing constructors to initialize new state fields is often the cause for oblivious updates, as constructor changes will not have any effect on already created objects.

5.5   Broken Assumption

Broken Assumption may surface when constraints governing the interrelationship between program state and program logic change between successive revisions. If, for instance, the value of a member field, e.g. a counter, depends on some other member field, e.g. a constant, then changing either the value of the constant or the logic of the code maintaining this interdependency may break objects when moved to the new class. Exception-based program termination is often the result.

5.6   Transient Inconsistency

Transient Inconsistency refers to the situation where an updated application is temporally brought into a run-time state that the new version of the application would never enter after a cold restart. If the updated application does not enter a valid run-time state in the new version after a finite period of time, it is said to be captured in an erroneous state. Erroneous state can be caused by a Broken Assumption that does not produce any run-time exceptions.

5.7   Observations Based on Phenomena

An interesting example of the Phantom Object and Lost State phenomena can be observed if we perform a dynamic roll-back by dynamically updating revision 4 back to revision 3 in the middle of a level. The resulting run-time effect of dynamic update is shown in Fig. 4. Here we see that the special bricks introduced in revision 4 disappear after the roll-back to revision 3. This happens because revision 4 uses subclasses of the abstract parent class (Brick.class) to model special feature bricks, such as concrete bricks and bonus bricks that drop bonuses when hit. This roll-back corresponds to a class-removed code change, as the subclasses do not exist in revision 3. Hence, the roll-back resulted in a run-time behavior that is different from that of a cold restart, where the brick wall would have appeared solid consisting of only blue bricks. However, this

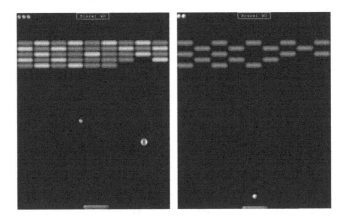

Fig. 4. Disappearing objects after class removals.

effect is a Transient Inconsistency as the brick wall is drawn correctly when continuing to the next game level.

We observed during our experiments with dynamically updating of the Breakout game that the result of a dynamic update is highly dependent on application design. The roll-back goes through despite the occurrence of run-time phenomena, because of a loosely coupled design that uses a lookup service for storing the brick wall. An alternative design storing the brick wall in an array of type Brick[][] would result in program termination due to a null pointer exception, because the state-migration mechanism in Gosh! cannot map objects of subclasses for special feature bricks in revision 4 to any objects in revision 3, as the subclasses do not exist here. Hence, the state-migration mechanism will instead insert null references in place of the original special brick objects in the array. It is these null-references that cause program termination due to a null pointer exception when traversing the array. More examples on the run-time phenomena and their causes are given in [28].

6 Merging Gosh! Dynamic Updating Model with JRebel

As said in Sect. 3, Zeroturnaround acquired what was formerly known as Javeleon, in order to fill out the missing gap in JRebel's current updating model, where changes to the inheritance hierarchy are not supported. This section will explain some of the new challenges that arise when merging those very different dynamic updating models. This section reports what have shown to be the most challenging tasks in the process of fitting the Gosh! model to the existing JRebel plug-ins. This is done by first listing the top 3 challenges followed by more detailed explanations in separate subsections.

The top 3 challenges (in non-prioritized order) have been:

1. Bootstrapping the JVM.
2. Context-specific runtime updates.
3. Determining which classes are updateable in general.

6.1 Bootstrapping the JVM

The updating model in Gosh! requires that even classes that are never updated are transformed to accommodate changes to subclasses. This accounts for all classes in the system, and therefore also the classes that are loaded in the very early phase of the JVM startup, called the bootstrap classes. Gosh! has previously solved this by using a so-called Java agent which can hook into class loading events before they are defined into the JVM. The main difficulty with the bootstrap classes is that these classes are already defined within the JVM and therefore they can only be changed in accordance to the built-in HotSwap mechanism. Hence only method body modifications are possible, which does not provide the change flexibility required by Gosh!. In Gosh! this was solved by taking a novel approach that allowed to transform the bootstrap classes without re-defining them into the existing JVM, then saving the transformed bootstrap classes at a well-defined location (e.g. user home dir or temp folder). Having the transformed bootstrap classes at hand, a new Java process was spawned using a special JVM option to prepend the transformed bootstrap classes, thereby allowing the new process to be bootstrapped with already transformed classes. Unfortunately, this had the effect (due to technicalities that are omitted here) that debugging was not possible in this special first run (any subsequent run would simply use the prepend bootstrap classes option). Furthermore, since the set of bootstrap classes are very different across JVM vendors and even changes from one Java update to another, hard to track JVM crashes and weird exception could happen when developers updated the JDK version in use. In order to fix those issues, the only way was to tell developers to delete the bootstrap classes, allowing for the special run to re-generate the bootstrap classes with the changed JDK version in use. In practice, such a solution does not work very well.

The first step towards a more user transparent solution was to hide the bootstrap generation behind IDE plug-ins. The idea was simple, just coding up functionality that could hook into the launch process provided by the IDE. At that time, the bootstrap classes could be generated even before starting up the application for the first time. More importantly, a check for a valid set of bootstrap classes could be made, and if found invalid, regeneration of the bootstrap classes would happen without user intervention. Already this was a big step forward. However, there were still problems, because some developers do not run their applications or startup application servers from within an IDE, rather they sometimes use special startup scripts which circumvents the hook in the IDE launch process.

Having not found the silver bullet, prototyping a native agent that could intercept the JVM process even before any classes are loaded began. The benefits of such an approach are obvious, since the code that checks for a valid set of bootstrap classes can be executed before loading any classes. The price to pay is the necessity for having to compile the C code for different platforms and OS, which is due to higher maintenance.

6.2 Context-Specific Runtime Updates

When dealing with modern frameworks in the Java ecosystem, lots of configuration changes, rescanning for changed framework-specific entities (e.g. XML or properties files) need to be applied in accordance to what actually changed within particular Java source files. Sometimes, the internal functionality of the frameworks requires specific operations to be executed within a certain context. Therefore, if the dynamic updating system operates by picking up class file changes, then applying updates in a special update thread, it may not be possible to perform the needed changes inside the frameworks, because it may hold thread local state. The Gosh! updating model does exactly that, which quickly showed to be a concern in many existing JRebel framework integrations. In some cases the problems could be resolved by postponing parts of the reconfiguration until the application thread itself was run. In other cases new integrations were needed, which added to the effort of bytecode patching the frameworks to match capabilities of Gosh!.

6.3 Determining Which Classes are Updateable in General

Both JRebel and Gosh! dynamic updating systems are based upon patching bytecode at load-time to allow for changes to the patched classes at runtime. In order to minimize the patching overhead (e.g. to reduce startup overhead, runtime overhead etc.) as much as possible, it is extremely important to be able to determine upfront which classes should be made updateable. As said before, in Gosh! all classes including system classes must be patched to allow for updates in updateable subclasses. This is not the case for JRebel, which only needs to patch the updateable part of the application. However, even in Gosh! the set of transformations needed to make a system class behave correctly is much smaller than what is required for updateable classes. Therefore, the goal is still to make as few classes updateable as possible without having to ask users to specify exactly which ones (for better ease of use). A naive approach that is partly taken by JRebel, is to make all classes that can be found from a path that is not inside a jar file updateable. This simple approach actually works quite well in many situations. However, there are some cases where users have jar files that they would also like to update at runtime. For that reason JRebel provides the ability to pickup user-specific directories and jar files from special XML-files called rebel.xml. For the Gosh! updating model things are a bit more complicated, because even if some classes will definitely not change at runtime (inside static jar files) some of these classes may actually have updateable types in their public interface (API). This becomes troublesome after applying updates to the updateable types within the API, once client code later calls into those interface methods with updated objects for which their classes by nature of the Gosh! model are distinct types from what is linked into the JVM. This will lead to some very hard to track no such method errors at runtime.

Therefore, special care must be taken in order to determine whether or not there are conflicting types within the public API of what appears to be pure "static" classes. If such occurrences are found, the conflicting classes can simply be made updateable, ensuring that they will be lifted to the parallel universe also.

7   Conclusion

In this paper, we have provided an overview of the current state-of-the-art of the DSU systems targeting Java, by comparing the set of code changes they support. The comparison shows that Gosh! is currently the most comprehensive publicly available DSU system available. Furthermore, we have benchmarked Gosh! against the only commercially available DSU system JRebel and shown that Gosh! delivers comparable run-time performance before updating and considerable better performance after updating. Whereas JRebel's updating model introduces a significant overhead for handling changed code, Gosh!'s updating model scales and continues to perform with the same constant run-time overhead. Hence, Gosh! shows the capability to provide support for dynamic updating of long-lived applications, like application- and web-servers. To evaluate Gosh!, we made four updates using five revisions of an in-house developed version of the classical arcade game Breakout. The experiment showed that it was possible to incrementally update the consecutive revisions of the Breakout game. However, what the experiment also showed was that dynamic updating may result in so-called run-time phenomena. I.e., situations where the run-time behavior of the updated application diverges from the behavior expected after a cold restart. Hence, to increase predictability of DSU systems there is a need for creating dynamic impact analysis tools that can determine whether code changes differentiating successive revisions may potentially lead to manifestation of run-time phenomena or not. Dynamic analysis is necessary as both the run-time state and the time of updating have significant impact on the result of an update, hence static impact analysis alone cannot determine whether a dynamic update will be successful, it can only identify potential risks of run-time phenomena. The advent of dynamic analysis tools will, among other things, determine the future success and feasibility of dynamic updating for mission critical software systems. Finally, we described the main challenges of integrating the Gosh! dynamic updating model, formerly known as Javeleon, with JRebel, after Zeroturnaround acquired it in spring 2013.

References

1. Lehman, M.M.: Laws of software evolution revisited. In: Montangero, C. (ed.) EWSPT 1996. LNCS, vol. 1149, pp. 108–124. Springer, Heidelberg (1996)
2. Neamtiu, I., Hicks, M., Stoyle, G., Oriol, M.: Practical dynamic software updating for C. In: Proceedings of PLDI 2006
3. Chen, H., Yu, J., Chen, R., Zang, B., Yew, P.C.: POLUS: A POwerful live updating system. In: Proceedings of ICSE 2007
4. Makris, K., Bazzi, R.: Multi-threaded dynamic software updates using stack reconstruction. In: Proceedings of USENIX Annual Technical Conference 2009
5. Altekar, G., Bagrak, I., Burstein, P., Schultz, A.: OPUS: Online patches and updates for security. In: Proceedings of USENIX Security 2005
6. Soules, C., Appavoo, J., Hui, K., Da Silva, D., Ganger, G., Krieger, O., Stumm, M., Wisniewski, R., Auslander, M., Ostrowski, M., Rosenburg, B., Xenidis, J.: System support for online reconfiguration. In: Proceedings of USENIX Annual Technical Conference 2003
7. Baumann, A., Appavoo, J., Da Silva, D., Kerr, J., Krieger, O., Wisniewski, R.W.: Providing dynamic update in an operating system. In: Proceedings of USENIX Annual Technical Conference 2005
8. Baumann, A., Appavoo, J., Wisniewski, R.W., Da Silva, D., Krieger, O., Heiser, G.: Reboots are for hardware: challenges and solutions to updating an operating system on the fly. In: Proceedings of USENIX Annual Technical Conference 2007
9. Makris, K., Ryu, K.D.: Dynamic and adaptive updates of non-quiescent subsystems in commodity operating system kernels. In: Proceedings of EuroSys 2007
10. Chen, H., Chen, R., Zhang, F., Zang, B., Yew, P.C.: Live updating operating systems using virtualization. In: Proceedings of VEE 2006
11. Arnold, J., Kaashoek, F.: Ksplice: Automatic rebootless kernel updates. In: Proceedings of EuroSys 2009
12. Sun Microsystems. Java Platform Debugger Architecture, 2004. This supports class replacement. See http://java.sun.com/javase/6/docs/technotes/guides/jpda/
13. Microsoft Corporation. Edit and continue (2008). http://msdn2.microsoft.com/en-s/library/bcew296c.aspx
14. Mort Bay Consulting web site, vol. 2002, (2002). http://jetty.mortbay.org/jetty/index.html
15. Gustavson, J.: A Classification of Unanticipated Runtime Software Changes in Java. In Proc, ICSM (2003)
16. Ritzau, T., Andersson, J.: Dynamic deployment of Java applications. In Proc, Java for Embedded Systems Workshop (2000)

17. Malabarba, S., Fabrikant, A., Gragg, J., Barr, E., Barnes, J.: Runtime support for type-safe dynamic java classes. In: Bertino, E. (ed.) ECOOP 2000. LNCS, vol. 1850, pp. 337–361. Springer, Heidelberg (2000)
18. Orso, A., Rao, A., Harrold, M.J.: A technique for dynamic updating of Java software. In: Proceedings of ICSM 2002
19. Bierman, G., Parkinson, M., Boyland, J.: UpgradeJ: incremental typechecking for class upgrades. In: Vitek, J. (ed.) ECOOP 2008. LNCS, vol. 5142, pp. 235–259. Springer, Heidelberg (2008)
20. Kabanov, J.: JRebel tool demo. In: Proceedings of Bytecode 2010 (2010)
21. Würthinger, T., Wimmer, C., Stadler, L.: Dynamic code evolution for Java. In: Proceedings of PPPJ 2010
22. Dmitriev, M.: Safe evolution of large and long-lived java applications. Ph.D. Thesis, Department of Computing Science, University of Glasgow, Glasgow G12 8QQ, Scotland (2001)
23. Subramanian, S., Hicks, M., McKinley, K.S.: Dynamic software updates: a VM-centric approach. SIGPLAN 44(6), 1–12 (2009)
24. Gregersen, A.R., Rasmussen, M., Jørgensen, B.N.: Dynamic software updating with Gosh! - current status and the road ahead. In: Proceedings of ICSOFT 2013 (2013)
25. Gregersen, A.R., Jørgensen, B.N.: Dynamic update of Java applications—balancing change flexibility vs programming transparency. J. Softw. Maint. Evol. Res. Pract. 21, 81–112 (2009)
26. Sato, Y., Chiba, S.: Loosely-separated "Sister" namespaces in Java. In: Black, A.P. (ed.) ECOOP 2005. LNCS, vol. 3586, pp. 49–70. Springer, Heidelberg (2005)
27. Gregersen, A.R., Hadaytullah, K.K., Jørgensen, B.N.: an integrated platform for dynamic software updating and its application in self-* systems. In: Proceedings of SCET 2012
28. Gregersen, A.R., Jørgensen, B.N.: Run-time phenomena in dynamic software updating: causes and effects. In: Proceedings of IWPSE-EVOL 2011
29. Lanza, M., Ducasse, S., Gall, H., Pinzger, M.: CodeCrawler: an information visualization tool for program comprehension. In: Proceedings of ICSE 2005

Compiling Functional to Scripting Languages

Paola Giannini and Albert Shaqiri[✉]

Computer Science Institute, DiSIT, Università del Piemonte Orientale,
Alessandria, Italy
albert.shaqiri@yahoo.com
http://www.di.unipmn.it

Abstract. In this paper we consider the problem of translating a core typed functional language, F#(including mutable variables), into scripting languages such as JavaScript or Python. We abstract the most significant characteristics of such scripting languages in an intermediate language (IL for short), which is an imperative language, with constructs for handling safely pieces of code containing free variables. We define an operational semantics for IL and highlight the proof of correctness of the translation.

Keywords: Scripting languages · Functional languages · Intermediate language · Translation

1 Introduction

Programming in JavaScript (or any other dynamically typed language) optimizes the programming time, but can cause problems when big applications are created. The absence of type checking, may cause unexpected application behaviour followed by onerous debugging, and introduce serious difficulties in the maintenance of medium to large applications. For this reason dynamically typed languages are used mostly for prototyping and quick scripting.

To deal with these problems we propose to use dynamically typed languages as "assembly languages" to which we translate the source code from F# which is statically typed. In this way, we take advantage of the F# type checker and type inference system, as well as other F# constructs and paradigms such as pattern matching, classes, discriminated unions, namespaces, etc., and we may use the safe imperative features introduced via F# mutable variables. There are also the advantages of using an IDE such as Microsoft Visual Studio (code organization, debugging tools, IntelliSense, etc.).

To provide translation to different target languages we introduce an intermediate language, IL for short. This is useful, for instance, for translating to Python that does not have complete support for functions as first class concept, or for translating to JavaScript, using or not libraries such as jQuery.

This work has been partially supported by Progetto MIUR PRIN CINA Prot. 2010LHT4KM.

J. Cordeiro and M. van Sinderen (Eds.): ICSOFT 2013, CCIS 457, pp. 114–130, 2014.
DOI: 10.1007/978-3-662-44920-2_8

Our aim is to prove the correctness of the compilers produced. To do that we formalize IL, and the translation from the source language to IL. The language IL is imperative, and has some of the characteristics of the scripting languages that makes them flexible, but difficult to check, such as blocks in which definition and use of variables may be interleaved, and in which use of a variable may precede its definition. (IL is partly inspired by IntegerPython, see [1].) Therefore, the proof of correctness of the translation from the source language F# to IL already covers most of the gap from F# to the target scripting languages. In IL we also have some construct that may be used to manipulate safely fragments of open code.

The paper is organized as follows. In Sect. 2, we introduce the challenges of the translation from F# to Python and JavaScript via some examples, that led us to introduce our intermediate language. We also outline the translation from IL to both JavaScript and Python. In Sect. 3 we define the fragment of F# used as source language, and in Sect. 4 we formalize IL. The formal translation from F# to IL is defined in Sect. 5, where it is also outlined the proof of preservation of the dynamic semantics of F#. In Sect. 6 we compare our work with the work of others, and finally in Sect. 7 we summarize our work, discussing briefly the implementation issues and highlighting our plans for future work.

2 Translation by Examples: Design Choices

In the fragment of F# we consider as source of our translation we have the typical functional language constructs: function definition, integers, booleans, addition and the conditional expression, and an imperative fragment including mutable variables, assignment, and sequences of expressions. On the left-hand-side of an assignment there must be a variable that was introduced with the `mutable` modifier.

Sequences of Expressions. Many F# constructs can be directly mapped to JavaScript (or Python), but when this is not the case we obtain a semantically equivalent behaviour by using the primitives offered by the target language. E.g., in F# a sequence of expressions is itself an expression, while in JavaScript and Python it is a statement. Suppose our application often requires to sum the elements of a list and immediately after it needs to search for an element in that same list. Instead of doing two runs, we could write a function that in a single run does both. On the left-hand side of Fig. 1 we have one possible implementation. The variable `res` holds the result of the sum of the elements of the list, and it is used to illustrate some theoretical problems that arise during the translation process.

As we can see, on the right-hand-side of "`let res=`" we have a sequence of expressions: the definition of the mutable variable `sum` followed by a for loop that at the same time calculates the sum and searches for an element, etc. This sequence is, in F#, an expression. If we directly map this code into JavaScript we obtain the syntactically incorrect code on the right-hand side of Fig. 1.

```
let SumContains lst x =              function SumContains(lst) {
  let mutable found = false           return function(x) {
  let res =                             var found = false;
    let mutable sum = 0                 var res =
    for el in lst do                      var sum = 0;
      sum <- sum + el                     lst.forEach(function(el) {
      if el = x then                        sum = sum + el;
        found <- true                       if (el == x) found = true;
    sum                                 });
  res, found                            sum;
                                        return [res,found];
                                      }
                                    }
```

Fig. 1. F# program containing sequence of expressions and the corresponding naive translation into JavaScript.

```
function SumContains(lst){           def temp2(found,lst,x):
  return function(x){                  res = 0
    var found = false;                 for el in lst:
    var res = (function(){               res = res + el
      var sum = 0;                       if el == x:
      lst.forEach(function(el){            found.value = True
        sum = sum + el;                 return res
        if (el == x)
          found = true;               def temp1(lst,x):
      });                              found = ByRef(False)
      return sum;                      sum = temp2(found,lst,x)
    })();                              return (sum,found.value)
    return [res,found];
  }                                   def SumContains(lst):
}                                       return lambda x: temp1(lst, x)
```

Fig. 2. Correct JavaScript and Python translations.

This program is syntactically wrong, since on the right-hand-side of an assignment we must have an expression, while a sequence of expressions is, in JavaScript, a statement. To transform a sequence of statements in an expression, in JavaScript, we wrap the sequence into a function, and to execute it we call the function, i.e., we use a JavaScript closure and application. In this way, the code on the left-hand-side of Fig. 2 is the correct translation of our F# function.

Unfortunately, the same cannot be done in Python as its support for closures is partial. So we have to define a temporary function, say temp2, in the global scope, and to execute it we have to call temp2 in the place where the original sequence of expressions should be. However, the variables found, lst, and x will be out of the scope of their definitions, and this would make the translation wrong. To obtain a behavior semantically equivalent, we have to pass to temp2 the variables lst and x by value, and found by reference, since it may be modified in the body of temp2. Note that, this problem is not present in JavaScript where the closure is defined and called in the scope of found, 1st, and x. Another problem in Python is related to lambdas, whose body must be an expression (not a sequence). So we define the function temp1 whose body contains the statements that should be placed where an expression is expected. On the right-hand-side of Fig. 2 we can see the translation of the F# code into Python.

The class ByRef is used to wrap the mutable variable found to obtain a parameter called by reference. The Python code generator inserts the needed wrapping and unwrapping before and after the call of temp2, and in the body of temp1.

The problem we illustrated above occurs whenever in the target language we get a statement where an expression is expected. Since target languages handle the situation differently, we abstract from this specific problem, and consider the more general problem of moving "open code" from its context, replacing it with an expression having the same behavior. Taking inspiration from work on dynamic binding, see [2] and recent work by the authors, see [3], we define a pair of boxing/unboxing contructs, that we call: code, and exc. The construct code wraps "open code" (in this case a sequence of expressions) providing the information on the environment needed for its execution, that is the mutable and immutable variables occurring in it. This construct defines a value, similar to a function closure. The construct exc is used to execute the code contained in code. To do this it must provide values for the immutable variables (in our example 1, and u), and bindings for the mutable variables (in our example w) to variables in the current environment.

With these constructs, the F# code on the left-hand-side of Fig. 1 would be translated into the IL code in Fig. 3.

All the let constructs are translated to variable definitions. The sequence of statements on the right-hand-side of "let res=" is packed into a code expression. Its first component is the translation of the sequence of expressions, the second w->EV says that in the execution environment there should be a rebinding of the global name EV to a variable. Such variable may (in this case will) be modified by the execution of the code through assignment to the local variable w.

```
def y = code(
    def sum = 0
    for el in l do
        sum <- sum + el
        if el = u then w <- true
    sum,
    w->EV, l,u
)

def SumContains = fun lst ->
    fun x ->
        def found = false
        def res = exc(y, EV->found,lst,x)
        (res, found)
```

Fig. 3. Translation of F# sequence of expressions in the intermediate language.

The third and fourth components provide a value for l, and u. Such variables are not modified by the execution of the code. We choose to use global names to unbind/rebind mutable variables, w in our example, so that the local variables can be consistently renamed without affecting the semantics of the construct as formal parameters of functions. Instead names such as EV are global to the whole program.

To obtain the result that we would have by evaluating the sequence of statements in the current environment, to the variable res it is assigned the exc expression applied to y, which is bound to code($\cdots$). The name EV is bound to the (mutable) variable found and the variables l and u to the values of the variables lst and x, respectively. Regarding the different treatment of mutable and immutable variables, notice that, even though our intermediate language is imperative, we know, since we are translating F# code that some variables are immutable, so we have to provide just the initial value.

The constructs code and exc have a different translation into the target languages JavaScript and Python, in particular for JavaScript we can take advantage from the fact that the closure wrapping the code can be inlined in the position where we have exc, so we can substitute both the mutable and immutable variables, instead the translation to Python treats the two kind of variables differently.

Dynamic Type Checking. JavaScript, and many dynamically typed languages, lack a rigorous type system. On the contrary, in F# if we write a function that adds two integers, like the one on the left-hand side of Fig. 4, we get the type in the right-hand side of Fig. 4, because, even though we do not specify type information, the interpreter infers the type shown after the function definition. Therefore, there is no way of calling add with arguments that are not of type integer. However, if our translation in the intermediate code would produce a function whose body was simply x+y, which in turn could be translated in the corresponding expression in both JavaScript and Python, the target JavaScript function could be called, e.g., add("foo")(1) and obtain the string "foo1" which is not what we wanted. In Python the situation would be better, in the sense that we cannot call add on a string and an integer, however, due to overloading we can call it on two floating points obtaining a floating point. This problem arises for top-level functions, that is functions which are not local to the F# code, because these functions may be called with actual parameters which are not the translation of F# expressions. To prevent this, the translation in the intermediate language, which follows, insert dynamic checks on parameters of functions (see Fig. 5). These checks are translated into dynamic type checking in JavaScript and Python. In JavaScript we use the function checkInt (that we defined) that returns its argument if it is an integer, and fails, raising an exception, if the parameter is not an integer.

```
let add x y = x + y              val add : int -> int -> int
```

Fig. 4. F# type inference.

```
def add = fun x ->              var add = function (x) {
  def x1 = check(int, x);         var x1 = checkInt(x);
  fun y ->                        return function(y) {
    def y1= check(int, y);          var y1 = checkInt(y);
    x1 + y1;                        return x1 + y1 } }
```

Fig. 5. Type checking code injection.

3 Core F#

In the syntax for the core F# language, presented below, we did not include the
for construct, tuples and lists, which are, anyway, part of the source language
of our implementation, see [4], instead we included constructs, such as let, let
mutable, and let rec that are used in the practice of programming and that raise
challenges in the translation to dynamic languages. We also did not introduce
imperative features through reference types, but through mutable variables, since
this is closer to the imperative style of programming. We present a typed version
of F#, and in the types we omit type variables, as they do not add complexity
to the translation. The following is the grammar for F# expressions:

$$e ::= x \mid n \mid \mathtt{tr} \mid \mathtt{fls} \mid e+e \mid \mathtt{if}\ e\ \mathtt{then}\ e\ \mathtt{else}\ e \mid \mathtt{fun}\ x{:}T\mathtt{->}e \mid e\ e$$
$$\mid \mathtt{let}\ [\mathtt{mutable}]\ x{=}e\ \mathtt{in}\ e \mid \mathtt{let}\ \mathtt{rec}\ x{:}T{=}v\ \mathtt{in}\ e \mid x{<}\mathtt{-}e \mid e,e$$
$$T ::= \mathtt{int} \mid \mathtt{bool} \mid T \to T$$
$$v ::= n \mid \mathtt{tr} \mid \mathtt{fls} \mid \mathtt{fun}\ x{:}T\mathtt{->}e\ (FV(e) \subseteq \{x\})$$

In the previous grammar, the square brackets "[. . .]" delimit an optional part of
the syntax, we use x, y, z for variable names, and the overbar sequence nota-
tion is used according to [5]. For instance: "$\overline{x{:}T}{=}\overline{v}$" stands for "$x_1{:}T_1{=}v_1 \cdots x_n{:}$
$T_n{=}v_n$". The empty sequence is denoted by "$\emptyset$". For an F# expressions e the
free variables of e, $FV(e)$ are defined in the standard way. An expression e *is
closed* if $FV(e) = \emptyset$. The let rec construct introduces mutually recursive variables. Variable names, in this constructs are meant to be bound to functions.
The let construct (followed by an optional mutable modifier) binds the variable
x to the value resulting from the evaluation of the expression on the right-hand-
side of = in the evaluation of the body of the construct. As usual the notation
let f $x{=}e_1$ in e_2 is a short hand for let $f{=}\mathtt{fun}\ x{:}T\mathtt{->}e_1$ in e_2 where T is the
type of e_1. Similarly for let rec. In the (concrete syntax) of the examples, as in
F#, "," and in are substituted by a return without indentation. When the let
construct is followed by mutable the variable introduced is mutable. Only mutable variables may be used on the left-hand-side of an assignment. This restriction
is enforced by the type system of the language. The type system enforces also
the restriction that the body of a function cannot contain free mutable variables,
even though it may contain bound mutable variables.

$$\Gamma \vdash n : \texttt{int} \quad \text{(TyNum)} \qquad\qquad \Gamma \vdash \texttt{tr}, \texttt{fls} : \texttt{bool} \quad \text{(TyBool)}$$

$$\frac{\Gamma \vdash e_1 : \texttt{int} \quad \Gamma \vdash_e e_2 : \texttt{int}}{\Gamma \vdash e_1 + e_2 : \texttt{int}} \text{ (TySum)} \qquad \frac{\Gamma \vdash e : \texttt{bool} \quad \Gamma \vdash e_1 : T \quad \Gamma \vdash e_2 : T}{\Gamma \vdash \texttt{if } e \texttt{ then } e_1 \texttt{ else } e_2 : T} \text{ (TyIf)}$$

$$\frac{\Gamma'[x : T] \vdash e : T' \quad \forall y, T'' \; y : T''! \notin \Gamma'}{\Gamma[\Gamma'] \vdash \texttt{fun } x{:}T\texttt{->}e : T \rightarrow T'} \text{ (TyAbs)} \qquad \frac{\Gamma \vdash e_1 : T \rightarrow T' \quad \Gamma \vdash e_2 : T}{\Gamma \vdash e_1 \; e_2 : T} \text{ (TyApp)}$$

$$\frac{x : T \dagger \in \Gamma}{\Gamma \vdash x : T} \text{ (TyVar)} \qquad \frac{\Gamma \vdash e_1 : T \quad \Gamma[x : T] \vdash e : T'}{\Gamma \vdash \texttt{let } x = e_1 \texttt{ in } e_2 : T'} \text{ (TyLet)}$$

$$\frac{\Gamma[\overline{x{:}T}] \vdash v_i : T_i \; (1 \leq i \leq n)}{\Gamma[\overline{x{:}T}] \vdash e : T} \text{ (TyRec)} \qquad \frac{\Gamma \vdash e_1 : T \quad \Gamma[x : T!] \vdash e : T'}{\Gamma \vdash \texttt{let mutable } x = e_1 \texttt{ in } e_2 : T'} \text{ (TyLetMut)}$$

$$\frac{\Gamma \vdash e : T \quad x : T! \in \Gamma}{\Gamma \vdash x \texttt{<-} e : T} \text{ (TyAssign)} \qquad \frac{\Gamma \vdash e_1 : T \quad \Gamma \vdash e_2 : T'}{\Gamma \vdash e_1, e_2 : T'} \text{ (TySeq)}$$

Fig. 6. Typing rules of core `F#`.

A type environment Γ is defined by: $\Gamma ::= x{:}T, \Gamma \mid x{:}T!, \Gamma \mid \emptyset$ that is Γ associates variables with types, possibly followed by !. If the type is followed by ! this means that the variable was introduced with the `mutable` modifier. Let $\dagger$ denote either ! or the empty string, and let $dom(\Gamma) = \{x \mid x{:}T \dagger \in \Gamma\}$. We assume that for any variable x, in Γ there is at most an associated type. With $\Gamma \vdash e : T$ we mean that the *expression e is well-typed and has type T in the environment Γ*. The rules are standard and can be found in Fig. 6.

Our core `F#` language has imperative features, so for the definition of the operational semantics we use a store. The *runtime configurations* are pairs "expression, store", $e \mid \rho$, where a *store* ρ is a mapping between locations and values: $l_1 \mapsto v_1, \ldots l_n \mapsto v_n$. In Fig. 7 we define: *runtime expressions*, which are expressions including locations (generated by the evaluation of mutable variables definitions); *evaluation contexts* defining, in conjunction with rule (Ctx-F), the reduction strategy of the language, which is call-by-value, with evaluation left-to-right, and *rules for the evaluation relation*, $\longrightarrow$.

In the rules, with $e[x := e']$ we denote the result of *substituting x with e' in e* with renaming if needed. Moreover, $\rho[x \mapsto v]$ is defined by: $\rho[x \mapsto v](x) = v$, and $\rho[x \mapsto v](y) = \rho(y)$, when $x \neq y$. Note that if the `let` introduces a `mutable` variable, rule (LetMut-F), a new location l is generated, added to the store with the initial value v, and the variable x is substituted with l. Therefore, during evaluation, expressions may contain locations. Indeed, since variables on the left-hand-side of assignments where always introduced by `let mutable`, when an assignment is evaluated, rule (Assign-F), we have a configuration: $l \texttt{<-} v \mid \rho$ which is

$$e ::= \cdots \mid l$$
$$\mathcal{E} ::= [] \mid \mathcal{E}+e \mid n+\mathcal{E} \mid \text{if } \mathcal{E} \text{ then } e \text{ else } e \mid \mathcal{E} \; e \mid v \; \mathcal{E}$$
$$\mid \text{let [mutable] } x=\mathcal{E} \text{ in } e \mid u<\text{-}\mathcal{E} \mid \mathcal{E}, e$$

$$n_1+n_2 \mid \rho \longrightarrow n \mid \rho \qquad\qquad\qquad\qquad \text{if} \quad \tilde{n} = \tilde{n}_1 +^{\text{int}} \tilde{n}_2 \;\; (\text{SUM-F})$$
$$\text{if tr then } e_1 \text{ else } e_2 \mid \rho \longrightarrow e_1 \mid \rho \qquad\qquad\qquad\qquad\qquad (\text{IFTRUE-F})$$
$$\text{if fls then } e_1 \text{ else } e_2 \mid \rho \longrightarrow e_2 \mid \rho \qquad\qquad\qquad\qquad\qquad (\text{IFFALSE-F})$$
$$(\text{fun } x{:}T\text{->}e) \; v \mid \rho \longrightarrow e[x := v] \mid \rho \qquad\qquad\qquad\qquad (\text{APP-F})$$
$$\text{let } x=v \text{ in } e \mid \rho \longrightarrow e[x := v] \mid \rho \qquad\qquad\qquad\qquad\qquad (\text{LET-F})$$
$$\text{let rec } \overline{x}{:}\overline{T}=\overline{v} \text{ in } e \mid \rho \longrightarrow$$
$$\quad e[x_i := (\text{let rec } \overline{x}{:}\overline{T}=\overline{v} \text{ in } v_i) \mid 1 \le i \le n] \mid \rho \qquad\qquad (\text{REC-F})$$
$$\text{let mutable } x=v \text{ in } e \mid \rho \longrightarrow e[x := l] \mid \rho[l \mapsto v] \quad l \notin \text{dom}(\rho) \text{ new} \quad (\text{LETMUT-F})$$
$$l<\text{-}v \mid \rho \longrightarrow v \mid \rho[l \mapsto v] \qquad\qquad\qquad\qquad l \in \text{dom}(\rho) \qquad (\text{ASSIGN-F})$$
$$v, e \mid \rho \longrightarrow e \mid \rho \qquad\qquad\qquad\qquad\qquad\qquad\qquad\qquad (\text{SEQ-F})$$
$$l \mid \rho \longrightarrow v \mid \rho \qquad\qquad\qquad\qquad\qquad\qquad \text{if } \rho(l) = v \qquad (\text{VAR-F})$$

$$\frac{e \mid \rho \longrightarrow e' \mid \rho' \quad \mathcal{E} \ne []}{\mathcal{E}[e] \mid \rho \longrightarrow \mathcal{E}[e'] \mid \rho'} \; (\text{CTX-F})$$

Fig. 7. Operational semantics of core F#.

evaluated by changing the value of the location l to be v. The evaluation of let rec, rule (LET-F), produces the body e in which each variable x_i is substituted with a let rec expression with body v_i, so that if x_i is evaluated all the variables $\overline{x}$ will be substituted with their definitions $\overline{v}$.

The typing rules in Fig. 6 are for the (source) expression language, so they do not include a rule for locations. To type run-time expressions we need a store environment Σ assigning types to locations. The type judgement should therefore be: $\Gamma \mid \Sigma \vdash e : T$ and the typing rule for locations $\Gamma \mid \Sigma \vdash l : \Sigma(l)$ (TYLOCF). All the other rules are obtained by putting $\Gamma \mid \Sigma$ on the left-hand-side of $\vdash$ in the typing rules of Fig. 6. Let $Loc(e)$ be the *set of locations occurring in e*. In the following we define well-typed stores, and well-formed configurations.

Definition 1.   *1. A store ρ is well-typed with respect to a store environment Σ, written $\Sigma \vdash \rho$, if $dom(\rho) = dom(\Sigma)$, and for all $l \in \rho$, we have that $\emptyset \mid \Sigma \vdash \rho(l) : \Sigma(l)$.*
2. *The configuration $e \mid \rho$ is well-formed w.r.t. Σ, written $\Sigma \vdash e \mid \rho$, if $\Sigma \vdash \rho$, $FV(e) = \emptyset$, and $Loc(e) \subseteq dom(\rho)$.*

Note that since values are closed, in the definition of well-typed stores, the values associated to locations must be well-typed from the empty type environment. Types are preserved by reduction, and progress holds, as the following two theorems state.

Theorem 1 (Preservation). *Let $\Gamma \mid \Sigma \vdash e : T$, and ρ be such that $\Sigma \vdash e \mid \rho$. If $e \mid \rho \longrightarrow e' \mid \rho'$, then $\Gamma \mid \Sigma' \vdash e' : T$, for some $\Sigma' \supseteq \Sigma$ such that $\Sigma' \vdash e' \mid \rho'$.*

Theorem 2 (Progress). *Let* $\emptyset \mid \Sigma \vdash e : T$, *then either* e *is a value or for any store* ρ *such that* $\Sigma \vdash \rho$ *there are,* e', *and* ρ' *such that* $e \mid \rho \longrightarrow e' \mid \rho'$.

4 Intermediate Language

The intermediate language, IL, is an imperative language with three syntactic categories: expressions, statements and blocks. We introduce the construct that wraps code that need to be moved from its definition environment, and the one that executes such code in the runtime environment. The syntax of IL is given below:

$$
\begin{array}{lcl}
bl & ::= & st; bl \mid e; bl \mid e \\
st & ::= & x\texttt{<-}e \mid \textbf{def } x\texttt{=}e \\
e & ::= & x \mid n \mid \texttt{tr} \mid \texttt{fls} \mid e\texttt{+}e \mid \textbf{fun } x\texttt{->}\{bl\} \mid e\ e \mid \textbf{if } e \textbf{ then } \{bl\} \textbf{ else } \{bl\} \mid \texttt{check}(T_g, e) \\
& & \mid \texttt{code}(\{bl\}, y \mapsto Y, x) \mid \texttt{exc}(e, Y \mapsto y, e) \\
T_g & ::= & \texttt{int} \mid \texttt{bool} \mid \texttt{fun} \\
v & ::= & n \mid \texttt{tr} \mid \texttt{fls} \mid \textbf{fun } x\texttt{->}\{bl\} \, (FV(bl) \subseteq \{x\}) \mid \texttt{code}(\{bl\}, y \mapsto Y, x) \, (FV(bl) \subseteq \{x, y\})
\end{array}
$$

There are three syntactic categories: *blocks*, *statements*, and *expressions*. We introduce the distinction between expressions and statements as many target languages do. This facilitates the translation process and prevents some errors while building the intermediate abstract syntax tree, see [6] for a similar choice. Blocks are sequences of statements or expressions ended by an expression. In our translation we flatten the nested structure of let constructs so we need blocks in which definitions and expressions/statements may be intermixed. Moreover, since we do not have a specific let rec construct use of a variable may precede its definition, e.g., when defining mutually recursive (or simply recursive) functions. Statements may be either assignments or variable definitions. Our compiler handles many more statements, but these are enough to show the ideas behind the design of IL. Our intermediate language is inspired (especially for the block structure) to IntegerPython, see [1]. Variables are statically scoped, in the sense that, if there is a definition of the variable x in a block, all the free occurrences of x in the block refer to this definition. However, we can have occurrences of x preceding its definition. E.g.,

```
def f=fun y->x;def x=5;f 2
```

correctly returns 5, whereas the following code would produce a run-time error:

```
def x=7;if (x>3) then {def f=fun y->{x};f 2;def x=5; 3} else {4}
```

since when f is called the variable x, defined in the inner block, has not yet been assigned a value. Instead, if x was not defined in the inner block, like in the following

```
def x7;if (x>3) then {def f=fun y->{x};f 2} else {4}
```

the block would return 7, since x is bound in the enclosing block. This is also the behaviour in JavaScript and Python. We have checks on primitive types (int and bool) and on functions (fun) which are generated during the translation of top-level function definitions, as we will see in the next section. The construct

$$e ::= \cdots \mid l \mid \{bl\} \mid \mathbf{eval}(bl)$$
$$\mathcal{S} ::= l\text{<-}\mathcal{E}; bl \mid \mathbf{def}\ l\text{=}\mathcal{E}; bl \mid \mathcal{E}; bl \mid \mathcal{E}$$
$$\mathcal{E} ::= [\,] \mid \mathcal{E}+e \mid n+\mathcal{E} \mid \mathcal{E}\ e \mid v\ \mathcal{E} \mid \mathbf{if}\ \mathcal{E}\ \mathbf{then}\ \{bl\}\ \mathbf{else}\ \{bl\} \mid \mathbf{check}(T_g, \mathcal{E})$$
$$\mid \mathbf{exc}(\mathcal{E}, \overline{Z} \mapsto \overline{l}, \overline{e}) \mid \mathbf{exc}(v, \overline{Z} \mapsto \overline{l}, \overline{v}\,\mathcal{E}\,\overline{e}) \mid \mathbf{eval}(\mathcal{S})$$

$\{bl\} \mid \rho \longrightarrow bl[\overline{x} := \overline{l}] \mid \rho[\overline{l} \mapsto \overline{?}]$	$\text{if}\ \overline{x} = def(bl)$	(ALLOC)
	$\overline{l} \notin dom(\rho)\ \mathbf{new}$	
$l\text{<-}v; bl \mid \rho \longrightarrow bl \mid \rho[l \mapsto v]$		(ASSIGN)
$\mathbf{def}\ l\text{=}v; bl \mid \rho \longrightarrow bl \mid \rho[l \mapsto v]$		(DEF)
$v; bl \mid \rho \longrightarrow bl \mid \rho$		(EXP)
$n_1+n_2 \mid \rho \longrightarrow n \mid \rho$	$\text{if}\quad \tilde{n} = \tilde{n}_1 +^{\mathrm{int}} \tilde{n}_2$	(SUM)
$(\mathbf{fun}\ x\text{->}\{bl\})\ v \mid \rho \longrightarrow \{bl[x := l]\} \mid \rho[l \mapsto v]$	$l \notin dom(\rho)\ \mathbf{new}$	(APP)
$\mathbf{if}\ \mathtt{tr}\ \mathbf{then}\ bl_1\ \mathbf{else}\ bl_2 \mid \rho \longrightarrow \{bl_1\} \mid \rho$		(IFTRUE)
$\mathbf{if}\ \mathtt{fls}\ \mathbf{then}\ bl_1\ \mathbf{else}\ bl_2 \mid \rho \longrightarrow \{bl_2\} \mid \rho$		(IFFALSE)
$\mathbf{check}(T_g, v) \mid \rho \longrightarrow v \mid \rho$	$\text{if}\quad typeof(v) = T_g$	(TYPEYES)
$\mathbf{check}(T_g, v) \mid \rho \longrightarrow typeErr$	$\text{if}\quad typeof(v) \neq T_g$	(TYPENO)
$\mathbf{exc}(code(\{bl\}), \overline{y} \mapsto \overline{Y}, \overline{x}), \overline{Z} \mapsto \overline{l'}, \overline{v}) \mid \rho \longrightarrow$	$\text{if}\quad \overline{Y} \subseteq \overline{Z}$	(CODE)
$\quad \mathbf{eval}(\{(bl[\overline{x} := \overline{v}])[y_i := l'_j \mid Y_i = Z_j\ 1 \leq i \leq n]\}) \mid \rho$		
$\mathbf{eval}(v) \mid \rho \longrightarrow v \mid \rho$		(EVAL)
$l \mid \rho \longrightarrow v \mid \rho$	$\text{if}\ \rho(l) = v$	(LOCDEF)
$l \mid \rho \longrightarrow undErr \mid \rho$	$\text{if}\ \rho(l) =?$	(LOCUND)

$$\frac{e \mid \rho \longrightarrow e' \mid \rho'\quad \mathcal{S} \neq [\,]}{\mathcal{S}[e] \mid \rho \longrightarrow \mathcal{S}[e'] \mid \rho'}\ (\text{CTX}) \qquad \frac{e \mid \rho \longrightarrow err\quad err = typeErr \vee undErr\quad \mathcal{S} \neq [\,]}{\mathcal{S}[e] \mid \rho \longrightarrow err}\ (\text{CTXERROR})$$

Fig. 8. Runtime expressions, evaluation contexts and operational semantics rule for IL.

code is used to move a block, bl, outside its definition context. To produce a closed term, the *mutable variables* free in bl, $\overline{y}$, are unbound by associating them to *global names* $\overline{Y}$ not subject to renaming. The variables $\overline{x}$, instead, are *immutable variables* free in bl, i.e., they are not modified by the execution of bl. The metavariables, X, Y, Z are used to denote names. Values are integers, booleans, closed functions (as for F#), and closed code.

The operational semantics of IL, see Fig. 8, is given, by defining a reduction relation for blocks. So our configurations will be pairs: "block, store". In order to specify the order of reduction we define evaluation contexts for blocks, $\mathcal{S}$, containing evaluation contexts for expressions, $\mathcal{E}$. As for F# we have to add to the syntax of expressions locations, l, as they are generated during the evaluation of blocks. Moreover, we add two constructs wrapping blocks: $\{bl\}$ and $\mathbf{eval}(bl)$. The first will be used to do the initial allocation of variables needed to reproduce the previously described semantics, and the second to execute a block in a position where an expression would be required. Note that these expressions are not in IL but are just introduced to describe its semantics.

As for F#, the evaluation contexts of Fig. 8 specify a call-by-value, left-to-right reduction strategy.

The first rule, (ALLOC), is used before the evaluation of a block to allocate the variables defined in a block. The function def mapping a block to the set of variables defined in it is defined by: $def(e) = \emptyset$, $def(e; bl) = def(x\texttt{<-}e; bl) = def(bl)$, and $def(\texttt{def } x\texttt{=}e; bl) = \{x\} \cup def(bl)$. The initial value of the locations is set to undefined, ?, so if an access to a variable is done before the evaluation of an assignment or a definition for this variable $undErr$ is returned. Note that, *this will never happen for* IL *programs which are translation of* F# *programs*. After this initial allocation a block will not contain free variables (but locations). Rules (ASSIGN) and (DEF) continue the execution of the expressions/statements in a block in a store in which the value of location l is v. So, after this, the value of l is not undefined. Rule (EXP) throws away the value of an expression and continues the execution of the block. The rules for $+$, and $\texttt{if}$ are trivial. Rule (APP) allocates a location in the memory, assigning the value of the actual parameter to it, then the location is substituted for the formal parameter in the body of the function. Note that, being in an imperative language, the formal parameter could be modified in the body of the function, however, this change would not be visible in the calling environment, since the location is new. After this allocation the execution continues with the evaluation of the body $\{bl\}$, i.e., applying rule (ALLOC). The rules (TYPEYES), and (TYPENO) check whether a value is of the right primitive type. The function $typeof$ from values to types is defined by: $typeof(\texttt{tr}) = typeof(\texttt{fls}) = \texttt{bool}$, $typeof(n) = \texttt{int}$, $typeof(\texttt{fun } x\texttt{->}\{bl\}) = \texttt{fun}$, and undefined for the other values. The evaluation of the $\texttt{exc}$ construct, rule (CODE), expects the first argument to be a $\texttt{code}$, such that the names of its unbindings are a subset of the one of the rebindings provided by $\texttt{exc}$. If this is the case, it substitutes the values for the immutable variables $\overline{x}$, instead, for the unbound variables $\overline{y}$ it substitutes the associated locations (via the correspondence of the names in $\overline{Y}$ and $\overline{Z}$). So through assignment to the (local) variables in $\overline{y}$ the execution environment may be modified. The resulting block is wrapped in the $\texttt{eval}$ construct. Rule (EVAL) returns its value. (Evaluation inside $\texttt{eval}$ is done by the (CTX) rule.) Finally, access to a location may return $undErr$ if the location has not been initialized with an assignment of or a definition statement. Rule (CTX) evaluates the first sub-expression selected by the evaluation context. In case the evaluation produces and error rule (CTXERROR) returns the error at the top level. Note that, given a block bl if there is $\mathcal{S}$ and e such that $bl = \mathcal{S}[e]$, then $\mathcal{S}$ is unique. So evaluation is deterministic.

In order to introduce the notion of well-formed configuration, we have to define the *free variables of a block*, $FV(bl)$. We first define the *free variables of an expression*, $FV(e)$, by:

- $FV(x) = \{x\}$, $FV(n) = FV(\texttt{tr}) = FV(\texttt{fls}) = \emptyset$,
- $FV(e_1\texttt{+}e_2) = FV(e_1\ e_2) = FV(e_1) \cup FV(e_2)$,
- $FV(\texttt{fun } x\texttt{->}\{bl\}) = FV(bl) - \{x\}$,
- $FV(\texttt{if } e \texttt{ then } \{bl_1\} \texttt{ else } \{bl_2\}) = FV(bl_1) \cup FV(bl_2) \cup FV(e)$,
- $FV(\texttt{check}(T_g, e)) = FV(e)$, $FV(\texttt{code}(\{bl\}, \overline{y} \mapsto \overline{Y}, \overline{x}))) = FV(bl) - \{\overline{x}, \overline{y}\}$, and
- $FV(\texttt{exc}(e, \overline{Y} \mapsto \overline{y}, \overline{e})) = FV(e) \cup \{\overline{y}\} \cup \bigcup_{0 \leq i \leq n} FV(e_i)$.

Since we may have forward definitions, to define the free variable of a block we first define the *variables of a block*, $Var(bl)$, by

- $Var(x\texttt{<-}e; bl) = FV(e) \cup Var(bl) \cup \{x\}$,
- $Var(\texttt{def }x\texttt{=}e; bl) = FV(e; bl) = FV(e) \cup Var(bl)$, and
- $Var(e) = FV(e)$.

Then $FV(bl) = Var(bl) - def(bl)$.

Definition 2. *The* IL *configuration* $bl \mid \rho$ *is well-formed, if*

- $FV(bl) = \emptyset$, $Loc(bl) \subseteq dom(\rho)$,
- *for all* $l \in dom(\rho)$, *we have that* $FV(\rho(l)) = \emptyset$, *and* $Loc(\rho(l)) \subseteq dom(\rho)$.

The operational semantics of Fig. 8 preserves well-formed configurations, as the following proposition states.

Proposition 1. *Let* $bl \mid \rho$ *be well-formed, if* $bl \mid \rho \longrightarrow bl' \mid \rho'$, *then* $bl' \mid \rho'$ *is well-formed.*

An IL *program* is a closed block, bl. The *initial configuration* for a program is $\{bl\} \mid []$. Since an initial configuration is well formed, all the configurations that we obtain during a computation are well formed.

5 Translation of Core F# to IL

In our translation we flatten the `let` constructs transforming them into definitions of the corresponding variables followed by the translation of the expression in their body. Therefore, we have to take into account the fact that in an IL block we may have forward binding. E.g., if the translation of the F# program that follows on the left is the IL code on the right: the translation is incorrect, since in the IL code the occurrence of y in the body of f is bound to the definition of y that follows. Therefore the F# expression evaluates to 3 whereas its translation in IL evaluates to 5. In the translation we use renaming to resolve this problem.

```
let y = 3 in                        def y = 3;
    if ( y = 3) then (                  if ( y = 3) then (
        let f = (fun x -> y)                def f = (fun x -> { y });
        let y = 5                           def y = 5;
        (f 0)    )                          (f 0)    )
    else 4                              else 4
```

We define two translations of F# expressions. The first to IL expressions, $[\![\cdot]\!]_{ex}^{I,M}$, and the second to IL blocks, $[\![\cdot]\!]_{bl}^{I,M}$. The translations are parametrized by the sets of the immutable variables, I, and mutable variables, M, of the context of the F# expression that is translated. The translations produce, in addition to an IL expression/block also a sequence of top level variable definition of variables bound to code expressions. The metavariable δ denotes a declaration of a variable "$\texttt{def }x\texttt{=}e$" and $\overline{\delta}$ a sequence of declarations separated by ";" (semicolon).

Formal Definition of the Translation. Before giving some (the most significant) clauses of the formal translation, we introduce the definition of the wrapping needed to extrude a block from its definition environment and how the construct exc rebinds it in the run-time environment.

Definition 3. *Given an* IL *block, and the disjoint sets of variables* $I = \{\overline{x}{:}\overline{T}\}$ *and* $M = \{\overline{y}{:}\overline{T'}\}$, *let* $blockToExp(bl, I, M)$ *be* $(\mathtt{exc}(z, \overline{Y} \mapsto \overline{y}, \overline{x}), \delta)$ *where:* δ *is* def $z{=}\mathtt{code}(bl, \overline{y} \mapsto \overline{Y}, \overline{x})$, z *is a new variable, and* $\overline{Y}$ *are new names.*

Let $blockToExp(bl, I, M) = (e, \delta)$, the evaluation of the block in which the definition δ is followed by the expression, e, produces the same result as the evaluation of the original block, $\{bl\}$.

To give the translation of both sequences of expressions and of the let constructs, we introduce the formal definition of the top level variable definition of F# expressions, then we define the renaming needed to avoid the capture of forward definitions described at the beginning of this section.

Definition 4. 1. *Let* e *be an* F# *expression, the function* $def^{\#}(e)$ *returning the set of variables defined at the top level of* e *is defined as follows:*
   - $def^{\#}(\mathtt{let}\ [\mathtt{mutable}]\ x{=}e_1\ \mathtt{in}\ e_2) = \{x\} \cup def^{\#}(e_2)$,
   - $def^{\#}(\mathtt{let}\ \mathtt{rec}\ \overline{x}{:}\overline{T}{=}\overline{v}\ \mathtt{in}\ e) = \{\overline{x}\} \cup def^{\#}(e)$,
   - $def^{\#}(e_1, e_2) = def^{\#}(e_1) \cup def^{\#}(e_2)$, *and*
   - $def^{\#}(e) = \emptyset$ *for all other expressions* e.
2. *Let* e *be an* F# *expression, and* $\overline{x}$ *a set of variables,* $rn(e, \overline{x})$, *renames the top level definitions of the variables* $\overline{x}$ *in* e *as follows:*
   - *if* e *is* let [mutable] $x{=}e_1$ in e_2, *then* $rn(e, \overline{x})$ *is*
     let [mutable] $x{=}e_1$ in $rn(e_2, \overline{x})$ *if* $x \notin \overline{x}$
     let [mutable] $z{=}e_1$ in $rn(e_2\{x \mapsto z\}, \overline{x})$ *if* $x \in \overline{x}$ *and* z *is new*
   - *if* e *is* let rec $\overline{y}{:}\overline{T}{=}\overline{v}$ in e, *then* $rn(e, \overline{x})$ *is*
     let rec $\overline{y}{:}\overline{T}{=}\overline{v}$ in $rn(e, \overline{x})$ *if* $\overline{y} \cap \overline{x} = \emptyset$
     let rec $\overline{z}{:}\overline{T}{=}(\overline{v}\{\overline{y} \mapsto \overline{z}\})$ in $rn(e\{\overline{y} \mapsto \overline{z}\}, \overline{x})$ *if* $\overline{y} \cap \overline{x} = \emptyset$ *and* $\overline{z}$ *are new*
   - *if* e *is* e_1, e_2 *then* $rn(e, \overline{x})$ *is* $rn(e_1, \overline{x}), rn(e_2, \overline{x})$
   - $rn(e, \overline{x})$ *is* e *for all other expressions* e.

In the following we present the translations for function definitions, sequence of expressions, and the let construct, which exemplify the technique used. The *translation of* F# *integer or boolean values to* IL *is the identity function.*

The *translations of* F# *function definitions to* IL *blocks or expressions*:

$$\llbracket \mathtt{fun}\ x{:}T{-}{>}e \rrbracket_{bl}^{I,M} \qquad \llbracket \mathtt{fun}\ x{:}T{-}{>}e \rrbracket_{ex}^{I,M}$$

are both equal to: (fun $x{-}{>}\{bl\}, \overline{\delta}$) where $\llbracket e \rrbracket_{bl}^{I \cup \{x{:}T\},M} = (\,bl, \overline{\delta}\,)$. So the translation of a function produces a function whose body is the translation of the body (to a block) of the original function. In the translation of the body of the function the typed variable x is added to the set of free immutable variables I.

In case of top-level definitions, that is functions that could be called with actual parameters which are not the translation of F# expressions we have to add the check on the input values, so the translation is as follows:

$$(\,\mathtt{fun}\ x{-}{>}\{\mathtt{def}\ y{=}\mathtt{check}(T', x); bl[x := y]\}, \overline{\delta}\,)$$

where $T = T'$ if T is equal to int or bool, and $T' =$ fun if T is equal to $T_1 \rightarrow T_2$. We can see that the formal parameter is replaced with a new variable resulting from the dynamic type checking of the original parameter. See the discussion about dynamic type checking in Sect. 2.

The *translations of an* F# *sequence of expressions to a* IL *block* is: $[\![e_1, e_2]\!]_{bl}^{I,M} = (\, bl_1; bl_2, \overline{\delta}; \overline{\delta}'\,)$ where: $[\![e_1]\!]_{bl}^{I,M} = (\, bl_1, \overline{\delta}\,)$, $[\![rn(e_2, \overline{z})]\!]_{bl}^{I,M} = (\, bl_2, \overline{\delta}'\,)$ and $\overline{z} = def^{\#}(e_2) \cap FV(e_1)$. The translation of the sequence is the sequence of blocks which are the translations of the two expressions to blocks. However, before translating the second expression, e_2, we rename all the variables defined in it that are free in e_1, since in e_1 these variables are bound to their definitions in the enclosing environment. In this way we preserve the semantics of the source language F#.

The *translations of an* F# *sequence of expressions to an* IL *expression* is: $[\![e_1, e_2]\!]_{ex}^{I,M} = (\, e, \delta; \overline{\delta}\,)$ where: $[\![e_1, e_2]\!]_{bl}^{I,M} = (\, bl, \overline{\delta}\,)$ and $blockToExp(bl, I, M) = (\, e, \delta\,)$. That is we first translate the sequence to a block, and then return an exc expression, and the definition of a new variable bound to an code expression, see Definition 3. Note that the sets of mutable and immutable variable of the environment are needed to generate the correct matching for the expressions exc and code.

The *translation of the let construct to an* IL *block* is:

$$[\![\text{let } x = e_1 \text{ in } e_2]\!]_{bl}^{I,M} = (\, \text{def } x = e_1'; bl, \overline{\delta}, \overline{\delta}'\,)$$

where $[\![e_1]\!]_{ex}^{I,M} = (\, e_1', \overline{\delta}\,)$ and $[\![rn(e_2, \overline{z})]\!]_{bl}^{I \cup \{x : T\}, M} = (\, bl, \overline{\delta}'\,)$ with $\overline{z} = def^{\#}(e_2) \cap FV(e_1)$, and $I, M \vdash e_1 : T$. That is, we translate e_1 into an IL expression and the body of the let e_2 into a block. For the translation of e_2 the variable x is added to the immutable variables of the context. Before translating e_2 we rename all the variables defined in e_2 that are free in e_1 (as for the translation of sequences of expressions). Note that, this translation produces a block, the definition of x followed by a block. Moreover, the translation of the expression on the right-hand-side of the definition of x, that is e_1, must be an IL expression, which is a sequence of expressions, must be translated to an IL expression.

The *translation of the let construct to an* IL *expression*, is: $[\![\text{let } x = e_1 \text{ in } e_2]\!]_{ex}^{I,M} = (\, e, \delta; \overline{\delta}\,)$ where $[\![\text{let } x = e_1 \text{ in } e_2]\!]_{bl}^{I,M} = (\, bl, \overline{\delta}\,)$, and $blockToExp(bl, I, M) = (\, e, \delta\,)$. That is, as for sequences, we first translate the let construct to a block, and then return an exc expression.

The translation of let mutable differs only in the fact that in translation of e_2, the variable x, being mutable, is added to M.

Properties of the Translation. The translation preserves the dynamic semantics of the F# expressions, that is if we have an F# program, that is a closed expression e, and $[\![e]\!]_{bl}^{\emptyset, \emptyset} = (\, bl, \overline{\delta}\,)$. Then $e \mid [\,] \longrightarrow^* v \mid \rho$ (where v is and int or bool value) if and only if $\{\overline{\delta}; bl\} \mid [\,] \longrightarrow^* v \mid \rho'$ for some ρ'. From this result and the fact that F# programs do not get stuck, we can also derive that: the IL translation of an F# program does not evaluate to an error or gets stuck.

First of all observe that the translation of an F# value is an IL value. In fact, the translation of an F# function produces and IL function. In addition, some definitions of associations between variables and code expressions may be generated.

To prove the result we need to analyse the behaviour of expressions/blocks which are intermediate results of the translation of a whole program. Such expressions contain free mutable and immutable variables. Let e be an F# expression. Let $I = \overline{x}{:}\overline{T}$, $M = \overline{y}{:}\overline{T}'$, and Σ be such that $I, M \mid \Sigma \vdash e : T$ for some T. To execute e in a store ρ such that $\Sigma \vdash \rho$ we close the expression substituting values for the free immutable variables, $\overline{x}$, and locations for the mutable variables, $\overline{y}$. Let $\overline{v}$ be such that $\emptyset \mid \Sigma \vdash \overline{v} : \overline{T}$, $\Sigma' = \overline{l}'{:}\overline{T}'$, and $\rho' = \overline{l}' \mapsto \overline{v}'$ be such that $dom(\Sigma') \cap dom(\Sigma) = \emptyset$, and $\Sigma[\Sigma'] \vdash \rho'$. We consider the F# reduction applied to $e_0 \mid \rho_0$, where $e_0 = (e[\overline{x}{:=}\overline{v}])[\overline{y}{:=}\overline{l}']$ and $\rho_0 = \rho[\rho']$, which is a well formed configuration w.r.t. $\Sigma[\Sigma']$. We show that, if we consider the IL configuration, $\{bl\} \mid \rho'_0$ in which bl is the translation of e_0, and ρ'_0 associates locations with the translation of the value associated in ρ_0, we get that if $e_0 \mid \rho_0 \longrightarrow e_1 \mid \rho_1$, then $\{bl\} \mid \rho'_0 \longrightarrow^\star \{bl'\} \mid \rho'_1$ where bl' is the translation of e_1 and for all $l \in dom(\rho_1)$, $\rho'_1(l)$ is the translation of $\rho_1(l)$.

6   Comparisons with Other Work

Similar projects exist and are based on similar translation techniques, although, as far as we know, we are the first to introduce an intermediate language allowing to translate to many target languages. Pit, see [7], and FunScript, see [8], are open source F# to JavaScript compilers. They support only translation to JavaScript. FunScript ha support for integration with JavaScript code. Websharper, see [9], is a professional web and mobile development framework. As of version 2.4 an open source license is available. It is a very rich framework offering extensions for ExtJs, jQuery, Google Maps, WebGL and many more. Again it supports only JavaScript. F# Web Tools is an open source tool whose main objective is not the translation to JavaScript, instead, it is trying to solve the difficulties of web programming: "the heterogeneous nature of execution, the discontinuity between client and server parts of execution and the lack of type-checked execution on the client side", see [10]. It does so by using meta-programming and monadic syntax. One of it features is translation to JavaScript. Finally, a translation between Ocaml byte code and JavaScript is provided by Ocsigen, and described in [11].

On the theoretical side, a framework integrating statically and dynamically typed (functional) languages is presented in [12]. Support for dynamic languages is provided with ad hoc constructs in Scala, see [13]. A construct similar to code, is studied in recent work by one of the authors, see [3], where it is shown how to use it to realize dynamic binding and meta-programming, an issue we are planning to address. The only work to our knowledge that proves the correctness of a translation between a statically typed functional language, with imperative features to a scripting language (namely JavaScript) is [14].

7   Conclusions and Future Work

In this paper we introduced IL an intermediate language for the translation of a significant fragment of F# to scripting languages such as Python and JavaScript.

The translation is shown to preserve the dynamic semantics of the original language. A preliminary version of this paper was presented at ICSOFT 2013, see [15]. We have a prototype implementation of the compiler that can be found at the project site [4]. The compiler is implemented in F# and is based on two metaprogramming features offered by the .net platform: *quotations* and *reflection*. Our future work will be on the practical side to use the intermediate language to integrate F# code and JavaScript or Python native code. (Some of the features of IL, such as dynamic type checking, were originally introduced for this purpose.) The current implementation also supports features such as namespacing, classes, pattern matching, discriminated unions, etc., some of which have poor or no support at all in JavaScript or Python. On the theoretical side, we are planning to complete the proofs of correctness of the translations. We need to formalize our target languages Python and JavaScript, and then prove the correctness of the translation from IL to them. (We anticipate that these proofs will be easier than the one from F# to IL.) Moreover, we want to formalize the integration of native code, and more in general meta-programming on the line of recent work by the authors, see [3]. We are also considering extending the type system for the intermediate language with polymorphic types, which is, as shown in [16], non trivial.

References

1. Ranson, J.F., Hamilton, H.J., Fong, P.W.L.: A semantics of python in isabelle/hol. Technical Report CS-2008-04, CS Department, University of Regina, Saskatchewan (2008)
2. Nanevski, A.: From dynamic binding to state via modal possibility. In: PPDP'03, pp. 207–218. ACM (2003)
3. Ancona, D., Giannini, P., Zucca, E.: Reconciling positional and nominal binding. In: ITRS 2012. EPTCS (2013)
4. Giannini, P., Shaqiri, A.: Blue storm project (2013). https://www.assembla.com/spaces/bluestorm
5. Igarashi, A., Pierce, B., Wadler, P.: Featherweight Java: a minimal core calculus for Java and GJ. ACM TOPLAS **23**(3), 396–450 (2001)
6. Appel, A.W.: Modern Compiler Implementation in ML. Cambridge University Press, New York (1998)
7. Fahad, M.S.: Pit - F Sharp to JS compiler, May 2012. http://pitfw.org/
8. Bray, Z.: Funscript, February 2013. http://tomasp.net/files/funscript/tutorial.html
9. Intellifactory: Websharper 2010 platform, May 2012. http://websharper.com/
10. Petříček, T., Syme, D.: AFAX: Rich client/server web applications in F#, May 2012. http://www.scribd.com/doc/54421045/Web-Apps-in-F-Sharp
11. Vouillon, J., Balat, V.: From bytecode to javascript: the js of ocaml compiler (2011). http://www.pps.univ-paris-diderot.fr/balat/publi.php
12. Matthews, J., Findler, R.B.: Operational semantics for multi-language programs. ACM Trans. Program. Lang. Syst. **31**(3), 144 (2009)
13. Moors, A., Rompf, T., Haller, P., Odersky, M.: Scala-virtualized. In: Kiselyov, O., Thompson, S. (eds.) Proceedings of PEPM 2012, Philadelphia, Pennsylvania, USA, pp. 117–120. ACM (2012)

14. Fournet, C., Swamy, N., Chen, J., Dagand, P.É., Strub, P.Y., Livshits, B.: Fully abstract compilation to javascript. In: POPL, pp. 371–384. ACM (2013)
15. Giannini, P., Shaqiri, A.: An intermediate language for compilation to scripting languages. In: ICSOFT-EA 2013 - Proceedings International Conference on Software Engineering and Applications, pp. 92–103. SCITEPRESS Digital Library (2013)
16. Ahmed, A., Findler, R.B., Siek, J.G., Wadler, P.: Blame for all. In: Proceedings of POPL 2011, Austin, TX, USA, pp. 201–214. ACM (2011)

Language Design and Implementation via the Combination of Embedding and Parsing

Gergely Dévai[✉], Dániel Leskó, and Máté Tejfel

Faculty of Informatics, Eötvös Loránd University,
Pázmány P. stny. 1/C, Budapest, Hungary
deva@elte.hu

Abstract. Language embedding is a method to implement a new language within the framework of an existing programming language. This method is known to speed up the development process compared to standalone languages using classical compiler technology. On the other hand, embedded languages may not be that convenient for the end-users as standalone ones with own concrete syntax. This paper describes a method that uses the flexibility of language embedding in the experimental phase of the language design process, then, once the language features are mature enough, adds concrete syntax and turns the language to a standalone one. Lessons learnt from a project, run in industry-university cooperation and using the presented method, are discussed. Based on these results, a cost model is established that can be used to estimate the potential benefits of this method in case of future language design projects.

Keywords: Domain specific languages · Embedding · Parsing · Concrete syntax

1 Introduction

1.1 Motivation

In special hardware or software domains the general purpose programming languages may not be expressive or efficient enough. This is why domain specific languages (DSLs) are getting more and more important. However, using classical compiler technology makes the development of new DSLs hard. The new language usually changes quickly and the amount of the language constructs increases rapidly in the early period of the project. Continuous adaptation of the parser, the type checker and the back-end of the compiler is not an easy job: It is time consuming and error prone.

Language embedding is a technique that facilitates this development process. In this case a general purpose language is chosen, which is called the *host language*, and its parser and type checker are reused for the purposes of the DSL. In fact, an embedded language is a special kind of library written in the host language. The DSL programs in this setup are programs in the host language that

© Springer-Verlag Berlin Heidelberg 2014
J. Cordeiro and M. van Sinderen (Eds.): ICSOFT 2013, CCIS 457, pp. 131–147, 2014.
DOI: 10.1007/978-3-662-44920-2_9

extensively use this library. The library is implemented in such a way that its users *have the impression* that they are using a DSL, even if they are producing a valid host language program.

In this paper we use the so called *deep embedding* technique. Implementation of a deeply embedded language consists of

- *data types* to represent the AST,
- *front-end:* a set of functions and helper data types which provide an interface to build ASTs,
- *back-end:* interpreter or compiler that inputs the AST and executes the DSL program or generates target code.

Not all general purpose programming languages are equally suitable to be host languages. Flexible and minimalistic syntax, higher order functions, monads, expressive type system are useful features in this respect. For this reason Haskell and Scala are widely used as host languages. On the other hand, these are not mainstream languages. As our experience from a previous project [1,8] shows, using a host language being unfamiliar to the majority of the programmers makes it harder to make the embedded DSL accepted in an industrial environment. In addition to this, error reporting and debugging are hard to solve in an embedded language.

For these reasons we have decided to create a standalone DSL as the final product of our current project. However, we did not want to go without the flexibility provided by embedding in the language design phase. This paper presents the experiment to combine the advantages of these two approaches.

1.2 Project Background

This paper is based on a university research project initiated by Ericsson. The goal of the project is to develop a novel domain specific language that is specialized in the IP routing domain as well as the special hardware used by Ericsson for IP routing purposes.

This paper does not introduce the DSL created by this project for two reasons. First, the language, being the result of an industry-university cooperation, is not publicly available at the moment. Second, the results presented in this paper concern the language development methodology used by the project. This methodology is general, and the concrete language it was applied to is irrelevant.

1.3 Main Messages

The most important lessons learnt from the experiment are the following. It was more effective to use an embedded version of the domain specific language for language experiments than defining concrete syntax first, because embedding provided us with flexibility so that we were able to concentrate on language design issues instead of technical problems. The way we used the host language features in early case studies was a good source of ideas for the standalone language design. Furthermore, it was possible to reuse the majority of the embedded language implementation in the final product, keeping the overhead of creating two front-ends low.

The paper is organized as follows. Section 2 introduces the architecture of the compiler. Then in Sect. 3 we analyze the implementation activities using statistics from the version control system used. Section 4 presents related work, then Sect. 5 presents the main messages of the paper and a cost model to estimate benefits of the approach for future projects.

2   Compiler Architecture

The architecture of the software is depicted in Fig. 1. There are two main dataflows as possible compilation processes: *embedded compilation* (dashed) and *standalone compilation* (dotted).

The input of the embedded program compilation is a Haskell program loaded in the Haskell interpreter. What makes a Haskell program a DSL program is that it heavily uses the *language front-end* that is provided by the embedded DSL implementation. This front-end is a collection of helper data types and functions that, on one hand, define how the embedded program looks like (its "syntax"), and, on the other hand, builds up the *internal representation* of the program. The internal representation is in fact the *abstract syntax tree (AST)* of the program encoded as a Haskell data structure. The embedded language front-end module may contain complex functions to bridge the gap between an easy-to-use embedded language syntax and an internal representation suitable for optimizations and code generation. However, it is important that this front-end does not run the DSL program: It only creates its AST.

The same AST is built by the other, standalone compilation path. In this case the DSL program has it's own concrete syntax that is parsed. We will refer to the result of the parsing as *concrete syntax tree (CST)*. This is a direct representation

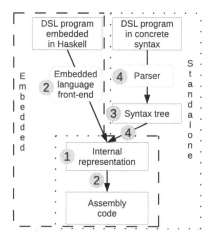

Fig. 1. Compiler architecture.

of the program text and may be far from the internal representation. For this reason the transformation from the CST to an AST may not be completely trivial.

Once the AST is reached, the rest of the compilation process (optimizations and code generation) is identical in both the embedded and the standalone version. As we will see in Sect. 3, this part of the compiler is much bigger both in size and complexity than the small arrow on Fig. 1 might suggest.

The numbers on the figure show the basic steps of the workflow to create a compiler with this architecture. The first step is to define the data types of the internal representation. This is the most important part of the language design since these data types define the basic constructs of the DSL. Our experience has shown that it is easier to find the right DSL constructs by thinking of them in terms of the internal representation then experimenting with syntax proposals.

Once the internal representation (or at least a consistent early version of it) is available, it is possible to create embedded language front-end and code generation support in parallel. Implementation of the embedded language front-end is a relatively easy task if someone knows how to use the host language features for language embedding purposes. Since the final goal is to have a standalone language, it is not worth creating too fine grained embedded language syntax. The goal of the front-end is to enable easy-enough case study implementation to test the DSL functionality.

Contrarily, the back-end implementation is more complicated. If the internal representation is changed during DSL design, the cost of back-end adaptation may be high. Fortunately it is possible to break this transformation up into several transformation steps and start with the ones that are independent of the DSL's internal representation. In our case this part of the development started with the module that pretty prints assembly programs.

When the case studies implemented in the embedded language show that the DSL is mature enough, it is time to plan its concrete syntax. Earlier experiments with different front-end solutions provide valuable input to this design phase. When the structure of the concrete syntax is fixed, the data types representing the CST can be implemented. The final two steps, parser implementation and the transformation of the CST to AST can be done in parallel.

3   Detailed Analysis

According to the architecture in Sect. 2 we have split the source code of the compiler as follows:

- *Representation:* The underlying data structures, basically the building data types of the AST.
- *Back-end:* Transforms the AST to target code. Mostly optimization and code generation.
- *Embedded front-end:* Functions of the embedded Haskell front-end which constructs the AST.
- *Standalone front-end:* Lexer and parser to build up the CST and the transformation from CST to AST.

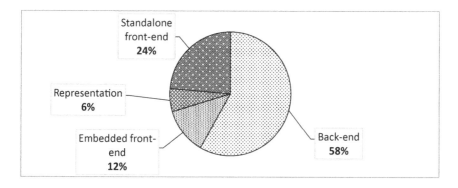

Fig. 2. Code size comparison by components.

The following figures are based on a dataset extracted from our version control repository[1]. The dataset contains information from 2012 late February to the end of the year.

Figure 2 compares the code sizes (based on the LOC, lines of code metric) of the previously described four components. The overall size of the project was around 13 000 LOC[2] when we summarized the results of the first year.

No big surprise there, the back-end is without a doubt the most heavyweight component of our language. The second place goes to the standalone front-end, partly due to the size of lexing and parsing codes[3]. The size of the embedded front-end is about the half of the standalone's. The representation is the smallest component by the means of code size, which means that we successfully kept it simple.

Figure 3 shows the exact same dataset as Fig. 2 but it helps comparing the two front-ends with the reused common components (back-end, representation).

The pie chart shows that by developing an embedded language first, we could postpone the development of almost one fourth of the complete project, while the so-called extra code (not released, kept internally) was only 12 %. Note that these figures are based on the code size at the end of the project. The actual amount of work will be discussed later in Sect. 5.4.

Figure 4 presents how intense was the development pace of the four components. The dataset is based on the log of the version control system. Originally it contained approximately 1000 commits which were related to at least one of the four major components. Then we split the commits by files, which resulted almost 3000 file-change. All of these changes were weighted by the number of inserted lines. So at the end we got 75 000 data-points, that we categorized by the four components. This way each data-point represents one line insertion.

---

[1] In this project we have been using *Subversion*.

[2] Note that this project was entirely implemented in Haskell, which allows much more concise code than the mainstream imperative, object oriented languages.

[3] We have been using the *Parsec* parser combinator library [10] of Haskell. Using context free grammars instead would have resulted in similar code size.

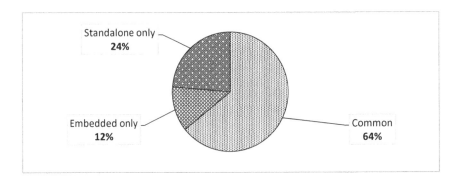

Fig. 3. Code size comparison for embedded / standalone.

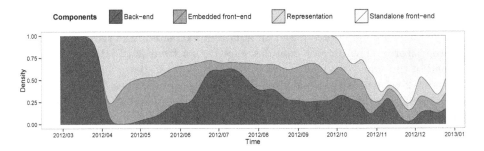

Fig. 4. Development timeline.

It may seem strange that we spent the first month of development with the back-end, without having any representation in place. This is because we first created a representation and pretty printer for the targeted assembly language.

The work with the representation started at late March and this was the most frequently changed component over the next two-three months. It was hard to find a proper, easy-to-use and sustainable representation, but after the first version was ready in early April, it was possible to start the development of the embedded front-end and the back-end.

The back-end and code generation parts were mostly developed during the summer, while the embedded front-end was slightly reworked in August and September, because the first version was hard to use.

By October we almost finalized the core language constructs, so it was time to start to design the standalone front-end and concrete, textual syntax. This component was the most actively developed one till the end of the year. Early November we had a slight architecture modification which explains the small spike in the representation and back-end related parts. Approaching the year end we were preparing the project for its first release: Every component was actively checked, documented and cleaned.

4   Related Work

Thomas Cleenewerck states that *"developing DSLs is hard and costly, therefore their development is only feasible for mature enough domains"* [5]. Our experience shows that if proper language architecture and design methodology is in place, the development of a new (not mature) DSL is feasible in 12 months. The key factors for the success are to start low cost language feature experiments as soon as possible, then fix the core language constructs based on the results and finally expand the implementation to a full-fledged language and compiler.

Frag is a DSL development toolkit [15], which is itself a DSL embedded into Java. The main goal of this toolkit is to support deferring architectural decisions (like embedded vs. external, semantics, relation to host language) in DSL software design. This lets the language designers to make real architectural decisions instead of ones motivated by technological constraints or presumptions. In our case there were no reason to postpone architectural decisions: It was decided early in the project to have an external DSL with a standalone compiler (see Sect. 1). What we needed instead was to postpone their realization and keep the language implementation small and simple in the first few months to achieve fast and painless experiment/development cycles.

Another approach to decrease the cost of DSL design is published by Bierhoff, Liongosari and Swaminathan [2]. They advocate incremental DSL development, meaning that an initial DSL is constructed first based on a few case studies, which is later incrementally extended with features motivated by further case studies. This might be fruitful for relatively established domains. In our case the language design iterations were heavier then simple extensions. We believe that creating a full fledged first version of the language and then considerably rewriting it in the next iterations would have wasted more development effort than the methodology we applied.

At the beginning of our project a set of separate embedded language experiments were started, each of them dedicated to independent language features. These components were loosely coupled at that time, therefore gluing them to form the first working version was a relatively simple task to do. This kind of architecture is very similar to keyword based programming [5], where the complete DSL is formed by loosely coupled and independent language components. Later on our components became more and more tightly coupled due to the need of proper error handling and reporting, type and constraint checking.

Languages like Java, Ruby, MetaOCml, Template Haskell, C++, Scala are used or are tried to be used as implementation languages for developing new DSLs [6,7,9,11]. These projects either used the embedded-only or the standalone-only approach and they all reported problems and shortcomings. We claim that many of these can be eliminated by combining the two approaches.

The Metaborg approach [3,4] (and many similar projects) extend the host language with DSL fragments using their own syntax. The applications are then developed using the mixed language and the DSL fragments are usually compiled to the host language. In our case the host language is only used for metaprogramming on top of the DSL, the embedding does not introduce concrete syntax and, finally, the host language environment is never used to execute the DSL programs.

David Wile has summarized several lessons learnt about DSL development [14]. His messages are mostly about how to understand the domain and express that knowledge in a DSL. Our current paper adds complementary messages related to the language implementation methodology.

Based on Spinellis's design patterns for DSLs [12], we can categorize our project. The internally used embedded front-end is a realization of a piggyback design pattern, where the new DSL uses the capabilities of an existing language. While the final version of our language, which employs a standalone front-end, is a source-to-source transformation.

5   Discussion and Conclusions

5.1   Lessons Learnt

This section summarizes the lessons learnt from the detailed analysis presented in Sect. 3.

Message 1: Do the language experiments using an embedded DSL then define concrete syntax and reuse the internal representation and back-end! Our project started in January 2012 and in December the same year we released the first version of the language and compiler for the industrial partner. Even if this first version was not a mature one, it was functional: the hash table lookups of the multicast protocol was successfully implemented in the language as a direct transliteration from legacy code. Since state of the art study and domain analysis took the first quarter of the year, we had only 9 months for design and implementation. We believe that using a less flexible solution in the language design phase would not have allowed us to achieve the mentioned results.

Message 2: Design the language constructs by creating their internal representation and think about the syntax later! The temptation to think about the new language in terms of concrete syntax is high. On the other hand, our experience is that it is easier to design the concepts in abstract notation. In our case this abstract notation was the algebraic data types of Haskell: The language concepts were represented by the data types of the abstract syntax tree. When the concepts and their semantics were clear there was still large room for syntax related discussions[4], however, then it was possible to concentrate on the true task of syntax (to have an easy to use and expressive notation) without mixing semantics related issues in the discussion. This is analogous to model driven development: It is easier to build the software architecture as a model and think about the details of efficient implementation later.

---

[4] *"Wadler's Law: The emotional intensity of debate on a language feature increases as one moves down the following scale: Semantics, Syntax, Lexical syntax, Comments."* (Philiph Wadler in the Haskell mailing list, February 1992, see [13].)

Message 3: Use the flexibility of embedding to be able to concentrate on language design issues instead of technical problems! Analysis of the compiler components in Sect. 3 shows that the embedded front-end of the language is lightweight compared to the front-end for the standalone language. This means that embedding is better suited for the ever-changing nature of the language in the design phase. It supports the evolution of the language features by fast development cycles and quick feedback on the ideas.

Message 4: No need for a full-fledged embedded language! Creating a good quality embedded language is far from trivial. Using different services of the host language (like monads and do notation, operator precedence definition, overloading via type classes in case of Haskell) to customize the appearance of embedded language programs can easily be more complex then writing a context free grammar. Furthermore, advocates of embedded languages emphasize that part of the semantic analysis of the embedded language can be solved by the host language compiler. An example in case of Haskell is that the internal representation of the DSL can be typed so that mistyped DSL programs are automatically ruled out by the Haskell compiler. These are complex techniques, while this paper has stated so far that embedding is lightweight and flexible — is this a contradiction? The goal of the embedded language in our project was to facilitate the language design process: It was never published for the end-users. There was no need for a mature, nicely polished embedded language front-end. The only requirement was to have an easy-to-use front-end for experimentation — and this is easy to achieve. Similarly, there was no need to make the Haskell compiler type check the DSL programs: the standalone language implementation cannot reuse such a solution. Instead of this, type checking was implemented as a usual semantic analyzer function working on the internal representation. As a result of all this, the embedded front-end in our project in fact remained a light-weight component that was easy to adapt during the evolution of the language.

Message 5: Carefully examine the case studies implemented in the embedded language to identify the host language features that are useful for the DSL! These should be reimplemented in the standalone language. An important feature of embedding is that the host language can be used to generate and to generalize DSL programs. This is due to the meta language nature of the host language on top of the embedded one. Our case studies implemented in the embedded language contain template DSL program fragments (Haskell functions returning DSL programs) and the instances of these templates (the functions called with a given set of parameters). The parameter kinds (expressions, left values, types) used in the case studies gave us ideas how to design the template features of the standalone DSL. Another example is the scoping rules of variables. Sometimes the scoping rules provided by Haskell were suitable for the DSL but not always. Both cases provided us with valuable information for the design of the standalone DSL's scoping rules.

Message 6: Plan enough time for the concrete syntax support, which may be harder to implement than expected! This is the direct consequence of the previous item. The language features borrowed from the host language (e.g. meta programming, scoping rules) have to be redesigned and reimplemented in the standalone language front-end. Technically this means that the concrete syntax tree is more feature rich than the internal representation. For this reason the correct implementation of the transformation from the CST to the AST takes time. Another issue is the development of a symbol table, which should store exact source positions in order to support good quality error messages, traceability, debugging and profiling. The symbol table is also useful for detecting the violations of scoping rules. This infrastructure is usually not (completely) present in an embedded language. To tell the truth, our embedded language implementation was not well prepared for the addition of this infrastructure. The lesson we have learnt here is that the embedded language implementation should be created keeping in mind that it will be turned to a standalone one later.

5.2   Plans and Reality

Our original project plan had the following check points:

– By the end of March: State of the art study and language feature ideas.
– By the end of June: Ideas are evaluated by *separate* embedded language experiments in Haskell.
– By the end of August: The language with concrete syntax is defined.
– By the end of November: Prototype compiler is ready.
– December was planned as buffer period.

While executing it, there were three important diverges from this plan that we recommend for consideration.

First, the individual experiments to evaluate different language feature ideas were quickly converging to a joint embedded language. Project members working on different tasks started to add the feature they were experimenting with modularly to the existing code base instead of creating separate case studies.

Second, the definition of the language was delayed by three months. This happened partly because it was decided to finish the spontaneously emerged embedded language including the back-end, and partly because a major revision and extension to the language became necessary to make it usable in practice. As a result, the language concepts were more or less fixed (and implemented in the embedded language) by September. Then started the design of the concrete syntax which was fixed in October. At first glance this seems to be an unmanageable delay. However, as we have pointed out in this paper, it was then possible to reuse a considerable part of the embedded language implementation for the standalone compiler.

Third, we were hoping that, after defining the concrete syntax, it will be enough to write the parser which will trivially fit into the existing compiler as an alternative to the embedded language front-end. The parser implementation was, in fact, straightforward. On the other hand, it became clear that it cannot directly produce the internal representation of the embedded language. Recall what Sect. 5.1 tells about the template features and scoping rules to understand why did the transformation from the parsing result to the internal representation take more time than expected. Therefore the buffer time in the plan was completely consumed to make the whole infrastructure work.

In brief, we used much more time than planned to design the language, but the compiler architecture of Sect. 2 yet made it possible to finish the project on time.

5.3 Cost Model

The messages in Sect. 5.1 suggest that the presented method pays off if the flexibility of an embedded language provides more benefit in the language design phase than the additional cost of creating an embedded language front-end. This happens if the language experiments modify the code base intensively *and* the size of the embedded front-end is small enough compared to the size of the standalone front-end.

This section digs deeper into the analysis of this trade-off by setting up a cost model to predict the effort needed to create a new language by the following two methods:

- *Standard Method.* A standalone language is implemented from the beginning of the project, the parser is maintained in each iteration of the language design.
- *Combined Method.* The one described in this paper. That is, an embedded language is created for experimentation and the standalone language front-end is added when the language is fixed.

The first observation we have to make is that choosing the standard or the combined method does not influence the effort needed for the back-end implementation. This is because the back-end inputs the internal representation of the program, and the complexity to turn it to target code is not affected by the way this internal representation was built up: either embedding or parsing. As a consequence, the cost model has to deal only with the representation, embedded front-end and standalone front-end.

The effort needed to develop these components depends on their final *size* and their *variability*. We will use variability to measure the difficulty of reaching the final version of a given component: If the solution is straightforward, then the final version will likely be created by gradually adding new functionality to the code base. On the other hand, a development process that involves many experiments and dead-ends will have considerable amount of deletion and modification of existing code.

If we stick to the *insert* and *delete* operations widely used in software version control, we can treat modifications as the deletion of the old and insertion of the new versions. If #*ins* and #*del* denotes the number of insertions and deletions done to a component[5], then the following equations can be given for *size* and *variability*:

---

[5] The unit of measure can be anything from files to characters. Our statistics use lines.

$$size = \#ins - \#del$$

$$variability = \frac{\#del}{\#ins}$$

Zero variability means no deletions at all, while variability converging to 1 means that the amount of code added and later deleted overwhelms the size of the final product.

We argue that the *effort* needed to create a component is well characterized by the number of insertions during the development process, that is $\#ins$. From the two equations above, we get the following one:

$$effort = \frac{size}{1 - variability}$$

The effort is given by the size in case of projects with zero variability, while the effort converges to infinity, if variability gets close to 1.

Experiments in the language design phase introduce new language concepts, remove less successful ones or alter them. These changes alter the internal representation in the first place, but the front-end module (either embedded or standalone) has to be adapted to be able to build the code base and evaluate the experiment. How heavily does a representation change affect a front-end module? The amount might vary depending on the exact case, however, we argue that it will be proportional to the change in the representation: a small change in the representation induces a small change in the front-end and adding a completely new set of language concepts require an entirely new front-end module.

Let $variability_{exp}$ denote the variability experienced during the experimental phase. Later, when the language features and their semantics are fixed, one can expect considerably lower variability, since that part of the development process is well-specified. Ideally, the variability in that phase would be zero. However, even well specified and straightforward projects show a slight code variability due to refactoring steps and bugfixes. We will denote this value by $variability_{norm}$.

We are now prepared to calculate the effort needed for the whole project in case of standalone and combined strategies. (The component names *rep*, *sf* and *ef* will denote the representation, the standalone front-end and the embedded front-end respectively.)

$$effort_{standard} = \frac{size_{rep} + size_{sf}}{1 - variability_{exp}}$$

$$effort_{combined} = \frac{size_{rep} + size_{ef}}{1 - variability_{exp}} + \frac{size_{sf}}{1 - variability_{norm}}$$

The equation for the standalone case is the direct consequence of the equation for *effort* above. In the combined case, the variability of experimentation only affects the representation and the embedded front-end. The standalone front-end is free from the effects of the language experiments, since its development only starts when the language is fixed. For this reason the normal variability is applicable for that component.

The combined development method is beneficial if

$$effort_{combined} < effort_{standard},$$

which is equivalent to the following condition:

$$\frac{size_{ef}}{1 - variability_{exp}} + \frac{size_{sf}}{1 - variability_{norm}} < \frac{size_{sf}}{1 - variability_{exp}}$$

The first observation is, that the size of the representation component disappeared from the condition as the result of simplification, so the actual size of the language to be designed is irrelevant when choosing between the two design strategies.

Further transforming the condition results in the following form:

$$\frac{size_{ef}}{size_{sf}} < \frac{variability_{exp} - variability_{norm}}{1 - variability_{norm}}$$

Note that, if $variability_{norm}$ is close to its ideal zero value, then the right hand size is close to $variability_{exp}$. This suggests the following rule of thumb: *The combined method can be beneficial if the ratio of the sizes of the embedded front-end and the standalone front-end is smaller than the variability during the experiments.*

How to estimate this ratio and the two variabilities when starting a new language development project? The ratio of the front-end sizes depends on the host language to be used for the embedding and also on the tools, libraries to be used for lexing and parsing. It seems to be a good idea to implement both the embedded and standalone version of a toy language using the selected implementation language and toolset to estimate the required size ratio.

The value of $variability_{norm}$ mainly depends on the developer team and its ways of working. Measuring the variability in an earlier, relatively well-specified project done by the same team gives a good basis to estimate this value.

Estimation of the variability during the experimental phase is more difficult, but it is still possible if one considers how stable is the concept of the language to be created. If the specification is clear and the solution is straightforward, one can expect that $variability_{exp}$ will be close to $variability_{norm}$. On the other hand, a lot of room for experimenting with different language features will certainly lead to much higher variability. Rephrasing the question might help: *Will we delete half of the code that we create during the experiments in order to get to the version that is more or less fixed?* If the answer is yes, one can expect $variability_{exp}$ around 0.5.

Once there is an estimation for the three parameters, the condition discussed above can be used to make a decision how the language should be developed.

5.4   Was It Worth It?

As discussed in Sect. 5.1, our impression was that using the combined development method was actually beneficial for the project we have been working on. Does the cost model introduced above confirm this?

Analysing the statistics of the SVN repository used, we got that the final size of the embedded front-end was 1592 lines, while the standalone front-end consists of 3092 lines. The size ratio is therefore 0.515.

Regarding variability, 0.765 was measured for the representation and 0.725 for the embedded front-end. This confirms the assumption of the model that the variability of the representation is close to that of the front-end used in the experimental phase. The weighted variability of these two components is 0.738. In contrast, the variability of the standalone front-end was only 0.260.

The condition suggested by the cost model is therefore

$$\frac{1592}{3092} < \frac{0.738 - 0.260}{1 - 0.260},$$

which boils down to $0.515 < 0.646$. That is, also the cost model suggests that combining embedding and parsing was actually worth it in our case.

We have seen the ratio of each component in terms of the final code size earlier, on Fig. 2. Figure 5, in contrast, shows their relation in terms of the *effort* needed to develop them. Note that the standalone front-end shrank to less then its half, while the other three components grew equally. This is the consequence of the low variability of the standalone front-end, due to its postponed development.

One can argue that the benefit of the combined development strategy is negligible compared to the maintenance cost of the back-end: Every change in the representation induces a change in the back-end, which is by far the most heavyweight component.

On the other hand, a change in the representation only affects a limited segment of the back-end. To measure this impact precisely, we analysed the commits of our version control system. If a change to a back-end file was made in such a commit which also changed a representation file, then we consider this back-end change a result of the change in the representation, otherwise it is independent.

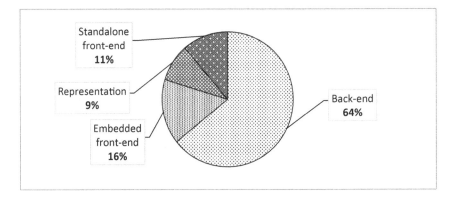

Fig. 5. Implementation effort by components.

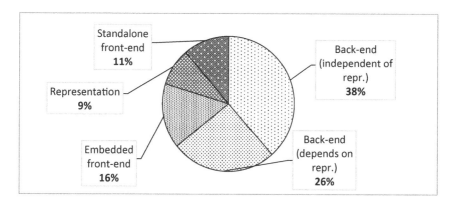

Fig. 6. Implementation effort by components (back-end partitioned).

The results show that only 40 % of the back-end changes are directly related to a change in the representation, the other 60 % is low level code generation and optimization related change. This is demonstrated by Fig. 6 where the back-end component (precisely its *effort*) is divided to a representation dependent and to a non-dependent part.

5.5 Future

At the moment it is unclear what will happen to this compiler architecture in the future when more language features will be added.

In 2013 only minor new features have been implemented, not requiring intensive language experiments. These low variability implementation tasks are cheaper to be done directly in the standalone version of the language.

However, conclusions of this paper suggest that if we will need to develop more complex new features in the future we shall continue with the successful strategy and experiment with new language features by modifying, extending the embedded language and, once the extensions are proved to be useful and are stable enough, add them to the standalone language.

On the other hand, this comes at a cost: The consistency of the embedded and standalone language front-ends have to be maintained. Whenever slight changes are done in the internal representation, the embedded language front-end has to be adapted. Many trivial new features added only to the standalone front-end, like the ones we have developed in 2013, make the two front-ends diverge. We still do not know if the adaptation costs overwhelm the advantage that the embedded language offers for the language design.

Furthermore, since the standalone syntax is more convenient than the embedded language front-end, it might not be appealing to experiment with new language concepts in the embedded language. It also takes more effort to keep in mind two different variants of the same language.

Even if it turns out that it is not worth maintaining the embedded language front-end and it gets removed from the compiler one day, its important positive role in the design of the first language version is indisputable.

6 Summary

This paper evaluates a language development methodology that starts the design and implementation with an embedded language, then defines concrete syntax and implements support for it. The main advantage of the method is the flexibility provided by the embedded language combined by the advantages of a standalone language. We have demonstrated that most of the embedded language implementation can be reused for the standalone compiler. A cost model has been presented that tells if our method is rewarding in case of future projects.

Acknowledgements. We would like to thank the support of Ericsson Hungary and the grant EITKIC 12-1-2012-0001 that is supported by the Hungarian Government, managed by the National Development Agency, and financed by the Research and Technology Innovation Fund.

References

1. Axelsson, E., Claessen, K., Dévai, G., Horváth, Z., Keijzer, K., Persson, A., Sheeran, M., Svenningsson, J., Vajda, A., et al.: Feldspar: a domain specific language for digital signal processing algorithms. In: Proceedings of the 8th ACM/IEEE International Conference on Formal Methods and Models for Codesign. IEEE (2010)
2. Bierhoff, K., Liongosari, E.S., Swaminathan, K.S.: Incremental development of a domain-specific language that supports multiple application styles. In: OOPSLA 6th Workshop on Domain Specific Modeling, pp. 67–78 (2006)
3. Bravenboer, M., de Groot, R., Visser, E.: MetaBorg in action: examples of domain-specific language embedding and assimilation using Stratego/XT. In: Lämmel, R., Saraiva, J., Visser, J. (eds.) GTTSE 2005. LNCS, vol. 4143, pp. 297–311. Springer, Heidelberg (2006)
4. Bravenboer, M., Visser, E.: Concrete syntax for objects: domain-specific language embedding and assimilation without restrictions. SIGPLAN Not. **39**(10), 365–383 (2004). http://doi.acm.org/10.1145/1035292.1029007
5. Cleenewerck, T.: Component-based DSL development. In: Pfenning, F., Macko, M. (eds.) GPCE 2003. LNCS, vol. 2830, pp. 245–264. Springer, Heidelberg (2003)
6. Cunningham, H.C.: A little language for surveys: constructing an internal DSL in Ruby. In: Proceedings of the 46th Annual Southeast Regional Conference on XX. ACM-SE 46, pp. 282–287. ACM, New York (2008). http://doi.acm.org/10.1145/1593105.1593181
7. Czarnecki, K., O'Donnell, J.T., Striegnitz, J., Taha, W.: DSL implementation in MetaOCaml, Template Haskell, and C++. In: Lengauer, C., Batory, D., Blum, A., Odersky, M. (eds.) Domain-Specific Program Generation. LNCS, vol. 3016, pp. 51–72. Springer, Heidelberg (2004)

8. Dévai, G., Tejfel, M., Gera, Z., Páli, G., Nagy, G., Horváth, Z., Axelsson, E., Sheeran, M., Vajda, A., Lyckegård, B., Persson, A.: Efficient code generation from the high-level domain-specific language Feldspar for DSPs. In: ODES-8: 8th Workshop on Optimizations for DSP and Embedded Systems (2010)

9. Freeman, S., Pryce, N.: Evolving an embedded domain-specific language in Java. In: Companion to the 21st ACM SIGPLAN Conference. OOPSLA'06, pp. 855–865, Portland, Oregon, USA (2006). http://www.mockobjects.com/files/evolving_an_edsl.ooplsa2006.pdf

10. Leijen, D., Meijer, E.: Parsec: Direct style monadic parser combinators for the real world. Electron. Notes Theoret. Comput. Sci. **41**(1) (2001). Technical Report UU-CS-2001-35

11. Sloane, A.M.: Experiences with domain-specific language embedding in Scala. In: Lawall, J., Réveillére, L. (eds.) International Workshop on Domain-Specific Program Development (DSDP), Nashville, Tennessee, USA. vol. 7 (2008)

12. Spinellis, D.: Notable design patterns for domain-specific languages. J. Syst. Softw. **56**(1), 91–99 (2001). http://dx.doi.org/10.1016/S0164-1212(00)00089-3

13. Wadler, P.: Wadler's "Law" on language design. Haskell mailing list (1992). http://code.haskell.org/~dons/haskell-1990-2000/msg00737.html

14. Wile, D.: Lessons learned from real DSL experiments. Sci. Comput. Program. **51**(3), 265–290 (2004). http://dx.doi.org/10.1016/j.scico.2003.12.006

15. Zdun, U.: A DSL toolkit for deferring architectural decisions in DSL-based software design. Inf. Softw. Technol. **52**(7), 733–748 (2010). http://eprints.cs.univie.ac.at/2288/

Enabling Informed Decision Making Through Mobile Technologies: A Challenge for Software Engineering

Xavier Franch[1(✉)], Anna Perini[2], and Norbert Seyff[3]

[1] Universitat Politècnica de Catalunya (UPC), Barcelona, Spain
franch@essi.upc.edu
[2] Fondazione Bruno Kessler (FBK), Trento, Italy
perini@fbk.eu
[3] University of Zurich (UZH), Zurich, Switzerland
seyff@ifi.uzh.ch

Abstract. The potential of mobile technologies is not fully exploited by current software services. One of the most influencing reasons for this problem is the lack of novel software engineering methods and tools that can master the complexity of mobile environments. Looking at a person in a smart environment, where mobile technologies and sensors are installed to support daily activities, it is observed that informed decision-making with the help of mobile technologies is beyond what users can expect from current software services. In this paper we present a motivating scenario to highlight the limitations of current decision support approaches. Based on this discussion we identify significant software engineering challenges, which currently hinder the realization of advanced decision support. In our research we have developed an initial version of a comprehensive framework that allows overcoming the challenges identified. It furthermore highlights which software engineering research lines may help to realize this vision.

Keywords: Software engineering · Software services · Apps · Mobile platforms · Service-oriented computing · Personal cloud · Decision-making · Thoughtful living

1 Introduction

The number and variety of software services (e.g., web services, mobile apps) dramatically increases every year. Service providers continuously emerge and the portfolio they offer grows steadily. Mobile technologies provide access to these services and are therefore becoming ubiquitous in our society. This leads to a magnitude of growth that was hardly conceivable in the recent past (e.g., the number of mobile phone subscriptions reached 5.000 million in 2010). Furthermore, it opens a lot of unforeseen opportunities for citizens worldwide and has improved citizenship's quality of life [31].

We are particularly interested in supporting informed decision-making with novel mobile applications and services. We envision that such services can further improve individual citizen's quality of life and will also lead to more thoughtful use of resources

© Springer-Verlag Berlin Heidelberg 2014
J. Cordeiro and M. van Sinderen (Eds.): ICSOFT 2013, CCIS 457, pp. 148–163, 2014.
DOI: 10.1007/978-3-662-44920-2_10

and therefore thoughtful living of citizens. However, this vision currently goes beyond state of the art software engineering techniques and approaches.

In order to realize our vision we have identified promising work in areas such as context-awareness, personalization and evolution of services. In this paper, we present a proposal to improve existing work in these areas to boost the impact of current software service technologies at the individual and the society level. For awareness, we propose to include knowledge about the individual and about the environment in the heart of mobile technologies. For personalization, we propose (semi-)automatic orchestration and enactment of software services according to a user's past behaviour. For evolution, we propose that it is driven by needs of individual citizens rather than developer assumptions.

We foresee that achieving these goals in the near future is plausible due to the significant and continuous advances in mobile technologies. However, in our opinion software engineering methods and tools are lacking behind the fast advances in mobile technologies. We have identified several challenges within the above-mentioned areas. Among them the fact that services nowadays lack a semantic layer and push their users to learn new rules which are imposed by their providers. This lack of standardization can demotivate potential platform users and contradicts with the interest of service providers to increase the usage rate of their services.

In this paper we also present our vision of a semantic service engineering framework, which could allow users to interact seamlessly with mobile technologies. Such an easy-to-use approach would encourage all different kinds of potential users to adopt the framework. Automatic service enactment would allow exploiting techniques from other fields, such as machine learning.

The rest of the paper is organized as follows (see Fig. 1). Section 2 presents a scenario highlighting today's decision-making approaches and Sect. 3 discusses issues with regard to the presented scenario. Section 4 highlights how decision-making support could look like in the future. In Sect. 5 we discuss software engineering challenges in order to achieve our vision. Section 6 provides a first solution idea by depicting the emerging ecosystem behind our vision and outlining a semantic platform supporting informed decision-making. Section 7 discusses the lines of research where advancement is needed to realize our vision. In Sect. 8 we highlight related work and Sect. 9 concludes the paper.

Fig. 1. Organization of the paper.

2 Motivating Scenario

Katie is the head of the paediatrics surgery unit at the Feeling Better International Hospital in Barcelona. Every day, her unit works with more than 100 patients. This work includes standard treatments that require only 30 min of their time, but also complex surgery lasting for several hours and involving several doctors. Her unit includes 30 doctors, 40 nurses and 10 administrative staff members. Most of the doctors are also academic staff of the Medical School at the Barcelona University. This means that on top of their medical duties, they have teaching responsibilities and need to take care of research projects (which might involve travelling).

Therefore, it is normal that members of her team are active from early morning to late at night. Although a daily schedule is available, it has to be reorganized in many cases as unexpected events are occurring (e.g., an operation takes longer). Observing the everyday work of her team, Katie has learnt that when this happens doctors feel distracted and even might think about possible appointments they have to cancel or reschedule while performing surgery. Furthermore, working late causes that doctors are tired and stressed. This is also worsened by the fact that most staff members live outside the city and have to travel for more than an hours on the average. Therefore, Katie has set up a new policy. In case a doctor finishes work later than 8 pm, the hospital offers free accommodation for the night including the transportation to and from the selected hotel. Furthermore, the hospital offers the doctors to manage their agenda and to inform family and friends about re-scheduling and delays.

Although Katie was confident on the success of the initiative, she observed problems. Managing the transportation and accommodation issue was not trivial because a doctor has to finish the on-going task before he can be asked about his preferences, therefore: (1) secretarial support staff complained about staying longer to take care of this service, (2) the doctor had to wait for the service, (3) different approaches to make a booking caused further delays, (4) spontaneous booking of a room or transportation was problematic, and (5) some doctors rejected to use the provided agenda management services, as they did not want to provide open access to their personal calendar. Katie concluded that a different solution was needed.

3 Analysis of the Current Scenario

The scenario above presents some issues that make the current support for doctors unsatisfactory:

Individuality. Every doctor is an individual with very different preferences, abilities, resources, etc. A one-fits-all solution might not be applicable. Katie is aware of this and, thus, she would like to offer services negotiated on an individual basis.

Privacy. Doctors are reluctant to make their private agenda public at the level required by the novel services offered. They do not want hospital staff to know about their private appointments and only share this information with the other parties involved and (possibly) their family. Therefore, Katie cannot have all the information needed to make the best possible decisions.

Service Heterogeneity. Different hotels use different booking strategies which complicates the booking. Secretaries first have to identify the suitable booking procedure and often have to perform time consuming activities while booking (e.g., re-entering personal information of a doctor).

Lack of Information. The information on which hotels and transportation options are still available for that day is not upfront available to the secretarial staff. They often have to fill in request forms to later find out that no more room is available.

Agility. As a consequence, the envisioned processes are not as agile and flexible as Katie would like them to be. Furthermore, the current solution often results in loosing time and requires additional resources, which negatively affects the hospital.

It is worth to mention that other scenarios could eventually reveal similar problems. For instance, doctors use to work in teams that may be preconfigured (e.g., same speciality) or dynamic (e.g., for a particular surgery). Sharing documents and information through hospital-centric applications may seem useful at a first sight, but may raise similar problems (e.g., privacy of confidential patient data records).

These limitations make Katie wonder about the possibility of alternative scenarios that are able to better exploit current mobile technologies.

4 Envisaged Scenario

Katie consults the software engineering research team from the local university to find out how mobile technologies could support her in finding a solution. The researchers highlight that one possibility to achieve her goal could be to shift the focus from a central, hospital-based perspective, to a distributed, person-based point of view where doctors themselves are the ones who have full responsibility. Provided services would then fit with their own individual needs (also regarding privacy). Together with the researchers, Katie discusses a scenario where personal mobile devices suggest actions to doctors, or even execute them on their behalf. This approach avoids the assignment of new tasks to the hospital administrative staff, and simultaneously simplifies doctors' daily life. Austin, who is one of the most prestigious surgeons in the Feeling Better International Hospital, is the key person within this scenario. He is young, ambitious and loves his job, so he often accepts a certain overload in his daily work. On a particular day, he was expecting to finish at 7.30 pm but an unexpected problem with medical supplies has postponed the start of the last operation of the day (Norman's cardio-surgery) from 5 pm to 8 pm. Katie offered him to delay the operation until tomorrow, but the next day Austin is flying to Brussels for a project meeting early in the morning, so he decided to go ahead.

Luckily, he recently bought a smartphone with access to a novel platform supporting informed decision-making. This smartphone offers a lot of capabilities whilst being quite simple to use. It reacts to changes in the agenda and reschedules appointments accordingly. The following activities happen:

– Katie reschedules Norman's cardio-surgery in the hospital information system to start at 8 pm. This change is propagated to Austin's personal agenda.
– Two events are still scheduled in Austin agenda for after the operation. The first one is "buying a present for his mother's birthday next week". The platform just reallocates this task to another possible day before the birthday.
– The second event is different, a romantic dinner with his friend Angie at 9.30 pm. Since the operation is expected to last 2.5 h, the platform knows that it has to cancel

this appointment (differently from above, the event cannot be rescheduled without interacting with the interested parties). The platform sends Angie a nice apology message, specially designed by Austin in advance.

- The platform also detects the early morning flight to Brussels (leaving at 6 am). Considering Austin's travelling record track, the platform decides to book Austin a room in a hotel near the airport. Since the platform knows that, unless otherwise stated, Austin always drives his own car to the hospital, no taxi is needed.
- Finally, the platform sends Austin an e-mail with the summary of actions. This also includes a booking reference for the hotel and the parking space at the airport.

Once Austin leaves the operating room, he checks his smartphone and reads those messages. He feels reassured that his new device works correctly. He remembers, that after he started to use the novel platform he needed some time to get familiar with the system and also the idea that the platform has access to all his personal data. With the current level of configuration and the history available, he is more than happy with the way it behaves.

Not only Austin is impressed by the mobile platform, also Katie can see that this new approach allows overcoming the issues identified in Sect. 3:

- No other person (e.g., secretary) is needed to take care of individual user preferences. The user-centric system is able to tailor itself to the individual needs of a person. The mobile platform knows a user's preferences and analyses the decisions taken by a user. This allows the platform to make suggestions and to handle situations intelligently, which makes it the ideal companion.
- Advanced privacy mechanisms give Austin full control about privacy relevant data and letting him actively decide which information is shared and with whom. Furthermore, the device automatically identifies certain levels of trust based on Austin's past sharing activities, which it follows when sharing information on Austin's behalf.
- Different services and technical details, this all is transparent for Austin as a user. The new platform takes care of identifying relevant services and presents information in an easy to understand and personalized way.
- This also means that there is no lack of information any longer. As everything is automated, the mobile platform can highlight the availability of rooms and transportation options in real time.
- This finally leads to the envisioned agile process and gives doctors the needed freedom, so that they can focus on work. No additional resources are needed and a certain improvement can be obtained.

5   Software Engineering Challenges

In the following we highlight key challenges towards strengthening user-centrality and enabling a user-driven evolution of software applications. Overcoming these challenges would allow implementing the scenario described in Sect. 4. The relationship between these challenges and the open issues mentioned in Sect. 3 is visualized in Fig. 2.

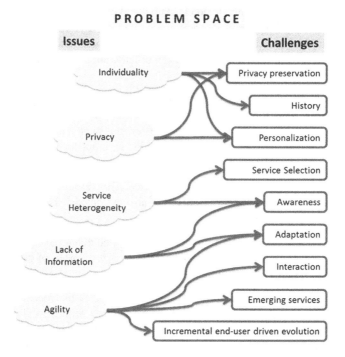

Fig. 2. Issues and associated challenges.

5.1 Strengthening User Centrality

Modern mobile devices, such as smartphones, are equipped with numerous sensors. However, approaches that allow determining a user's context are still limited. Furthermore, services still require the end-user to make a tedious personalization job. The support given by providers to adapt services to the needs of an individual user is quite limited and just includes some basic characteristics (e.g., language selection). These issues limit current services to react based on the given environment and particular user profiles and needs. In our scenario the hotel booking action is an example. Selecting a hotel that fits best may depend on the place of the first morning commitment. As Austin needs to be ready for his 8 am class on a Tuesday, the system will book a room near the university. Current software engineering approaches and tools do not sufficiently support such considerations and the following challenges have been identified:

Privacy Preservation. Success of an IT product heavily relies on respecting privacy. Sensible data must be kept inside the individual's boundary. For example, Austin prefers to keep his friendship with Angie confidential. The communication of information needs to be balanced. While some kind of aggregated, anonymous data sent to the service providers may help them to analyse service usage and improve their products in the future, private data needs to stay under user control.

History. Individuals tend to apply patterns of behaviour. These patterns may be tacit and usually will emerge after some time. For instance, being young and energetic,

Austin does not mind sleeping in hotels paid by the hospital, whilst other doctors (e.g. with children) will prefer to sleep at home and take a taxi to the airport early in morning. Their decisions along time will reflect their preferences. This means that decisions need to be monitored and analysed in order to support decision-making in the future.

Personalization. A selected service furthermore needs to be tailor to individual customer preferences. This for example includes how the service presents its functionalities to the user (the look and feel of the service), but personalization also needs to consider the data that the user is willing to provide as input for the service.

Service Selection. Several services might be available to support a selected task. The service providing the best value needs to be selected. This does not only mean to select the service providing the best performance, but also to consider the costs of a service.

Awareness. Decision-making may be improved by increasing the awareness about the environment. For instance, the platform could be informed about the current location of Austin's car. This could improve decision-making so that the need of calling a taxi for bringing him to the airport is automatically identified.

Adaptation. The increasing availability of information paves the road for better decision-making. The best decision today may not be the best tomorrow. For instance, a hotel, which now has good ratings, might be a bad choice next year. Furthermore, sudden adaptation is required as unexpected events might occur (e.g., bad weather forecast in Brussels) may require an unexpected reaction (e.g., Austin going back to his house for taking his coat). This means that services need to adapt constantly to a changing environment.

Interaction. As part of the individualization aspect, some citizens may rely more than others on technology. Whilst Austin seems to be fully confident in the mobile platform, other doctors who have similar smartphones may choose the "Always Require Confirmation" option. Therefore, we need to be aware of and respect different ways of interacting with a possible solution.

5.2   Enabling User-Driven Evolution

Literature highlights that software must be adapted and enhanced continuously to remain satisfactory [5]. User needs and expectations change over time and services should provide the desired new features. Furthermore, they need to improve in quality. Currently, methods and approaches to identify changing user needs are limited and do not allow to continuously involve end-users in service evolution.

Emerging Services. The dramatic increment of available apps and services requires improved mechanisms to identify interesting functionalities that emerge from providers of any kind. For instance, Austin should be offered new services on transportation. In case Austin is interested to try these services should be automatically integrated into the workflow required. Filtering, recommendations and crowdsourcing become cornerstones of this idea. Individuals may play a part in this scene by publishing (i.e., sharing) their own services thus actively contributing to the service marketplace population.

Incremental End-user Driven Evolution. Functionality provided by a service platform may grow by increments, as an average user needs some time to master a new service. Then new needs may be identified. For instance, Austin may at some time investigate how to use the invoice generation facilities by hotels in order to store a copy of such an invoice in his Dropbox account for his own purposes or post this need to developers if not yet provided.

In the next section we propose a high-level architecture that aims to overcome these challenges.

6 A Platform for Semantic Service Engineering

The envisioned scenario can be generalized in terms of an emerging ecosystem. Citizen using smart devices are the key component. We envision that the mobile device can make suggestion to the user based on analysing existing information. Information can be gathered via the smart environment (environmental data) or services and apps. Communication with other systems and users can furthermore include relevant information. Results of the analysis of the gathered information might also be communicated to other systems and users. A particular example is the communication of feedback to developers in order to ensure continuous service evolution. Figure 3 depicts this ecosystem. Given their current predominance in society, smart mobile devices (smartphones, tablets, etc.) provide all necessary functionalities to help people, e.g. citizens of a smart city, organizing their daily activities and accessing a variety of services through apps. We envision that over time, the appropriate apps are discovered and installed according to the citizen's profile. This profile resides in the citizen's personal cloud that contains all sensible information that needs to be private. Being in the cloud, this information is shared by all mobile devices used by the citizen, thus preventing problems in synchronization of data and profiles. The profile goes beyond the typical concept that is applied for using applications today, we envision a social profile that emerges from past actions and feedback given by the citizen to suggestions that the mobile devices provide over time, which can be analysed by developers and

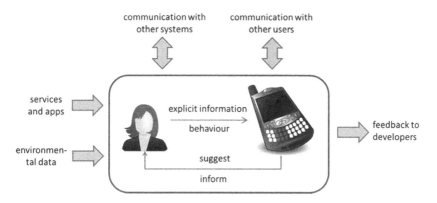

Fig. 3. The emerging ecosystem.

motivate them to evolve the service or app it refers to. The mobile device is tightly connected to the environment, especially to the smart city that surrounds the citizen, and any possible sensor that the citizen may use (e.g., smart clothes for medical monitoring). With all this information and also interoperating with more classical information systems that are of interest for the citizen (e.g., at work), the mobile device may take decisions on the go and inform other individuals about the consequences of these decisions.

Focusing on the logical architectures of the software platform that can enable the described ecosystem, and allow addressing the previously discussed challenges, we can first recognize that the choice of whether to put a decision-making component on-board of the mobile device or in the personal cloud or distributed on both, brings to a family of possible architectures. Figure 4 shows one of these possible architectures, adopting distributed decision-making (i.e., the decision-making component is embedded in the mobile device). Its three main logical components are presented next.

Table 1 at the end of the section shows how the different mentioned platform elements are involved in the software engineering challenges identified in Sect. 5).

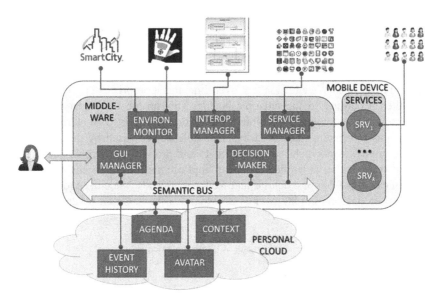

Fig. 4. High-level architecture of a platform for enabling informed decision-making.

6.1   The Personal Cloud

Within the personal cloud component we identify four main resources, each controlled by a specific manager (not shown in the figure):

- *Agenda.* Keeps track of the citizen's daily activities. This agenda needs to be seen as multidimensional, in which the usual time arrangement is just one possible viewpoint; others like location, people met, etc., should be easily retrieved in order to facilitate later management.

- *Context.* Represents the context of the user, continuously updated. Under this context, we may identify the following dimensions: time, location, environment (e.g., low battery), type of activity (e.g., work, leisure, family), user skills (novice, experienced; may be application-dependant), etc.
- *Event History.* Stores the activities of the citizen in the past. In the general case, activities, even if represented in the form of a list (time-ordered), encode complex workflows that represent processes followed by the user.
- *Avatar.* Creates a representation of the citizen that is used for decision-making. This can be done exploiting decision-making algorithms executing in the personal cloud, which, for instance, dynamically rank alternatives (e.g. services, or products) along the user's preferences.

6.2   The Mobile Device

The *mobile device* includes the following elements:

- *GUI Manager.* Intelligent interface of the mobile device with the user, supporting agile composition and personalization.
- *Decision-maker.* This is the real core of the platform. It continuously decides about the next actions to make.
- *Environmental Monitor and Interoperability Manager.* Communicate with the outside world (smart cities, body sensors, information systems, etc.) and also get the relevant environmental information from the mobile device (battery level, etc.).
- *Service Manager.* Discovers and, when appropriate, installs services in the mobile device. This installation includes an initial automatic personalization.
- *Service Space.* Set of services installed on the device, including those modified or defined by the user. Some of them may be used to inform other users affected by decision-making, some others to provide explicit or implicit (i.e., logs of service/ app usage) feedback to service and app developers.

Table 1.   Relating the solution space with the problem space.

		Personal Cloud				Mobile device					Semantic bus
		Agenda	Context	Event history	Avatar	GUI manager	Decision maker	Environ. monitor	Service manager	Service space	Semantic bus
	Privacy preservation	+			+	+				+	+
	History	+		+		+			+		
	Personalization	+		+	+	+			+		
	Service selection			+	+	+	+	+	+		
	Awareness	+	+			+	+	+			
	Adaptation	+	+	+		+			+		
	Interaction				+	+					
	Emerging services	+	+	+		+			+	+	+
	Incremental evolution			+		+			+		+

6.3   The Semantic Bus

The semantic bus component is a classical interoperability bus for event-driven communication, with the particularity that events have a high semantic content. It implements a publisher-observer pattern.

7   The Way Ahead

The realization and adoption of the envisaged platform, and the need to enable seamless evolution of services and applications in the emerging ecosystem, ask for advances in software engineering research, which may also take advantages of results and techniques from different research fields. In this section we enumerate emerging synergies and promising research lines as a preliminary step towards setting up a research agenda.

Semantic Interoperability. In order to allow interoperability among all the platform components and the external services, ontologies are needed to represent the information that flows around according to some agreed conceptual reference framework [28]. General ontologies for time, localization, etc., from organizations like W3C, could be adopted to serve as lingua-franca for the platform. Data produced and consumed by services should be compliant to these ontologies in order to allow interconnection through the platform.

Knowledge Representation and Reasoning Techniques. In order to build an accurate and trustable knowledge base and infer the behaviour that better matches users' expectations, AI techniques for knowledge representation and automated reasoning are promising. Recommender systems [2] may provide (even automatically execute) recommendations on which services to apply; some applications in the marketing context, e.g. (de Bruin et al., 2008), have explored this particular aspect. Case-based reasoning [1] may be useful to improve the knowledge and reasoning capabilities of individual users case by case. More recently, the use of ontology in combination with statistical models is proposed to provide models of human behaviours in a given context [8].

Service Solutions. A great deal of existing proposals in the service-oriented computing field clearly transfers into our envisaged platform. Approaches for service discovery [23], service composition [24] (in particular using AI techniques [4]) and service adaptation [9] are of application to satisfy some of the envisaged challenges.

Social Collaboration. The active participation of a large number of people to perform particular tasks or solve problems, as emerging in the so called social computing [30], is of great interest for our work, and has been pointed out as an opportunity to exploit in different software engineering processes, from requirements engineering to software testing. Lim and Finkelstein [17] have investigated first approaches towards large-scale requirements elicitation using social networks. These approaches complement classical market-driven requirements elicitation methods [14]. The potential of social collaboration (via social network platform), to tackle the issue of "unknown unknown" requirements is pointed out also in [27]. Crowdsourcing for addressing the Oracle problem in software testing has been also recently investigated [21]. Furthermore, Onnela and Reed-Tsochase [20] provide first insights on social influence within social networks.

Participatory Sensing. Gathering contextual information in order to allow services to adapt to a particular user context is a key aim of our work. Research on participatory sensing [7] focuses on communities that use sensors as provided by mobile devices to retrieve information about the environment.

Change Management. Different sources of change need to be identified, classified and analysed. Research on self-adaptive software services focus on defining solutions to managing dynamic changes in the environment, mainly by adopting a monitor-eval-adapt control loop [9]. Most of the proposed approaches focus on design-time methods, while more recent work aim at equipping service-based systems with mechanisms for managing changes of user requirements and preferences at run-time, e.g. [22]. In this light, also traditional software evolution approaches require rethinking. Service providers need to be aware not just of new needs coming from the potential customers but also new opportunities coming from other services and applications. To this end, very agile change management processes need to be designed. The concept of "fluidity of design" [13] should be accommodated somehow in these processes. One crucial question here is timing: when is the right moment to update the service, for which selected requirements?

Personal and Social Values. Beyond pure technological knowledge, personal and social factors need to be considered in this kind of solutions. Long ago Goguen [10] already recognized this link in requirements engineering. The key value of requirements in this context was also recently highlighted by Milne and Maiden [19] who demonstrated that requirements are socially constructed in a political context. This means that decision-making needs to consider all type of factors surrounding individuals. Towards this objective, studies in the area of social science, which are based on empirical survey techniques conducted on large user population can contribute with statistically relevant data about the relationship between lifestyle traits, social influence, people's attitudes towards mobile innovations and the adoption of various types of mobile services [6]. Indeed, our vision includes the idea that people should benefit individually from the proposed solution, in harmony with the goals of a sustainable society, such thoughtful use of resources and energy.

Feedback/Communication Channels. Continuous feedback on services is needed in order to ensure long-term user satisfaction. Approaches which allow end-user to give feedback on current context-aware services [25] and which allow them to document their ideas on services in situ [26] build a basis to satisfy some of the depicted issues.

Process Mining. The fact that the proposed platform includes an activity history in the form of list makes process mining [29] an interesting research field. In other words, the activity history may be considered as a personal process log in which existing techniques may be assessed and applied if adequate.

Table 2 sketches an overview on the relationships we can see so far between these research lines and the challenges, and solution elements above discussed.

8   Related Work

In this paper we have proposed a novel approach to close the gap among regular citizens and software services available in mobile technologies. We aim at simplifying the interaction of multiple internet services by means of a dedicated platform that is able to make decisions autonomously and also to learn from past decisions from the user. Our vision relies on several existing works both in the form of scientific contributions and existing technologies that we survey below.

Table 2. Research lines vs. solution elements they can contribute for.

		SOLUTION SPACE		
		Personal Cloud	Mobile device	Semantic bus
	Semantic interoperability		+	+
	Knowledge represen-tation and reasoning	+	+	
	Service solutions	+	+	
	Social collaboration	+	+	
	Participatory sensing		+	
	Change management		+	
	Personal and social values	+		
	Feedback/Communi-cation channels		+	+
	Process mining	+	+	

(left vertical label: RESEARCH LINES)

The IFTTT Project (https://ifttt.com/) supports user-designed service composition. For example, a user can create a rule that is triggered when he uploads an image to Instagram that saves this image in his Dropbox account. Such rules (called recipes), can be shared among users or created in a personalised basis. A similar approach is followed by the SATIN project (http://www.satinproject.eu/mission). Although the system is not designed to learn from the user behavior, it opens the path to communication between applications. Such a technology could be integrated into the GUI manager with the purpose of supporting the user to configure his personalized workflows.

Similarly, the on{X} project (https://www.onx.ms/#!landingPage) lets the user control and extend the capabilities of his Android smartphone using a JavaScript API. on{X} provides an API that allows the device to detect several user events, as for example the speed of movement or the arrival to the office. Applications can use this API to react to these events. This type of technology can be integrated in the environment monitor e.g. to update doctors' context when they park the car at the hospital.

Also several applied research projects tackle related issues. The PERSIST project (http://www.ict-persist.eu/) envisions a Personal Smart Space (PSS) that is associated with the personal devices carried by the user and which follows him, providing uninterrupted context-aware pervasiveness. This concept of PSS could be the basis of the avatar component in our platform. The SOCITIES project (http://www.ict-societies.eu/)

aims at improving on-line community services, creating new ways of communicating, working and socialising. In their own words, "the vision of SOCITIES is to develop a complete integrated Community Smart Space, which extends pervasive systems beyond the individual to dynamic communities of users".

MUSIC (http://ist-music.berlios.de/site) developed an open framework for the development and deployment of context aware and self-adaptive mobile applications targeted for ubiquitous and service oriented environments. The framework offers a distributed context sensing and management system and supports self-adapting distributed mobile services collaborating in dynamically adapting ensembles. With the help of MUSIC, a developer can implement and deploy a custom context sensor specific to a given device (e.g. a sensor for handling compass data). Still, the framework requires significant effort and a case-by-case study to integrate new services into the user environment.

Some platforms start to be also available in mobile infrastructure. BLOCCO [12] is a service linking system available in Android platform that enables the building of new application mash-ups by linking other existing Android applications. This was delivered in the form of an Android application. The main goal of the project was to enable users to combine functionalities provided by different applications and to implement automatic execution of applications according to user configuration. In addition, various events happening in one application could be detected and they could be used to trigger execution of other services, using parameter passing and processing techniques. Similar to IFTTT, BLOCCO focused on constant rules for end-user configuration and enabled end-users to build new applications according to their specific needs, in a user-centred fashion.

Finally, some academic works have already explored similar features or functionalities. An event-driven approach for business process modeling [3] was introduced to enhance agility by means of learning rules between events and actions. Similarly, the integration of adaptive process management and case handling was used to create a more flexible and user-friendly approach to process management [11]. Another noteworthy work [18] studies end-user service composition from the perspective of users. With this goal, the authors review users' perceptions, intuitions and requirements regarding bridging different services. Finally, Semantic Web Pipes [16] is a mechanism that supports fast implementation of semantic data mash-ups while preserving abstraction, encapsulation, component-orientation, code re-usability and maintainability.

9   Conclusions

In this paper we have identified challenges for software engineering based on an envisioned example focusing on decision-making support of the future. Furthermore we have presented a first solution idea of a platform which could provide the envisioned decision support. However, in order to achieve this vision several advances regarding software engineering methods and tools are required. We discuss an initial research agenda where we have reflected on the different research lines that may contribute to the realization of our vision.

Whilst certainly there is a long path to achieve the scenario presented in Sect. 4, we have tried to show that a lot of work is already there and can be used as the baseline for building such a platform. Still, many fundamental questions need to be addressed. For instance, recent findings dispute the idea that people are rational decision-makers [15]. This opens an interesting debate: is it cost-effective to try to embody all possible preferences and attitudes of citizens in a computational form? Answers to this kind of fundamental questions allow us envisaging new emerging interdisciplinary research lines.

Acknowledgements. This work has been supported by the Spanish project TIN2010-19130-C02-01.

References

1. Aamodt, A., Plaza, E.: Case-based reasoning: foundational issues, methodological variations, and system approaches. AI Commun. **7**(1), 39–59 (1994)
2. Adomavicius, G., Tuzhilin, A.: Toward the next generation of recommender systems: a survey of the state-of-the-art and possible extensions. IEEE Trans. Knowl. Data Eng. **17**(6), 734–749 (2005)
3. Alexopoulou, N., Nikolaidou, M., Chamodrakas, Y., Martakos, D.: Enabling on-the-fly business process composition through an event-based approach. In: HICSS 2008 – Proceedings of 41st Hawaii International Conference on System Sciences. IEEE Press (2008)
4. Beauche, S., Poizat, P.: Automated service composition with adaptive planning. In: Bouguettaya, A., Krueger, I., Margaria, T. (eds.) ICSOC 2008. LNCS, vol. 5364, pp. 530–537. Springer, Heidelberg (2008)
5. Bennett, K.H., Rajlich, V.T.: Software maintenance and evolution: a roadmap. In: ICSE 2000 – Proceedings of Conference on The Future of Software Engineering. ACM Press 2000
6. Bouwman, H., López-Nicolás, C., Molina-Castillo, F.J., van Hattum, P.: Consumer lifestyles: alternative adoption patterns for advanced mobile services. IJMC **10**(2), 169–189 (2012)
7. Burke, J., Estrin, D., Hansen, M., Parker, A., Ramanathan, N., Reddy, S., Srivastava, M.B.: Participatory sensing. In: WSW 2006 – Proceedings of Workshop on World-Sensor-Web: Mobile Device Centric Sensor Networks and Applications (2006)
8. Codescu, M., Horsinka, G., Kutz, O., Mossakowski, T., Rau, R.: Osmonto - an ontology of openstreetmap tags. In: State of the map Europe (SOTM-EU) (2011)
9. Di Nitto, E., Ghezzi, C., Metzger, A., Papazoglou, M., Pohl, K.: A journey to highly dynamic, self-adaptive service-based applications. Autom. Softw. Eng. **15**, 313–341 (2008)
10. Goguen, J.: Requirements engineering as the reconciliation of social and technical issues. In: Goguen, J., Jirotka, M. (eds.) Requirements Engineering: Social and Technical Issues. Academic Press Professional, San Diego (1994)
11. Gunther, C., Reichert, M., van der Aalst, W.: Supporting flexible processes with adaptive workflow and case handling. In: WETICE 2008 – Proceedings of Workshops on Enabling Technologies: Infrastructure for Collaborative Enterprises. IEEE Press (2008)
12. Hagino, H., Fujii, K., Murakami, J., Hara, M.: The BLOCCO service linking system, enabling combination of services through user configuration. NTT DOCOMO Tech. J. **12** (4), 30–37 (2011)

13. Jarke, M., Loucopoulos, P., Lyytinen, K., Mylopoulos, J., Robinson, W.: The brave new world of design requirements. Inf. Syst. J. **36**, 992–1008 (2011)
14. Karlsson, L., Dahlstedt, A.G., Regnell, B., och Dag, J.N., Persson, A.: Requirements engineering challenges in market-driven software development - an interview study with practitioners. Inf. Syst. Technol. **49**(6), 588–604 (2007)
15. Lehrer, J.: How we Decide. Houghton Mifflin Harcourt, Boston (2009)
16. Le-Phuoc, D., Polleres, A., Hauswirth, M., Tummarello, G., Morbidoni, C.: Rapid prototyping of semantic mash-ups through semantic web pipes. In: WWW 2009 – Proceedings of International World Wide Web Conference 2009. ACM Press (2009)
17. Lim, S.L., Finkelstein, A.: StakeRare: using social networks and collaborative filtering for large-scale requirements elicitation. IEEE Trans. Softw. Eng. **38**(3), 707–735 (2012)
18. Mehandjiev, N., Namoune, A., Wajid, U., Macaulay, L., Sutcliffe, A.: End user service composition. In: WWW 2009 – Proceedings of International World Wide Web Conference 2009. ACM Press (2009)
19. Milne, A., Maiden, N.: Power and politics in requirements engineering: a proposed research agenda. In: RE 2011 – Proceedings of the 19th IEEE International Requirements Engineering Conference (2011)
20. Onnela, J.-P., Reed-Tsochase, F.: Spontaneous emergence of social influence in online systems. Proc. Nat. Acad. Sci. U.S.A. **107**(43), 18375–18380 (2010)
21. Pastore, F., Mariani, L., Gordon F.: Crowdoracles: can the crowd solve the oracle problem. In: International Conference on Software Testing, Verification and Validation (ICST) (2013)
22. Qureshi, N.A., Perini, A.: Requirements engineering for adaptive service based applications. In: Proceedings of the 18th IEEE International Requirements Engineering Conference, pp. 108–111 (2010)
23. Ran, S.: A model for web services discovery with QoS. ACM SIGecom Exch. **4**(1), 1–10 (2003)
24. Rao, J., Su, X.: A Survey of automated web service composition methods. In: Cardoso, J., Sheth, A.P. (eds.) SWSWPC 2004. LNCS, vol. 3387, pp. 43–54. Springer, Heidelberg (2005)
25. Schneider, K., Meyer, S., Peters, M., Schliephacke, F., Mörschbach, J., Aguirre, L.: Feedback in context: supporting the evolution of IT-ecosystems. In: Ali Babar, M., Vierimaa, M., Oivo, M. (eds.) PROFES 2010. LNCS, vol. 6156, pp. 191–205. Springer, Heidelberg (2010)
26. Seyff, N., Graf, F., Maiden, N.A.M.: Using mobile RE tools to give end-users their own voice. In: RE 2010 – Proceedings of the 19th International Requirements Engineering Conference (2010)
27. Sutcliffe, A., Sawyer, P.: Requirements elicitation: towards the unknown unknowns. In: RE 2013 – Proceedings of the 21th International IEEE Requirements Engineering Conference (2013)
28. Uschold, M., Gruninger, M.: Ontologies: Principles, Methods and Applications. Knowl. Eng. Rev. **11**(2), 93–136 (1996). Cambridge University Press
29. van der Aalst, M.P.: Process Mining - Discovery, Conformance and Enhancement of Business Processes, pp. I–XVI, 1–352. Springer, Berlin (2011). (ISBN 978-3-642-19344-6)
30. Wang, F.-Y., Carley, K.M., Zeng, D., Mao, W.: Social computing: from social informatics to social intelligence. IEEE Intell. Syst. **22**(2), 79–83 (2007)
31. West, D.: How mobile devices are transforming healthcare. Issues Technol. Innov. **18**, 1–14 (2012)

Early Verification and Validation According to ISO 26262 by Combining Fault Injection and Mutation Testing

Rakesh Rana[1]([✉]), Miroslaw Staron[1], Christian Berger[1], Jörgen Hansson[1], Martin Nilsson[2], and Fredrik Törner[2]

[1] Computer Science and Engineering, Chalmers/University of Gothenburg, Gothenburg, Sweden
rakesh.rana@gu.se
[2] Volvo Car Corporation, Göteborg, Sweden

Abstract. Today software is core part of modern automobiles. The amount, complexity and importance of software components within Electrical/Electronics (E/E) systems of modern cars is only increasing with time. Several automotive functions carrying software provide or interact with safety critical systems such as systems steering and braking and thus assuring functional safety for such systems is of high importance. Requirements for the safety assurance are specified partially by such functional safety standards as ISO 26262. The standard provides the framework and guidelines for the development of hardware and software for components deemed to be safety critical. In this chapter we argue that traditional approaches for safety assurance such as fault injection and mutation testing can be adapted and applied to functional models to enable early verification and validation according to the requirements of ISO 26262. We show how to use fault injection in combination with mutation based testing to identify defects early in the development process - both theoretically and on a case of self-driving miniature vehicles. The argument is grounded upon the current best practices within the industry, a study of ISO 26262 standard, and academic and industrial case studies using fault injection and mutation based testing applied to the functional model level. In this paper we also provide the initial validation of this approach using software of a self-driving miniature vehicle.

Keywords: Fault injection · Mutation testing · ISO 26262 · Simulink · Model based development · Automotive domain · Safety critical software

1 Introduction

Nowadays, a typical premium car has up to 70 ECUs, which are connected by several system buses to realize over 2,000 functions [1]. As around 90 % of all innovations today are driven by electronics and software the complexity of cars embedded software is expected to grow. The growth is fuelled by cars beginning

© Springer-Verlag Berlin Heidelberg 2014
J. Cordeiro and M. van Sinderen (Eds.): ICSOFT 2013, CCIS 457, pp. 164–179, 2014.
DOI: 10.1007/978-3-662-44920-2_11

to act more proactively and more assistive to its drivers, which requires software to interact with hardware more efficiently and making more decisions automatically (e.g. collision avoidance by braking, brake-by-wire or similar functions). In total with about 100 million lines of code (SLOC), premium segment vehicles carry more software code than in modern fighter jets and airliners [2]. Software for custom functionality in modern cars is usually developed by multiple suppliers although it is designed by a single OEM (Original Equipment Manufacturer) like Volvo Cars. The distributed development and use of standards like AUTOSAR aims to facilitate reuse of software and hardware components between different vehicle platforms, OEMs and suppliers [3]. However, testing of such systems is more complex and today testing of software generally accounts for almost 50 % of overall development costs [4].

ISO-26262 in automotive domain poses stringent requirements for development of safety critical applications and in particular on the testing processes for this software. These requirements are intended to increase the safety of modern cars, although they also increase the cost of modern cars with complex software functions influencing safety or car passengers.

The position for which we argue in this paper is that *efficient verification and validation of safety functions requires combining Model Based Development (MBD) with fault injection into models with mutation testing*. This position is based on the studies of the ISO 26262 standard (mainly Chap. 6 that describes requirements on software development but also Chap. 4, which poses requirements on product development [5]). It is also based on previous case studies of the impact of late defects on the software development practices in the automotive section [6].

The requirements from the ISO 26262 standard on using fault injection techniques is challenging since it relates to the development of complete functions rather than components of sub-components of software. The current situation in the automotive sector is that fault injection is used, but it is used at the level of one electronic component (ECU) or one software system, rarely at the function level [7,8].

The current state of art testing is not enough for detecting safety defects early in the automotive software development process since fault injection is done late in the development (when ECUs are being developed), which usually makes the detection of specification-related defects difficult and costly [6]. This detection should be done in the model level when the ECUs functionality is still under design and thus, it is relatively cheap to redesign. The evidence from literature on successful use of fault injection shows that the technique indeed is efficient in finding dependability problems of hardware and software systems when applied to computer systems [9]. To be able to increase the effectiveness of the fault injection strategies and identify whether the faults should be injected at the model, software or ECU level - mutation testing should be applied to verify the adequacy of test cases. And finally we need to assess how to combine these approaches and apply them at the model level that will enhance our ability to detect safety related defects right at the design stage.

In this paper we provide a roadmap, which shows how to introduce fault injection and mutation testing to modelling of automotive software in order to avoid costly defects and increase the safety of modern and future cars. This paper is the extended version of our previous work [10] where we presented the theoretical approach. In this paper we include a validation of this framework on a set of software components of self-driving miniature vehicles. The system used for initial validation is developed using a code-centric approach which makes the framework more generic as the initial evaluation in [10] was conducted on model-based development.

The remaining of the paper is structured as follows: In the next Sect. 2 we provide an overview of software development in automotive domain and associated concepts. This is followed by brief discussion on related work in Sect. 3 and our position is presented and discussed in Sect. 4. Section 5 presents the initial validation case for the framework and Sect. 6 provides conclusions.

2   Background

In this section we take a brief overview on the current state of automotive software development process and environment, how safety is important in safety critical applications and overview of theoretical background on fault injection techniques and mutation testing.

2.1   Automotive Software Development and ISO 26262

Various software functions/applications developed within the automotive industry today are classed as safety critical for example Volvo's City Safety consists of components that are safety critical (Fig. 1).

Broy [1] gives examples of functions/areas within automotive domain of recent development which includes crash prevention, crash safety, advanced energy management, adaptable man-machine interface, advanced driver assistance, programmable car, car networking etc., much of these fall within the safety critical functionality and demands high quality and reliability. Also a number of on-going projects are directed towards the goal of self-driving cars.

Software development in automotive sector in general follows the 'V' process, where OEMs take the responsibility of requirement specification, system design, and integration/acceptance test. This is followed by the suppliers, where the actual code that runs on ECUs is developed. Although the code is tested at the supplier level (mainly unit testing), the OEMs are responsible for the final integration, system and acceptance testing to ensure that the given implementation of a software (SW) meets its intended functional and safety goals/demands.

In this model of software/product development (see Fig. 2) testing is usually concentrated in the late stages of development, which also implies that most of the defects are discovered late in the development process. In a recent study using real defect data from an automotive software project from the industry showed that late detection of defects is still a relevant problem and challenge yet

Fig. 1. Volvo Cars city safety function, image provided by Volvo Car Corporation.

to overcome [6]. The defect inflow profile presented in this study is presented in Fig. 3 for reference, which exhibits a clear peak in number of open defects in the late stages of function development/testing.

Testing the software is an important tool of ensuring correct functionality and reliability of systems but it is also a very resource intensive activity accounting for up to 50 % of total software development costs [11] and even more for safety/mission critical software systems. Thus having a good testing strategy is critical for any industry with high software development costs. It has also been shown that most of the defects detected during testing do not depend on actual implementation of code, about 50 % of defects detected during testing in

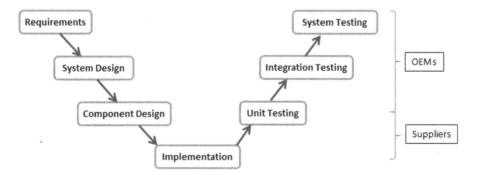

Fig. 2. The V-model in the automotive industry with distinction between the OEM and supplier contributions.

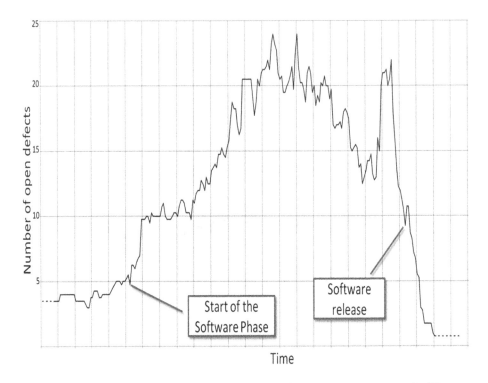

Fig. 3. Defect inflow profile for automotive software project, as given in [6].

the study by Megen and Meyerhoff [12] were found during the test preparation, an activity independent of the executable code. And since automotive sector has already widely adopted MBD for the software development of embedded systems, a high potential exists for using the behavioural modes developed at the early stages of software development for performing some of the effort spent on V&V (Verification & Validation). Early V&V by helping to detect defects early will potentially save significant amount of cost for the projects.

2.2 ISO 26262

ISO/IEC 26262 is a standard describing safety requirements. It is applied to safety-related systems that include one or more electrical and/or electronic (E/E) systems. The overview of safety case and argumentation is represented in Fig. 4.

Written specifically for automotive domain, the ISO-26262 standard is adapted for the V-model of product development corresponding to the current practice in the industry. The guidelines are laid out for system design, hardware and software design and development and integration of components to realize the full product. ISO-26262 includes specifications for MBD and provides recommendations for using fault injection techniques for hardware integration and testing, software unit testing, software integration testing, hardware-software

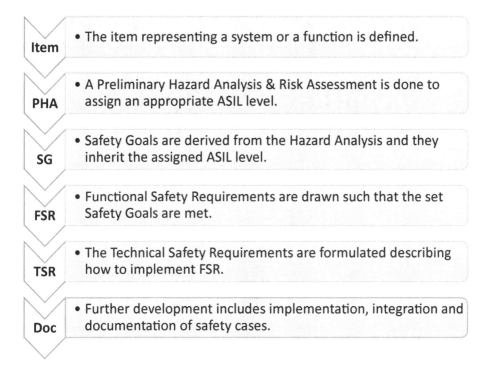

Fig. 4. Overview of ISO-26262 safety case & argumentation process.

integration testing, system integration testing and vehicle integration testing. Although the functional safety standard specifies clearly the recommendations for using fault injection during various stages of testing but does not recommend anything with respect to using mutation testing. This also reflects the current standard practice within the automotive industry where mutation testing is not widely adopted yet.

2.3 Fault Injection

Fault injection techniques are widely used for experimental dependability evaluation. Although these techniques have been used more widely for assessing the hardware/ prototypes, the techniques are now about to be applied at behavioural models of software systems [13], thus enabling early verification of intended functionality as well as enhancing communication between different stakeholders. Fault injection techniques applied at models level offer distinct advantages especially in an industry using MBD, but use of these techniques at model level in automotive industry is currently at its infancy. Figure 5 shows a mind map of classification of fault injection techniques based on how the technique is implemented; some of the tools which are developed based on given approach are also listed for reference. For a good overview of fault injection techniques readers are referred to [9,14].

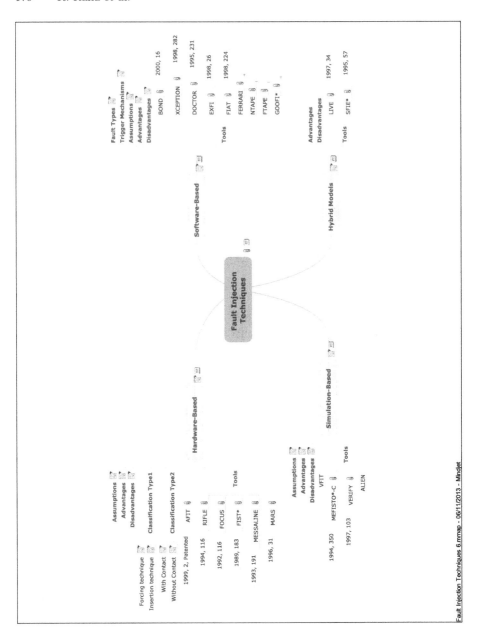

Fig. 5. Common classification of fault injection techniques and implementation tools, description available in [9,14].

2.4 Mutation Testing

Mutation testing is technique for assessing the adequacy of given test suite/set of test cases. Mutation testing includes injection of systematic, repeatable seeding of faults in large number thus generating number of copies of original software artefacts with artificial fault infestation (called a mutant). And on the basis of what percentage of these mutations are detected by the given test cases/suite gives a metrics (called "mutation adequacy score" [15]) which can be used for measuring the effectiveness of given test suite. Faults for mutation testing approach can be either hand written or auto-generated variants of original code. The effectiveness of this approach in mimicking the real faults has also been established [16] i.e. mutants do reflect characteristics of real faults. Mutation theory is based on two fundamental hypotheses namely Competent Programmer Hypothesis (CPH) and the Coupling Effect, both introduced by DeMillo et al. [17]. CPH at its core reflects the assumption that programmers are competent in their job and thus would develop programme close to correct version while coupling effect hypothesis according to Offutt is "Complex mutants are coupled to simple mutants in such a way that a test data set that detects all simple faults in a program will detect a high percentage of the complex defects" [18].

3 Related Work

A number of European Union sponsored projects have within the area of embedded software development and safety critical systems have looked at and developed techniques to effectively use fault injection for safe and reliable software development. The examples include the ESACS [19] (Enhanced Safety Assessment for Complex Systems), the ISAAC [20] (Improvement of Safety Activities on Aeronautical Complex systems). These projects have used the SCADE (Safety-Critical Application Development Environment) modelling environment to simulate hardware failure scenarios to identify fault combinations that lead to safety case violations.

A model-implemented fault injection plug-in to SCADE called FISCADE is introduced in [21] which utilizes approach similar to mutation based testing and replaces the original model operators by equivalent fault injection nodes. The derived models are then used to inject the fault during execution and log the results which are analysed later. Dependability evaluation of automotive functions using model based software implemented fault injection techniques have also been studied in [22].

A generic tool capable of injecting various types of faults on the behavioural or functional Simulink models is also developed and introduced [13]. The tool called MODIFI (or MODel-Implemented Fault Injection tool) can be sued to inject single or multiple point faults on behavioural models, which can be used to study the effectiveness/properties of fault tolerant system and identify the faults leading to failure by studying the fault propagation properties of the models.

Another work [23] with its root in the European CESAR (Cost-efficient methods and processes for safety relevant embedded systems) project provides a good

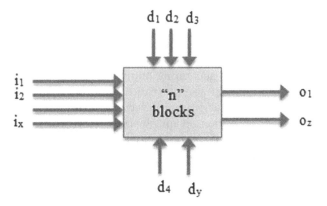

Fig. 6. MBD based representation of a general system with inputs, outputs and dependencies.

theoretical overview of how fault and mutation based test coverage can be used for automated test case generation for Simulink models. We provide a practical framework on how fault injection combined with mutation testing within an MDB environment can be used in the industry. And how will this practice enhance the verification and validation of software under development, its functional validation that would generates statistics for the effective argumentation of ISO 26262 compliance.

4   Framework for Early Verification and Validation According to ISO 26262

We contend that fault injection can be effectively used at the model level to verify and validate the attainment or violation of safety goals. By applying mutation testing approach at the model level enough statistical evidence will be provided for the coverage needed for argumentation of fulfilment of safety goals as per the ISO26262 safety standard requirements.

A major challenge in successful argumentation of ISO-26262 compliance is to provide statistical evidence that Safety Goals (SGs) would not be violated during operation and doing this within reasonable testing efforts.

If we are able to differentiate early between defects that will or not cause the violation of SGs, the amount of testing required will be manageable. With MBD the testing for functionality under these defect conditions could be modelled using fault injection techniques, while the possibility of implementation bugs in the actual code can be checked using the mutation testing approach. The framework on how this could be achieved in practice is as follows:

As illustrated in Fig. 6, a given system/function generally has following common features (in context of model based development): firstly it will have x inputs $(i_{1,2,...x})$; it would have dependencies to other y components/functions $(d_{1,2,...y})$;

it will have z outputs $(o_{1,2,...z})$; and it will have a number of sub-units/modules within it that implements the intended functionality, let us assume that this part contains n basic blocks in the modelling environment corresponding to n statements for a hand written code. To verify and validate the correct functionality and ISO 26262 compliance of this generic function using fault and mutation testing approach we can follow the steps as:

- Assign or define the Functional Safety Requirements (FSRs) and Technical Safety Requirements (TSRs) for the z outputs of the given system/function in accordance to ISO 26262.
- Use fault injection technique to inject common occurring defects and other theoretically possible fault conditions at the x inputs.
- By studying the fault propagation of different injected faults at inputs and their effect on outputs, the individual faults and combinations of it that violate the FSRs for given system can be noted.
- Steps (b) & (c) should also be done to test and validate the given system/function dependencies on other functions/components.
- Mutation approach is then used to inject faults (or cause mutations) to the n basic blocks of given functional model and assess the detection effectiveness of test suite/cases for possible implementation bugs.
- The mutants which are not killed by given set of test cases/suits are examined for their effect on given functions FSRs, if the given mutation violates the SGs/FSRs then a suitable test case will be created to detect/kill such mutants i.e. detect such bugs in actual code.

Thus by following the above mentioned steps we not only ensure that the given function works as intended, does not violate the SGs and FSR/TSRs under faulty inputs and/or due to dependencies on other functions, but we can also identify possible implementation defects using the mutation approach and ensure that we have test cases ready to catch such faults that can potentially violate the SGs/TSRs even before the code is implemented/generated.

Further to make this framework/approach more effective in industrial practice we identify some best practices that will have positive impact on detecting defects early in the development process and thus have effective V&V of ISO26262.

- Model evolution corresponding to different levels of software/product development.
- Specification and testing for SGs, FSRs and TSRs on the behavioural models.
- Identification of different types of defects/types of faults and at what stage they could be modelled/injected at models to ensure that models are build robust right from the start instead of adding fault tolerance in later stages of development.

5   Case Study: Validation

In this section we present the validation of proposed framework on a set of components for self-driving miniature vehicles. The software for the miniature

Fig. 7. Self-driving miniature vehicle [25].

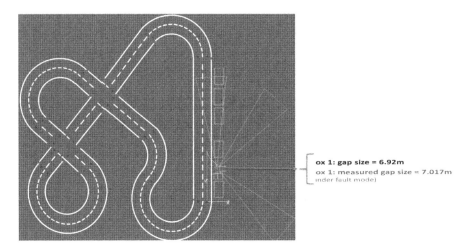

Fig. 8. Test track for the experiment with parking gap from our simulation environment.

vehicles is build using similar methods and tools as professional software in the automotive industry, although on a smaller scale. In the validation we use the self-parking function of a self-driving miniature vehicle [24]. The architecture of the software is described in detail in [25] and one of our miniature vehicles using the self-driving vehicle software and a scenario for a sideways parking realized in our simulation environment are illustrated in Figs. 7 and 8. The miniature vehicles are in the scale 1:10 compared to the normal cars.

For understanding the initial validation of this framework it is sufficient to note that the functionality we are dealing with is self-parking for on a sideways parking strip. The self-parking algorithm expects a gap size of at least 7 m to park in one turn without using an additional correction trajectory. This scenario is presented in Fig. 8.

We applied the framework for early verification and validation following the steps given in Sect. 4 as follows:

- Assign FSR/TSR: An example of obvious functional safety requirement (FSR) for self-parking functionality is parking without hitting any other object. The corresponding technical safety requirement (TSR) can thus be parking only when gap size exceeds 7 m (minimum gap size requirement).
- Using fault injection to simulate common fault scenario: A fault scenario is created by injecting a fault in the returned value for the travelled path by adding an error value of maximum 3.4 % for the relatively travelled path increment. Thus, the size for measured gaps (due to faulty sensor input) increases for example by 9.7 cm to 7.01678 m.
- Identify fault scenarios leading to FSR/TSR violations: Since in the experiment with fault injection, the parking algorithm depends on the travelled path; thus the algorithm parks the car in the lower gap which leads to a safety case violation because the cars collides with the obstacle at the rear side.
- Repeat steps (b) & (c) for all inputs: For this experiment, we focused on the fault injection for a single signal.
- Cause mutations: Single point mutations are caused by changing the logical operators in the self-parking function code, the standard test protocol to test the expected functionality was then applied to evaluate the generated mutants.
- Examine mutants & create new test cases: The mutants and the results whether they were successfully detected are provided in Table 1. In this simple case itself with only 24 mutations, to our surprise two mutations produced unexpected results and violated the assigned FSR. While previously the test protocol has been deemed being sufficient for this function, the experiment clearly demonstrated the need for adding further test cases to reliably spot these failures and to detect possible faults leading to FSR violations.

5.1   Lessons Learned

The initial validation experiment presented in this section for the proposed framework is the first step towards a complete validation of this framework in an industrial setting. Although the framework is focused on using fault injection and mutation testing at functional model level in model-based development to shift some of the verification and validation efforts to early stages of development, the example here demonstrated its applicability of given framework in a code-centric development environment as well.

The experiments using the software of a miniature vehicle provided a proof-of-concept for the framework and provide a frame of reference with respect to

Table 1. Mutation testing output, case with and without fault mode scenario.

ID	Mutant	Change description	Test case result using regular vehicle simulation	Test case result using vehicle simulation with fault injection
1	Unmodified	Original self-parking algorithm	Passed as expected	Failed as not expected, vehicle took first gap, collided (expected: robust algorithm dealing with varying travelled distance data)
2	68	Changed == to >	Failed as expected, vehicle did not start	Failed as expected, vehicle did not start
3	73	Changed first > to ==	Failed as expected, vehicle started hardly noticeable (v < 0.009m/s)	Failed as expected, vehicle started hardly noticeable (v < 0.009m/s)
4	73	Changed && to ||	Failed as expected, vehicle moved forwards slightly and pull back while turning to left	Failed as expected, vehicle moved forwards slightly and pull back while turning to left
5	73	Changed second < to >	Failed as expected, vehicle moved to the end of the second parking spot but did not start parking	Failed as expected, vehicle moved to the end of the first parking spot but did not start parking
6	79	Changed first >= to <=	Failed as expected, vehicle did not start	Failed as expected, vehicle did not start
7	79	Changed && to ||	Failed as expected, vehicle moved backwards while turning to left	Failed as expected, vehicle moved backwards while turning to left
8	73	Changed second < to >	Failed as expected, vehicle moved to the end of the second parking spot but did not start parking	Failed as expected, vehicle moved to the end of the first parking spot but did not start parking
9	85	Changed first >= to <=	Failed as expected, vehicle moved backwards while turning to right	Failed as expected, vehicle moved backwards while turning to right
10	85	Changed && to ||	Failed as expected, vehicle moved backwards while turning first to right and then to left (S-shaped)	Failed as expected, vehicle moved backwards while turning first to right and then to left (S-shaped)
11	85	Changed second < to >	Failed as expected, vehicle moved to the end of the second parking spot but did not start parking	Failed as expected, vehicle moved to the end of the first parking spot but did not start parking
12	91	Changed first >= to <=	Failed as expected, vehicle moved backwards while turning to left	Failed as expected, vehicle moved backwards while turning to left
13	91	Changed && to ||	Failed as expected, vehicle moved backwards while turning to left	Failed as expected, vehicle moved backwards while turning to left
14	91	Changed second < to >	Failed as expected, vehicle moved to the end of the second parking spot, started parking, but stopped after the first right turn	Failed as expected, vehicle moved to the end of the first parking spot, started parking, but stopped after the first right turn
15	97	Changed >= to <=	Failed as expected, vehicle did not start	Failed as expected, vehicle did not start
16	115	Changed first > to <	Failed as expected, vehicle did not find the parking stop and continues driving	Passed as not expected, vehicle parked in the second parking spot because the noise added to the travelled distance resulted in a valid parking gap size
17	115	Changed && to ||	Failed as expected, stopped before the first parking gap, collided with parked car	Failed as expected, stopped before the first parking gap, collided with parked car
18	115	Changed second > to <	Failed as expected, stopped before the first parking gap, collided with parked car	Failed as expected, stopped before the first parking gap, collided with parked car
19	126	Changed first > to <	Failed as expected, vehicle took first gap, collided	Failed as expected, vehicle took first gap, collided
20	126	Changed && to ||	Failed as expected, vehicle did not find the parking stop and continues driving	Failed as expected, vehicle did not find the parking stop and continues driving
21	126	Changed second > to <	Failed as expected, vehicle did not find the parking stop and continues driving	Failed as expected, vehicle did not find the parking stop and continues driving
22	135	Changed first > to <	Failed as expected, vehicle did not find the parking stop and continues driving	Failed as expected, vehicle did not find the parking stop and continues driving
23	135	Changed && to ||	Failed as expected, stopped before the first parking gap, collided with parked car	Failed as expected, stopped before the first parking gap, collided with parked car
24	135	Changed second > to <	Failed as expected, stopped before the first parking gap, collided with parked car	Failed as expected, stopped before the first parking gap, collided with parked car

its possible effectiveness. While in full scale safety evaluations following the ISO 26262, a given function depending on its functionality may be subjected to tens of safety goals and even larger number of corresponding FSR/TSRs, we only evaluated one such scenario. Still with only a single fault scenario - we were able to identify faults leading to safety case violation. Also the mutation approach applied to this exemplary scenario by using 24 mutations, 2 out of these 24 mutants produced unexpected results and exposed the deficiency of the current test protocol, which was considered as adequate for the given functionality.

Therefore while these are encouraging results pointing towards applicability and effectiveness of the proposed framework, we also learned that we need further validation on industrial scale projects to increase the external validity of these results. Further for this framework to be successful in any organization much of the steps of described framework will have to be automated and supported by appropriate tools. As explained in Sects. 2 and 3, a number of tools for fault injection and mutation testing based approaches are available for code-centric development making this framework practical for implementation on large scale with high automation. But corresponding tools to support fault injection and mutation based testing at functional model level in model-based development are not widely available and the few tools currently available are in their early stages of development where reliability of such tools will be an issue at least for some time in near future.

6 Conclusions

In this paper we have examined the growing importance of software in automotive domain. The development of software in automotive and other similar industries has widely adopted the paradigm of model based development and by the nature of application much of the functionality developed and implemented in these sectors is safety critical. Safety critical software/application development requires observation of stringent quality assessment and adherence to functional safety standards such as ISO 26262 in automotive and DO-173 in aerospace industry.

Development of behavioural models in MBD offers significant opportunity to do functional testing early in the development process. Fault injection and mutation testing approach in combination can be used to effectively verify and validate the functional properties of a software system/function. The approach will also provide the required statistics for the argumentation of safety standards compliance. In this paper the need for such validation and a framework on how this could be achieved in practice is discussed. More research and tools are needed to bring this approach into wider industrial adoption.

Initial validation of our proposed framework provided a proof-of-concept and produced encouraging results indicating its usefulness and effectiveness in practice. It is also noted that the framework will become much more effective and easy to use for model-based development as tools related to fault injection and mutation testing at model level matures over time. In the meantime, validation on industrial scale functions will provide further evidence to evaluate the applicability and effectiveness of the proposed framework in practice.

By detecting defects early and being able to do much of verification and validation of intended functionality, robustness and compliance to safety standards on the models the quality and reliability of software in automotive domain will be significantly enhanced. More effective approaches and tools support will also reduce the V&V costs and lead to shorter development times. High quality, reliable and dependable software in automobiles brings innovative functionality sooner, keeps product costs lower and most importantly ensures that automobiles are safer than ever before.

Acknowledgements. The work has been funded by Vinnova and Volvo Cars jointly under the FFI programme (VISEE, Project No: DIARIENR: 2011-04438).

References

1. Broy, M.: Challenges in automotive software engineering. In: Proceedings of the 28th International Conference on Software Engineering, pp. 33–42 (2006)
2. Charette, R.N.: This car runs on code. IEEE Spectr. **46**(3), 3 (2009)
3. Fennel, H., Bunzel, S., Heinecke, H., Bielefeld, J., Fürst, S., Schnelle, K.P., Grote, W., Maldener, N., Weber, T., Wohlgemuth, F., et al.: Achievements and exploitation of the autosar development partnership. In: Convergence 2006, October 2006
4. Boehm, B., Basili, V.: Defect reduction top 10 list. Computer **34**, 135–137 (2001)
5. ISO, C.: 26262, road vehicles-functional safety (2011)
6. Mellegård, N., Staron, M., Törner, F.: A light-weight defect classification scheme for embedded automotive software and its initial evaluation. In: 2012 IEEE 23rd International Symposium on Software Reliability Engineering (ISSRE), pp. 261–270. IEEE (2012)
7. Hillenbrand, M., Heinz, M., Adler, N., Müller-Glaser, K.D., Matheis, J., Reichmann, C.: ISO/DIS 26262 in the context of electric and electronic architecture modeling. In: Giese, H. (ed.) ISARCS 2010. LNCS, vol. 6150, pp. 179–192. Springer, Heidelberg (2010)
8. Schätz, B.: Certification of embedded software – impact of ISO DIS 26262 in the automotive domain. In: Margaria, T., Steffen, B. (eds.) ISoLA 2010, Part I. LNCS, vol. 6415, p. 3. Springer, Heidelberg (2010)
9. Hsueh, M., Tsai, T., Iyer, R.: Fault injection techniques and tools. Computer **30**(4), 75–82 (1997)
10. Rana, R., Staron, M., Berger, C., Hansson, J., Nilsson, M., Törner, F.: Increasing efficiency of iso 26262 verification and validation by combining fault injection and mutation testing with model based development. In: 8th International Joint Conference on Software Technologies-ICSOFT-EA, Reykjavík, Iceland, July 2013
11. Jones, E.L.: Integrating testing into the curriculumarsenic in small doses. In: ACM SIGCSE Bulletin, vol. 33, pp. 337–341
12. Megen, R., Meyerhoff, D.: Costs and benefits of early defect detection: experiences from developing client server and host applications. Software Qual. J. **4**(4), 247–256 (1995)
13. Svenningsson, R., Vinter, J., Eriksson, H., Törngren, M.: MODIFI: a MODel-implemented fault injection tool. In: Schoitsch, E. (ed.) SAFECOMP 2010. LNCS, vol. 6351, pp. 210–222. Springer, Heidelberg (2010)
14. Ziade, H., Ayoubi, R., Velazco, R., et al.: A survey on fault injection techniques. Int. Arab J. Inf. Technol. **1**(2), 171–186 (2004)
15. Jia, Y., Harman, M.: An analysis and survey of the development of mutation testing. IEEE Trans. Softw. Eng. **37**(5), 649–678 (2011)

16. Andrews, J., Briand, L., Labiche, Y.: Is mutation an appropriate tool for testing experiments? [software testing]. In: Proceedings of the 27th International Conference on Software Engineering, ICSE 2005, pp. 402–411 (2005)
17. DeMillo, R., Lipton, R., Sayward, F.: Hints on test data selection: help for the practicing programmer. Computer **11**(4), 34–41 (1978)
18. Offutt, A.: Investigations of the software testing coupling effect. ACM Trans. Softw. Eng. Methodol. (TOSEM) **1**(1), 5–20 (1992)
19. ESAC: Enhanced safety assessment for complex systems. FP5-GROWTH contract no. G4RDCT-2000-00361
20. ISAAC: Improvement of safety activities on aeronautical complex systems. FP6-AEROSPACE project reference 501848 (2007)
21. Vinter, J., Bromander, L., Raistrick, P., Edler, H.: Fiscade - a fault injection tool for scade models. In: 2007 3rd Institution of Engineering and Technology Conference on Automotive Electronics, pp. 1–9 (2007)
22. Plummer, A.: Model-in-the-loop testing. Proc. Inst. Mech. Eng. Part I: J. Syst. Control Eng. **220**(3), 183–199 (2006)
23. Brillout, A., He, N., Mazzucchi, M., Kroening, D., Purandare, M., Rümmer, P., Weissenbacher, G.: Mutation-based test case generation for simulink models. In: de Boer, F.S., Bonsangue, M.M., Hallerstede, S., Leuschel, M. (eds.) FMCO 2009. LNCS, vol. 6286, pp. 208–227. Springer, Heidelberg (2010)
24. Berger, C., Chaudron, M., Heldal, R., Landsiedel, O., Schiller, E.M.: Model-based, composable simulation for the development of autonomous miniature vehicles. In: Mod4Sim'13: 3rd International Workshop on Model-driven Approaches for Simulation Engineering at SCS/IEEE Symposium on Theory of Modeling and Simulation in Conjunction with SpringSim 2013 (2013)
25. Berger, C., Hansson, J., et al.: Cots-architecture with a real-time os for a self-driving miniature vehicle. In: Proceedings of Workshop ASCoMS (Architecting Safety in Collaborative Mobile Systems) of the 32nd International Conference on Computer Safety, Reliability and Security (2013)

Platform-Independence in Model-Driven Development of Graphical User Interfaces for Multiple Devices

David Raneburger[1]([✉]), Gerrit Meixner[2], and Marco Brambilla[3]

[1] Institute of Computer Technology, Vienna University of Technology,
Gusshausstrasse 27-29, 1040 Vienna, Austria
`david.raneburger@tuwien.ac.at`
[2] Faculty of Computer Science, Heilbronn University,
Max-Planck-Str. 39, 74081 Heilbronn, Germany
`gerrit.meixner@hs-heilbronn.de`
[3] Dipartimento di Elettronica, Informazione e Bioingegneria,
Politecnico di Milano, Via Ponzio 34/5, 20133 Milan, Italy
`marco.brambilla@polimi.it`

Abstract. We would like to encourage you to list your keywords within Model-driven development of Graphical User Interfaces (GUIs) for multiple devices involves the transformation of the same platform-independent model to several platform-dependent GUI models. A clear definition of which characteristics comprise a platform is important, because the platform definition determines which characteristics must not be considered in platform-independent models. In this chapter we compare the notion of platform and the corresponding implications in two conceptual approaches that support multi-device GUI generation – the Model Driven Architecture (MDA) proposed by OMG and the Cameleon Reference Framework (CRF), a framework that has been developed to classify model-based user interface generation approaches. We discuss the relation between MDA and CRF in the context of multi-device GUI generation and illustrate their correspondence through classifying state-of-the-art GUI generation approaches. This classification also allows us to illustrate three different mechanisms for achieving multi-device GUI generation in practice.

Keywords: Multi-device · Platform · Model-driven development · Model-based development · User interface · Model Driven Architecture · Cameleon Reference Framework

1 Introduction

Model-driven software development uses automated transformations to transform high-level models, which specify all platform-independent aspects of the

© Springer-Verlag Berlin Heidelberg 2014
J. Cordeiro and M. van Sinderen (Eds.): ICSOFT 2013, CCIS 457, pp. 180–195, 2014.
DOI: 10.1007/978-3-662-44920-2_12

software to build, to different platform-specific models. A clear platform definition is a prerequisite to distinguish between platform-independent and platform-specific models. In the context of Graphical User Interface (GUI) generation for multiple devices, such a platform is a computing device (e.g., desktop PC or smartphone), which displays the GUI of an application. The corresponding platform model needs to consider hardware (e.g., available screen space) and software (e.g., graphical toolkit) characteristics to allow for multi-device GUI generation.

The Object Management Group (OMG) has defined its own comprehensive proposal for applying model-driven practices to systems development. This goes under the name of MDA (Model Driven Architecture). The definition of platform provided by MDA [1] has understandably a very wide scope, as it has been designed to support model-based application development for a wide range of different application domains. It does not require the explicit consideration of hardware characteristics. An MDA compliant platform model may consider hardware and software characteristics, or software characteristics only.

MDA compliant UI generation approaches typically support multi-modal user interface (UI) development. Such multi-modal UIs typically combine different modalities (e.g., graphical, speech, or gesture UIs) to allow for a more natural and more robust interaction. GUIs are special in comparison to serial modalities like speech or gesture, as they allow for parallel information exchange. GUIs shall fit the screen of a certain device to achieve a good level of usability. If hardware characteristics like screen size are not considered in the platform model they have either to be considered by the transformations, or during the creation of the high-level model that specifies the flow of information (e.g., which information is exchanged in parallel).

Models that implicitly consider hardware features of the target platform are still platform-independent models according to the MDA definition, as they do not consider software features of the target device, but they do not support multi-device UI development. For supporting multi-device UI generation, platform-independence must include independence of a certain software *and* independence of a certain hardware. A *device* can thus be modeled through a platform definition that considers software and hardware characteristics. Such a platform definition is provided by the Cameleon Reference Framework (CRF) [2] that supports the classification of UI generation approaches and their models in the context of Model-based User Interface Development (MBUID). The CRF platform definition and model classification scheme is compliant to the MDA and can be seen as specialization in the context of UI development.

This chapter recaptures the MDA and CRF platform definitions, relates them and shows that both definitions support the consideration of hardware characteristics in addition to software characteristics in the platform model, based on [3]. Relying on such a platform definition, we illustrate the relation between MDA and CRF in the context of multi-device GUI development, through classifying state-of-the-art UI generation approaches. This classification also allows us to illustrate three different mechanisms for achieving multi-device GUI generation, which we illustrate each through presenting a corresponding state-of-the-art GUI generation approach in detail. In particular we present the recently adopted Object Management Group (OMG) standard IFML[1] (Interaction Flow Modeling Language) [4], the Model-based Useware-Engineering (MBUE) [5] approach that contributes to a currently ongoing W3C standardization effort[2], and a Communication-Model-based transformation approach that supports automated GUI optimization for different devices [6] in more detail.

2 Conceptual Approaches – MDA and CRF

This section presents the platform definitions and the model classification schemes of the MDA and the CRF, together with the context in which they have been developed.

2.1 Model Driven Architecture

The Object Management Group's (OMG) MDA [1] distinguishes three different types of models that reside on different levels of abstraction. These levels are (from abstract to concrete): the Computation Independent Model (CIM), the Platform Independent Model (PIM) and the Platform Specific Model (PSM).

The *Computation Independent Model* is a high-level view of the problem, which describes some basic abstractions without considering how problems will be actually solved in terms of systems. It describes the usage scenarios in which the system will be used, specifying exactly what the system is expected to do. These models are sometimes referred to as domain, business, or requirement models in the context of MDA. The *Platform Independent Model* describes the system to be built, without specifying details of the implementation platform that will be used. It will be suited for a particular architectural style, but can be mapped onto different platforms. Requirements specified through a certain platform model must not be considered in a PIM.

The *Platform Specific Model* specifies how a system is implemented upon, or uses a particular platform. This model needs to specify all details necessary to derive the *Implementation* of the system.

MDA applies *Model Transformations* to transform PIMs to PSMs. Such transformations need to provide the additional information required to produce the PSM from the PIM. Sometimes, no transformation between CIM and PIM is possible, as CIMs may not be specified in a formal way, or could describe completely manual behaviors, not implemented on any platforms.

Platform is a fundamental concept in MDA, as its promises of resilience to technology obsolescence, rapid portability, increased productivity, shorter time-to-market, consistency and reliability of produced artifacts [7] are based on the abstraction from a certain platform.

According to MDA, a *"platform is a set of subsystems and technologies that provide a coherent set of functionality through interfaces and specified usage patterns, which any application supported by that platform can use without concern*

---

[1] http://www.omg.org/spec/IFML/, http://www.ifml.org

[2] http://www.w3.org/wiki/Model-Based_User_Interfaces

for the details of how the functionality provided by the platform is implemented
[1]." Such a platform is represented through a platform model.

This platform definition does not distinguish hardware and software of a
system explicitly. MDA compliant platform models may consider hardware characteristics in addition to software characteristics, but they do not have to. The
GUI-specific aspects of system design are captured by the IFML (Interaction
Flow Modeling Language) standard [4], which covers user interaction specification and binding to the business logic and persistence layers.

2.2 Cameleon Reference Framework

Model-based UI Development (MBUID) has a long research history [8] and
it uses models to specify all aspects that are involved in the development of
user interfaces. MBUID approaches typically refine high-level interaction models over different levels of abstraction to source code that represents the UI. The
Cameleon Reference Framework (CRF) supports the classification of UIs that
support multiple targets, or multiple contexts of use [2]. Classifying transformation methods and tools for UI generation according to the CRF, facilitates
understanding and comparing them. The CRF introduces four levels of abstraction, which are (from abstract to concrete): Tasks & Concepts, Abstract User
Interface (AUI), Concrete User Interface (CUI) and Final User Interface (FUI).

The *Tasks & Concepts* level contains task models, specifying the tasks of the
user with the system to be built, and models of the domain of activity.

The *Abstract User Interface* level typically contains a presentation and a
dialog model that render the domain concepts into canonical expressions that
are independent from any concrete interactors available on a certain platform.

The *Concrete User Interface* level contains models in which the canonical
expressions have been replaced through concrete interactors that specify the look
and feel of the user interface, but are still independent from a certain toolkit.

The *Final User Interface* represents the UI source code that can be compiled
and run.

Model-driven UI generation typically applies model-to-model transformations between the upper three levels of abstraction and model-to-code transformations for concrete to final UI transformations.

The notion of *platform* is here tailored to UI development and defined as part
of the *context of use*, together with the *user* and the *environment*[3]. The platform
consists of *"a set of hardware (e.g., processor, screen, and mouse) and software
resources (e.g., operating system, technological space) that function together to
form a working computational unit whose state can be observed and/or modified
by a human user. Single resources (processor, peripheral devices etc.) are unable,
individually, to provide this functionality. A platform may be either elementary
or form a cluster of platforms."*

The CRF platform definition explicitly distinguishes hardware and software
of a computational unit. The consideration of both, hardware and software

---

[3] see also http://www.w3.org/wiki/Model-Based_User_Interfaces

characteristics, is important in the context of UI development as it allows to achieve a good level of usability through tailoring a UI to a certain device.

2.3 Relating MDA and CRF for Multi-device GUI Development

A platform definition that shall support multi-device UI development needs to consider software and hardware characteristics of a device. Encapsulating this information in the platform model supports the creation of platform-independent high-level models, adding the platform-specific information only during their transformation to PSMs.

An MDA platform specifies a coherent set of functionalities through interfaces and usage patterns. Examples are operating systems, programming languages, databases, middleware solutions or user interfaces [7]. However, the MDA platform definition is very generic and does not inhibit its interpretation as depending on software alone or on software and hardware together (e.g., a smartphone with a certain operating system and physical characteristics like memory or screen size).

It is recommendable to refine the MDA platform definition for a certain application domain to facilitate its applicability and avoid misunderstandings. The CRF platform definition can be seen as such a refined definition for the MBUID domain. A CRF platform consists of hardware (physical) properties (e.g., screen size and resolution, supported interaction modalities) and software properties, meaning toolkits that implement a certain modality (e.g., Java Swing or HTML). Such a platform definition that contains software and hardware characteristics supports multi-device UI development and allows to establish a clear one-to-one correspondence between MDA models and CRF levels [9]. Table 1 illustrates this correspondence.

Table 1. Correspondence between MDA and CRF levels.

MDA	CRF
CIM ↔ Tasks & Concepts Level
PIM ↔ AUI Level
PSM ↔ CUI Level
ISM ↔ FUI Level

High-level task models, typically used to specify the tasks of the user with a system, together with models that specify the concepts of a certain application domain (i.e., domain models) are CIMs. Such models reside on the Tasks & Concepts level and can be used as a starting point for multi-device UI development, if they do not consider any platform characteristics.

A PIM that is derived from a CIM is still platform-independent. AUI models derived from platform-independent models that reside on the Tasks & Concepts level correspond to PIMs.

Platform specific information is added during the transformation of an AUI model to a certain CUI model, which means that PSMs reside on CUI level.

Finally the PSM is transformed to the source code that implements the UI. Thus, the implementation (or Implementation Specific Model (ISM)) corresponds to the FUI.

So, what does this assignment imply for models on Tasks & Concepts level and implicitly also for AUI models derived from them? Models on these levels must not restrict the rendering possibilities that are supported through the platform model.

The implication for the domain model is that it needs to define all concepts of the application domain, regardless whether they are used by a certain model (that may already be device-dependent) or not.

The implication for the high-level interaction model is that it must not constrain the amount of exchanged information (e.g., based on the available screen space). This means that all information that can be exchanged at a certain point in time needs to be modeled as concurrently available.

The same implication as for the high-level interaction model is valid for the abstract user interface model. An AUI model still needs to specify all canonical expressions that render the information specified as concurrently available in the high-level interaction model, as part of the same presentation (i.e., presentation or dialog model unit).

In terms of GUI development this means that both, the high-level task models and AUI models, assume a "potentially infinite" screen. Specifying information as concurrently available on Tasks & Concepts and on AUI level allows for splitting it to different (smaller) screens according to platform constraints on CUI level. Tailoring the UI to fit a limited screen on CUI level allows for top-down multi-device UI generation (i.e., starting from the Tasks & Concepts or AUI level). Doing it the other way round (i.e., combining information bottom up from the CUI level) is hard to achieve in an automated way, as it requires the analysis of dependencies between the exchanged information to detect which information can be exchanged in parallel on a device with a larger screen.

The remainder of this chapter illustrates how state-of-the-art UI generation approaches support multi-device UI generation and discusses whether the meta-models of the corresponding models can be assigned according to the one-to-one correspondence scheme presented in Table 1. Based on this discussion we illustrates three mechanisms of how multi-device GUI generation is typically achieved, which we illustrate each with a corresponding GUI generation approach.

3   Multi-device GUI Generation in Practice

The presentation of model-driven UI development approaches that support multi-platform development typically focuses on the involved models and does not provide a clear definition of the platform model used [10]. We classified the models of six state-of-the-art UI generation approaches that support multi-platform development, considering how this is achieved by the transformation method, to test the correspondence scheme introduced in Table 1. Table 2 shows our classification of the interaction/UI models of each approach to MDA levels using the CRF platform definition and assuming that the designer will model all information that can be exchanged at a certain point in time as concurrently available when she creates an instance of a certain CIM or PIM model.

Table 2. Classification of UI generation approach models.

	IFML	TERESA	MARIA	MBUE	UsiXML	UCP
CIM	BPMN	CTT	CTT	useML	Task Model	Communication Model
PIM	IFML (and WebML)	CTT	MARIA	DISL	AUI	UI Behavior Model
PSM	Presentation + SW Model	CTT/AUI/CUI	MARIA	UIML	CUI	Screen Model
ISM	FUI	FUI	FUI	FUI	FUI	FUI

IFML shows a one-to-one correspondence between meta-models and MDA levels and has been adopted as OMG standard in March 2013. MARIA [11], MBUE [5] and UsiXML[4] also show a one-to-one correspondence and strongly contribute to an ongoing W3C standardization effort for task and AUI models. In addition to these two UI generation standards, we included TERESA [12] and the Unified Communication Platform (UCP) [13] approach in our comparison. UCP was selected because its support for multi-device GUI generation differs from how this is achieved by IFML or the task-based approaches and TERESA was added, because it allows us to illustrate that instances of the same meta-model can be assigned to more than one MDA level.

All approaches except for TERESA show a one-to-one correspondence, because they use a platform definition that considers software and hardware characteristics. TERESA, in contrast, defines a platform as "*a class of systems that share the same characteristics in terms of interaction resources (e.g., the graphical desktop, PDAs, mobile phones, vocal systems). Their range varies from small devices such as interactive watches to very large flat displays [12]*". The corresponding transformation method requires the manual refinement of the platform-independent CTT model to different platform-dependent System Task Models (e.g., a desktop, a cellphone or a voice System Task model, still specified in CTT), which are subsequently refined to an AUI, a CUI and finally the FUI for the corresponding platform.

The System Task Models that are derived from the platform-independent task model are platform dependent, but are still assigned to the Tasks & Concepts level of the CRF. This means that TERESA does not allow the designer to

---

[4] http://www.usixml.org

specify all information that can be exchanged at a certain point in time as concurrently available and is therefore not compliant to the correspondence scheme defined in Table 1. Its models are assigned to the MDA models as specified in Table 2, because its transformation approach requires the System Task Models already to take platform specific information into account. This allows for a more straight forward transformation approach, but reduces the re-usability of involved models to the topmost CTT models.

The remainder of this section presents IFML, MBUE and UCP in detail and illustrate three different mechanisms for achieving multi-device GUI generation. We use a short flight-selection scenario where the user selects a departure, a destination airport and enters a travel date in a first step, and is provided with a list of flights that match the entered data in a second step, to illustrate each approach and its mechanism to tailor the resulting GUI for a specific device.

3.1   Interaction Flow Modeling Language (IFML)

The Interaction Flow Modeling Language[5] (IFML) [4] supports the creation of visual models of user interactions and front-end behavior in software systems, independently of a certain execution platform and has been adopted as a standard by the OMG[6] in March 2013. IFML is a PIM-level language in MDA parlance, and it perfectly fits into the AUI level of the CRF. The Business Process Model and Notation (BPMN) language may be used in the context of IFML to provide CIM models. The Web Extension of IFML, called WebML[7] [14] extends the general purpose IFML concepts with some more precise UI characteristics, considering the peculiarity of the user interaction on the Web, while still keeping a platform-independent vision (both in terms of independence from software and hardware features). WebML also includes a presentation model that covers the PSM level, by describing the graphical style and positioning of elements in the screen, depending on various device properties such as screen size, allowed user events, and so on. The WebRatio tool-suite automatically generates industrial-strength running applications [15] from WebML/IFML models, exploiting the presentation model at the PSM level. The IFML standardization document includes a set of guidelines for the mapping of IFML models to PSMs, namely software platform models, such as Java, .Net WPF, and HTML.

IFML supports multi-device UI generation through the definition of rules at the PIM level for self-adaptation of user interfaces depending on the device, screen size, or location. It also allows to incorporate platform-specific aspects in the transformation towards the PSM level. IFML therefore satisfies the correspondence scheme shown in Table 2. Additionally, IFML includes some support of platform-specific definition through the concepts of ViewPoint and Context, which can comprise context dimensions (such as screen size, or user position). Therefore, IFML can be used in two ways regarding platform adaptation: as a

---

[5] http://www.ifml.org/
[6] http://www.omg.org/spec/IFML/
[7] http://www.webml.org

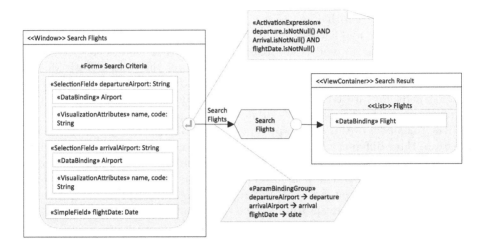

Fig. 1. PIM-level IFML model for the running case of flight selection.

PIM including some model adaptation rules based on the device; or as a pure PIM, with delegation of adaptation to transformation rules or even run-time rules that check the state of the context (i.e., platform). To demonstrate how IFML actually works, Fig. 1 shows the IFML model for the running example adopted in this chapter: a the *Search Flights* Window contains a Form called *Search Criteria*, including two SelectionFields that let users choose departure and arrival airports and a SimpleField for selecting the date. The submission of the form (conditioned by the ActivationExpression that checks that the three fields must not be null) triggers the business logics Search Flights, which in turn returns a list of flights, shown in the *Search Results* ViewContainer. This model is defined at the PIM level, and thus it can be rendered on any platform. This can be obtained either by designing different model transformations that generate the UIs for the different platforms, or by adding adaptation rules in the graphical style that adapt at run-time to the device consuming the UI (e.g., this can be obtained through HTML5 responsive templates).

3.2   Model Based Useware-Engineering (MBUE)

The Useware-Engineering (UE) process is a human-centered development process according to ISO 9241-210. The UE process is divided into 4 main phases accompanied by a supporting evaluation phase. To support the developers of user interfaces at development time, the Useware-Engineering process has been enhanced with a model-based user interface development methodology [16]. Models, process phases and levels of the CRF are interrelated in the architecture of MBUE [5].

The MBUE architecture has been derived and refined on the basis of the (meta-)architecture of the CRF [5]. Therefore, the levels of the MBUE correspond to the levels of the CRF as shown in Table 2. The use model (described with the Useware Markup Language (useML) 2.0) adheres to the CIM level. Accordingly, the use model abstracts platform independent tasks into use objects (UO) that make up a hierarchically ordered structure. Furthermore, the leaf tasks of a use model are described with a set of elementary use objects (eUO) representing atomic interactive tasks: inform, trigger, select, enter and change. In Version 2.0, useML was extended by five temporal operators to support temporal relationships as well as it provides the possibility to define multiple executions or (pre-/post-) conditions that can be attached to tasks of the model. useML is supported by Udit - an interactive editor and simulator for use models [17], which is able to transform use models into AUI models (corresponding to the PIM level of the MDA). The AUI model is specified with the Dialog and Interface Specification Language (DISL), a modeling language for platform- and modality-independent UIs for mobile devices which has originally been developed at the University of Paderborn. DISL focuses on scalability, reactivity, easy usability for developers, and low demands on processing power and memory consumption. An important precondition to the systematic development of UI is the strict separation of structure, presentation and behavior of a UI. DISL supports only 8 generic (meaning platform and modality-independent) widgets, but allows the extension for future generic widgets. The CUI model is described with the User Interface Markup Language (UIML). UIML has been developed as a specification for a meta-language that can provide a canonical XML representation of any UI and has been standardized in version 4.0 by the OASIS. The UI description is implementation-language-independent since it uses a generic vocabulary to specify the interaction objects and is thus implementation independent. UIML specifies the presentation of the UI together with its behavior and corresponds to the PSM level in MDA. These interaction objects can be translated into interaction objects by using the peers-element, which is an addition to the vocabulary to map the concrete interaction objects to their representation in the target language. There are peers for several languages, including Java Swing, XHTML and the .NET components.

Fig. 2. Screenshots of the authoring tools: in the left part Udit shows the task model for the flight scenario and in the right part the DISL authoring tool shows three dialogues.

The MBUE approach relies on the CRF platform definition and its transformation approach ensures that the models can be assigned according to the correspondence scheme defined in Table 1. It is noteworthy that MBUE applies task annotations in its useML task model that assign tasks to a certain context of use (i.e., platform and/or user and/or environment). This way MBUE supports the automated tailoring of the UIs to a certain context of use. Such annotations are similar to the Web-service annotations used in MARIA. Similar to the platform-independent AUI model in MARIA, there is only one platform-independent (annotated) task (i.e., useML) model in MBUE which can be used for multi-device UI generation.

To demonstrate (parts of) the MBUE development environment Fig. 2 illustrates on the left the flight scenario task model (described with useML 2.0 in the Udit tool) and on the right our currently developed authoring tool for the AUI model (specified with DISL). In Future we expect to extend our toolchain with more tools concerning the authoring of UIML and adding different transformations.

3.3 Unified Communication Platform (UCP)

The Unified Communication Platform[8] (UCP) supports the automated generation of GUIs that are optimized for different devices (e.g., smartphone or tablet PC) [13]. This approach relies on Discourse-based Communication Models [18] to model the high-level interaction between a user and the system platform-independently. Communication Models are CIMs and can be transformed automatically to a UI Behavior model that resides on AUI level [19] and is still platform-independent, and to a Screen Model that is tailored for a certain device and thus already platform-dependent. The Screen Model corresponds to the CUI level of the CRF and is finally transformed to HTML code that represents the FUI/ISM.

Table 2 shows that a one-to-one correspondence can be established for UCP. A platform in UCP is defined through software (e.g., supported GUI toolkits) and hardware characteristics (e.g., screen size) of a certain device. In particular, UCP uses a so-called "Application-tailored Device Specification" [20] to specify how the application to built uses a specific device, for example in terms of screen space or pointing granularity (e.g., finger or pen operated). The properties of an application-tailored device specification are shown in Table 3.

The properties `resolution`, `dpi`, `scrollWidth` and `scrollHeight` determine the available screen space and define the boundaries into which the framework tries to fit the GUI. The properties `pointingGranularity` and `toolkits` can be used to filter the transformation rules upfront, for example, to discard rules that created widgets that are not supported by the target toolkit. The property `defaultCSS` references a Cascading Style Sheet (CSS) where styles for custom transformation rules can be defined.

---

[8] http://ucp.ict.tuwien.ac.at

Table 3. Application tailored device specification properties.

name	Defines the name of a certain device
resolution	Specifies the x and y resolution of the device's display
dpi	Specifies the dots per inch of the device's display
defaultCSS	Specifies the default CSS to be used for the device (e.g., to specify the minimum size of a button)
pointingGranularity	Specifies whether the application is going to be operated using the fingers (i.e., Pointing Granularity COARSE) or a mouse (Pointing Granularity FINE)
toolkits	Specifies which graphical toolkits are supported by the device (e.g., Java Swing or HTML)
scrollWidth	Specifies the maximum horizontal scroll width in multiples of the screen width (i.e., 1 means no scrolling)
scrollHeight	Specifies the maximum vertical scroll height in multiples of the screen width (i.e., 1 means no scrolling)

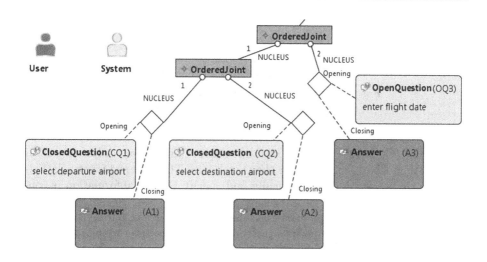

Fig. 3. FlightSelection Communication Model.

Figure 3 shows the Communication Model [21] excerpt for the first step of our simple flight selection scenario. This model specifies the interaction between the User and the System, which are depicted as interacting agents in the upper left corner. Communication Models use so-called Adjacency Pairs (depicted as diamonds in Fig. 3) to model typical turn-takings like Question-Answer, through relating an opening Communicative Act (depicted as rounded rectangles in Fig. 3) with 0 to 2 closing Communicative Acts. The Communicative Acts are assigned to one of the interacting agents through their fill color (yellow/light for the System and green/dark for the User). The ClosedQuestion-Answer

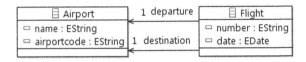

Fig. 4. FlightSelection Domain-of-Discourse Model.

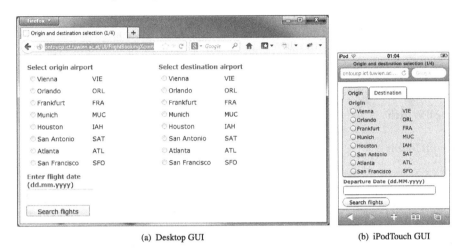

(a) Desktop GUI   (b) iPodTouch GUI

Fig. 5. Flight Selection GUIs generated with UCP.

Adjacency Pairs model the selection of the departure (CQ1-A1) and the destination (CQ2-A2) airport. The `OpenQuestion-Answer` Adjacency Pair (OQ3-A3) models the question for the travel date. The `OrderedJoint` relations structure the interaction hierarchically and specify that all information is concurrently available.

Figure 4 depicts the Domain-of-Discourse (DoD) model for our flight selection scenario. The DoD model specifies the concepts that the interacting parties can "talk" about. These concepts are referenced through the propositional content of the Communicative Acts (for details please refer to [21]). The propositional content of CQ1, for example, is specified as a list of `Airport` concepts specified in the DoD model.

Figure 5 shows GUIs generated with UCP for our running example, one for a desktop device and one for a iPodTouch device. Figure 5(a) shows the desktop screen, where all widgets required for the interaction fit the screen. The iPod-Touch screen space was too small to fit all widgets, so the optimization algorithm split the selection of the departure and the destination airports into separate tabbed panels. We omitted the second step of our running example, because the list of flights was rendered equally as radio-button list on both devices.

UCP uses an automated GUI optimization algorithm to tailor the resulting GUI for a given device according to the objectives (maximum use of available space, minimum amount of navigation clicks and minimum scrolling) and the device constraints specified trough the corresponding application tailored device specification [6]. Rendering a GUI for a new device simply requires the designer to provide the corresponding application tailored device specification.

4   Discussion

The classification of the MBUID approaches presented above reveals that no simple one-to-one correspondence between MDA and CRF, as presented in Table 1, can be established in general. A one-to-one correspondence requires a platform model that considers and encapsulates software and hardware characteristics, which must not be considered in CIMs or PIMs. All approaches whose classification shows a one-to-one correspondence support multi-device UI generation, which can be used as a criteria to detect such approaches.

Our classification of UI generation approaches showed that device specific transformation/adaptation rules, model annotations and automated optimization are established mechanisms to achieve multi-device GUI generation. All approaches presented above are applied at design-time, but run-time GUI generation typically applies similar mechanisms. SUPPLE for example applies automated GUI optimization at run-time [22] through adaptations of a given device-dependent GUI model (i.e., a PSM) according to the needs of motor-impaired users. Run-time UI generation typically requires explicit presentation models [23,24] and does not derive the GUI from a PIM.

We conjecture that a clear definition of the notion platform is also important in other application domains of model-based software development to support multi-device development. The encapsulation of platform characteristics in the corresponding platform model, together with the use of annotations as used in MBUID to avoid dependencies between a high-level model and a certain platform, is a generally applicable way to separate platform specific information from the model itself. Alternatively the platform-tailoring can be automated according to given optimization objectives, as shown for GUI optimization in [6]. This saves the time and effort required for creating annotations manually, but may not produce the exact result expected by the designer. So, there is a trade-off between better predictability of the resulting GUIs through the manual specification of transformation/adaptation rules or annotations and less effort through automated optimization with a lower predictability.

5   Conclusions

Platform-independence for a model requires that this information has to be encapsulated in the corresponding platform model and *must not* be considered in the CIM and PIM model. A platform in the context of multi-device GUI generation must specify software and hardware characteristics. We showed that both the MDA and the CRF platform definition support multi-device UI development, but that no general one-to-one correspondence between the meta-models involved in a certain MBUID approach classified as MDA models, and the CRF levels can be established. The reason is that the use of a certain meta-model instance strongly depends on the transformation approach. For example, task models are platform-independent if they use annotations to specify which task is available on a certain device, or platform-dependent if they consider hardware characteristics like screen-size when specifying which information is concurrently available. However, a one-to-one correspondence indicates that a certain approach supports multi-device UI generation. Our classification of state-of-the-art UI generation approaches revealed specific transformation/adaptation rules, annotations and automated device optimization as three major mechanisms for achieving multi-device GUI generation with a trade-off between manual effort and predictability of the resulting GUI.

References

1. Miller, E.J., Mukerjij, J.: MDA guide version 1.0.1. Technical report, Object Management Group (OMG) (2003)
2. Calvary, G., Coutaz, J., Thevenin, D., Limbourg, Q., Bouillon, L., Vanderdonckt, J.: A unifying reference framework for multi-target user interfaces. Interact. Comput. **15**(3), 289–308 (2003)
3. Raneburger, D., Meixner, G., Brambilla, M.: Platform-independence in model-based multi-device UI development. In: Proceedings of the 8th International Joint Conference on Software Technologies (ICSOFT'13), SciTePress, July 2013
4. Brambilla, M., Bongio, A., Butti, S., Fraternali, P., Kling, W., Molteni, E., Seidewitz, E.: Interaction Flow Modeling Language (IFML). Standardization specification ptc/2013-03-08, Object Management Group (OMG), March 2013. http://www.omg.org/spec/IFML/
5. Meixner, G., Seissler, M., Breiner, K.: Model-driven useware engineering. In: Hussmann, H., Meixner, G., Zuehlke, D. (eds.) MDD of Advanced User Interfaces. SCI, vol. 340, pp. 1–26. Springer, Heidelberg (2011)
6. Raneburger, D., Popp, R., Kavaldjian, S., Kaindl, H., Falb, J.: Optimized GUI generation for small screens. In: Hussmann, H., Meixner, G., Zuehlke, D. (eds.) MDD of Advanced User Interfaces. SCI, vol. 340, pp. 107–122. Springer, Heidelberg (2011)
7. Truyen, F.: The Fast Guide to Model Driven Architecture - The basics of Model Driven Architecture, January 2006
8. Meixner, G., Paternò, F., Vanderdonckt, J.: Past, present, and future of model-based user interface development. i-com **10**(3), 2–10 (2011)
9. Vanderdonckt, J.: A MDA-compliant environment for developing user interfaces of information systems. In: Pastor, Ó., Falcão e Cunha, J. (eds.) CAiSE 2005. LNCS, vol. 3520, pp. 16–31. Springer, Heidelberg (2005)
10. Van den Bergh, J., Meixner, G., Sauer, S.: MDDAUI 2010 workshop report. In: Proceedings of the 5th International Workshop on Model Driven Development of Advanced User Interfaces (MDDAUI 2010) (2010)
11. Paternò, F., Santoro, C., Spano, L.D.: Maria: a universal, declarative, multiple abstraction-level language for service-oriented applications in ubiquitous environments. ACM Trans. Comput. Hum. Interact. **16**, 19:1–19:30 (2009)
12. Mori, G., Paternò, F., Santoro, C.: Design and development of multidevice user interfaces through multiple logical descriptions. IEEE Trans. Softw. Eng. **30**(8), 507–520 (2004)

13. Popp, R., Raneburger, D., Kaindl, H.: Tool support for automated multi-device GUI generation from discourse-based communication models. In: Proceedings of the 5th ACM SIGCHI Symposium on Engineering Interactive computing systems, EICS '13. ACM, New York (2013)
14. Ceri, S., Brambilla, M., Fraternali, P.: The history of WebML lessons learned from 10 years of model-driven development of web applications. In: Borgida, A.T., Chaudhri, V.K., Giorgini, P., Yu, E.S. (eds.) Mylopoulos Festschrift. LNCS, vol. 5600, pp. 273–292. Springer, Heidelberg (2009)
15. Acerbis, R., Bongio, A., Brambilla, M., Butti, S., Ceri, S., Fraternali, P.: Web applications design and development with WebML and WebRatio 5.0. In: Paige, R., Meyer, B. (eds.) TOOLS EUROPE 2008. LNBIP, vol. 11, pp. 392–411. Springer, Berlin Heidelberg (2008)
16. Meixner, G.: Model-based useware engineering. In: W3C Workshop on Future Standards for Model-Based User Interfaces, Rome, Italy (2010)
17. Meixner, G., Seissler, M., Nahler, M.: Udit a graphical editor for task models. In: Proceedings of the 4th International Workshop on Model-Driven Development of Advanced User Interfaces (MDDAUI), Sanibel Island, USA (2009)
18. Falb, J., Kaindl, H., Horacek, H., Bogdan, C., Popp, R., Arnautovic, E.: A discourse model for interaction design based on theories of human communication. In: Extended Abstracts on Human Factors in Computing Systems (CHI '06), pp. 754–759. ACM Press, New York (2006)
19. Popp, R., Falb, J., Arnautovic, E., Kaindl, H., Kavaldjian, S., Ertl, D., Horacek, H., Bogdan, C.: Automatic generation of the behavior of a user interface from a high-level discourse model. In: Proceedings of the 42nd Annual Hawaii International Conference on System Sciences (HICSS-42), Piscataway, NJ, USA. IEEE Computer Society Press (2009)
20. Kavaldjian, S., Raneburger, D., Falb, J., Kaindl, H., Ertl, D.: Semi-automatic user interface generation considering pointing granularity. In: Proceedings of the 2009 IEEE International Conference on Systems, Man and Cybernetics (SMC 2009), San Antonio, TX, USA, October 2009
21. Popp, R., Raneburger, D.: A high-level agent interaction protocol based on a communication ontology. In: Huemer, C., Setzer, T. (eds.) EC-Web 2011. LNBIP, vol. 85, pp. 233–245. Springer, Heidelberg (2011)
22. Gajos, K.Z., Weld, D.S., Wobbrock, J.O.: Automatically generating personalized user interfaces with supple. Artif. Intell. **174**(12–13), 910–950 (2010)
23. Pastor, O., España, S., Panach, J.I., Aquino, N.: Model-driven development. Informatik Spektrum **31**(5), 394–407 (2008)
24. Roscher, D., Lehmann, G., Schwartze, V., Blumendorf, M., Albayrak, S.: Dynamic distribution and layouting of model-based user interfaces in smart environments. In: Hussmann, H., Meixner, G., Zuehlke, D. (eds.) MDD of Advanced User Interfaces. SCI, vol. 340, pp. 171–197. Springer, Heidelberg (2011)

Software Paradigm Trends

Controllability for Nondeterministic Discrete-Event Systems with Data

J. Markovski[(⊠)]

Eindhoven University of Technology,
Den Dolech 2, 5612MH Eindhoven, The Netherlands
j.markovski@tue.nl

Abstract. Supervisory control ensures safe coordination of the discrete-event behavior of the components of a given system. Models of supervisory control software are automatically synthesized based on formal models of the unsupervised system and the coordination requirements. To provide for a greater modeling convenience and to better the expressivity of the model-based systems and software engineering framework, several extensions of supervisory control theory with variables have been proposed. Supervisory control theory studies automated synthesis of supervisory controllers, where the central notion of controllability characterizes the notion of a model of a supervisory controller. One of the most prominent extensions of the theory with data is implemented by means of extended finite automata with variables. We revisit the notion of controllability for these models and we show that the relations that capture existing notions of controllability for finite automata with variables do not have desirable algebraic properties, i.e., they are not a preorders. We propose an alternative notion of controllability based on a behavioral relation termed partial bisimulation. We show that the proposed extension of partial bisimulation for finite automata with variables subsumes existing notions and we discuss its role in a proposed model-based engineering framework.

Keywords: Supervisory control theory · Controllability · Finite automata with variables · Partial bisimulation

1 Introduction

Development of quality control software is becoming an increasingly difficult task due to high complexity of high-tech systems, promoting the former as an important bottleneck in the design and production process as already noted in [11]. Traditional techniques are not able to satisfactorily cope with the challenge due to the frequent design changes in the control requirements, which gave rise to supervisory control theory of discrete-event systems postulated in [4,18].

The work presented in this paper is supported by the Dutch NWO project ProThOS, no. 600.065.120.11.

J. Cordeiro and M. van Sinderen (Eds.): ICSOFT 2013, CCIS 457, pp. 199–214, 2014.
DOI: 10.1007/978-3-662-44920-2_13

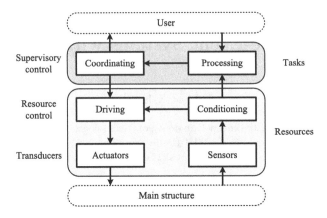

Fig. 1. Supervisory control architecture.

Supervisory control theory studies automatic synthesis of models of supervisory control software that provide for safe and nonblocking behavior of the controlled system by coordinating high-level discrete-event behavior of the concurrent system components.

Supervisory controllers rely on discrete-event observations made regarding the discrete-event system behavior by using sensory information, as depicted in Fig. 1. Based upon the observed signals, these controllers decide which activities are allowed to be carried out safely and do not lead to potentially dangerous or otherwise undesired situations, and send back control signals to the hardware actuators. Under the assumption that the supervisory controller can react sufficiently fast on machine input, one can model this *supervisory control feedback loop* as a pair of synchronizing processes in line with [4,18]. The model of the uncontrolled system is typically referred to as *plant* and it is restricted by the model of the supervisory controller, which referred to as *supervisor*. The coupling of the supervisor and the plant, results in the *supervised plant*, which models the supervisory control loop, i.e., it specifies the behavior of the controlled system.

Traditionally, the activities of the machine are modeled as discrete events, whereas the supervisor is a process that synchronizes with the plant. The supervisor can enable or disable available events in the plant by synchronizing or not synchronizing with them, respectively. The events are split into *controllable* and *uncontrollable events*, the former typically modeling interaction with actuators, whereas the latter model observation of sensory information. Therefore, the supervisor is allowed to disable controllable events, e.g., if the boiler pressure is above the safe threshold, then the heater should be switched off, but it is not allowed to disable any available uncontrollable events, e.g., by ignoring the pressure sensor of the boiler, one reaches a potentially dangerous situation.

Additionally, the supervised plant must also satisfy a given set of *control requirements*, which model the safe or allowed behavior of the machine. Furthermore, it is typically required that the supervised plant is nonblocking, meaning

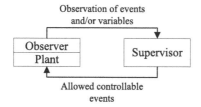

Fig. 2. Supervisory control feedback loop with data-based observations.

that it comprises no deadlock and no livelock behavior. To this end, every state is required to be able to reach a so-called *marked* or final state, following the notation of [4, 18], which denotes the situation that the plant is considered to have successfully completed its execution. The conditions that define the existence of such a supervisor are referred to as (nonblocking) *controllability* conditions. In the setting of this paper we will not consider in detail the process of modeling and ensuring that the (nonblocking) control requirements hold for the given plant and, instead we refer the reader to the model-based engineering framework of [15, 20].

Depending on the observational power of the supervisor, we deal with event-based supervision, studied in [18], state-based supervision as studied in [12, 15], or data-based supervision along the lines of [14, 16], respectively. The first approach relies on building a history of observed events to deduce the state of the system as suggested in [4], whereas the second and the third approaches employ observers and guards that directly convey the state of the system to the supervisor in the vein of [12, 14], as depicted in Fig. 2. With respect to the control architecture of Fig. 1, the second and the third approach suggest that the interface between the layers of resource and supervisory control is unified, e.g., by employing shared variables or publisher/subscriber services, which is typical for implementations in the artificial intelligence domain. The event-based approach suggests direct observation of activities of the system, which are typically triggered by the system to be supervised, relying on some input/output interface. The extensions of supervisory control theory with variables and data aim at a two-fold improvement: more concise specification due to parametrization of the systems, as suggested in [5, 16] and greater expressiveness and modeling convenience, as shown in [8, 21]. The extensions range over the most prominent models of discrete-event systems like finite-state machines developed in [5], labeled transition systems, considered in [14], and automata extensions, provided in [8, 21].

With the development of new models, the original notion of controllability for deterministic discrete-event systems of [4, 18] is subsequently extended to the corresponding settings with variables and data parameters. We note that the controllability is originally defined as a language-based property and, thus, meant for deterministic discrete-event systems. Extensions of controllability for parameterized languages are proposed in [5, 8]. For nondeterministic discrete-event systems, there are several proposed notions, relying on commonly observed traces in [7,23], failure semantics in [17], or (bi)simulation semantics in [2]. For nondeterministic extended finite automata with variables, introduced in [21], the proposed notion of so-called state controllability of [16] relies on an extension of the work of [7]. Both works of [17] and [2] rely on preorder behavioral relations to formulate the notion of controllability, the former relying on failure-trace semantics, whereas the latter is (bi)simulation-based. Even though, it has been argued that refinements based on these two types of semantics have similar properties, cf. [6], (bi)simulation-based refinements are finer notions that are supported by more efficient algorithms, like [13].

To capture the notion of controllability, we rely on a behavioral preorder termed *partial bisimulation*, first introduced in the co-algebraic characterization of [19] and, subsequently, lifted to a process theory in [2]. In essence, we employ this preorder to state a relation between the supervised plant and the original plant allowing controllable events to be simulated, while requiring that uncontrollable event are bisimulated. This ensures that the supervisor does not disable uncontrollable events, while preserving the branching structure of the plant. We will show that this notion subsumes the notion of state controllability for finite automata with variables. Moreover, we will show that state controllability is not a preorder and that some plants are considered as uncontrollable, even though there exist suitable supervisory controllers. Finally, by employing the proposed notion of controllability, we will show that it is possible to eliminate spurious plant nondeterminism, i.e., nondeterminism can be eliminated without sacrificing supervised plant behavior.

2   Finite Automata with Variables

In order to directly relate our notion of controllability with previous work, we model nondeterministic discrete-event systems by means of finite automata with variables. For a full treatment of supervisory control theory in a process-theoretic setting, we refer to [2,3,14] for event-, state-, and data-based supervision, respectively. In general, we allow arbitrary variable domains, even though variables with finite domains can be eliminated in order to employ more efficient synthesis procedures, as suggested in [21]. We suppose that the variables are given by the set V, where given a variable $X \in \mathsf{V}$, its domain is denoted by $\mathrm{D}(X)$. (Standard arithmetical) expressions over a set of variables $V \subset \mathsf{V}$ are denoted by $\mathsf{F}(V)$ and they are evaluated with respect to $e_\delta \colon \mathsf{F}(V) \to \mathrm{D}(V)$, where $\delta \colon V \to \mathrm{D}(V)$ holds the variable assignments. We note that for the sake of clarity of presentation, we do not take into consideration the expressions that do not evaluate within the variable domain and extensions to inconsistent processes can be handled by a straightforward extension of the approach of [3]. By $\mathsf{B}(V)$ we denote Boolean expression over the set of variables $V \subset \mathsf{V}$ where the atomic propositions are given by some set of predefined predicates, the logical constants false F and true T, and the set of standard logical operators. The obtained Boolean expressions are evaluated with respect to a given valuation $v_\delta \colon \mathsf{B}(V) \to \{\mathsf{F}, \mathsf{T}\}$, where again $\delta \colon V \to \mathrm{D}(V)$.

$$s \xmapsto{a} s', \; v_\delta(\gamma(s,a,s')) = \mathrm{T},$$

$$\delta'(X) = \begin{cases} e_\delta(\alpha((s,a,s'),X)), & \text{if } ((s,a,s'),X) \in \mathrm{D}(\alpha) \\ \delta(X), & \text{otherwise} \end{cases}$$

$$\overline{\qquad (s,\delta) \xrightarrow{a} (s',\delta') \qquad}$$

Fig. 3. Operational semantics of finite automata with variables.

Definition 1. *A finite automaton with variables G is given by the tuple $G = (S, A, V, \longmapsto, [4]\gamma, \alpha, (s_0, \delta_0))$, where*

- *S is a finite set of states;*
- *A is a finite set of event labels;*
- *$V \subset \mathsf{V}$ is a finite set of variables;*
- *$\longmapsto \; \subset S \times A \times S$ is a labeled transition relation;*
- *$\gamma \colon \longmapsto \; \to \mathsf{B}(V)$ are transition guards;*
- *$\alpha \colon (\longmapsto \times V) \rightharpoonup \mathsf{F}(V)$ is a partial updating function; and*
- *(s_0, δ_0) is the initial state $s_0 \in S$ and initial data assignment $\delta_0 \colon V \to \mathrm{D}(V)$.*

If the set of variables of a finite automaton with variables G, as given by Definition 1, is empty, then G is a standard automaton with labeled transitions. For the transition relations, we will employ infix notation and write $s \xmapsto{a} s'$ for $(s, a, s') \in \longmapsto$.

The dynamics of the finite automaton with variables G is given by the transition relation $\longrightarrow \; \subseteq S \times (V \to \mathrm{D}(V)) \times A \times S \times (V \to \mathrm{D}(V))$, which is determined by the actual evaluation of the guards with respect to the value assignments. In order to keep track of the updated variable values, we employ the data assignment function $\delta \colon V \to \mathrm{D}(V)$. Now, the semantics of G is given by $\longrightarrow$, where initially the automaton is in state s_0 with environment δ_0, denoted by (s_0, δ_0). The dynamics of (s, δ) is captured by the operational rule depicted in Fig. 3, following the notation of structural operational semantics of [1], where the premise must hold, so that the bottom transition can be taken.

The rule states that a transition is possible if such labeled transition is defined in the automaton, the guard of that transition evaluates to true, whereas the variables are updated according to the partial updating function. It is not difficult to observe that the transition relation $\longrightarrow$ induces a labeled transition system with state space $S \times \mathrm{D}(V)$, set of labels A, and initial state (s_0, δ_0).

Definition 2. *Given an automaton with variables $G = (S, A, V, \longmapsto, \gamma, \alpha, (s_0, \delta_0))$, we define the induced labeled transition system by $\mathrm{T}(G) = (S \times \mathrm{D}(V), A, \longrightarrow, (s_0, \delta_0))$, where:*

- *$S \times \mathrm{D}(V)$ is a set of states;*
- *A is the set of events taken over from G;*
- *$\longrightarrow \; \subseteq S \times (V \to \mathrm{D}(V)) \times A \times S \times (V \to \mathrm{D}(V))$ is the instantiated labeled transition relation as given by the operational rule of Fig. 3; and*

– (s_0, δ_0) *is the initial state of the labeled transition system induced by the initial state of* G *and its initial variable valuation.*

If the set of variables is empty, i.e., $V = \emptyset$, then $\longmapsto$ and $\longrightarrow$ coincide, provided that the (then trivial) transition guards are set to be true, and G reduces to a standard automaton.

In order to define the language generated by automaton G, we extend the transition relation $\longrightarrow$ to a multistep transition relation $\longrightarrow^*$. By A^* we define the set of strings made from the labels in A that label the transitions of $\longrightarrow^*$, where ϵ denotes the empty string and st denotes the concatenation of the strings s and t for $s, t \in A^*$. Now, the multistep transition relation is given by the operation rules (1):

$$\frac{\overline{(s, \delta) \xrightarrow{\epsilon}^* (s, \delta)}}{(s, \delta) \xrightarrow{t}^* (s'', \delta''), \ (s'', \delta'') \xrightarrow{a} (s', \delta)', \ t \in A^*, \ a \in A}{(s, \delta) \xrightarrow{ta}^* (s', \delta')}. \tag{1}$$

By $(s, \delta) \xrightarrow{t}^*$ we denote that there exists (s', δ') such that $(s, \delta) \xrightarrow{t}^* (s', \delta')$. Now, the language generated by the automaton G is given by $L(G)$, where $L(G) = \{t \in A^* \mid (s_0, \delta_0) \xrightarrow{t}^* \}$.

In order to couple the plant and the supervisor, we define a synchronous composition of two automata that synchronizes on transitions with the same labels and interleaves on the other transitions. We note that, in general, the synchronous composition cannot be defined due to conflicts induced by the partial assignment functions α. A simple counterexample is the situation where two automata need to synchronize on transitions with the same label that update the same variable to two different values, as noted in [21]. Again, for the sake of clarity, we do not consider conflicting situations, which are easily detectable as none of the conditions for the partial updating functions in Definition 3 apply.

Definition 3. *Let* $G_1 = (S_1, A_1, V_1, \longmapsto_1, \gamma_1, \alpha_1, (s_{01}, \delta_0))$ *and* $G_2 = (S_2, A_2, V_2, \longmapsto_2, \gamma_2, \alpha_2, (s_{02}, \delta_0))$. *The synchronous composition of* G_1 *and* G_2 *is given by* $G_1 \parallel G_2 = (S_1 \times S_2, A_1 \cup A_2, V_1 \cup V_2, \longmapsto, \gamma, \alpha, ((s_{01}, s_{02}), \delta_0))$, *where* $\longmapsto$, γ, *and* α *are defined in Fig. 4, where* $\wedge$ *denotes logical conjunction.*

Definition 3 is given directly in terms of automata with variables, unlike the work of [21], where it is given in terms of the underlying labeled transition system. Now, given two finite automata with variables G_1 and G_2, we can derive the underlying transition systems $T(G_1)$ and $T(G_2)$. It is not difficult to show that $T(G_1 \parallel G_2)$ coincides with $T(G_1) \parallel T(G_2)$, where the synchronization on the relation $\longrightarrow$ is defined as for $\longmapsto$.

Proposition 1. *Let* $G_i = (S_i, A_i, V_i, \longmapsto_i, \gamma_i, \alpha_i, (s_{0i}, \delta_0))$ *for* $i \in \{1, 2\}$ *be such that* $G_1 \parallel G_2$ *is well-defined. Let* $(S_i \times \delta_i, A_i, \longrightarrow_i, (s_{0i}, \delta_0))$ *be the underlying labeled transition systems, where* $\longrightarrow_i$ *is induced by the operational rule of Fig. 3 and* $\delta_i \colon V_i \to D(V_i)$, *for* $i \in \{1, 2\}$. *Let* $T(G_1) \parallel T(G_2) = ((S_1 \times \delta_1) \times (S_2 \times \delta_2),$

$$(s_1, s_2) \xmapsto{a} \begin{cases} (s_1', s_2), & \text{if } s_1 \xmapsto{a}_1 s_1', a \in A_1 \setminus A_2 \\ (s_1, s_2'), & \text{if } s_2 \xmapsto{a}_2 s_2', a \in A_2 \setminus A_1 \\ (s_1', s_2'), & \text{if } s_1 \xmapsto{a}_1 s_1', s_2 \xmapsto{a}_2 s_2', a \in A_1 \cap A_2 \end{cases}$$

$$\gamma((s_1, s_2), a, (s_1', s_2')) = \begin{cases} \gamma_1(s_1, a, s_1'), & \text{if } s_1 \xmapsto{a}_1 s_1', a \in A_1 \setminus A_2 \\ \gamma_2(s_2, a, s_2'), & \text{if } s_2 \xmapsto{a}_2 s_2', a \in A_2 \setminus A_1 \\ \gamma_1(s_1, a, s_1') \wedge \gamma_2(s_2, a, s_2'), & \text{if } \begin{array}{l} s_1 \xmapsto{a}_1 s_1', s_2 \xmapsto{a}_2 s_2', \\ a \in A_1 \cap A_2 \end{array} \end{cases}$$

$$\alpha(((s_1, s_2), a, (s_1', s_2')), X) =$$
$$\begin{cases} \alpha_1((s_1, a, s_1'), X), & \text{if } ((s_1, a, s_1'), X) \in D(\alpha_1), ((s_2, a, s_2'), X) \notin D(\alpha_2) \\ \alpha_2((s_2, a, s_2'), X), & \text{if } ((s_2, a, s_2'), X) \in D(\alpha_2), ((s_1, a, s_1'), X) \notin D(\alpha_1) \\ \alpha_1((s_1, a, s_1'), X), & \text{if } \begin{array}{l} ((s_1, a, s_1'), X) \in D(\alpha_1), ((s_2, a, s_2'), X) \notin D(\alpha_2), \\ \alpha_1((s_1, a, s_1'), X) = \alpha_2((s_2, a, s_2'), X) \end{array} \end{cases}$$

Fig. 4. Definition of $\longmapsto$, γ, and α of Definition 3.

$$((s_1, \delta_1), (s_2, \delta_2)) \xrightarrow{a} \begin{cases} ((s_1', \delta_1'), (s_2, \delta_2)), & \text{if } (s_1, \delta_1) \xrightarrow{a}_1 (s_1', \delta_1'), a \in A_1 \setminus A_2 \\ ((s_1, \delta_1), (s_2', \delta_2')), & \text{if } (s_2, \delta_2) \xrightarrow{a}_2 (s_2', \delta_2'), a \in A_2 \setminus A_1 \\ ((s_1', \delta_1'), (s_2', \delta_2')), & \text{if } \begin{array}{l} (s_1, \delta_1) \xrightarrow{a}_1 (s_1', \delta_1'), \\ (s_2, \delta_2) \xrightarrow{a}_2 (s_2', \delta_2'), a \in A_1 \cap A_2 \end{array} \end{cases}.$$

Fig. 5. Definition of $\longrightarrow$ of Proposition 1.

$A_1 \cup A_2, \longrightarrow, ((s_{01}, \delta_0), (s_{02}, \delta_0)))$, where $\longrightarrow$ is defined as in Fig. 5. Then, $\mathrm{T}(G_1 \parallel G_2)$ is isomorphic to $\mathrm{T}(G_1) \parallel \mathrm{T}(G_2)$.

The proof of Proposition 1 is meticulous, but straightforward, by showing that the constructions given in Definition 3 form an isomorphic transition system as the one defined in the proposition. It is worthwhile noting that the definition of $\longrightarrow$ in Proposition 1 does not impose an additional condition for the situation when $((s_1, \delta_1), (s_2, \delta_2)) \xrightarrow{a} ((s_1', \delta_1'), (s_2', \delta_2'))$ that δ_1' and δ_2' should coincide on the common updated variables. This is directly implied by the construction of α in Definition 3.

A direct corollary of Definition 3 and Proposition 1 is that the language of the synchronization is an intersection of the languages of the components of the composition, i.e., $L(G_1 \parallel G_2) = L(G_1) \cap L(G_2)$. This enables a connection with the original supervisory control theory of finite automata of [4,18].

3   Controllability

Given an automaton with a set of labels A, we split the labels to set of controllable C and uncontrollable U labels such that $C \cap U = \emptyset$ and $C \cup U = A$. To model the plant we can take an unrestricted finite automaton with variables

$$P = (S_P, A_P, V_P, \longmapsto_P, \gamma_P, \alpha_P, (s_{0P}, \delta_0)), \tag{2}$$

as the uncontrolled system is allowed to have every possible type of behavior. We note that the plant is typically obtained as a (well-defined) parallel composition of multiple concurrent components, which ultimately results in the process modeled by P.

The supervisor, however, is required to be a deterministic process, as it has to send unambiguous feedback to the plant and it is not allowed to alter the state of the plant, i.e., it must not comprise variable assignments, as suggested in [14]. The supervisor can rely either on synchronization of events that keeps the history of the plant as in the original setting of [4,18] or on data observation from the plant to make supervision decisions in the vein of [14,16]. In both cases, we can assume that the supervisor is given as an deterministic automaton

$$S = (S_S, A_S, V_S, \longmapsto_S, \gamma_S, \emptyset, (s_{0S}, \delta_0)), \tag{3}$$

where $C \subseteq A_S \subseteq A_P$, $V_S \subseteq V_P$, and the labeled transition function $\longmapsto_S$ is such that if $s \overset{a}{\longmapsto}_S s'$ and $s \overset{a}{\longmapsto}_S s''$, then $s' = s''$ for every $s, s', s'' \in S_S$ and $a \in A_S$.

We note that the supervisor can choose not to synchronize on some uncontrollable event from the plant, but its alphabet must comprise all controllable events as the supervisor must supply the control signals. Furthermore, the supervisor has no need of additional variables, as it does not update any variables, i.e., $\alpha_S = \emptyset$. Consequently, there is never a conflict in the synchronization between the plant and the supervisor, and the composition $P \parallel S$ is well-defined. If the supervisor does not rely on data-based observations, but employs synchronization of events to keep track of the state of the plant, then additionally $\gamma_S(s, a, s') = T$ for all $(s, a, s') \in \longmapsto$.

The composition $P \parallel S$ models the supervised plant, i.e., the behavior of the controlled system as given by the supervisory feedback loop of Fig. 2. We note that the transition system

$$\mathrm{T}(P \parallel S) = (S_P \times S_S \times \delta_P, A_P, \longrightarrow, (s_{0P}, s_{0S}, \delta_0)), \tag{4}$$

where $\delta_P \colon V_P \to \mathrm{D}(V_P)$ and $\longrightarrow$ is defined by the operational rule of Fig. 3.

To state that the supervisor has no control over the uncontrollable events, the language-based controllability of the original setting of [4,18] is stated as:

$$L(P \parallel S)U \cap L(P) \subseteq L(P \parallel S), \tag{5}$$

where $L(P \parallel S)U$ denotes the concatenation of the language of the supervised plant and the set of uncontrollable labels. Intuitively, the controllability relation (5) demands that all uncontrollable events available in reachable states of the original plant by traces enabled by the supervisor, must also be available in the supervised plant. This ensures that the supervisor does not disable any uncontrollable events when forming the supervised plant.

This definition has been subsequently extended to so-called state controllability in [7, 16, 21, 23] for nondeterministic discrete-events systems (with variables). Given an automaton $G = (S, A, V, \longmapsto, \gamma, \alpha, (s_0, \delta_0))$ with a transition relation $\longrightarrow$, let $\mathrm{E}(s, \delta)$ denote the set of enabled transitions of the state (s, δ) for $s \in S$ and $\delta \colon V \to \mathrm{D}(V)$, i.e., $\mathrm{E}(s, \delta) = \{a \in A \mid (s, \delta) \xrightarrow{a} \}$.

Definition 4. *Let P and S be finite automata with variables, representing the plant and the supervisor. A state $(s_P, (s_P, s_S), \delta_P)$ of the transition system $\mathrm{T}(P \parallel (P \parallel S))$ is defined as controllable, if it holds that*

$$A_S \cap U \cap \mathrm{E}(s_P, \delta_P) \subseteq \mathrm{E}((s_P, s_S), \delta_P).$$

A plant P is state controllable with respect to S if and only if all reachable states of $\mathrm{T}(P \parallel (P \parallel S))$ are state controllable.

Intuitively, the parallel composition between of the plant and the supervised plant helps identify all states in the original and the supervised plant that can be reached by the same trace. According to Definition 4, controllable states ensure that all uncontrollable events that are synchronized between the plant and the supervisor, given by $A_S \cap U$, that are also enabled in the reached plant state (s_P, δ_P) by following the same trace, must be enabled in the reached supervised plant state $((s_P, s_S), \delta_P)$. Note that both states must have the same variable assignment function δ_P as the supervisor has an empty updating function, so it does not influence the updating of the variables.

We note that the definition relies on the underlying transition system, employing it to identify the necessary control actions. It is not difficult to show that state controllability implies language controllability, as given in (5), for deterministic automata, see [21]. The key observation is that $P \parallel P$ coincides with P for deterministic systems, implying that $P \parallel S$ can act as a supervisor and lead to the same supervised behavior as S.

Here, we take a closer look at the state controllability condition for nondeterministic plants. Condition (4) essentially requires that all states that are reachable by the same trace, must also enable the same uncontrollable events. This proves to be too strict in some situations. Consider the automata depicted in Fig. 6, where state names are given inside the circles, all guards are set to be true, there are no variables, the event labeled by c is controllable, whereas the events labeled by u_1 and u_2 are uncontrollable. Suppose that a plant is given by automaton P and a supervisor by automaton S. As the supervisor does not disable any events, we can assume that the control requirements do not restrict the behavior of the plant, i.e., the supervised plant depicted by automaton $P \parallel S$ coincides with the plant. In such reflexive situations, it is always possible to find a supervisor that simply allows all events of the plant, trivially "controlling" the plant.

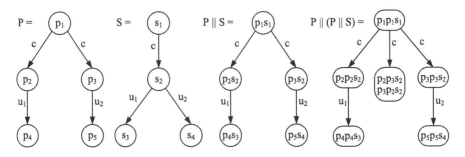

Fig. 6. A nondeterministic plant P, a deterministic supervisor S, and the resulting state uncontrollable nondeterministic supervised plant $P \parallel S$.

Now, putting in parallel plant P and supervised plant $P \parallel S$, leads to automaton $P \parallel (P \parallel S)$ as depicted in Fig. 6. This parallel composition reveals that states p_2 of P and (p_3, s_2) of $P \parallel S$ are reachable by the same trace. However, state $(p_2, \emptyset)$ of the transition system $T(P)$ enables the uncontrollable transition labeled by u_1, whereas state $((p_3, s_2), \emptyset)$ of transition system $T(P \parallel S)$ enables only the uncontrollable transition labeled by u_2. This directly implies that plant P is state uncontrollable with respect to $P \parallel S$, i.e., it is not state controllable with respect to itself. Thus, state controllability is not a preorder relation, as plants that have states that enable different sets of uncontrollable events in states that can be reached by the same trace are deemed uncontrollable, despite the existence of a trivial supervisor that enables all transitions.

4   Partial Bisimulation

We propose to employ the behavioral relation termed partial bisimulation to defined controllability for finite automata with variables. Partial bisimulation was first introduced in [19] to capture language controllability in a coalgebraic setting. It was lifted in [2] to a process theory for supervisory control of nondeterministic discrete-event systems. Here, we provide an interpretation for finite automata with variables and discuss its relationship with state controllability.

Partial bisimulation is parameterized by a so-called bisimulation action set B. The relation requires that the labeled transitions of the first transition system are simulated by the second transition system, whereas only the labels of the second transition system that are in the bisimulation action set B are bisimulated back by the first one. The intuition behind this definition is that the bisimulation action set plays the role of the uncontrollable actions that must always be enabled both in the original and the supervised plant, whereas it is sufficient to only simulate controllable events, as these can be restricted by the supervisor.

Definition 5. Let $T_i = (S_i, A_i, \longrightarrow_i, s_{0i})$ for $i \in \{1, 2\}$ be two transition systems. A relation $R \subseteq S_1 \times S_2$ is said to be a partial bisimulation with respect to a bisimulation action set $B \subseteq A_2$, if for all $(s_1, s_2) \in R$, it holds that:

1. if $s_1 \xrightarrow{a} s_1'$ for $a \in A_1$ and $s_1' \in S_1$, then there exist $a \in A_2$ and $s_2' \in S_2$ such that $s_2 \xrightarrow{a} s_2'$ and $(s_1', s_2') \in R$;

2. if $s_2 \xrightarrow{b} s_2'$ for $b \in B$ and $s_2' \in S_2$, then there exist $b \in A_1$ and $s_1' \in S_1$ such that $s_1 \xrightarrow{a} s_1'$ and $(s_1', s_2') \in R$;

If R is a partial bisimulation relation such that $(s_{01}, s_{02}) \in R$, then T_1 is partially bisimilar to T_2 with respect to B and we write $T_1 \leq_B T_2$. If $T_2 \leq_B T_1$ holds as well, we write $T_1 =_B T_2$.

We note that due to condition 1. of Definition 5, it must hold that $A_1 \subseteq A_2$, whereas due to condition 2. it holds that $B \subseteq A_1$ as well. It is not difficult to show that partial bisimilarity is a preorder relation [2]. In addition, following the guidelines of [19], it can be shown that $\leq_B$ is a partial bisimulation relation with respect to B. Thus, we obtain standard results for the partial bisimulation preorder and equivalence, similarly as for the simulation preorder and equivalence of [9]. Moreover, the partial bisimulation preorder is shown a precongruence for the most prominent processes operations following the guidelines of [2]. Finally, we note that $T_1 =_{A_1 \cup A_2} T_2$ amounts to bisimulation, whereas $T_1 \leq_\emptyset T_2$ reduces to simulation preorder and $T_1 =_\emptyset T_2$ reduces to simulation equivalence, as noted in [2].

Now, suppose that as before, the plant is given by finite automaton with variables P, whereas the supervisor is given by S, and the supervised plant is given by $P \parallel S$. Then, the supervisor may restrict some controllable events from the plant, whereas all available uncontrollable events in the reachable states should be enabled. This can be expressed by requesting that the transition system of the supervised plant is partially bisimulated by the transition system of the original plant with respect to the uncontrollable events, i.e.,

$$\mathrm{T}(P \parallel S) \leq_U \mathrm{T}(P). \tag{6}$$

It is immediate that $\mathrm{T}(P) \leq_U \mathrm{T}(P)$, when $P \parallel S$ coincides with P as in the example of Fig. 6. It is also not difficult to show that for deterministic processes, relation (6) reduces to language controllability of (5), see [2,19]. Next, we show that controllability as defined in (6) by means of partial bisimulation is a coarser notion than state controllability of Definition 4.

Theorem 1. Let P and S be finite automata with variables representing the plant and the supervisor. If P is state controllable with respect to S according to Definition 4, then relation (6) holds.

Proof. Let us assume that $P = (S_P, A_P, V_P, \longmapsto_P, \gamma_P, \alpha_P, (s_{0P}, \delta_0))$ and $S = (S_S, A_S, V_S, \longmapsto_S, \gamma_S, \emptyset, (s_{0S}, \delta_0))$. We define the relation

$$R = \{(((p, s), \delta_P), (p, \delta_P)) \mid$$
$$\exists t \in A_P^* \colon (p_0, (p_0, s_0), \delta_0) \xrightarrow{t}{}^* (p, (p, s), \delta_P)\}.$$

We show that R is a partial bisimulation relation between $\mathrm{T}(P \parallel S)$ and $\mathrm{T}(P)$ with respect to the uncontrollable labels $U \subseteq A_P$. Suppose that $(((p, s), \delta_P), (p, \delta_P))$

$\in R$ for some states $((p, s), \delta_P) \in S_P \times S_S \times (V_P \to D(V_P))$ and $(p, \delta_P) \in S_P \times (V_P \to D(V_P))$.

Let $((p, s), \delta_P) \xrightarrow{a} ((p', s'), \delta'_P)$ for some $a \in A_P$. Then, according to Definition 3 and the operational rule of Fig. 3, either $a \in A_P \setminus A_S$ or $a \in A_S$. In the former case, we have that $s = s'$, so $(p, \delta_P) \xrightarrow{a} (p', \delta'_P)$ and $(((p', s), \delta'_P), (p', \delta'_P)) \in R$. In the latter case, we have that $((p, s), \delta_P) \xrightarrow{a} ((p', s'), \delta'_P)$ for some $s' \in S_S$. However, since the updating function of the supervisor S is empty and the action $a \in A_S$ is synchronizing, we have that again $(p, \delta_P) \xrightarrow{a} (p', \delta'_P)$ with $(((p', s'), \delta'_P), (p', \delta'_P)) \in R$.

Now, suppose that $(p, \delta_P) \xrightarrow{u} (p', \delta'_P)$ for some $u \in U$. Again, either $u \in U \setminus A_S$ or $u \in U$. If $u \notin A_S$, then u is not a synchronizing label, implying that $((p, s), \delta_P) \xrightarrow{u} ((p', s), \delta'_P)$ with $(((p', s), \delta'_P), (p', \delta'_P)) \in R$. If u is a synchronizing label, then by the condition for controllable states of Definition 4, we have $u \in E((s_P, s_S), \delta_P)$, i.e., $((p, s), \delta_P) \xrightarrow{u} ((p', s'), \delta'_P)$ for some $((p', s'), \delta'_P) \in S_P \times S_S \times (V_P \to D(V_P))$ and $(((p', s'), \delta'_P), (p', \delta'_P)) \in R$, which completes the proof.

We have shown that every state controllable plant is also controllable with respect to condition (6). That the inclusion is strict follows immediately from the counterexample of Fig. 6.

Condition (6) additionally implies that the same supervised behavior given by $P \parallel S$ is preserved for every plant P' such that $P' =_U P$, i.e., we have that $P' \parallel S =_U P \parallel S$, which is the basis of the algorithms developed in [13]. This enables us to detect spurious nondeterministic behavior for which state controllability cannot be applied in general. We given an example from the literature of such nondeterministic behavior.

In Fig. 7, plant P_{orig} represents a model of a faulty automated scanner that makes a shopping list of items to be purchased by the user. The scanner is faulty as sometimes it does not give an option to cancel a scanned item, e.g., when the

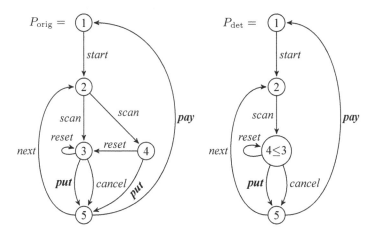

Fig. 7. Checkout scanner of [23] - A plant with spurious nondeterminism.

user wants to return the product or just wants to check the price, and in that case the scanner needs to be reset. As suggested in [23] the set of uncontrollable events is given by $U = \{pay\}$ as payment cannot be avoided, even though we also suggest to treat the event *put* as uncontrollable.

The interpretation is that if there is no cancelation of some scanned product, after a possible timeout, it should automatically be placed on the shopping list. It is easily observed that state 4 is partially bisimulated by state 3 and, thus, state 3 can be safely removed without any loss in behavior (the only situation where state 3 could not be removed arises if the event *cancel* is uncontrollable, which here is not the case). The resulting deterministic plant P_{det} reveals that P_{orig} actually contains no real nondeterministic behavior with respect to controllability. In the original setting of [23] that employs state controllability for nondeterministic discrete-event systems, this observation was not possible and the plant P_{orig} is treated as nondeterministic.

5   Synthesis-Centric Model-Based Engineering

We employ the framework depicted in Fig. 8 in order to structure the process of supervisory control software synthesis [15, 20]. We start with informal specifications of the controlled system, i.e., the desired product, given as documents that are written by domain engineers. Based on these documents, an architectural design of the controlled system is made by the domain and software engineers together. This design defines the appropriate modeling level of abstraction and it specifies the control architecture. Based on the architectural design, a decision is made to which extent the control is managed by the software, and which part is implemented in hardware. The resulting (informal) documents specify the requirements of the supervised system. In the following, we omit the roles of the engineers as they are clear from the context.

Most system models, i.e., plants, contain mixed discrete-event and continuous or hybrid behavior. As discussed above, supervisor synthesis requires a discrete-event abstraction, which inevitably leads to nondeterministic behavior. This is where our approach to nondeterministic discrete-event systems discussed in this paper comes into place. The hybrid model is often made for validation purposes, e.g., for discrete-event simulation [4,18]. In the design of the plant, decisions are made on the level of abstraction that is used, and what is significant discrete-event behavior. In parallel, a formal specification of the control requirements is made, which together with the plant serve as input to the synthesis tool. The synthesis tool automatically synthesizes a supervisor. Our preliminary investigation in synthesis algorithms for the notion of controllability proposed in this paper is given in [10].

To validate the obtained supervisors, software-in-the-loop simulation can be employed, coupled with the discrete-event or the hybrid model of the system. One also has the option of early integration, by employing hardware-in-the-loop simulation, which is used to validate the supervisor against a prototype of the plant. If the validation is not satisfactory, the control requirements and/or the

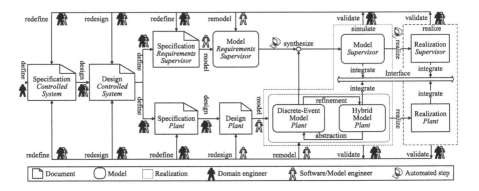

Fig. 8. Model-based systems engineering framework for supervisory controller synthesis.

system model need to be revised. Finally, the control software code is generated automatically based on the validated models.

We note that the proposed framework directly affects the software development process. It switches the focus of the software engineers from interpreting requirements, coding, and testing to analyzing requirements, modeling, and validating system behavior. Admittedly, use of formal methods requires a substantial initial effort during the development and design phases. However, early model validation and employment of unambiguous formal specifications decrease the number of testing and integration errors. In this way, the overall product-development time and costs are mitigated, while increasing product quality [22].

6   Concluding Remarks

We defined a notion of controllability for finite automata with variables based on the behavioral preorder termed partial bisimulation. We showed that the proposed notion of controllability subsumes the prominent previous notion of state controllability, which was specifically tailored for nondeterministic finite automata with variables. Moreover, we showed that state controllability is not a preorder and that there exist state-uncontrollable plants for which it is possible to synthesize viable supervisory controllers. This situation was remedied by the new definition, which does not exclude the investigated cases. Furthermore, we showed that the proposed setting enables detection of spurious nondeterministic behavior, i.e., it is possible to eliminate nondeterministic behavior that does not contribute to the behavior of the supervised system. Finally, we outlined the use of the proposed theory in a synthesis-centric model-based systems and software engineering framework.

References

1. Baeten, J.C.M., Basten, T., Reniers, M.A.: Process Algebra: Equational Theories of Communicating Processes. Cambridge Tracts in Theoretical Computer Science, vol. 50. Cambridge University Press, Cambridge (2010)
2. Baeten, J.C.M., van Beek, D.A., Luttik, B., Markovski, J., Rooda, J.E.: A process-theoretic approach to supervisory control theory. In: Proceedings of ACC 2011, pp. 4496–4501. IEEE (2011)
3. Baeten, J., van Beek, D., van Hulst, A., Markovski, J.: A process algebra for supervisory coordination. In: Proceedings of PACO 2011. EPTCS, vol. 60, pp. 36–55. Open Publishing Association (2011)
4. Cassandras, C., Lafortune, S.: Introduction to Discrete Event Systems. Kluwer Academic Publishers, Dordrecht (2004)
5. Chen, Y.L., Lin, F.: Modeling of discrete event systems using finite state machines with parameters. In: Proceedings of CCA 2000, pp. 941–946 (2000)
6. Eshuis, R., Fokkinga, M.M.: Comparing refinements for failure and bisimulation semantics. Fund. Inform. **52**(4), 297–321 (2002)
7. Fabian, M., Lennartson, B.: On non-deterministic supervisory control. In: Proceedings of the 35th IEEE Decision and Control, vol. 2, pp. 2213–2218 (1996)
8. Gaudin, B., Deussen, P.: Supervisory control on concurrent discrete event systems with variables. In: Proceedings of ACC 2007, pp. 4274–4279 (2007)
9. van Glabbeek, R.J.: The linear time-branching time spectrum I. In: Bergstra, J.A., et al. (eds.) Handbook of Process Algebra, Chap. 1, pp. 3–99. Elsevier, Amsterdam (2001)
10. Kirilov, A., Martinovikj, D., Mishevski, K., Petkovska, M., Trajcheska, Z., Markovski, J.: A supervisor synthesis tool for finite nondeterministic automata with data. In: Counsell, S., Núñez, M. (eds.) SEFM 2013. LNCS, vol. 8368, pp. 101–112. Springer, Heidelberg (2014)
11. Leveson, N.: The challenge of building process-control software. IEEE Softw. **7**(6), 55–62 (1990)
12. Ma, C., Wonham, W.M.: Nonblocking Supervisory Contr. LNCIS, vol. 317, pp. 1–9. Springer, Heidelberg (2005)
13. Markovski, J.: Coarsest controllability-preserving plant minimization. In: Proceedings of WODES 2012, pp. 251–258. IFAC (2012)
14. Markovski, J.: Communicating processes with data for supervisory coordination. In: Proceedings of FOCLASA 2012. EPTCS, vol. 91, pp. 97–111. Open Publishing Association (2012)
15. Markovski, J., van Beek, D.A., Theunissen, R.J.M., Jacobs, K.G.M., Rooda, J.E.: A state-based framework for supervisory control synthesis and verification. In: Proceedings of CDC 2010, pp. 3481–3486. IEEE (2010)
16. Miremadi, S., Akesson, K., Lennartson, B.: Extraction and representation of a supervisor using guards in extended finite automata. In: Proceedings of WODES 2008, pp. 193–199. IEEE (2008)
17. Overkamp, A.: Supervisory control using failure semantics and partial specifications. IEEE Trans. Autom. Control **42**(4), 498–510 (1997)
18. Ramadge, P.J., Wonham, W.M.: Supervisory control of a class of discrete-event processes. SIAM J. Control Optim. **25**(1), 206–230 (1987)
19. Rutten, J.J.M.M.: Coalgebra, concurrency, and control. In: Proceedings of WODES 2000, pp. 31–38. Kluwer Academic Publishers, Dordrecht (2000)

20. Schiffelers, R.R.H., Theunissen, R.J.M., van Beek, D.A., Rooda, J.E.: Model-based engineering of supervisory controllers using CIF. Electron. Commun. EASST **21**, 1–10 (2009)
21. Skoldstam, M., Akesson, K., Fabian, M.: Modeling of discrete event systems using finite automata with variables. In: Proceedings of CDC 2007, pp. 3387–3392. IEEE (2007)
22. Woodcock, J., Larsen, P.G., Bicarregui, J., Fitzgerald, J.: Formal methods: practice and experience. ACM Comput. Surv. **41**(4), 1–36 (2009)
23. Zhou, C., Kumar, R., Jiang, S.: Control of nondeterministic discrete-event systems for bisimulation equivalence. IEEE Trans. Autom. Control **51**(5), 754–765 (2006)

A Computer-Aided Process from Problems to Laws in Requirements Engineering

Stephan Faßbender$^{(\boxtimes)}$ and Maritta Heisel

Paluno - The Ruhr Institute for Software Technology,
University of Duisburg-Essen, Essen, Germany
{Stephan.Fassbender,Maritta.Heisel}@paluno.uni-due.de

Abstract. In today's world many products and services are highly dependent on software and information systems. With the growing importance of IT systems, legislators worldwide decided to regulate and enforce laws for IT systems. With respect to this situation, the impact of compliance on the development of IT systems becomes more and more severe. Hence, software engineers have a need for techniques to deal with compliance. But identifying relevant compliance regulations for IT systems is a challenging task. We proposed patterns and a structured method to tackle these problems [1]. A crucial step is the transformation of requirements into a structure, which allows for the identification of laws. The transformation step was described in general in [2]. This work describes a method to structure the requirements, elicit the needed domain knowledge and transform requirements into law identification pattern instances. The manual execution of this method was reported by us to be time consuming and tedious. Hence, in this work we identify the points for (semi-)automation, and we outline a first implementation for the automation. We present our results using a voting system as an example, which was obtained from the ModIWa DFG (Juristisch-informatische Modellierung von Internetwahlen (II). A Deutsche Forschungsgemeinschaft project: http://cms.uni-kassel.de/unicms/index.php?id=38536) project and the common criteria profile for voting systems.

Keywords: Compliance · Law · Voting system · Requirements engineering · Model transformation

1 Introduction

In today's world many products and services are highly dependent on software and information systems. With the growing importance of IT systems over the past decades, legislators worldwide decided to regulate and enforce laws regarding IT systems. The permanently evolving technology inevitably leads to ever

Part of this work is funded by the German Research Foundation (DFG) under grant number HE3322/4-2 and the EU project Network of Excellence on Engineering Secure Future Internet Software Services and Systems (NESSoS, ICT-2009.1.4 Trustworthy ICT, Grant No. 256980).

© Springer-Verlag Berlin Heidelberg 2014
J. Cordeiro and M. van Sinderen (Eds.): ICSOFT 2013, CCIS 457, pp. 215–234, 2014.
DOI: 10.1007/978-3-662-44920-2_14

increasing legal requirements and regulations with severe penalties for non-conformance. Many emerging information-driven businesses deploy information services without adequately considering illegal misuse. But compliance is critical for such systems as they are governed by regulations and law, especially given that non-compliance can result in both financial and criminal penalties.

One emblematic example is the case of the information broker "ChoicePoint" for which an identity theft of more than 163.000 consumers was reported. An assessment of the company's products indicated that these were developed without proper security controls as mandated by the Fair Credit Reporting Act. Since ChoicePoint failed to comply with these regulations, it was fined $10 million in civil damages and $5 million for consumer redress. Further, the settlement requires ChoicePoint to implement new procedures to ensure that it provides consumer reports only to legitimate businesses for lawful purposes, to establish and maintain a comprehensive information security program, and to allow audits by an independent third-party security professional every other year until 2026 [3]. Violations similar to this example are considered to be due to the subjective interpretation of regulations by companies in the context of their information systems' landscape. Ultimately, the law is valid for all software products, regardless of size, revenues or scale of the producer.

The identification and analysis of relevant laws is considered to be difficult because it is a cross-disciplinary task in laws as well as in software and systems engineering [4]. Otto and Antón [5] conclude in their survey about research on laws in requirements engineering that there is a need for techniques to identify relevant laws based on requirements, analyze them, and to derive requirements from them.

Pattern-based approaches capture the knowledge of domain experts. In this way, the knowledge is made explicit and can be re-used for recurring problems. Hence, we proposed a pattern-based approach for identifying and analyzing laws in one of our earlier works [1]. These patterns already allow the identification of relevant laws.

However, the identification of a relevant law alone is not sufficient for software engineers. They require a structured method that uses this approach to derive software requirements and further implementable software specifications. In [6] we present such a structured method. One crucial step within this method is the transformation of functional requirements into law identification pattern instances, which allows the matching with law pattern instances. How to do the transformation manually is described in another work of ours [2]. But the method execution is reported by us to be time consuming and tedious. Hence, in this paper we present an improved method with tool-support.

In the following, we present a guided and tool-supported transformation of requirements into law identification pattern instances, using a voting system as an example. We make use of the problem-based requirements engineering approach proposed by Jackson [7] to structure the requirements in terms of problem diagrams in the first place. We decided to use problem frames because they have a kind of semi-formal structure and can be modeled. Furthermore, they already embody descriptions of common problems. Thus, they are suitable as an input for a transformation as they have a predictable structure, and transformation rules can be set up on the basis of the generic problems. Then we show how to turn these problem diagrams into law identification patterns using our tool. We provide detailed transformation rules for different requirement patterns, as described by Côté et al. [8], to obtain the corresponding law identification pattern instances. All these information needed for matching, and transformation is provided by means of *transformation cards* (see Sect. 5). In this way, the identification of laws gains precision and is less error-prone, for example due to forgetting important domain knowledge.

In Sect. 2 we introduce the problem frame terminology and notation, and the pattern for law identification. Next, we briefly introduce the voting system case in Sect. 3. For our case study, we structure the problem, ending up with a set of problem diagrams in Sect. 4. In Sect. 5 we present a structured method, which guides requirements engineers through the process of transforming the problem into relevant law identification pattern instances. Section 6 outlines the result of a validation. Section 7 discusses the related work, and Sect. 8 concludes the paper.

2   Background

We use the problem frames [7] approach to structure functional requirements and corresponding domain knowledge. And we make use of the problem frames to facilitate the transformation to the law identification pattern.

Problem Frames. Jackson [7] introduced the concept of *problem frames*, which is concerned with describing, analyzing, and structuring of software development problems. A problem frame represents a class of software development problems. It is described by a *frame diagram*, which consists of domains, interfaces between them, and a requirement. Domains describe entities in the environment. Jackson distinguishes the domain types **biddable domains** that are usually people, **causal domains** that comply with some physical laws, and **lexical domains** that are data representations. To describe the problem context, a **connection domain** between two other domains may be necessary. Connection domains establish a connection between other domains by means of technical devices. Examples are video cameras, sensors, or networks. Finally, we introduced **display domains** [8] which serve to display information to some biddable domain.

Interfaces connect domains, and they contain *shared phenomena*. Shared phenomena may be events, operation calls, messages, and the like. They are observable by at least two domains, but controlled by only one domain, as indicated by the name of that domain and "!". For example, shared phenomenon *displayBallot* in Fig. 1 is observable by the domains **ShowBallotClient** and **Voter**, but controlled only by the domain **Voter**. We describe problem frames using UML class diagrams, extended by stereotypes, as proposed by Hatebur and Heisel [9].

The objective is to construct a *machine* (i.e., software) that controls the behavior of the environment (in which it is integrated) in accordance with the requirements. When we state a requirement, we want to change something in

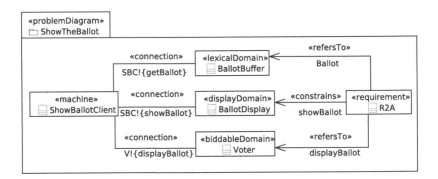

Fig. 1. Problem diagram for R2A.

the environment. Therefore, each requirement *constrains* at least one domain. A requirement may also *refer* to several domains in the environment of the machine.

The problem frames approach distinguishes therefore between the *requirements (R)*, the *domain knowledge (D)*, and the *specification (S)*. The requirements describe the desired system after the machine is built. The domain knowledge represents the relevant parts of the problem world. The specifications describe the behavior of the software in order to meet the requirements.

Beside the requirements, the domain knowledge about the environment of the machine to be built is crucial for understanding the problem and specifying the machine behavior later on. Unlike Jackson, we distinguish between *assumptions*, *facts*, and *definitions and designations*. Assumptions describe conditions fulfilled by the environment that are needed, so that the requirements can be fulfilled by the machine. However, these may be violated in certain situations. Facts describe fixed properties of the environment irrespective of how the machine is built. Definitions and designations specify a set of special terms used for formulating requirements, assumptions and facts.

Problem-oriented requirements analysis starts with representing the environment using a *context diagram*. Such a diagram describes *where* the problem is located by stating the relevant domains and their interfaces, including the machine to be built. Problem-oriented requirements analysis proceeds with a decomposition of the overall problem into sub-problems, which are represented by *problem diagrams*. The problem diagrams should be instances of problem frames, thereby representing *simple* development problems. In contrast to context diagrams, problem diagrams contain the requirements belonging to the sub-problem. An example of a problem diagram can be found in Fig. 1.

Figure 1 shows a problem diagram in UML notation. The biddable domain (UML class with stereotype ≪biddableDomain≫) **Voter** controls the *display ballot* command (Name of the UML association with the stereotype ≪connection≫ between the classes **Voter** and **ShowBallotClient**), which is observed by the machine domain **ShowBallotClient** (UML class with stereotype ≪machine≫).

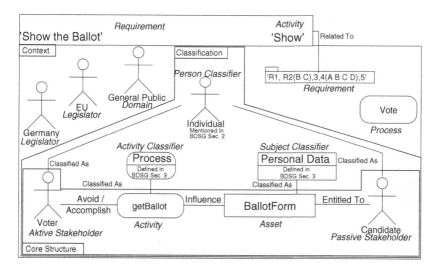

Fig. 2. One law identification pattern instance for R2A.

The **ShowBallotClient** controls the phenomenon *getBallot*, which is obtained from the lexical domain **BallotBuffer**(UML class with stereotype ≪lexicalDomain≫). Additionally, the **ShowBallotClient** *shows the ballot* using the **BallotDisplay**. The requirement **R2A** (for a textual description see Sect. 4) constrains the **BallotDisplay** and refers to the **Voters**, and the **BallotBuffer**.

Patterns for Requirement-based Law Identification. Commonly, laws are not adequately considered during requirements engineering [5]. Therefore, they are not covered in the subsequent system development phases. One fundamental reason for this is that the involved engineers are typically not cross-disciplinary experts in law and software and systems engineering. To bridge this gap, we developed law patterns and a general process for law identification which relies on these patterns.

We investigated how judges and lawyers are supposed to analyze a law, based upon legal literature research. These insights lead to a basic structure of laws and the contained sections. One result of our investigations is a common structure of laws. Based on this structure of laws, we defined a *law pattern*. The law pattern itself is discussed in detail in [1].

Identifying relevant laws based on functional requirements is challenging. Functional requirements are often too imprecise for a sufficient law analysis, they contain important information only implicitly, and use a different wording than in laws. Therefore, we developed a *law identification pattern*, which structures requirements in a way that important terms of a requirement can be mapped to the legal wording and then matched with law pattern instances (Fig. 2 shows an instance).

The light-gray words in italics indicate the general elements of the law identification pattern, while the black words represent the current instantiation.

First of all, a *Requirement* dictates a certain behavior of the machine and it can be *Related To* other *Requirements*. A behavior can be a certain *Activity* or an entire *Process*. The machine resides in one or more jurisdictions represented by their *Legislators*. And the problem the machine has to solve is a problem of one or more *Domains*. The fundamental parts of the requirements are described in the *Core Structure*. An *Activity* involves an *Active stakeholder* and in some cases an *Asset*. Additionally, an *Activity Influences* a *Passive Stakeholder* in a direct way or indirectly through an *Asset*, to which the *Passive Stakeholder* is *entitled to*. The terms used for *Activities*, *Stakeholders*, and *Assets* can be *Classified* in the *Classification* part, using terms of the legal domain.

The general process for identifying relevant laws consists of five steps [6]. The first step is to set up a database of all laws which might be of relevance for a scenario. Therefore, laws have to be analyzed and stored in the structure of the law pattern. Thus, they are stored as law pattern instances. The second step uses information from functional requirements and their context to instantiate the core structure and the context of the according law identification pattern. Third, the relation between laws and software requirements has to be established to prepare the identification of relevant laws for the given system. Hence, a mapping between the terms and notions of the software requirements to legal terms and notions is derived. Fourth, the law pattern instances and law identification pattern instances have to be matched. This results in a set of laws which might be of relevance for the software. Fifth, the found laws are the basis for further investigations.

In order to accomplish this process described, law experts and software engineers have to work together for the necessary knowledge transfer. Step one can be performed by legal experts alone and for step two only software engineers are needed. But in steps three and four both groups are needed to bridge the gap between the legal and technical world. The last step can be accomplished by legal experts alone. In this paper, we focus on the transformation step (step two) and how to turn requirements, in our case in terms of problem diagrams, into law identification pattern instances.

3   Case Study: Voting System for Germany

Electronic voting enjoys an ever-increasing interest from governments as they seek to facilitate and simplify their election procedures. In several countries like Australia, Brasil, Belgium, Canada, India, UK, and Spain electronic voting systems are already in use [10]. In Germany there are also some activities on introducing such a voting system.

By its very nature, the field of electronic voting is an interdisciplinary field in which legal and computer scientists work together. During the development of the first voting system used in Germany, this fact was neglected or inadequately considered. Hence, the federal constitutional court of Germany judged in 2009 that using this system for votings in 2005 was unconstitutional [11].

A general problem description of this voting system and which functionality it has to provide was derived from [12,13]. The former work was conducted in the context of the ModIWa II project, while the latter work was elaborated in the context of a Common Criteria (CC) Profile [14] for online voting systems. These documents are used in Sect. 4 for detailing the requirements and knowledge about the involved stakeholder and systems, and their relation to each other.

4 Structuring the Problem

As proposed by Jackson [7], we derive requirements and domain knowledge from the problem description, and decompose the overall problem into sub-problems using problem diagrams. Note that for presenting our transformation method we only use functional requirements. Non-functional requirements are left aside. Nevertheless, the found laws demand further quality requirements, for example privacy requirements.

Requirements and Domain Knowledge. The CC profile for online voting systems [14] only deals with the polling phase. The preliminary election preparation and the tallying are not considered in detail. Hence, the profile only defines functional requirements for the voter and the election officer who represents the election authority. In total, the machine to be built is described in terms of 21 requirements by the CC profile. Later on we split some of the requirements for handling reasons. We only consider one requirement of the voter at this point. It is sufficient for the rest of the paper. The requirement texts are directly taken from the CC profile [14]. (Note that the abbreviation TOE stands for target of evaluation, which is, in terms of the CC, the machine to be built.)

(R2A) show the ballot "[...] involves the ballot being displayed to a voter [...]. [...]usually in the form of a corresponding on-screen display. [...] The [...] ballot is held in the buffer from the point that the casting of the vote is initiated to the storage of the vote in the ballot box.[...]"

Besides the requirements themselves, the knowledge about the environment of the machine to be built is crucial for understanding the problem and specifying the machine behavior later on. We only present the assumptions and facts we derived from CC profile [14] which are of relevance in the following. In total, the CC profile states 21 assumptions, 14 facts and 35 definitions and designations.

(A3) ballot display "Vote casting [...] takes place [...] from a vote-casting device which is able to display the full contents of the ballot and to implement the responsible election authority's specifications for the type of display, in particular the order of voting options.[...] The voter acts responsibly in securing the vote-casting device. It is assumed that each voter that installs or uses the client-sided TOE does so in such a way that the vote-casting device can neither observe nor influence the vote casting process. This includes the assumption that the voter does not manipulate his vote-casting device on purpose. The vote-casting device is able to properly display the ballot, to properly transfer the voters input to the election server and to delete the vote after the polling process."

(**A10**) **observation** "The voter ensures that nobody is watching him while he casts his vote. The responsible election authority accounts for appropriate advice for the voter regarding how to cast his vote unobserved."

(**F6**) **ballot** "Displayed form (conforming to a ballot paper). This can be blank or completed. It can also offer the opportunity to deliberately cast an invalid vote. The completed ballot is held in the buffer from the point that the casting of the vote is initiated to the storage of the vote in the ballot box. According to which conditions a vote is valid is dependent on the election regulation. An example of an invalid vote is when the voter has selected no or too many voting options."

For analyzing and structuring requirements we use problem diagrams. Figure 1 shows the problem diagram for the requirement R2A. The diagram was already described in Sect. 2.

5   Transforming Problem Diagrams to Law Identification Pattern Instances

So-called transformation cards are the central tool for executing the transformation in the following. We developed a transformation card for each problem frame, which helps requirements engineers to fit the problem diagrams into the according law identification pattern instances. The transformation card contains information used for *matching problem diagrams and frames*, and information how the problem frame, and therefore the matching problem diagram, is related to the *core structure* of the law identification pattern. It also contains information for *collecting potentially missing domain knowledge*, which is important for transforming problem diagrams into core structures, and the *transformation rules* themselves. As a result, the transformation card supports and guides requirements engineers when preparing the requirements for the matching with relevant laws. In this way, the identification of laws gains precision and is less error-prone, for example due to forgetting important domain knowledge. Beside improving the precision and reducing the chance of an error, transformation cards are the basis for the semi-automatic tool-support. The description of the tool-support will be also given in the following paragraphs highlighted with a different font.

For the tool-support, all information given by the transformation cards is modeled using the UML and a specific transformation card profile. The model containing all transformation cards is then the input for the tool. The tool itself is realized with the Eclipse Epsilon framework[1]. The result is an Eclipse plugin which integrates into the UML4PF tool[2].

The process for using the transformation cards, and therefore the tool, is shown in Fig. 3. It starts with the *identification of applicable transformation*

---

[1] http://www.eclipse.org/epsilon/

[2] http://www.uml4pf.org

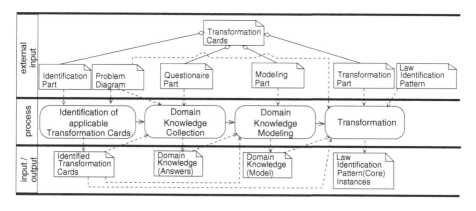

Fig. 3. The transformation process.

cards for the problem diagrams. The *problem diagrams* are a necessary external input like the *identification part* of the transformation cards. The problem diagrams have to be modeled beforehand. Then the *questionnaire part* of the *identified transformation cards* is used for a *domain knowledge collection*. Next, the *answers* and the *modeling part* of the identified transformation card serve as input for *domain knowledge modeling*. The modeling part contains detailed rules how to model legal domain knowledge. Finally, the *transformation* is executed using information contained problem diagrams and the according *domain knowledge models*. The used transformation rules are obtained from *transformation part* of the identified transformation cards. The transformation results in *law identification pattern (core) instances*.

Identification of Applicable Transformation Cards. Table 1 shows the part of a transformation card, which can help to identify the matching problem frame. In the problem frame part, the structure of the problem frames by means of contained domains, phenomena, their sequence, and *refers to and constrains* relations to the requirement are described. A matching problem diagram must

Table 1. Query transformation card: identification part.

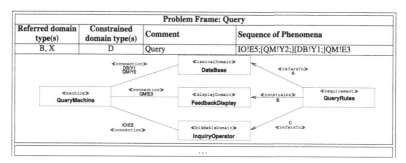

have the same characteristics as described in this part of the transformation card.

The problem diagrams have sometimes to be modified for matching. For example, big and complex problem diagrams have to be partitioned, or domains have to be merged for fitting the problem diagram at hand to a problem frame. For reasons of space we skip the full discussion. The interested reader is referred to Hatebur and Heisel [9].

For selecting the applicable transformation cards, the tool provides a selection of transformation cards which might be applicable to the problem. For this task we use the Epsilon comparison language. For each transformation card it calculates a fitting indicator for a given problem diagram. In case that all domains and necessary interfaces are found in a problem diagram, and the correct domains are referred and constrained. Hence, the fitting indicator is 1. The indicator is decreased for each missing domain, additional domain or differing interface. The selection of an applicable transformation card itself has to be done by the user. It cannot be done automatically because the sequence of phenomena, for example, cannot be checked automatically. But for the selection, the user has only to analyze the transformation cards with a high indicator and not all transformation cards.

For our example (Fig. 1), we now check if a transformation card is applicable or not. First, the tool calculates the fitting indicator. The **Voter** is a biddable domain and the **BallotBuffer** is a lexical domain. R2A refers to both. This matches the *Referred domain type(s)* of the identification part of the query transformation card. This is also true for the *Constrained domain type(s)* which has to be a display domain. The constrained domain **BallotDisplay** in our problem diagram is a display domain. As all phenomena necessary for the sequence of phenomena are also given in the problem diagram (e.g. *QM!E3* matches *SBC!{showBallot}*), the fitting indicator is 1.

Last, we have to check whether the implicitly described sequence of phenomena of the problem frame, matches the phenomena of the problem diagram or not. The sequence of *V!{login}*; *VISM!{getIdentifictaion}*; *VICM!{showLoginResult}* matches the regular expression as given by the *Sequence of Phenomena* in the transformation card. As a result, the transformation card for the problem frame Query has to be applied.

Domain Knowledge Collection. After the successful matching, the transformation card contains further guidance for preparing the transformation. It contains several core structure variants, which describe the possible *core structure* instantiations of the law identification pattern for the problem frame at hand.

The core structure variants not only relate problem frame and core structure, but also consider typical domain knowledge for a problem frame. To ensure that this domain knowledge is collected properly, there is a questionnaire for each core structure variant. The questionnaire is structured into the parts "Necessary Information", which describes for which information we are looking for, "Details", which states which domain is the target of the question, the "Question" itself, and "Result", which describes how to model the collected domain

Table 2. Query transformation card: questionnaire and transformation part.

Problem Frame: Query
...

Core Structure Variant 2

Machine Stakeholder — Avoid / Accomplish — QM!Y2 — Activity — Influence — DataBase (part) — Asset — Entitled To — DataBase Stakeholder / DataBase Information Stakeholder

Aktive Stakeholder / *Passive Stakeholder*

Necessary Information	Details	Question	Result
Structure Database	DataBase	Which information is contained in the database and which structure does it have?	**For each** new found part of the database : **Add** a «lexical» domain for the part to the model. **Add** a aggregation relation between database and database part domain to the model.**roF**
Database Stakeholder	-	Who are the stakeholders owning the database?	**For each** found stakeholder : **If** stakeholder does not exists in model **then Add** new «biddable» domain for the stakeholder to the model.**fI Add** a «entitledTo» association between database (part) domain and stakeholder domain.**roF**
Database Information Stakeholder	-	Who are the stakeholders entitled to information contained in the database (part)?	**For each** found stakeholder : **If** stakeholder does not exists in model **then Add** new «biddable» domain for the stakeholder to the model.**fI Add** a «entitledTo» association between database (part) domain and stakeholder domain.**roF**
Machine Stakeholder	-	Who is responsible and in control of the machine?	**For each** found stakeholder : **If** stakeholder does not exists in model **then Add** new «biddable» domain for the stakeholder to the model.**fI Add** a «controls» association between stakeholder domain and machine.**roF**
Instantiation Rule:		**For each** database and its parts: **For each** machine stakeholder: **For each** database (information) stakeholder: Instantiate core structure variant 2. **roF roF roF**	

...

knowledge. While answering these questions, necessary domain knowledge which might be missing is collected.

The tool uses the Epsilon generation language and pdflatex to prepare an adjusted questionnaire for each core structure variant. Table 3 shows such a generated questionnaire. The shown questionnaire only contains questions regarding core structure variant 2 and before the first iteration. Indeed, the tool does not generate one questionnaire for each problem diagram and related core structure variants separately. Instead, it generates one coherent questionnaire for a complete set of problem diagrams and related transformation cards. This way, repetition of questions can be avoided. Several iterations are possible as an answer can lead to new questions. For example, discovering a new sub-art of the ballot buffer leads to new questions regarding this new part. Thus, the tool indicates the need of an additional iteration and provides a new questionnaire. The new questionnaire only contains the newly occurred questions. In this way, the generated questionnaires guide through the domain knowledge elicitation.

Table 2 shows one core structure variant. There are three more variants, which we have to skip due to reasons of space. The first information, which might be missing, is about the structure of the **DataBase**. Normally, in problem diagrams a lexical domain represents information, which can be regarded as part

Table 3. Catalog of questions for core structure variant 2.

Necessary Information	Details	Question
Structure BallotBuffer	BallotBuffer	Which information is contained in the BallotBuffer and which structure does it have?
BallotBuffer Stakeholder	-	Who are the stakeholders owning the BallotBuffer?
BallotBuffer Information Stakeholder	-	Who are the stakeholders entitled to information contained in the BallotBuffer?
ShowBallotClient Stakeholder	-	Who is responsible and in control of the ShowBallotClient?

of the overall database. But for law identification we need to know the specific piece(s) of information which is/are relevant for the problem at hand. In case the database can be partitioned further, we have to add a separate lexical domain for each found piece of information. For the **BallotBuffer** we already collected the information by means of the fact **F6**. Hence, we know that ballot form for displaying the ballot is part of the buffer. Additionally, the information about the data the voter has already entered is stored in the buffer. Thus, we add the ballot form and entered data as part of the ballot buffer. The ballot buffer is related to one **DataBase Stakeholder**. Thus is the **Voter**, who owns the voting device and therefore the buffer. The ballot buffer is related to two **DataBase Information Stakeholders** to which the next question refers. The first one is the **Voter** because entered data represents the decisions of the voter. The second ones are the party candidates because the ballot form contains their names and relations to the parties. After answering the questionnaire, all necessary domain knowledge is available in terms of natural language answers.

Domain Knowledge Modeling. The natural language answers given in the previous step have to be made available in the model for the next steps. Therefore, we use domain knowledge diagrams [15] and a UML profile for legal domain knowledge modeling.

The modeling of domain knowledge is completely tool-supported. Using the Epsilon wizard language, the answers to the questions can be added within guided wizards. The domain knowledge diagrams according to the answers themselves are then automatically set up. Only the graphical representation has to be generated manually if needed.

Transformation. With the newly obtained domain knowledge at hand, we can transform the problem diagram into law identification pattern core structure instances. How often a core structure has to be instantiated is described in the instantiation rule (see Table 2) of each core structure variant part of the transformation card. Hence, it is possible that one problem diagram is transformed into several law identification pattern instances.

For **R2A** (Fig. 1) and *Core Structure Variant 2* (Table 2) we have to instantiate the core structure for each combination of **Database (part)**, **Machine Stakeholder**, **DataBase Stakeholder** and **DataBase Information Stakeholder**. The *Activity* is the same for all core structures of variant 2. This results in a core structure for **Voter**, *getBallot*, **BallotBuffer**, and **Voter**, a core structure for **Voter**, *getBallot*, **BallotForm**, and **Candidate**, and a core structure for **Voter**, *getBallot*, **EnteredData**, and **Voter**. The second core structure is shown in Fig. 2. The *Active Stakeholder* is instantiated as **Voter**, the *Passive Stakeholder* as **Candidate**, the *Asset* as **BallotForm**, and the *Activity* is instantiated as *getBallot*.

The transformation from problem diagrams to core structures can be performed fully automatically by the tool. For this task we use the Epsilon transformation language and a UML profile for representing law identification patterns in UML. Note that the core structures are added to the same UML model where also the problem diagrams reside. In this way, we have one model storing all information allowing information tracing and coherence checks. In a second step, the UML representation is transformed into a law pattern specific form, which allows the matching with laws.

After adding the context information to the pattern and discussing the mappings of terms with a legal expert, we obtain a law identification pattern instance as shown in Fig. 2. For the process of adding the classification and context, and finally the matching to laws, we refer the interested reader to [1,6].

6   Validation

For the validation of our proposed method we analyzed the voting system in a case of action research in [2]. There were two hypotheses to be tested, namely *"H1: The transformation cards are sufficient to be integrated into the overall identification process as described by [6]"* and *"H2: Using the transformation cards leads to an identification of all relevant laws"*. For this paper, we made a re-run for the voting system using our tool-supported improved method.

The re-run should ensure that the integration of the tools does not negatively influence the results reported in our previous paper [2]. Additionally, the hypotheses *"H3: Using tool-support improves the execution of the transformation as described in [2]"* was tested.

To decide the first and the third hypotheses, we tested the usage of transformation cards by integrating the transformation process in the overall process as described in [6]. To be able to discuss the sufficiency of the transformation cards and tool support, we tracked the generation of core structures in terms of number and effort. These results were compared to the previous results, which were obtained facilitating purely manual work, as reported in [2].

To decide the second hypothesis, we already conducted a literature research about the voting system and the relevant German laws for this matter in [2]. The main source was the judgment of 2009 by the Federal Constitutional Court of

Germany [11], followed by discussions with several domain and/or legal experts. These insights lead to expectations whether a requirement will match with a particular law or not. These expectations were documented in terms of a table listing the expectations for each law and requirement. This table was compared to the matching based on the generated law identification pattern. The result is of a quantitative nature in terms of false positives and false negatives, and evidence by the number of matches.

For the validation, we excluded some laws even though they were identified as relevant based on the literature research and discussions. We selected the highly relevant laws as discussed by the Federal Constitutional Court. These laws are necessary to find the weaknesses of our method in terms of false negatives. A false negative would be a missing match with a law for a certain requirement. To identify false positives, we also added laws which are somehow related to voting systems, but not relevant. Hence, here we expected to find matches which are not of real relevance. For the validation, we selected the four following laws:

– The BDSG as highly relevant law concerning personal data.
– The BWahlG (Bundeswahlgesetz), which is the law for federal state elections in Germany and also highly relevant.
– The SigG (Signatur Gesetz), a law which regulates the use of digital signatures. This particular law was selected not due to its relevance, but it is related in terms of the technological background. Therefore, it is interesting whether such a law, which is only related in the used wording, will match or not.
– The PassG (Pass Gesetz), which regulates the use of passports in Germany. This law is clearly irrelevant, nevertheless the passport is a possible authentication means during elections.

From our observations, the transformation cards integrated well in the overall law identification process. After the core structures were generated, no further modifications were required for instantiating the full law identification patterns. The preparations of the core structures were more structured and detailed and therefore less error-prone compared to the hands on instantiation we used previously.

A major downside is the sheer number of generated core structures. And there is a high share of duplicates. But as the core structures are generated automatically, the additional effort spent is zero at this point. And the tool is able to remove the duplicates. From our experience, none of the non-duplicated core structures can be removed as they are all necessary for a detailed detection of relevant laws. Sometimes only the minor differences between core structures revealed the most important parts of a requirement for the relevance of a law. These differences then help to understand how to address the law. Furthermore, we could not identify common characteristics for filtering out the core structures which match all relevant laws. The laws are too different to do so. Hence, the big number of core structures is necessary and even helpful.

Speaking of the effort, there are several things to consider (see overview Table 4). The matching of problem diagrams with problem frames is straightforward and takes almost no time. The modeling of the problem diagrams by

Table 4. Effort spent for conducting the method.

			Method Step				
			Modeling of Problem Diagrams	Identification of applicable transformation cards	Domain Knowledge Collection	Domain Knowledge Modeling	Transformation
Method execution	Manually	Per Item	30 min per Problem Diagram	5 min per Problem Diagram	45 min per Problem Diagram	15 min per Problem Diagram	4 minutes per core structure
	(reported in [2])	Total	5 person hours	1 person hour	7.5 person hours	2.5 person hours	8 person hours
	Tool	Per Item	30 min per Problem Diagram	1 min per Problem Diagram	45 min per Problem Diagram	5 min per Problem Diagram	0 minutes per core structure
	Supported	Total	5 person hours	0.125 person hour	7.5 person hours	1 person hour	0 person hours

an experienced user took about 5 person hours (0.5 h for one requirement). This seems reasonable if the law identification gives sufficient results afterward. Answering the questionnaire and modeling the resulting information takes some more time. But this process of answering and modeling speeds up significantly with a growing number of already analyzed requirements. Mostly, the questions consider the domains directly. And as the number of domains is limited, so is the information needed about them. Thus, most information is already known and modeled for later requirements. It took about 8.5 person hours for this step including discussions (about 1 h for one requirement). This seems to be a significant amount of work, but the information collected is crucial for the success of the application of the transformation card. Hence, we spent some more time for this discussions and searching for the necessary information (e.g. in the protection profile [14]). Setting up the core structures is an easy task, and automated it takes no time. In total, executing the proposed method took 13.5 person hours.

This effort seems to be significantly high. But there are two things to consider: First, modeling problem diagrams enables one to use several other methods available for analyzing problem diagrams. For example, they can be analyzed for privacy [16] or standard-related issues [17]. Second, the effort for the elicitation of law-relevant information has to be invested even if someone uses another method to find relevant laws. Thus, the effort related to the use of transformation cards is limited to the modeling of problem diagrams and modeling of the collected information. And this pays off as it enables the automated generation and guided analysis. Hence, the overall effort to be spent seems to be reasonable, as long as the results of the identification process are precise enough.

Result H1: From our experience, the transformation card method using tool-support is still sufficient to integrate in the overall identification process as described by [6].

For assessing the precision and recall of the law identification using transformation cards, we set up Table 5. Symbols should be read the following way:

– A normal cross indicates an expected and observed match.
– A bold cross indicates an unexpected but correct match.

Table 5. Validation results: expected and found matches.

		Requirement									
		R1 identification voter	R2 A show ballot	R2 B complete ballot	R2 C correct ballot	R3 init vote	R4 A hasty vote protection	R4 B cast vote	R4 C ack vote	R4 D clear buffer	R5 abort vote
Law	BDSG	X	X	X	X	X	X	X	X	X	
	BwahlG		X̶	X	X	X	X	X̶	X̶		
	SigG	X̲									
	PassG										

– A canceled cross indicates an expected but not observed match and the missing cross turned out to be correct.
– An underlined cross indicates an unexpected and irrelevant match.

For the precision the identification turned out to be remarkable. The precision for the voting system and the four selected laws is at 0.94 (true positive/(true positive + false positive) = 16/(16 + 1)). Thus, almost every match points out a relevant law.

For the recall the result is perfect. The recall is at 1 (true positive/(true positive + false negative) = 16/(16 + 0)). Thus, not a single relevant law is missed.

Having a high recall is more important than a high precision in our case. The method should find all relevant laws. The impact of a missed law is much more serious to the development and success of the system-to-be than the extra effort spent on the legal revision for an irrelevant law. Hence, having recall value near to 1.0 is the main objective of our method. But a precision of 0.94 adds some surplus value. In terms of precision and recall, it is reasonable to use our method.

Compared to our expectations based on the requirements and legal insights alone, using the identification method is superior. For the BDSG we neglected the fact that the information about the candidates and their relation to parties is personal information which falls under the BDSG. In fact, this issue is not of high importance as this information is publicly available. But nevertheless, it makes the BDSG relevant for these requirements. For the BWahlG it turned out that this law and its sections only deal with the expression of opinion alone. Thus, those requirements that are not directly related to the voting itself are not in the focus of this particular law. The only point in favor of our manual prediction is that we rejected the SigG, while it was matched once by the law identification process. Integrating the tool into the method did not change any matching. Hence, the precision and recall of the law identification process is significantly higher than for our educated prediction.

"Result H2: To sum up, using the transformation cards and the tool leads to an identification of all relevant laws with a high precision". And it significantly improves the situation compared to an unguided method.

We have to consider two different aspects when deciding the third hypothesis. First, did the tool have an impact on the results of the method itself? Second, did it improve the effort to be spent? For the impact aspect we experienced no significant change. Only in the generated core structures we discovered three additional core structures. They were generated by the tool but overlooked when doing the generation manually. In our case, this did not change anything regarding the matching. Thus, using the tool does not add a benefit compared to conducting the method manually in an accurate way. But we assume that such a benefit would be visible if the method had been executed by an inexperienced user or users in a rush. For the effort aspect, Table 4 shows a significant improvement. We lowered the effort by 1/3. For the manual method execution we spent 24 person hours, while using the tool we only spend 13.5 h. *Result H3: Hence, the tool improves the execution of the transformation as described in* [2].

7 Related Work

Breaux et al. [18,19] present a framework for analyzing the structure of laws using a natural language pattern. This pattern helps to translate laws into a more structured restricted natural language and then into a first-order logic. The idea of using first-order logic in the context of regulations is not a new one. For example, Bench-Capon et al. [20] made use of first-order logic to model regulations and related matters. In contrast to our work, the authors of those methods assume that the relevant laws are already known and thus do not support identifying legal texts based on functional requirements.

Siena et al. [21] describe the differences between legal concepts and requirements. They model the regulations using an ontology, which is quite similar to the natural language patterns described in the methods mentioned previously. The ontology is based in the Hohfeld taxonomy [22], which describes the means and relations between the different means of legal texts in a very generic way. Thus Hohfeld does not structure a certain law at all, but aims at the different meanings of laws. Hence, the resulting process in [21] to align legal concepts to requirements and the given concepts are quite high-level and cannot be directly applied to a scenario. In a second work Siena et al. [23] try to bridge the gap between the requirements engineering process and compliance using a goal-oriented method. In this work they propose to derive goals from regulations and apply those goals to the actors within a requirements engineering scenario. In contrast to our method, they do not identify relevant laws and do not intertwine compliance regulations with already elicited requirements.

Maxwell et al. [24] developed an method to check existing software requirements for regulatory compliance, i.e., to discover violations and missing requirements. While our approach focuses on the identification of relevant laws, we could imagine using it to detect violations, too. We consider dependencies between different laws or regulations, which the approach from Maxwell et al. neglects.

Álvarez et al. [25] describe reusable legal requirements in natural language, based on the Spanish adaption of the EU directive 95/46/CE concerning personal data protection. We believe that the work by Álvarez et al. complements our work, i.e., applying our law identification method can proceed using their security requirements templates.

8 Conclusions

In this work, we introduced a structured method for transforming functional requirements into law identification pattern instances using transformation cards and tool-support. The transformation makes use of problem diagrams for structuring the functional requirements, problem frames for transformation instructions, domain knowledge for considering the context of the system, and questionnaires for refining the domain knowledge. We illustrated the method using a case study in the field of online voting. The contributions of this work are:

- Reuse of results of an existing requirements engineering (here problem frames) method for law identification.
- Transformation cards with tool-support, which enable software engineers to
  - identify the problem class of the requirement at hand
  - identify the needed domain knowledge for the transformation
  - model the domain knowledge
  - execute the transformation
- A structured and guided method for software engineers to transform functional requirements into law identification pattern instances.
- An improvement of law identification in requirements engineering by augmenting a crucial step of the law identification process as described in Beckers et al [6].
- A semi-automatic tool-support.

For the future we plan to investigate the matter of quality requirements. Quality requirements themselves are too vague to be directly transformed into law identification pattern instances. But they contain additional, relevant information about the functionality and context of a system. It seems to be promising to integrate this information to improve the precision of our method.

In general, our law identification process was used in the field of cloud computing, health-care and for this paper in the domain of voting systems. The transformation cards were only used for the latter. From our experience, our method is usable regarding the German law for different domains without adaption. We found evidence that this observation is also true for laws from other countries, as long as the law system of the country is a statue law. For example, Biagioli et al. [4] describe the very same structure for Italian laws as we use for German laws. For case law systems, like the one of the US, our method needs to be adapted. The use of our method on more domains, for other countries with statue law, and even for case law countries is under research.

References

1. Beckers, K., Faßbender, S., Küster, J.-C., Schmidt, H.: A pattern-based method for identifying and analyzing laws. In: Regnell, B., Damian, D. (eds.) REFSQ 2011. LNCS, vol. 7195, pp. 256–262. Springer, Heidelberg (2012)

2. Faßbender, S., Heisel, M.: From problems to laws in requirements engineering using model-transformation. In: ICSOFT 2013 - Proceedings of the 8th International Conference on Software Paradigm Trends, INSTICC. pp. 447–458. SciTePress (2013)
3. Federal Trade Commission: Choicepoint settles data security breach charges. Technical report, Federal Trade Commission (2006). http://www.ftc.gov/opa/2006/01/choicepoint.shtm
4. Biagioli, C., Mariani, P., Tiscornia, D.: Esplex: A rule and conceptual model for representing statutes. In: ICAIL, pp. 240–251. ACM (1987)
5. Otto, P.N., Antón, A.I.: Addressing legal requirements in requirements engineering. In: Proceedings of the International Conference on Requirements Engineering. IEEE (2007)
6. Beckers, K., Faßbender, S., Schmidt, H.: An integrated method for pattern-based elicitation of legal requirements applied to a cloud computing example. In: ARES, pp. 463–472 (2012)
7. Jackson, M.: Problem Frames: Analyzing and Structuring Software Development Problems. Addison-Wesley, Boston (2001)
8. Côté, I., Hatebur, D., Heisel, M., Schmidt, H., Wentzlaff, I.: A systematic account of problem frames. In: Proceedings of the European Conference on Pattern Languages of Programs (EuroPLoP), pp. 749–767. Universitätsverlag Konstanz (2008)
9. Hatebur, D., Heisel, M.: Making pattern- and model-based software development more rigorous. In: Dong, J.S., Zhu, H. (eds.) ICFEM 2010. LNCS, vol. 6447, pp. 253–269. Springer, Heidelberg (2010)
10. Kumar, S., Walia, E.: Analysis of electronic voting system in various countries. Int. J. Comput. Sci. Eng. (IJCSE) **3**, 1825–1830 (2011)
11. Federal Constitutional Court of Germany: Verwendung von Wahlcomputern bei der Bundestagswahl 2005 verfassungswidrig (2009). https://www.bundesverfassungsgericht.de/pressemitteilungen/bvg09-019.html
12. Brehm, R.: Kryptographische verfahren in internetwahlsystemen, Technical report. Technical University of Darmstadt (2012)
13. Volkamer, M.: Requirements and evaluation procedures to support responsible election authorities. In: Volkamer, M. (ed.) Evaluation of Electronic Voting. LNBIP, vol. 30, pp. 37–57. Springer, Heidelberg (2009)
14. Volkamer, M., Vogt, R.: Common Criteria Protection Profile for Basic set of security requirements for Online Voting Products. Bundesamt für Sicherheit in der Informationstechnik (2008)
15. Alebrahim, A., Hatebur, D., Heisel, M.: A method to derive software architectures from quality requirements. In: Thu, T.D., Leung, K. (eds.) Proceedings of the 18th Asia-Pacific Software Engineering Conference (APSEC), pp. 322–330. IEEE Computer Society (2011)
16. Beckers, K., Faßbender, S., Heisel, M., Meis, R.: A problem-based approach for computer-aided privacy threat identification. In: Preneel, B., Ikonomou, D. (eds.) APF 2012. LNCS, vol. 8319, pp. 1–16. Springer, Heidelberg (2014)
17. Beckers, K., Côté, I., Faßbender, S., Heisel, M., Hofbauer, S.: A pattern-based method for establishing a cloud-specific information security management system. Requirements Eng. **18**(4), 1–53 (2013)
18. Breaux, T.D., Vail, M.W., Antón, A.I.: Towards regulatory compliance: extracting rights and obligations to align requirements with regulations. In: Proceedings of the International Conference on Requirements Engineering (RE), pp. 46–55. IEEE (2006)

19. Breaux, T.D., Antón, A.I.: Analyzing regulatory rules for privacy and security requirements. IEEE Trans. Softw. Eng. **34**, 5–20 (2008)
20. Bench-Capon, T.J.M., Robinson, G.O., Routen, T.W., Sergot, M.J.: Logic programming for large scale applications in law: a formalization of supplementary benefit legislation. In: Proceedings of the International Conference on Artificial Intelligence and Law. ACM (1987)
21. Siena, A., Perini, A., Susi, A.: From laws to requirements. In: Proceedings of the International Workshop on Requirements Engineering and Law (RELAW), pp. 6–10. IEEE (2008)
22. Hohfeld, W.N.: Fundamental legal conceptions as applied in judicial reasoning. Yale Law J. **26**, 710–770 (1917)
23. Siena, A., Perini, A., Susi, A., Mylopoulos, J.: A meta-model for modelling law-compliant requirements. In: Proceedings of the International Workshop on Requirements Engineering and Law (RELAW), pp. 45–51. IEEE (2009)
24. Maxwell, J.C., Antón, A.I.: Developing production rule models to aid in acquiring requirements from legal texts. In: Proceedings of the 17th IEEE International Requirements Engineering Conference, RE, Washington, DC, USA. IEEE Computer Society (2009)
25. Álvarez, J.A.T., Olmos, A., Piattini, M.: Legal requirements reuse: a critical success factor for requirements quality and personal data protection. In: Proceedings of the International Conference on Requirements Engineering (RE), pp. 95–103. IEEE (2002)

An Ambient ASM Model of Client-to-Client Interaction via Cloud Computing and an Anonymously Accessible Docking Service

Károly Bósa[(⊠)]

Christian Doppler Laboratory for Client-Centric Cloud Computing, JKU, Linz,
Softwarepark 21, 4232 Hagenberg im Mühlkreis, Austria
k.bosa@cdcc.faw.jku.at

Abstract. In our former work we have given a high-level formal model of a cloud service architecture in terms of a novel formal method approach which combines the advantages of the mathematically well-founded software engineering method called *abstract state machines* and of the calculus of mobile agents called *ambient calculus*. This paper presents an extension for this cloud model which enables client-to-client interaction in an almost direct way, so that the involvement of cloud services is transparent to the users. The discussed solution for transparent use of services is a kind of switching service, where registered cloud users communicate with each other, and the only role the cloud plays is to switch resources from one client to another. We also show in an example at the end of this paper how our novel client-to-client interaction mechanism can be utilized for the development of the anonymously accessible cloud services.

Keywords: Cloud computing · Ambient abstract state machines · Ambient calculus

1 Introduction

In [1] we proposed a new formal method approach which is able to incorporate the major advantages of the *abstract state machines (ASMs)* [2] and of *ambient calculus* [3]. Namely, one can describe formal models of distributed systems including mobile components in two abstraction layers such that while the algorithms of executable components (*agents*) are specified in terms of ASMs; their communication topology, locality and mobility described with the terms of ambient calculus in our method.

In [4] we presented a high-level formal model of a cloud service architecture in terms of this new method. In this paper, we extended this formal model with a *Client-to-Client Interaction (CTCI)* mechanism via a cloud architecture. Our envisioned cloud feature can be regarded as a special kind of services we call *channels*, via which registered cloud users can interact with each other in almost

© Springer-Verlag Berlin Heidelberg 2014
J. Cordeiro and M. van Sinderen (Eds.): ICSOFT 2013, CCIS 457, pp. 235–255, 2014.
DOI: 10.1007/978-3-662-44920-2_15

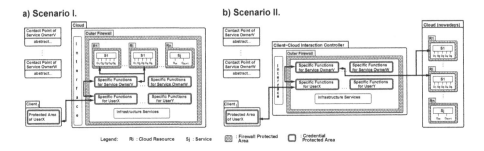

Fig. 1. Application of our model according to different scenarios.

direct way and, what is more, they are able to share available cloud resources among each other as well.

Some use cases, which may claim the need of such CTCI functions, can be for instance: dissemination of large or frequently updated data whose direct transmitting meets some limitations; or connecting devices of the same user (in the later case an additional challenge can be during a particular interpretation of the modeled CTCI functions, how to wrap and transport local area protocols, like *upnp* via the cloud).

The rest of the paper is organized as follows. Section 2 informally summarizes our formerly presented high-level cloud model. Section 3 gives a short overview on the related work as well as ambient calculus and ambient ASM. Section 4 introduces the definitions of some non-basic ambient capability actions which are applied in the latter sections. Section 5 describes the original model extended with the CTCI functions. Section 6 demonstrates how the CTCI architecture and the shared cloud resources can be applied for anonym usage of certain cloud services. Finally, Sect. 7 concludes this paper.

2   Overview on Our Model

Roughly our formal cloud model can be regarded as a pool of resources equipped with some infrastructure services, see Fig. 1a. Depending whether these abstract resources represent only physical hardware and virtual resources or entire computing platforms the model can be an abstraction of *Infrastructure as a Service (IaaS)* or *Platform as a Service (PaaS)*, respectively. The basic hardware (and software) infrastructure is owned by the cloud provider, whereas the softwares running on the resources are owned by some users. We assume that these softwares may be offered as a *service* and thus used by other users. Accordingly, we apply a relaxed definition of the term service cloud here, where a user who owns some applications running on some cloud resources may become a software service provider at the same time. Thus, from this aspect the model can be regarded as an abstraction of a mixture of *Software as a Service (SaaS)* and of IaaS (or a mixture of SaaS and PaaS).

We make a distinction between two kinds of cloud users. The normal *users* are registered in the cloud and they subscribe to and use some (software) services available in the cloud. The *service owners* are users as well, but they also rent some cloud *resources* to deploy some *service instances* on them.

For representing service instances, we adopt the formal model of *Abstract State Services (AS^{2}s)* [5,6]. In an AS^2 we have views on some hidden database layer that are equipped with *service operations* denoted by unique identifers $o_1,\ldots,o_n$. These service operations are actually what are exported from a service to be used by other systems or directly by users. The definition of AS^{2}s also includes the *pure data services* (service operations are just database queries) and the *pure functional services* (operation without underlying database layer) as extreme cases.

In our approach the model assumes that each service owner has a dedicated contact point which resides out of the cloud. It is a special kind of client that can also act as a server for the cloud itself in some cases. Namely, if a registered cloud user intends to subscribe to a particular service, she sends a subscription request to the cloud, which may forward it to such a special kind of client belonging to the corresponding service owner. This client responses with a special kind of action scheme called *service plot*, which algebraically defines and may constrain how the service can be used by the user[1]. (E.g.: it determines the permitted combination of service operations). This special kind of client is abstract in the current model.

The received service plots, which may be composed individually for each sub-scribing user by service owners, are collected with other cloud functions available for this particular user in a kind of personal user area by the cloud. Later, when the subscribed user sends a service request, it is checked whether the requested service operations are allowed by any service plot. If a requested operation is permitted then it is triggered to perform, otherwise it is blocked as long as a plot may allow to trigger it in the future. Each triggered operation request is authorized to enter into the user area of the corresponding service owner to whom the requested service operation belongs. Here a scheduler mechanism assigns to the request a one-off access to a cloud resource on which an instance of the corresponding service runs. Then the service operation request is forwarded to this resource, where the request is processed. Finally, the outcome of the performed operation returns to the area of the initiator user, where the outcome is either stored or send further to a given client device. In this way, the service owners have direct influence to the service usage of particular users via the provided service plots.

Regarding our proposed cloud model one of the major questions can be whether it is adaptable to the leading cloud solutions (e.g.: Amazon S3, Microsoft Azure, IBM SmartCloud, etc.). Since due to the applied ambient concept the relocation of the system components is trivial, we can apply our model according to different scenarios. For instance, all our novel functions including the client-to-client interaction can be shifted to the client side and wrapped into a

---

[1] For an algebraic formalization of plots *Kleene algebras with tests (KATs)* [7] has been applied.

Table 1. Definition of ambient calculus.

A. The Mobility and Communication Primitives		B. Reduction (Operational Semantics)	C. Structural Congruence (Operational Semantics)
			$P \equiv P$
$P, Q, R ::=$	processes	$P \equiv P', Q \equiv Q', P \longrightarrow Q \Longrightarrow P' \longrightarrow Q'$	$P \equiv Q \Longrightarrow Q \equiv P$
$P \mid Q$	parallel composition		$P \equiv Q, Q \equiv R \Longrightarrow P \equiv R$
$n[\,P\,]$	ambient	$P \longrightarrow Q \Longrightarrow P \mid R \longrightarrow Q \mid R$	$P \equiv Q \Longrightarrow \P \mid R \equiv Q \mid R$
$(\nu\, n)P$	restriction of name n within P^a		$P \equiv Q \Longrightarrow n[\,P\,] \equiv n[\,Q\,]$
0	inactivity (**skip** process)	$P \longrightarrow Q \Longrightarrow n[\,P\,] \longrightarrow n[\,Q\,]$	$P \equiv Q \Longrightarrow !P \equiv !Q$
$!P$	replication of P		$P \equiv Q \Longrightarrow (\nu\, n)P \equiv (\nu\, n)Q$
$M.\,P$	(capability) action M then P	$P \longrightarrow Q \Longrightarrow (\nu\, n)P \longrightarrow (\nu\, n)Q$	$P \equiv Q \Longrightarrow M.P \equiv M.Q$
$(x).\,P$	input action (the input value is bound to x in P)		$P \equiv Q \Longrightarrow (x).P \equiv (x).Q$
$\langle a \rangle$	async output action	$n[\,\text{IN}\, m.P \mid Q\,] \mid m[\,R\,] \longrightarrow m[\,n[\,P \mid Q\,] \mid R\,]$	$P \mid Q \equiv Q \mid P$
$M_1 . \ldots . M_k$	a path formation on actions		$(P \mid Q) \mid R \equiv P \mid (Q \mid R)$
		$m[\,n[\,\text{OUT}\, m.p \mid Q\,] \mid R\,] \longrightarrow n[\,P \mid Q\,] \mid m[\,R\,]$	$!P \equiv P \mid !P$
$M ::=$	capabilities		$(\nu\, n)(\nu\, m)P \equiv (\nu\, m)(\nu\, n)P$
$\text{IN}\, n$	entry capability (to enter n)	$\text{OPEN}\, n.P \mid n[\,Q\,] \longrightarrow P \mid Q$	$(\nu\, n)(P \mid Q) \equiv P \mid (\nu\, n)Q$ if $n \notin fn(P)$
$\text{OUT}\, n$	exit capability (to exit n)		$(\nu\, n)(m[\,P\,]) \equiv m[(\nu\, n)P\,]$ if $n \neq m$
$\text{OPEN}\, n$	open capability (to dissolve n's boundary)	$(x).P \mid \langle a \rangle \longrightarrow P(x/a)$	$P \mid 0 \equiv P$
			$!0 \equiv 0$
			$(\nu\, n)0 \equiv 0$

^{a} Name Restriction creates a new (unique) name n within a scope P. One must be careful with the term $!(\nu\, n)P$, because it provides a fresh value for each replica, so $(\nu\, n)!P \not\equiv !(\nu\, n)P$.

middleware software which takes place between the end users and cloud in order to control the interactions of them, see Fig. 1b. The specified communication topology among the distributed system components remains the same in this later case.

3   Related Work

It is beyond the scope of this paper to discuss the vast literature of formal modeling mobile systems and SOAs, but we refer to some surveys on these fields [8–10].

One of the first examples for representing various kinds of published services as a pool of resources, like in our model, was in [11].

In [12] a formal high-level specifications of service cloud is given. This work is similar to ours in some aspects. Namely, it applies the language-independent AS^2s with algebraic plots for representing services. But it principally focuses on service specification, service discovery, service composition and orchestration of service-based processes; and it does not apply any formal approach to describe either static or dynamically changing structures of distributed system components.

Another approach similar to ours is *Cloud Calculus* [13], which also uses ambient calculus for capturing the dynamic topology of cloud computing systems. Cloud Calculus is very effective to verify whether global security policies are preserved after virtual machine migrations, but it is a very specific tool which is not applicable for giving the formal specification of functionalities of cloud/distributed systems.

In the rest of this section, we give a short summary on ambient calculus and ambient ASM, respectively, in order to facilitate the understanding of the latter sections.

3.1   Ambient Calculus

The ambient calculus was inspired by the π-calculus [14], but it focuses primarily on the concept of locality and process mobility across well defined boundaries instead of channel mobility as π-calculus. The concept of *ambient* stands in the center of the calculus, see a summary of the definition of ambient calculus in Table 1.

The ambient calculus includes only the mobility and communication primitives depicted in Table 1A. The main syntactic categories are *processes* (including both ambients and agents) and *actions* (including both *capabilities* and *communication primitives*). A reduction relation $P \longrightarrow Q$ describes the evolution of a term P into a new term Q (and $P \to^* Q$ denotes a reflexive and transitive reduction relation from P to Q).

An ambient is defined as a bounded place where computation happens. An ambient is written as $n[P]$, where n is its name, which can be used to control access (entry, exit, communication, etc.), and a process P is running inside its *body* (P may be running even if n is moving). Ambient names may not be unique. Ambients can be embedded into each other such that they can form a hierarchical tree structure. An ambient body is interpreted as the parallel composition of its elements (its local ambients and its local agents) and can be written as follows:

$$n[\, P_1 \mid \ldots \mid P_k \mid m_1[\ldots] \mid \ldots \mid m_l[\ldots]\,] \text{ where } P_i \neq m_i[\ldots]$$

An ambient can be moved. When an ambient moves, everything inside it moves with it (the boundary around an ambient determines what should move together with it). An action defined in the calculus can precede a process P. P cannot start to execute until the preceding actions are performed. Those actions that are able to control the movements of ambients in the hierarchy or to dissolve ambient boundaries are restricted by capabilities. By using capabilities an ambient can allow some processes to perform certain operations without publishing its true name to them (see the entry, exit and open in Table 1). In case of the modeling of a real life system, communication of (ambient) names should be rather rare, since knowing the name of an ambient gives a lot of control over it. Instead, it should be common to exchange restricted capabilities to control interactions between ambients (from a capability the ambient name cannot be retrieved).

3.2   Ambient ASM

In [15] the ambient concept (notion of "nestable" environments where computation can happen) is introduced into the ASM method. In that article an ASM machine called MOBILEAGENTSMANAGER is described as well, which gives a natural formulation for the reduction of three basic capabilities (ENTRY, EXIT and OPEN) of ambient calculus in terms of the *ambient ASM* rules. For this machine an ambient tree hierarchy is always specified initially in a dynamic derived function called *curAmbProc*. The machine MOBILEAGENTSMANAGER transforms the current value of *curAmbProc* according to the capability actions given in *curAmbProc*. Since one of the main goals of [15] is to reveal the inherent opportunities of the new ambient concept introduced into ASMs, the presented definitions for moving ambients are unfortunately incomplete.

Table 2. A Summary of the definitions of some non-basic capabilities.

Names	New Reduction Relations (Based on the Definitions)	Definitions of the New Capabilities
1) Renaming	$n[\ n\ \text{BE}\ m.P \mid Q\ ] \longrightarrow^{*} m[\ P \mid Q\ ]$	$n\ \text{BE}\ m.P \equiv (\nu\ s)(s[\ \text{OUT}\ n \mid m[\ \text{OPEN}\ n.\text{OUT}\ s.P\ ]\,] \mid \text{IN}\ s.\text{IN}\ m)$
2) Seeing	$n[\,]\ \mid\ \text{SEE}\ n.P \longrightarrow^{*} n[\,] \mid P$	$\text{SEE}\ n.P \equiv (\nu\ r,\ s)(\ r[\ \text{IN}\ n.\text{OUT}\ n.r\ \text{BE}\ s.P\ ] \mid \text{OPEN}\ s\ )$
3) Wrapping	$n[\ m\ \text{WRAP}\ n.P\ ] \longrightarrow^{*} m[\ n[\ P\ ]\,]$	$m\ \text{WRAP}\ n.P \equiv$ $(\nu\ s,\ r)(\ s[\ \text{OUT}\ n.\text{SEE}\ n.s\ \text{BE}\ m.r[\ \text{IN}\ n\ ]\,] \mid \text{IN}\ s.\text{OPEN}\ r.P\ )$
4) Allowing Code	$\text{ALLOW}\ key.P \mid key[\ Q\ ] \longrightarrow^{*} P \mid Q$	$\text{ALLOW}\ key.P \equiv \text{OPEN}\ key.P$
5) Drawing in (an Ambient)	$m[\ Q \mid \text{ALLOW}\ key\ ] \mid n[\ n\ \text{DRAWIN}_{key}\ m.P\ ]$ $\longrightarrow^{*} n[\ Q \mid P\ ]$	$n\ \text{DRAWIN}_{key}\ m.P \equiv$ $key[\ \text{OUT}\ n.\text{IN}\ m.\text{IN}\ n\ ] \mid \text{ALLOW}\ m.P$
6) Drawing in Then Release a Lock	$m[\ Q \mid \text{ALLOW}\ key\ ] \mid$ $n[\ \text{DRAWIN}_{key}\ m\ \text{THENRELEASE}\ lock.P\ ]$ $\longrightarrow^{*} lock[\ n[\ Q \mid P\ ]\,]$	$n\ \text{DRAWIN}_{key}\ m\ \text{THENRELEASE}\ lock.P \equiv$ $key[\ \text{OUT}\ n.\text{IN}\ m.\text{IN}\ n\ ] \mid \text{SEE}\ m.lock\ \text{WRAP}\ n.\text{ALLOW}\ m.P$
7) Concurrent Server Process	$m[\ Q \mid \text{ALLOW}\ key\ ] \mid \text{SERVER}^{n}_{key}\ m.P$ $\longrightarrow^{*} \text{SERVER}^{n}_{key}\ m.P \mid n^{uniq}_{k}[\ Q \mid P\ ]$	$\text{SERVER}^{n}_{key}\ m.P \equiv$ $(\nu\ next)(next[\,] \mid$ $!(\nu\ n)(\text{OPEN}\ next.n[$ $n\ \text{DRAWIN}_{key}\ m\ \text{THENRELEASE}\ next.P\ ]))$

In [1] we extended this ASM machine given in [15], such that it fully captures the calculus of mobile agents and it can interpret the agents' algorithms (given in terms of ASM syntax in $curAmbProc$ as well) in the corresponding contexts. By this one is able to describe formal models of distributed systems including mobile components in the mentioned two abstraction layers.

Since the definition of ambient ASM is based upon the semantics of ASM without any changes, each specification given this way can be translated into a traditional ASM specification.

Ambient ASM is not the only research which aims to build in a concept of mobile ambients to the ASM method. In [16] some advantages of a simple ambient concept introduced into ASM are demonstrated. Although this work was also inspired by ambient calculus, it is by far not refined and versatile as ambient ASM.

4 Definitions

As Cardelli and Gordon showed in [3] the ambient calculus with the three basic capabilities (ENTRY, EXIT and OPEN) is powerful enough to be Turing-complete. But for facilitating the specification of such a compound formal model as a model of a cloud infrastructure, we defined some new *non-basic capabilities* encoded in terms of the three basic capabilities. Table 2 summarizes the definitions of these non-basic capabilities.

Below we give an informal description of each non-basic capability in Table 2. It is beyond the scope of the paper to present detailed explanations and reductions of their ambient calculus-based definitions, but we refer to our former works [4,17] for more details.

1. Renaming. This capability is applied to rename an ambient comprising this capability. Such a capability was already given in [3], but our definition differs from Cardelli's definition. In the original definition, the ambient m was not enclosed into another, name restricted ambient (it is called s in our definition), so after it has left ambient n, n may enter into another ambient called m (if more than one m exists as sibling of n).

2. Seeing. This operation was defined in [3] and it is used to detect the presence of a given ambient.

3. Wrapping. Its aim is to pack an ambient comprising this capability into another ambient.

4. Allowing Code. This capability is just a basic OPEN capability action. It is applied if an ambient allows/accepts an ambient construct (which may be a bunch of foreign codes) contained by the body of one of its sub-ambients (which may was sent from a foreign location). The name of the sub-ambient can be applied for identifying its content, since its name may be known only by some trusted parties.

5. Draw in (an Ambient). The aim of this capability is to draw in a particular ambient (identified by its name) into another ambient (which contains this capability) and then to dissolve this captured ambient in order to access to its content. For achieving this, a mechanism (contained by the ambient *key*) is applied which can be regarded as an abstraction of a kind of protocol identified by *key*. The ambient *key* enters into one of the available target ambients which should accept its content in order to be led into the initiator ambient.

6. Draw in then Release a Lock. This capability is very similar to the previous one, but after m has been captured by n (and before m is dissolved), n is wrapped by another ambient. The new outer ambient is usually employed as release for a lock[2].

7. Concurrent Server Process. This ambient construct can be regarded as an abstraction of a multi-threaded server process. It is able to capture and process several ambients having the same name in parallel. In the definition n is a replicated ambient whose each replica is going to capture another ambient called m. Since there is a name restriction quantifier in the scope of the replication sign, which binds the name n, a new, fresh and unique name (denoted by n_k^{uniq}) is generated for each replica of n. One of the consequences of this is that nobody knows from outside the true name of a replica of the ambient n, so each replica of n is inaccessible from outside for anybody (even for another replica of n, too).

5   The Extended Formal Model

In the formal model discussed in this section, we assume that there are some standardized public ambient names, which are known by all contributors. We distinguish the following kinds of public names: addresses (e.g.: *cloud*, *client*$_1$, ..., *client*$_n$), message types (e.g.: *reg*(*istration*), *request*, *subs*(*cription*), *returnValue*, etc.) and parts of some common protocols (e.g.: *lock*, *msg*, *intf*, *access*, *out*, o_1, ..., o_s, *op*). All other ambient names are non-public in the model which follows:

---

[2] In ambient calculus the capability OPEN $n.P$ is usually used to encode locks [3]. Such a lock can be released with an ambient like $n[Q]$ whose name corresponds with the target ambient of the OPEN capability.

$$curAmbProc := root[\ Cloud\ |\ Client_1\ |\dots|\ Client_n\ ]^3$$

In this paper, we focus on the cloud service side and we leave the client side abstract.

5.1 User Actions

In the model user actions are encoded as messages. A user can send the following kinds of messages to the cloud:

$MsgFrame \equiv msg[\ \text{IN}\ cloud.\text{ALLOW}\ intf.content\ ]$
where content can be:
  $RegMsg \equiv reg[\ \text{ALLOW}\ CID.\langle UID_x \rangle\ ]$

  $SubsMsg \equiv subs[\ \text{ALLOW}\ CID.\langle UID_x, SID_i, pymt \rangle\ ]$

  $RequestMsg \equiv request[\ \text{IN}\ UID_x.\text{ALLOW}\ CID\ |$
      $\langle o_i, client_k, args_i \rangle\ |\dots|\ \langle o_j, client_k, args_j \rangle\ ]$

  $AddClMsg \equiv addCl[\ \text{IN}\ UID_x\ |\ \text{ALLOW}\ CID.\langle client_k, path_l, UID_{(\text{on } client_l)} \rangle\ ]$

  $AddChMsg \equiv addCh[\ \text{ALLOW}\ CID.\langle UID_x, cname \rangle\ ]$

  $SubsToChMsg \equiv subsToCh[\ \text{ALLOW}\ CID.\langle UID_x, cname, uname, client_k, pymt \rangle\ ]$

  $ShareInfoMsg \equiv share[\ \text{IN}\ CHID_i\ |\ \text{ALLOW}\ CID.\langle sndr, rcvr, info \rangle\ ]$

  $ShareSvcMsg \equiv share[\ \text{IN}\ CHID_i\ |\ \text{ALLOW}\ CID.$
    $\langle sndr, rcvr, info, o_i, argsP, argsF \rangle\ ]$

In the definitions above: the ambient msg is the frame of a message; the term IN $cloud$ denotes the address to where the message is sent; the term ALLOW $intf$ allows a (server) mechanism on the target side which uses the public protocol $intf$ to capture the message; and the $content$ can be various kind of message types. The term ALLOW CID denotes that the messages are sent to a service of a particular cloud which identifies itself with the non-public protocol/credential CID (stands for *cloud identifier*).

The first three kinds of messages were introduced in the original model. In a $RegistrationMsg$ the user x provides her identifier UID_x that she is going to use in the cloud. By a $SubscriptionMsg$ a user subscribes to a cloud service identified by SID_i; the information represented by $pymt$ proves that the given user has paid for the service properly.

Again, cloud services provide their functionalities for their environment (users or other services) via actions called service operations in our model. In a $RequestMsg$ a user who has subscribed to some services before can request the cloud to perform some service operations belonging to some of these services. Service operation requests are denoted by triples, where o_i and o_j are the unique names of these service operations; $client_k$ is the identifer of a target location (usually a client device) to where the output of a given operation should

---

[3] The ambient called *root* is a special ambient which is required for the ASM definition of ambient calculus, see [1,15].

be sent by the cloud; and $args_i$ and $args_j$ are the arguments of the corresponding requested service operations. Furthermore, the term $\text{IN } UID_x$ represents the address of the target user area within the *Cloud*.

The rest of the message types is new in the model. With *AddClMsg* a user can register a new possible target (client) device or location for the outcomes of the requests initiated by her. Such a message should contain the chosen identifier $client_k$ of the new device, the address $path_l$ of the device and the user identifier $UID_{(\text{on } client_l)}$ used on the given target device.

By *AddChMsg* users can open new channels, by *SubsToChMsg* users can subscribe to channels and by *ShareInfoMsg* and *ShareSvcMsg* users can share information as well as service operations with some other users registered in the same channel. For the detailed description of the arguments lists of these last four messages, see Sect. 5.3.

5.2   The Cloud Service Architecture

The basic structure of the defined cloud model, which is based on the simplified *Infrastructure as a Service (IaaS)* specification given in [1], is the following:

$Cloud \equiv (\nu\ fw,\ q,\ rescr_1, \ldots rescr_m) cloud[$
  $interface\ |$
  $fw\ [\ rescr_1[\ service_1\ ]\ |\ldots|\ rescr_l[\ service_1\ ]\ |\ rescr_{l+1}[\ service_2\ ]\ |\ldots|\ rescr_m[$
$service_n\ ]\ |$
    $q[\ !\text{OPEN}\ msg\ |\ BasicCloudfunctions\ |\ CTCIfunctions\ |$
     $UID_x[userIntf]\ |\ldots|\ UID_y[userIntf]\ |$
     $UID_v^{owner}[ownerIntf]\ |\ldots|\ UID_w^{owner}[ownerIntf]\ ]\ ]\ ]$
where
  $interface \equiv \text{SERVER}_{intf}^n\ msg.\text{IN}\ fw.\text{IN}\ q.n\ \text{BE}\ msg$

In the cloud definition above, the names of the ambients fw, q and $rescr_1, \ldots rescr_m$ are bound by name restriction. The consequence of this is that the names of these ambients are known only within the cloud service system, and therefore the contents of their body are completely hidden and not accessible at all from outside of the cloud. So each of them can be regarded as an abstraction of a firewall protection.

The ambient expression represented by $interface$ "pulls in" into the area protected by the ambients fw and q any ambient construct which is encompassed by the message frame msg. The purpose of the restricted ambients fw and q is to prevent any malicious content which may cut loose in the body of q after a message frame (msg) has been broken (by $\text{OPEN}\ msg$) to leave the cloud together with some sensitive information. For more details we refer to [4].

The restricted ambients $resrc_1, \ldots,\ resrc_m$, represent computational resources of the cloud. Within each cloud resource some service instances can be deployed. A service may have several deployed instances in a cloud (see instances of $service_1$ in $resrc_1, \ldots,\ resrc_l$ above).

Every user area is represented by an ambient whose name corresponds to the corresponding user identifier UID_i. Furthermore, the user areas extended with service owner role are denoted by UID_i^{owner}. The terms denoted by $BasicCloudfunctions$ are responsible for cloud user registration and service subscription. Finally the terms denoted by $CTCIfunctions$ encode the client-to-client interaction.

It is beyond the scope of this paper to describe all parts of this model in details (e.g.: the structure of service instances $service_i$, functions of a service owner area $ownerIntf$, the service plots and the ASM agents in $BasicCloudfunctions$). For the specification of these components, we refer to [4].

User Access Layers. A user access layer (or user area) may contain the following mechanisms: accepting user requests and converting them to the format which is compatible with plots[4] ($requestPreprocessor$), accepting new plots (!ALLOW $newPlot$), accepting outputs of service operations (!ALLOW $returnValue$) and some service plots.

$userIntf \equiv$
$\quad requestPreprocessor \mid$!ALLOW $newPlot \mid clientRegServer \mid$!ALLOW $returnValue \mid$
$\quad sortingOutput \mid client_1[\, posting_{client_1}\,] \mid \ldots \mid client_k[\, posting_{client_k}\,]$
$\quad \text{PLOT}_{SID_i} \mid \ldots \mid \text{PLOT}_{SID_j} \mid$
where
$\quad requestPreprocessor \equiv \text{SERVER}_{CID}^n\ request.(o,\,c,\,args).o[\ \text{ALLOW}\ op.\langle c,\,args\rangle\,]$
$\quad sortingOutput \equiv\ !(o,\,client,\,a).output[\ \text{IN}\ client.\text{ALLOW}\ CID \mid \langle o, client, a\rangle\,]\,]$
$\quad clientRegServer \equiv \text{SERVER}_{CID}^n\ addCl.(client,\,path,\,UID).(n\ \text{BE}\ client \mid$
$\qquad posting_{client}\,)$
$\quad posting_{client_i} \equiv \text{SERVER}_{CID}^n\ output.(o,\,client,\,a).$
$\qquad \text{OUT}\ client_i.forwardTo_{client_i}.returnValue[\ \text{IN}\ UID_{(\text{on}\ client_i)} \mid \langle o, client, a\rangle\,]\,]$
$\quad forwardTo_{client_i} \equiv n\ \text{BE}\ outgoingMsg.\text{OUT}\ UID_x.leavingCloud.path_i$
$\quad leavingCloud \equiv \text{OUT}\ q.\text{OUT}\ fw.\text{OUT}\ cloud.outgoingMsg\ \text{BE}\ msg$

This paper extends the user areas with some new functionalities. $clientRegServer$ is applied to process every $AddClMsg$ sent by the corresponding user. It creates new communication endpoint for target (client) devices. Each such an endpoint is encoded by an ambient whose name $client_i$ corresponds the given identifier provided in a message $AddClMsg$. By these endpoints outputs of service operations can immediately be directed to registered (client) devices after they are available. Of course, if no target device or a non-registered one is given in a $RequestMsg$, the outcome will be stored in the area of the user.

Every service operation output, which is always delivered within the body of an ambient called $returnValue$, consists of three parts: the name of the performed service operation, the identifier of a target location to where the output should be sent back and the outcome of the performed service operation itself.

$sortingOutput$ distributes every service operation output among the communication endpoints in an ambient called $output$. The mechanism $posting_{client_i}$,

---

[4] Service plots can accept requests if they are encompassed by ambients whose names are correspond with the unique names of the requested operations ($o_i \ldots o_j$), see the definition of $requestPreprocessor$ above.

which resides in each such a communication endpoint, is responsible to wrap each output of service operations which reaches the corresponding endpoint again into an ambient $returnValue$ and to forward it to the specified user $UID_{(on\ client_i)}$ on the corresponding device $client_i$.

5.3   Client-to-Client Interaction

Again, the client-to-client interaction in our model is based on the constructs called *channels*. These are represented by ambients with unique names denoted by $CHID_i$ which contain some mechanisms whose purpose is to share some information and service operations among some subscribed users, see below:

$CTCI functions \equiv$
$CHID_1[\ channelIntf\ ]\ |\ldots|\ CHID_l[\ channelIntf\ ]\ |$
$\textsc{Server}^n_{CID}\ addCh.(UID,\ cname).\textsc{ChMgr}(n,\ UID_x,\ cname)\ |$
$\textsc{Server}^n_{CID}\ subsToCh.(UID,cname,uname,client,pymt).$
  $\textsc{ChSubsMgr}(n,\ UID,\ cname,\ uname,\ client,\ pymt)$
where
$channelIntf \equiv \textsc{Server}^n_{CID}\ share.(\ (sndr,\ rcvr,\ info).$
  $\langle sndr,rcvr,info, \textbf{undef}, \textbf{undef}, \textbf{undef}\rangle\ |$
  $(sndr,\ rcvr,\ info,\ o,\ argsP,\ argsF).$
  $\textsc{SharingMgr}(n,\ sndr,\ rcvr,\ info,\ o,\ argsP,\ argsF)\ )$

Every cloud user can create and own some channels by sending the message *AddChMsg* to the cloud, where an instance of the ASM agent ChMgr, which is equipped with a server mechanism, processes such a request and creates a new ambient with unique names for the requested channel, see Sect. 5.3.

If a user would like to subscribe to a channel she should send the message *SubToChMsg* to the cloud. The server construct belongs to the ASM agent ChSubsMgr is responsible for processing these messages, see Sect. 5.3. In the subscription process the owner of the channel can decide about the rights which can be assigned to a subscribed user. According to the presented high-level model, the employed access rights are encoded by the following static nullary functions: *listening* is a default basic right, because everybody who joins to a channel can receive shared contents; *sending* authorizes a user to send something to only one user at a time; and *broadcasting* permits a user to distribute contents to all member of the channel at once.

Both *ShareInfoMsg* and *ShareSvcMsg* are processed by the same server which belongs to the ASM agent SharingMgr and which is located in the body of each ambient $CHID_i$, see Sect. 5.3. In the case of *ShareInfoMsg* the server first supplements the arguments list of the message with three additional **undef** values, such that it will have the same number of arguments as *ShareSvcMsg* has. Then an instance of the ASM agent SharingMgr can process the *ShareInfoMsg* similarly to *ShareSvcMsg* (the first three arguments are the same for both messages).

Table 3. The ASM agents CHMGR and CHSUBSMGR.

CHMGR(n, UID, $cname$) ≡
  ctr_state : {$InitialState$, $EndState$}
  initially $ctr\_state := InitialState$

  if $ctr\_state = InitialState$ **then**
    $ctr\_state := EndState$
    if $UID ∈ userIds$ **then**
      if $ownerOfCh(cname) = $ **undef then**
        let $CHID = $ **new**($channelIds$) **in**
        STORECHANNEL($CHID$, $cname$, UID)
        let $CHConstruct = createChannel(CHID)$
  in
      NEWAMBIENTCONSTRUCT($CHConstruct$)
  where
    $CHConstruct ≡ CHID[$ OUT n | $channelIntf$]

CHSUBSMGR(n,UID,$cname$,$uname$,$client$,$pymt$) ≡
  ctr_state : {$InitialState$, $EndState$}
  initially $ctr\_state := InitialState$
  if $ctr\_state = InitialState$ **then**
    $ctr\_state := EndState$
    if $UID ∈ userIds$ **then**
      if $ownerOfCh(cname) ≠$ **undef then**
        if $uname ∉ members(cname)$ **then**
          let $owner = ownerOfCh(cname)$ **in**
          let $rights = $
            CONFIRMRIGHTS($owner$,$uname$,$cname$,$pymt$)
  in
          if $rights ≠ ∅$ **then**
          STOREMEM-
          BER(UID,$uname$,$client$,$cname$,$rights$)
            if $rights ≠ \{listening\}$ THEN
            let $CHID = idOfCh$(cname) **in**
            NEWAMBIENTCONSTRUCT($returnValue[$
            OUT n.IN UID.($cname$, $client$, IN $CHID$)])

Establishing a New Channel. CHMGR is a parameterized ASM agent, see in Table 3, which expects UID of the cloud user who is going to create a new channel and $cname$ which is the name of this channel as arguments. The additional argument n is the unique name of an ambient which was provided by the surrounding server construct and in which the current $AddChMsg$ is processed by an instance of this agent (such an argument is also applied in the case of the other ASM agents below).

First the agent checks whether the given UID has already been registered on the cloud and whether the given name $cname$ has not been used as a name of an existing channel yet (the unary function $ownerOfCh$ returns the value **undef** if there is no assigned owner to this name). If it is the case, the agent generates a new and unique identifier denoted by $CHID$ for the new channel with the usage of the function **new** which provides a unique and completely fresh element for the given set each time when it is applied. The abstract ASM macro STORECHANNEL inserts into an abstract database a new entry with all the details of the new channel which are the channel identifier, the channel name and the identifier of the owner.

Then it calls the abstract derived function $createChannel$, which creates an ambient called $CHID$ with the terms denoted by $channelIntf$ in its body which encode the functions of the new channel. By the abstract tree manipulation operation called NEWAMBIENTCONSTRUCT[5] introduced in [1], this generated ambient construct is placed into the ambient tree hierarchy as sibling of the agent.

Although a channel is always created as a sibling of the current instance of CHMGR, but as a first step it leaves the ambient n which was provided by the

---

[5] This is the only way how an ASM agent can make changes in the ambient tree hierarchy contained by dynamic derived function $curAmbProc$ [1].

surrounding server construct and in which the message was processed (see the underlined moving action in *CHConstruct* above). After that it is prepared to serve as a channel for client-to-client interaction (it is supposed that the name *cname* of every channel is somehow announced among the potential users).

Subscribing to a Channel. CHSUBSMGR is a parameterized ASM agent, see in Table 3, which expects the following as arguments: *UID* of the user who is going to subscribe to the channel, *cname* which is the name of the channel, *uname* is the name that the user is going to use within the channel, *client* which is the identifier of a registered client device to where the shared content will be forwarded and *pymt* which is some payment details if it is required. A user can register to a channel with different names and various client devices in order to connect these devices via the cloud.

First the agent checks whether the given *UID* and *cname* have already been registered on the cloud and whether the given *uname* has not been used as a name of a member of the channel yet. If it is the case, the agent informs the owner of the channel about the new subscription by applying the abstract ASM macro CONFIRMRIGHTS, who responses with a set of access rights to the channel that she composed based on the information given in the subscription.

If the subscription has been accepted by the owner and besides *listening* some other rights are granted to the new user, an ambient construct is created and sent as a message *returnValue* to the user by NEWAMBIENTCONSTRUCT. This message contains the capability IN *CHID* by which the new user can send messages called *ShareInfoMsg* and *ShareSvcMsg* into the ambient *CHID* which represents the corresponding channel (the owner of a channel also has to subscribe in order to receive this information and to be able to distribute content via the channel).

Sharing Information via a Channel. Every server construct in which the agent SHARINGMGR is embedded is always located in an ambient which represents a particular channel and whose name corresponds to the identifier of the channel. In order to be able to perform its task, it is required that each instance of SHARINGMGR knows by some static nullary function called *myChId* the name of the ambient in which it is executed.

SHARINGMGR is a parameterized ASM agent, see in Table 4, which expects the following arguments: *sndr* is the registered name of the sender, *rcvr* is either the registered name of a receiver or an asterisk "*", *info* is either the content of *ShareInfoMsg* or the description of a shared service operation in *ShareSvcMsg*. The last three arguments are not used in the case of the message *ShareInfoMsg* and the value **undef** is assigned to each of them by the surrounding server construct. In the message *ShareSvcMsg o* denotes the unique identifier of the service operation that *sndr* is going to share, *argsP* denotes the arguments of *o* that *rcvr* can freely modify if she calls the operation and *argsF* denotes those part of the argument list of *o*, whose value is fixed by *sndr*.

The agent first generates a new and unique operation identifier for the service operation *o* in the control state *InitialState*. This new identifier which is

Table 4. The ASM agent SHARINGMGR.

SHARINGMGR(n, $sndr$, $rcvr$, $info$, o, $argsP$, $argsF$)
$\equiv$
$ctr\_state : \{InitialState, SharingState,$
$EndState\}$
initially $ctr\_state := InitialState$

if $ctr\_state = InitialState$ **then**
  $ctr\_state := SharingState$
  if $o \neq$ **undef then**   //svc. sharing
    let $newOpId = $ **new**($sharedOpIds$) **in**
      $shOp = newOpId$
  else $shOp =$ **undef**   //msg. sharing

if $ctr\_state = SharingState$ **then**
  $ctr\_state := EndState$
  let $cname = getChannelName(myChId)$ **in**
  if $sndr \in members(cname)$ **then**
  let $rights = getRights(cname, sndr)$ **in**

> **if** $rcvr = $ "*" **then**   //broadcasting a msg.
>   **if** $boradcasting \in rights$ **then**
>   **forall** $M \in members(cname)$ **do**
>   **let** $UID = $ getId(M), $client = $ getAddress(M)
>   **in**
>   **if** $shOp =$ **undef then**
>   NEWAMBIENTCONSTRUCT(
> $sharedM_{content_1}$)
>   **else**
>   NEWAMBIENTCONSTRUCT(
> $sharedM_{content_2}$)
>   **let** $UID_{sndr} = $ getId($sndr$) **in**
>   NEWAMBIENTCONSTRUCT($sharedPlot$)

else   //sending a msg.
if $sending \in rights$ **and** $rcvr \in$ $members(cname)$
then
  let $UID = $ getId($rcvr$), $client=$ getAddress($rcvr$) **in**
    if $shOp = $ **undef then**
      NEWAMBIENTCONSTRUCT(
  $sharedM_{content_1}$)
    else
      NEWAMBIENTCONSTRUCT(
  $sharedM_{content_2}$)
      let $UID_{sndr} = $ getId($sndr$) **in**
      NEWAMBIENTCONSTRUCT($sharedPlot$)

where
  $sharedM_{content_i} \equiv returnValue[$
    OUT n.OUT $myChId$.IN $UID.\langle cname, client, content_i \rangle$
  ]

$content_1 \equiv \{$"sender:" $sndr$, "content:" $info\}$

$content_2 \equiv \{$"sender:" $sndr$, "operation:" $shOp$,
  "arguments:" $argsP$, "description:" $info\}$

$sharedPlot \equiv$
  $newPlot[$ OUT n.OUT $myChId$.IN UID | PLOT$_{shOp}$]

PLOT$_{shOp} \equiv$ SERVER$^s_{op}$ $shOp.trigger_o$

$trigger_o \equiv (\nu\ tmp)$
  $(client, argsP).($OUT UID.IN $UID_{sndr}.s$ BE $request$ |
  ALLOW $CID.\langle o, tmp, (argsP \setminus argsF) + argsF \rangle$ |
  $tmp[$ ALLOW $output$ | $CID[(o, c, a).$OUT UID_{sndr}.
  IN $UID.tmp$ BE $returnValue.\langle shOp, client, a \rangle$]])

stored in the nullary location function $shOp$ will be announced to the channel member(s) specified in $rcvr$. In the control state $SharingState$ the agent checks whether the $sndr$ is a registered member of the channel by calling the function $members(cname)$. Then if the given value of $rcvr$ is equal to "*" the agent broadcasts the content of the current message to all members of the channel, see code branch bordered by the first rectangular frame below. Otherwise if the value of $rcvr$ corresponds to the name of a particular member of the channel, the agent sends the content of the current message only to her, see the code branch bordered by the second rectangular frame below.

Apart from the number of users to whom the information is sent the both code branches mentioned above define the same actions. Accordingly at the end of the processing of $ShareInfoMsg$ the agent sends to the member(s) specified in $rcvr$ the message $sharedM_{content_1}$, which contains the sender $sndr$ and the shared information $info$.

At the end of the processing of $ShareSvcMsg$ two ambient constructs are created by NEWAMBIENTCONSTRUCT. The first one is the message $sharedM_{content_2}$ and it is sent to the member(s) specified in $rcvr$. It contains the sender $sndr$, the new operation identifier $shOp$, the list of public arguments $argsP$ and the informal description of the shared operation denoted by $info$.

The second ambient construct is the plot PLOT_{shOp} enclosed by the ambient *newPlot* and equipped with some additional ambient actions (see the underlined capabilities in the definition of *sharedPlot*) which move the entire construct into the user area of the channel member(s) specified in *rcvr*, where the plot will be accepted by the term !ALLOW *newPlot*.

The execution of the shared service operation *shOp* can be requested in a usual *RequestMsg* as normal service operations. The PLOT_{shOp} is a plot, which can accept service operation requests for *shOp* several times. It is special plot, because instead of triggering the execution of *shOp* as in the case of a normal operation a normal plot does, see [4], it converts the original request to another request for operation *o* by applying the term $trigger_o$. This means that it substitutes the operation identifier *o* for *shOp*, it completes its arguments list with *argsF* and it forwards the request for *o* to the user area of the user *sndr* who actually has right to trigger the execution of the operation *o*.

To the new request the name restricted ambient *tmp* is attached, whose purpose is similar to the communication endpoints of registered clients. Namely, it is placed into the user area of *sndr* temporary and it is responsible for forwarding the outcome of this particular request from the user area of *sndr* to the user area of the user who initiated the request. It is beyond the scope of this chapter to present a reduction how a particular request for a shared operation is processed in our model, but we refer to [18] for more details.

6   Anonymous Docking Service

If we apply the scenario proposed in Sect. 2 and depicted on Fig. 1b, according to which we shift (among others) the client-to-client functionality to client side and wrap into a middleware, then no traces of the user activities belonging to the shared services will be left on the cloud, since all the service operations which are shared via a channel are used on behalf of its initial distributor.

Many scenario can make a profit on this fact, which require some anonymously usable cloud services. For instance, one of the possible use cases arises in a *multi-clouds* approach which enables many-to-many relationship between cloud service providers and customers of the middleware, such that the middleware architecture is capable to treat intermediate results exchanged among the requested cloud services. It may become necessary to store intermediate results on a third party cloud exploiting infrastructure as a service, and to ensure that after completion of the temporary use of this *docking service* no trace of the customers is left.

In the case study discussed in this section, we introduce a new kind of requests called *pipelined requests*, which can be composed from some normal service operation requests such that the requested services are able to exchange data according to a predefined information flow pattern. Below we also extend our formal model to be able to process this new kind of requests in a distributed way and to be able to anonymously store the intermediate results exchanged among some requested services on (probably) a third-party IaaS.

In our approach we assume that the middleware mentioned above (or its provider) has access to such a third-party storage service, whose operations are shared with all users of the middleware via some kind of public channel. Since these users access to the third-party docking service on behalf of the middleware (provider), their personal data is not given/forwarded to any third-party for any service subscription.

A complex pipelined request can be regarded as an extension of $RequestMsg$ defined in Sect. 5.1, see an example below:

$$RequestMsg_{pipelined} \equiv request[\ \text{IN}\ UID_x.\text{ALLOW}\ CID\ |\ \langle P_1 \rangle\ |\ \langle P_2 \rangle\ |$$
$$\langle o_i, P_1, args_i \rangle\ |\ \langle o_j, P_2, args_j \rangle\ |\ \langle o_k, client, \{arg_1, \ldots, P_1, \ldots, P_2, \ldots, arg_n\} \rangle\ ]$$

$RequestMsg_{pipelined}$ also contains the triples which denote the usual service requests, but it can also contains some singletons which declare the names of some information flow (or pipe) denoted by $P_1, \ldots, P_n$. If such a pipe name appears as the target location of the output of a requested operation (see the request triples for o_i and o_j above), then this output should be stored on a docking service, instead of sending to the user who initiated the request.

If the name of some pipes appears in the argument list of some operation requests, then the execution of these requests is blocked as long as all the inputs provided via the mentioned pipes will be available. Every pipe always describes a one-to-one or a one-to-many relationships (one operation can provide data to many) and it is always local to its containing $RequestMsg$.

6.1   New Assumptions and Changes in the Model

Now, it is assumed that each user of the middleware has access to the following two shared service operations which were distributed on behalf of the middleware provider via some public channel after each user registration:

– *sharedStore* is a shared version of a service operation whose task is to store some data in a filesystem on a third-party IaaS. It has two arguments, which are freely modifiable by the users. The first is an identifier (a pipe name) and the second is the data which are going to be stored.
– *sharedReceive* is a shared version of another service operation which belongs to the same third party IaaS as *sharedStore*. It has only one freely modifiable argument, the identifier by which some stored data can be retrieved. If no data is stored with the given identifier, the operation blocks until some data bound to such an identifier appear on the third-party IaaS.

In order to adapt the model to the new pipelined requests only the ambient expression represented by *requestPreprocessor* has to be replaced which was given as a part of the definition of user areas in Sect. 5.2:

$$requestPreprocessor \equiv \text{SERVER}_{CID}^n\ request.($$
$$!(p).\text{LISTENER}_{pipe}(p)\ |\ !(o, c, args).\text{LISTENER}_{req}(o, c, args)\ |\ \text{REQUESTMGR}(n)\ )$$

Table 5. The ASM agents LISTENER$_{pipe}$ and LISTENER$_{req}$.

LISTENER$_{pipe}$ (p) ≡
  ctr_state : $\{InitialState, EndState\}$
  initially $ctr\_state := InitialState$
 	
  if ctr_state = $InitialState$ **then**
  $ctr\_state := EndState$
  ADD$(p, mailbox_{pipe})$
	LISTENER$_{req}$ $(o, c, args)$ ≡
	  ctr_state : $\{InitialState, EndState\}$
	  initially $ctr\_state := InitialState$
	
	  if ctr_state = $InitialState$ **then**
	  $ctr\_state := EndState$
	  ADD$(\langle o, c, args\rangle, mailbox_{req})$

The new expression is an ambient server construct that is able to capture (both normal and pipelined) service operation requests arriving at a user area and able to prepare them for execution with the help of the three ASM agents called LISTENER$_{pipe}$, LISTENER$_{req}$ and REQUESTMGR(n).

LISTENER$_{pipe}$ and LISTENER$_{req}$ are very simple parameterized ASM agents, see in Table 5, whose several instances are available in the server construct referred by *requestPreprocessor*. Each replica of LISTENER$_{pipe}$ can capture a singleton containing a pipe name and mediates it to the agent REQUESTMGR via the shared dynamic function $mailbox_{pipe}$[6]. Replicas of LISTENER$_{req}$ can capture request triples, respectively, and also forward them to the agent REQUESTMGR via the shared dynamic function $mailbox_{req}$.

6.2   Request Preprocessing

REQUESTMGR is a parameterized ASM agent, see in Table 6, whose only argument is n which is the unique name of an ambient provided by the surrounding server construct and in which the content of current *RequestMsg* is preprocessed by an instance of this agent.

In the control state *InitialState* the agent first waits until every singleton and every triple in n are captured by LISTENER$_{pipe}$ and LISTENER$_{req}$. Then in the control state *PreProcessing* all request triples contained by the captured message will be prepared for execution in parallel.

In the next step, each request triple $\langle o, c, args\rangle$ is checked whether its execution is independent from other requests or in other words none of the pipe names occurs in $args$. If it is the case, the agent also checks whether the target location c does not correspond with any pipe name. If this is true as well, then the current request is a normal request which is not connected to any pipe, so it is simply converted into a service plot compatible format as before with NEWAMBIENTCONSTRUCT (see $request(n, o, c, args)$ in Table 6).

In that case if a pipe denoted by P_{out} is specified as a target location in the request, the agent generates a new and unique global identifier denoted by PID for the pipe with the function **new**. PID substitutes for P_{out} in the request

---

[6] In our applied ambient ASM-based formal method, ASM agents can communicate with each other directly via shared functions if and only if they are sibling of each other [1].

Table 6. The ASM agent REQUESTMGR.

REQUESTMGR(n) $\equiv$
 ctr_state : {$InitialState$, $PreprocessingState$,
 $EndState$}
 initially ctr_state := $InitialState$

 if ctr_state = $InitialState$ then
  if all async outputs are captured in n then
   ctr_state := $PreprocessingState$
 if ctr_state = $PreprocessingState$ then
  ctr_state := $EndState$
  forall R = $\langle o,\ c,\ args \rangle \in mailbox_{req}$ do
   if $R \in$
$independentReq(mailbox_{req},\ mailbox_{pipe})$ then
    if forall $P_{out} \in mailbox_{pipe}$ $P_{out} \neq c$ then
     NEWAMBIENTCONSTRUCT($request(n, o, c,$
$args)$)
    else
     choose $P_{out} \in mailbox_{pipe}$ with P_{out} = c do
     let PID = **new**($pipeIds$) in
      NEWAMBIENTCONSTRUCT(
       $request(n, o, PID, args)$ |
$tmpEndPoint(PID, P_{out})$))
   else
    let RID = **new**($requestIds$) in
    forall $P_{in} \in mailbox_{pipe}$ with $P_{in} \in args$ do
     NEWAMBIENTCONSTRUCT($receiveMsg(RID,$
$P_{in})$)
     if forall $P_{out} \in mailbox_{pipe}$ $P_{out} \neq c$ then
      NEWAMBIENTCONSTRUCT(
       $blockedRequest(\ request(RID, o, c, args)$
))
    else

choose $P_{out} \in mailbox_{pipe}$ with P_{out} = c do
let PID = **new**($pipeIds$) in
 NEWAMBIENTCONSTRUCT(
  $blockedRequest(\ request(RID, o, PID,$
$args)$) |
   $tmpEndPoint(PID, P_{out})$))
where
 all async outputs are captured in n $\equiv$ forall $o, c, args, P,$
Q
  $(ambBody(n) \neq \langle o,\ c,\ args \rangle \mid Q \wedge ambBody(n)$
$\neq \langle P \rangle \mid Q)$

$independentReq(X,\ Y) \equiv$
 { $\langle o,\ c,\ args \rangle \in X$ | forall $P_{in} \in Y$ ($P_{in} \notin args$)
}

$request(amb, o, target, args) \equiv$
 $o[$ OUT amb.ALLOW $op.\langle target, args \rangle$]

$tmpEndPoint(PID, P_{out}) \equiv$
 $PID[$ OUT n.ALLOW $output$ | $CID[(o, c, a$
).$sharedStore[$
  OUT PID.ALLOW $op.\langle c, \{n{:}P_{out}, a\} \rangle$]]]]

$receiveMsg(RID, P_{in}) \equiv$
 $sharedReceive[$ OUT n.ALLOW $op.\langle RID, n{:}P_{in} \rangle$]

$blockedReq(request) \equiv$
 $RID[$OUT n | !ALLOW $output$.$CID[\ ]$ |
  !(o, c, a).LISTENER$_{output}(o, c, a)$ |
  REQTRIGGER($n, mailbox_{pipe}, request$)]

triple as the target location of the output. When the modified ambient request is created with NEWAMBIENTCONSTRUCT another ambient term denoted by $tmpEndPoint$ attached to it, whose purpose is similar to the communication endpoints of the registered clients. Namely, it refers to an ambient called PID, so the output of the service operation eventually arrives at the body of this ambient. The aim of the mechanism located in the body of the ambient PID is to trigger the shared operation $sharedStore$ which will store the output bound to the global pipe identifier $n{:}P_{out}$ on the third-party IaaS (P_{out} alone cannot be applied as a unique global identifier of the pipe on a third-party storage, since it is always given by a user; hence, it should be extended with n as prefix, because n always refer to a unique name in the case of each captured $RequestMsg$).

In that case if some of the pipe names occur in $args$ (non-independent request), the request must be blocked until all the inputs referred by these pipes are available. First a unique identifier denoted by RID is generated for the request, which is applied as the name of the ambient, into where the request is enclosed and at where the required inputs from the third-party IaaS arrive eventually. Then a request for shared service operation $sharedReceive$ is triggered in parallel for each such a pipe with the argument $n{:}P_{in}$ and with the target location RID (see $receiveMsg(RID, P_{in})$ in Table 6). These requests

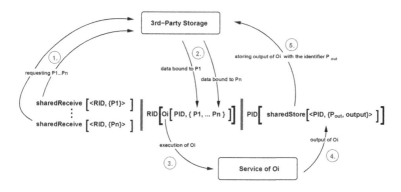

Fig. 2. Execution of pipelined service operation o_i.

block until some data bound to the global pipe identifer $n{:}P_{in}$ is not available on the third-party IaaS.

Concurrently with the sending of *sharedReceive* messages, an ambient construct called *blockedRequest* is created, which denotes the ambient RID and some ASM agents in its body. The ambient RID serves as the target location of the outputs of the triggered *sharedReceive* requests. This ambient also contains several replicas of the abstract ASM agent LISTENER$_{output}$ and one instance of the ASM agent REQTRIGGER. Each LISTENER$_{output}$ is responsible for capturing an output triple of an executed *sharedReceive* and for delivering it to REQTRIGGER via a shared dynamic function. REQTRIGGER is also an abstract ASM agent whose task is to add all the expected inputs provided by other services via pipes to the argument list of the current request and to then trigger this request as it is specified in the agent REQTRIGGER's argument list. If the target location of a non-independent request is also a pipe, then the original target location of this request is replaced with PID and $tmpEndPoint$ is attached to $tmpEndPoint$ like in the previous case above.

Figure 2 depicts a generalized summary how a request which is part of a pipelined $RequestMsg$ is processed in the model. According to it, if the request for the operation o_i requires inputs from other services, some *sharedReceive* requests are sent to the third-party IaaS on behalf of the middleware and the request for o_i is blocked in an ambient whose name is denoted by RID. After all the necessary data have arrived at the ambient RID and they have been added to the argument list, the request for o_i is triggered and executed. If the given target location of the output of o_i refers to another pipe, then this output is delivered into the ambient PID instead of a client. From here the output is forwarded in a *sharedStore* request message and stored on the third-party IaaS on behalf of the middleware as well.

7   Conclusions

In this paper we extended our formerly given cloud model with the high-level formal definitions of some client-to-client interaction functions, by which not only information, but cloud service functions can be also shared among the cloud users. Our approach is general enough to manage situation in which a user who has access to a shared service operation to share it again with some other users via a channel (who in turn may share it again, etc.).

Furthermore, if we apply the scenario proposed in Sect. 2 and depicted on Fig. 1b, according to which we shift (among others) the client-to-client functionality to client side and wrap into a middleware, then no traces of the user activities belonging to the shared services will be left on the cloud, since all the service operations which are shared via a channel are used on behalf of its initial distributor. As it was showed this consideration can facilitate the development of anonymously accessible cloud services. The consequence of this is that if a cloud user who has contracts with some service providers completely or partially shares some services via a channel, then she should be aware of the fact that all generated costs caused by the usage of these shared services will be allocated to her.

The specification described in Sect. 6 can lead to a solution of some problems regarding nowadays *(web) mashup* services, too. A mashup is a composed application, using elements from different sources. Namely, the examination of the security requirements for mashups [19] demands among others stronger separation guarantees between the executable components, but at the same time also require the possibility of interaction between these separated components. According to our opinion the formal specification defined above for complex pipelined requests can also be a good basis for overcoming these two problems of mashup services.

Acknowledgements. This research has been supported by the Christian Doppler Society.

References

1. Bósa, K.: Formal modeling of mobile computing systems based on ambient abstract state machines. In: Schewe, K.-D., Thalheim, B. (eds.) SDKB 2013. LNCS, vol. 7693, pp. 18–49. Springer, Heidelberg (2013)
2. Börger, E., Stark, R.F.: Abstract State Machines: A Method for High-Level System Design and Analysis. Springer, Secaucus (2003)
3. Cardelli, L., Gordon, A.D.: Mobile ambients. Theor. Comput. Sci. **240**, 177–213 (2000)
4. Bósa, K.: An ambient ASM model for cloud architectures. Formal Aspects of Computing (2013, submitted)
5. Ma, H., Schewe, K.-D., Thalheim, B., Wang, Q.: Abstract state services. In: Song, I.-Y., et al. (eds.) ER Workshops 2008. LNCS, vol. 5232, pp. 406–415. Springer, Heidelberg (2008)
6. Ma, H., Schewe, K.D., Thalheim, B., Wang, Q.: A theory of data-intensive software services. Serv. Orient. Comput. Appl. **3**, 263–283 (2009)
7. Kozen, D.: Kleene algebra with tests. Trans. Program. Lang. Syst. **19**, 427–443 (1997)

8. Boudol, G., Castellani, I., Hennessy, M., Kiehn, A.: A theory of processes with localities. Formal Aspects Comput. **6**, 165–200 (1994). doi:10.1007/BF01221098
9. Cardelli, L.: Mobility and security. In: Bauer, F.L., Steinbrüggen, R., (eds.) Proceedings of NATO Advanced Study Institute on Foundations of Secure Computation. Lecture Notes for Marktoberdorf Summer School 1999 (A Summary of Several Ambient Calculus Papers), pp. 3–37. IOS Press (1999)
10. Schewe, K.D., Thalheim, B.: Personalisation of web information systems - a term rewriting approach. Data Knowl. Eng. **62**, 101–117 (2007)
11. Tanaka, Y.: Meme Media and Meme Market Architectures: Knowledge Media for Editing, Distributing, and Managing Intellectual Resources. Wiley, New York (2003)
12. Ma, H., Schewe, K.D., Thalheim, B., Wang, Q.: A formal model for the interoperability of service clouds. Serv. Orient. Comput. Appl. **6**, 189–205 (2012)
13. Jarraya, Y., Eghtesadi, A., Debbabi, M., Zhang, Y., Pourzandi, M.: Cloud calculus: security verification in elastic cloud computing platform. In: Smari, W.W., Fox, G.C. (eds.) CTS, pp. 447–454. IEEE (2012)
14. Milner, R., Parrow, J., Walker, D.: A calculus of mobile processes, Parts I. and II. Inf. Comput. **100**, 1–77 (1992)
15. Börger, E., Cisternino, A., Gervasi, V.: Ambient abstract state machines with applications. J. CSS (Special Issue in Honor of Amir Pnueli) **78**, 939–959 (2012)
16. Valente, M., Bigonha, R., Loureiro, A., Maia, M.: Abstractions for mobile computation in ASM. In: Graham, P., Maheswaran, M. (eds.) Proceedings of the International Conference on Internet Computing, IC 2000, Las Vegas, Nevada, USA, 26–29 June 2000, pp. 165–172. CSREA Press (2000)
17. Bósa, K.: A formal model of a cloud service architecture in terms of ambient ASM. Technical report, Christian Doppler Laboratory for Client-Centric Cloud Computing (CDCC), Johannes Kepler University Linz, Austria (2012)
18. Bósa, K.: An ambient ASM model for client-to-client interaction via cloud computing. In: Proceedings of the 8th International Conference on Software and Data Technologies (ICSOFT), Reykjavik, Iceland, pp. 459–470 (Best Paper Award). SciTePress (2013)
19. De Ryck, P., Decat, M., Desmet, L., Piessens, F., Joosen, W.: Security of web mashups: a survey. In: Aura, T., Järvinen, K., Nyberg, K. (eds.) NordSec 2010. LNCS, vol. 7127, pp. 223–238. Springer, Heidelberg (2012)

Modeling a Flexible Replication Framework for Space-Based Computing

Stefan Craß[✉], Jürgen Hirsch, Eva Kühn, and Vesna Sesum-Cavic

Institute of Computer Languages,
Vienna University of Technology, Argentinierstr. 8, Vienna, Austria
{sc,jhirsch,eva,vesna}@complang.tuwien.ac.at

Abstract. Large-scale distributed systems often require complex interaction among dynamically joining and leaving participants. Compared
to classical approaches coordinated by a central authority, peer-to-peer
systems have been shown to provide a highly scalable and flexible architecture for such scenarios. Coordination middleware like tuple spaces
can help to unburden developers from coping with the complexity of distributed coordination by offering simple abstractions for the decoupled
interaction of autonomous peers. However, a fault-tolerant peer-to-peer
system can only be built if replication mechanisms exist to persist data
on several peers at once. To enrich space-based middleware with a flexible replication mechanism, we have designed a generic, plugin-based
replication framework that supports easy adaptation via configurable
replication schemes. The framework may act as a testbed to analyze the
efficiency and reliability of different replication strategies. Its architecture is built via highly composable coordination patterns that internally
interact via space containers. Using the generic framework, this paper
shows how different variants of multi-master replication can be realized
and how they can be adapted for various scenarios.

Keywords: Coordination middleware · Distributed systems · Peer-to-
peer · Replication framework · Tuple space

1   Introduction

The classical client-server paradigm is the usual way of communication between
computers across the Internet, but it implies severe problems as the server is a
single point of failure. If a huge number of clients communicate with the server,
they may overload it and decrease the performance of the entire system. Peer-to-
Peer (P2P) networks solve this problem as each peer works as client and server
at the same time, connects to other peers to request or transmit data and may
dynamically join and leave the network. Beside the advantages of P2P networks
like flexibility and a certain level of self-organization, they face problems of
increased complexity like lacking a central register describing which information
resides on which client or which clients are currently connected to the network.

© Springer-Verlag Berlin Heidelberg 2014
J. Cordeiro and M. van Sinderen (Eds.): ICSOFT 2013, CCIS 457, pp. 256–272, 2014.
DOI: 10.1007/978-3-662-44920-2_16

Once a peer leaves the network, its data is not available anymore and the only solution is to replicate each peer's data to other peers in the network.

In a distributed environment that enables clients to read and update generic data, replication is beneficial in two ways [5]: Firstly, it improves the scalability of a system as read access can be split among multiple replicas. Secondly, availability is increased as data is kept redundantly at multiple sites. However, replication also induces an overhead to synchronize replicas and keep them in a consistent state. Increasing the number of replicas also increases the management effort to ensure consistency. The situation becomes even more complex if an update operation fails on certain peers. In such a case error handling must be performed to decide if the overall operation was successful or not. In the worst case the operation has to be undone on all peers. According to the CAP theorem [10], a distributed system can, at any time, only provide two out of the three properties consistency, availability, and partition tolerance in an optimal way. Thus, if all replicas always have to be in the same, consistent state and lost messages or replica crashes occur, concurrently evaluated requests on different replicas either fail or block until the connection is restored.

Space-based middleware [18] provides an architectural style for distributed processes to collaborate in a decoupled way via a shared data space. This paradigm is based on the Linda tuple space model [9], which enables participants to write data tuples into a space and retrieve them using a query mechanism based on template matching. Tuple spaces can be used to synchronize independent processes via blocking queries that return their result as soon as a matching tuple is provided by another process. The XVSM (eXtensible Virtual Shared Memory) middleware model [8] adheres to this space-based computing style via space containers that are identified via a URI and support configurable coordination laws for writing and selecting data entries. Processes that access a container may write, read, or take (i.e. read and delete) entries, which generalize the tuple concept, using configurable coordination mechanisms like key-based access, FIFO queues, or template matching. Depending on the used coordination mechanism, queries for read and take operations include parameters like the key of a searched entry or the count of entries that shall be returned in FIFO order. If no matching result exists, the query blocks until it is fulfilled or a given timeout is reached, which enables decoupled communication.

If many distributed processes interact, a single space may form a performance bottleneck that hinders scalability. Replicated spaces would enable scalable P2P-based solutions, but currently only a few space-based middleware systems provide built-in replication mechanisms. However, even those that support replication usually assume a fixed mechanism, but there is not one optimal replication mechanism that serves all applications equally well. The trade-off between consistency, availability and partition tolerance must be negotiated for each use case. Thus, a replication mechanism should offer different replication strategies that can be configured by the user to enable adaption for any use case.

Therefore, we have designed a flexible replication framework for XVSM based on asynchronous replica management and replication strategies that can be configured via plugins. This paper is a revised version of [7], which describes a replication framework for the Java version of XVSM. While the original paper copes with the implementation and evaluation of two concrete replication plugins, this paper focuses on the generic framework approach and the design methodology for modeling new replication mechanisms. We have improved the initial framework architecture by decoupling components involved in the replication process via space containers. Thus, a replication mechanism for space containers is provided that itself is realized on top of space-based middleware, which is beneficial for the collaboration of autonomous, possibly mobile agents as it requires little mutual knowledge [4]. As we have already shown in earlier work on frameworks for load balancing [17] and load clustering algorithms [16], this approach allows for plugging and benchmarking different algorithms and configurable settings in a generic testbed, thus easing the task of finding the most suitable algorithm for a given scenario. For modeling the components of the replication mechanism and their interactions, we apply a flexible modeling technique based on services, space containers and dynamic links between them as introduced in [15].

A motivating use case can be found in the domain of traffic management for road or rail networks, were nodes are placed along the track to collect data from passing vehicles and inform them about relevant events (like congestions). As nodes may fail, data must be replicated to prevent data loss. For scalability reasons, a P2P-based approach is more feasible than a centralized architecture. As conditions are highly dynamic (e.g. number of vehicles and events), there might not be a single replication algorithm that performs well in every scenario. Thus a generic framework approach as proposed here appears very reasonable.

The paper is structured as follows: Sect. 2 describes related work for middleware replication. Section 3 presents the component-based design methodology and how it is used to create an architecture for the generic space-based replication framework. Section 4 shows different variants of a multi-master replication mechanism to proof the flexibility of the model. Section 5 evaluates the framework architecture and its plugin design methodology. Section 6 finally provides a conclusion and outlines future work.

2   Related Work

Replication for databases and data-oriented middleware like tuple spaces may be achieved via synchronous or asynchronous replica updates. Synchronous replication as defined by the ROWA (Read-One-Write-All) approach [1] forces any update operation to wait until the update has been propagated to all replicas. This scales well in a system that performs many read operations but few updates. In general, however, asynchronous replication mechanisms that use lazy update propagation increase the scalability and performance dramatically [13], but this is achieved at the cost of reduced consistency guarantees and more complex error handling. Depending on the requirements of a distributed application, strict consistency models based on ACID (Atomicity, Consistency, Isolation, Durability)

[11] or relaxed models like BASE (Basically Available, Soft state, Eventually consistent) [20] are more suitable for data replication. While ACID transactions guarantee consistent replica states, BASE uses a more fault-tolerant model that allows temporarily inconsistent states. In this paper, we present a replication mechanism that supports both consistency models.

Replication schemes define how operations are performed on specific replicas. For a space-based approach, master-slave and multi-master replication schemes are relevant. For master-slave replication, several slave nodes are assigned to a single master node. Read operations can be performed on any node while updates are restricted to the master node, which then propagates the changes to the slaves. If the master node fails, another node may be elected to be the new master. If many updates occur, the master may still become a bottleneck. In this case, a multi-master approach is more feasible, where every node may accept both read and update operations. However, an additional synchronization mechanism has to be introduced between the replicated nodes to guarantee that updates are performed in the same order on each replica. The proposed replication architecture supports both types depending on the used plugin.

Effective and fault-tolerant replication for space-based middleware can be achieved by letting distributed spaces collaborate using a P2P approach. Replication frameworks require a reliable way of coordinating replicas and exchanging meta data among nodes. One way to establish such a coordination channel is via distributed hash tables (DHT) [3], which distribute data as key-value pairs across the P2P network according to a deterministic hash function. The hashed key serves to retrieve a specific value from the network without knowing its actual storage location. In Sect. 4.2, we evaluate a DHT-based replication mechanism for XVSM based on the Hazelcast in-memory data grid [12], which provides dynamic node discovery, distributed locking and a map abstraction that transparently distributes data among several nodes in a fault-tolerant way. An alternative mechanism is based on group communication, where replicas subscribe to a specific topic, e.g. for a specific container, and are informed when a new message is published. Such a channel can be established using meta containers of the space itself, as shown with our native replication approach in Sect. 4.3.

Several related replication mechanisms have been invented for space-based middleware: GSpace [21] provides a Linda tuple space where every tuple type can be assigned to a specific replication policy, like replication to a fixed number of nodes or to dynamically evaluated consumers of a certain tuple type. Using a cost evaluation function based on the current space usage, the replication policy may be changed dynamically. DepSpace [2] examines Byzantine fault-tolerant replication for Linda spaces using a total order multicast protocol that works correctly if less than a third of the replicas are faulty. Corso [14] uses a replication mechanism based on a logical P2P tree-based overlay topology of replicas, where the master copy can be dynamically reassigned to another node through a primary copy migration protocol, to allow local updates on a data field. When using the eager propagation mode, updates are pushed to all replicated locations immediately, whereas for lazy propagation, updates are pulled on-demand when the corresponding data is accessed locally. LIME [19] provides an asynchronous master-slave replication approach for tuple spaces in mobile environments. Configurable replication profiles specify in which tuples a node is interested. If a matching tuple is found among neighboring nodes, it is automatically replicated to the local space.

Compared to the mentioned space-based solutions, the here proposed XVSM replication mechanism is able to cope with different coordination laws (label, key, queue, template matching etc.) and provides a more generic replication framework that supports the plugging of arbitrary replication mechanisms.

3   Generic Replication Framework

For designing a generic replication framework for XVSM, we rely on an architectural style termed *Peer Model* [15], which is based on coordination services that are encapsulated in components called *peers* and communicate with each other in a decoupled way using space containers. The following sections describe the general Peer Model concepts together with its graphical notation and how it can be applied to model the replication mechanism.

3.1   Peer Model Design Concepts

The Peer Model is a component-based programming model for developers of distributed applications that is based on asynchronous communication via space-based middleware, a staged event-driven architecture and data-driven workflow. The basic entity of a uniquely named peer is composed of a *peer-in-container (PIC)*, a *peer-out-container (POC)*, and its internal logic represented by *wirings* and *services*. The containers, which hold the system state, can be realized using XVSM or a similar middleware. A peer is invoked by writing one or more *entries*, which consist of properties represented by key/value pairs, into its PIC. Wirings describe the flow of entries among containers within peers and between them. Each wiring requires one or more entries as input, optionally processes them by calling a service containing the logic, and returns zero or more entries as output.

Figure 1 shows the graphical notation for a simple example with two peers. Within Peer1, there is a single wiring W1 with two *guard links* that describe its input and two *action links* as output. The circles on these links represent queries that denote the transported entries. The upper value represents the required entry type while the number below indicates how many entries of this type are needed to trigger the link. For this count parameter, either a concrete value, a minimum or a maximum can be specified. A filled circle means that the wiring takes the entry from the source container, while an unfilled one corresponds to a read operation. When all required entries are available, the guard links are triggered and the wiring becomes active. The service gets the input entries from the wiring, processes them and returns output entries that trigger the action links. In the example, the wiring takes one entry of type T1 and reads another entry of type T2. The service then creates one or more entries of type T3 and one entry of type T4. The T4 entry is written back to the peer's PIC, from where other wirings of Peer1 can access it, e.g. to retrieve state information for the current interaction. The T3 entries are moved to Peer1's POC, from where they are transferred to the PIC of another peer, whose internal behavior is not detailed here, to trigger the next stage of the computation. This is done by a so-called *move wiring*, which has a single input link, no service, and a single output link that simply moves the input entry to another container. In the graphical notation this is simplified using a solid arrow. Using count parameter 1 instead of >=1 means that each entry is moved separately in a possibly concurrent way, while using a minimum value, all available entries would be moved at once.

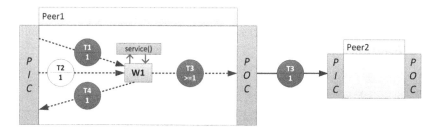

Fig. 1. Basic Peer Model notation.

To correlate the entries of a single flow (belonging to the same business process) across multiple stages and isolate them from unrelated flows that are executed concurrently, entries are enriched with a *flow identifier*. Wirings are only triggered if all of their input entries belong to the same flow. A flow's lifecycle either ends when all of its entries are consumed (e.g. because the result is returned), or after a specified *time-to-live (TTL)* has expired.

A distributed system is defined by specifying its components as peers, distributing them across the network and connecting them via inter-peer wirings. A Peer Model runtime environment, which is bootstrapped on top of XVSM containers, manages the peers on each host. Wiring execution can be realized via XVSM transactions, which encapsulate several read, take, and write operations into atomic actions. When specifying sources and targets of wirings, containers can be specified either via the unique address of their peer consisting of host URI and peer name, or via a logical lookup expression that is dynamically resolved by the runtime. To allow the dynamic selection of targets depending on application logic, services may also directly specify the destination of their output entries, which can be seen as a dynamic form of wiring.

3.2   Framework Architecture

We use the Peer Model to design a generic replication mechanism for XVSM containers where every component is modeled as a peer. As this approach achieves high decoupling between components and supports the composition of complex coordination patterns from simpler ones, it is ideal for the specification of a plugin-based framework that supports a wide range of different replication strategies. Figure 2 shows the basic architecture of the XVSM replication framework by using the Peer Model to describe the major components and their connections via move wirings. The *Replication API* is invoked by applications that want to access replicated XVSM containers through the framework. It transforms API calls into *Access Container Request (ACR)* entries for write, read, and take operations, and *Create Container Request (CCR)* entries for the creation of new containers. Deletion of containers is omitted here to simplify the model. These requests are written into the PIC of the configured *Replication Plugin* peer (short: *Plugin*), which performs the actual replication according to its strategy. Container replicas are spread among several distributed *XVSM Space* peers (short: *Space*) that are managed by the Plugin. Each space runtime acts as a peer that accepts request entries in its PIC and provides the corresponding *Result (RES)* entries in its POC.

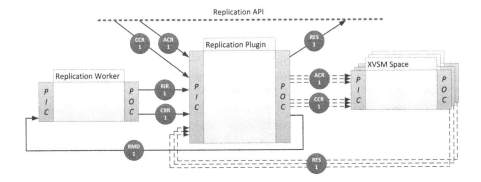

Fig. 2. Replication framework architecture.

For ACR entries, the Plugin dynamically selects one or more replicas according to the operation type and its policy. For each of these replicas, a corresponding ACR entry is created, which is dynamically routed to the respective Space (as indicated by the dashed lines). As the Plugin's PIC is specified as answer container in the ACR, the results are returned to the Plugin as RES entries, which can include query results (for read and take) or a success message (for write). If the operation could not be performed, an error message is included in the entry instead. Finally, the Plugin forwards the operation result to the Replication API. CCR entries are treated in a similar way by forwarding the requests to selected Spaces to initialize the replicas of a newly created container. As the Replication API uses the same request and result types as the Space itself, any application that directly accesses XVSM containers can be transparently ported to a replicated space version via the framework.

The *Replication Worker* peer ensures a configurable Quality of Service (QoS) for the replication mechanism by periodically checking the status of replicas via the Plugin. It monitors all replicas via *Replica Information Requests (RIR)* that are wired to the Plugin, which responds with *Replica Meta Data (RMD)* entries that indicate the status of the replicas. This information is obtained by the Plugin by sending ACR entries to all replica sites. If the number of valid replicas drops for any container below the configurable minimum, the Replication Worker reacts by triggering the creation of new replicas via a *Create Replica Request (CRR)*. The Plugin reacts to such a request by invoking CCR messages on Spaces that do not yet contain a replica of the container. The current container content is finally copied to the new replicas via ACR entries. The activation of the Replication Worker in regular intervals can be achieved by writing an initial entry (not shown in Fig. 2) with an attached *time-to-start (TTS)* property into its PIC. This entry triggers the wiring responsible for issuing the RIR entries after the TTS is reached. By writing this entry back into the PIC with an updated TTS, the wiring can delay its next execution, as an entry is not visible if its TTS is not yet reached. The advantage of this asynchronous approach is that Plugins do not need to check the status of replicas during a method invocation, which is a time-consuming operation. As the Replication Worker and the Plugin are running on each node of a P2P scenario, the system is able to recover from node failures as long as at least one replica of a container remains.

The Plugin defines the replication mechanism, the technology for inter-process communication and the type of replication (synchronous or asynchronous). In the following section, a Plugin using a distributed hash table and a native one using XVSM's own middleware mechanisms are realized, both resting upon a generic multi-master replication pattern. This framework approach does not impose any limitation on the replication strategy and thus ensures flexibility.

4 Plugin Design

To replicate an XVSM container, the entries as well as associated meta data have to be managed by the Plugin. Two types of meta data are considered: *Location meta data* is used to find available locations for new replicas and to locate existing containers. *Container meta data* consists of information for a particular container that is used when creating new replicas. Due to their flexible coordination laws like FIFO queues, key-based access or template matching, XVSM containers are not just lists of entries. For any container, each supported coordination mechanism is managed by a so-called coordinator, which stores an internal container view (e.g. a map) that is updated every time when entries are written to or taken from the container. This view determines which entries are selected by read or take queries. The container meta data therefore contains the registered coordinators, the container size, coordinator meta data (e.g. keys) and additional replication parameters supported by the Plugin. The meta data itself has to be replicated because otherwise it is neither possible to find other replicas, nor to create a new replica as an exact copy of an existing container.

Plugins are defined by specifying a peer that satisfies the interface described in Sect. 3.2. The behavior is described by defining the internal wirings and their services. The plugin mechanism may consist of a single peer or it may be composed of several sub-plugins that are invoked by the main Plugin peer, which is transparent for the surrounding framework. Plugins for both master-slave and multi-master replication can be designed with this approach. As multi-master replication provides more flexibility and does not limit the number of concurrent write operations, it is preferred for P2P scenarios. In the following, we present a generic multi-master replication pattern that utilizes an exchangeable component for managing meta data.

4.1   Generic Multi-master Replication Pattern

To model a generic coordination pattern for multi-master replication, coordination logic can be split into two parts. The main Plugin peer communicates with the framework and performs the actual replication, while a separate peer is used to manage replicated meta data. This second peer acts as an exchangeable component that does not affect the semantics of the general replication mechanism but mainly its QoS guarantees concerning scalability and consistency.

Figure 3 shows the design of a basic multi-master replication approach. Relevant entry properties are specified in square brackets next to the respective entries. Because of space limitations, only the wirings related to container access are shown. Wiring W1 processes ACR entries that are written by the framework into the Plugin's PIC. They include a container reference (cref) as well as different request parameters like operation type (write, read, or take) and coordination parameters (e.g. keys). The service associated with W1 creates a *Replica Directory Query (RDQ)* entry for the accessed container that is sent to the *Data Management Peer* via a move wiring. This peer then responds with a *Replica Locations (RL)* entry that lists available replica locations for the requested container. To store the state of the current replication flow, also an *Access Data (AD)* entry that includes the request information is written to the PIC.

Wiring W2 waits for the RL entry from the Data Management Peer and retrieves the state of the current operation by reading the AD entry. In case multiple ACR entries are processed concurrently by the Plugin, the correlation of associated entries is achieved via their flow identifiers, as the wiring automatically reads the AD entry with the same ID as the RL entry, whose IDs both originate from the initial ACR entry. The output of W2 is a set of multiple ACR entries that include the container reference and the parameters from the original request, as well as a special destination property (DEST) that indicates to which peers these entries should be dynamically wired by the Peer Model runtime. Thus, for each space URI included in the RL list, an asynchronous request is issued that distributes the container operation to all active replicas. Within the targeted Spaces the actual data containers (e.g. named C1 and C2) can be modeled as internal peers with merged PIC and POC. The semantics of the request handling in the XVSM runtime is, however, out of scope of this paper.

The final wiring W3 is triggered every time one or more RES entries, which contain the operation result and associated meta data, are returned to the Plugin's PIC. These entries are taken together with the previously created AD entry.

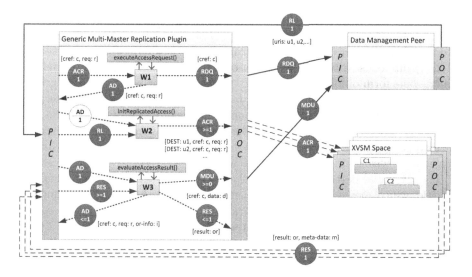

Fig. 3. Generic multi-master replication pattern (container access).

The service then determines if enough replicas have responded yet. While for a read operation, a single response is sufficient, a replicated take operation requires a minimum number of replicas to respond. If the replicated operation was successful, a new RES entry with the retrieved result data is written to the POC. Additionally, one or more *Meta Data Update (MDU)* entries may be emitted to the Data Management Peer if the operations require changes to the container meta data, which depends on the request information from the AD entry and the meta data included in the received RES entries. If the replicated operation has failed according to the service logic, this information is also written to the POC via an RES entry. It may also be possible that the service cannot decide yet if the operation was successful. In this case, it includes the currently available results in the AD entry, which is written back into the PIC. Wiring W3 is triggered again when new RES entries arrive.

This simple replication strategy provides only very basic consistency guarantees, but the pattern can be easily extended via new or adapted wirings and services. It is for example possible to use separate wirings for write, read, and take requests as they often require different handling. It is usually sufficient to read data only from a single container, as all replicas eventually contain the same data. Thus, the `initReplicatedAccess` service from wiring W2 can be modified to output only a single ACR entry for read operations. For synchronous write and take operations, it may be feasible to return only when all registered replicas were successfully updated. Therefore, wiring W2 must also update the AD entry instead of only reading it to include the number of issued ACR entries. Then the `evaluateAccessResult` service of W3 should only return a result when the number of received RES entries matches that count. In contrast, asynchronous behavior can be reached if an RES entry is written to the POC as soon as one space has responded (or already in W1 for write operations). Service semantics may also be dynamically configurable by writing specific configuration entries into the PIC, which are then read by wirings and passed to the associated service.

To ensure consistency in the case of concurrent updates on a replicated container, some form of locking is required. Global locks on container level prevent conflicts as updates must be performed on each replica in the same order. Different locking mechanisms can be supported by including their logic in the Data Management Peer. Integration with the provided Plugin can be achieved via asynchronous lock and unlock requests to the Data Management Peer that are triggered by wirings installed before W2 and after W3, respectively.

The presented pattern assumes that any container access operation is deterministic, which means that it is sufficient to replicate the operation request to all replica locations. XVSM, however, also supports non-deterministic coordination mechanisms. E.g., if on a container with five entries managed by the non-deterministic AnyCoordinator the same read operation is repeatedly performed, the results may differ as an arbitrary entry is selected each time. If a take operation is replicated, using this coordinator may result in replica inconsistencies, because the coordinator may delete a different entry in each replicated space container. In order to avoid an inconsistent state between the replicas, we distinguish between *strict* and *loose consistency models*, which are applied according to the used coordinators. For take operations using non-deterministic coordinators, a strict consistency approach is required, which means that when performing a take operation, the same entries must be removed from each replica container. All other operations may follow the loose consistency approach that simply replicates the request entries as shown before. With strict consistency, one space is invoked via a ACR entry to perform the initial take operation. The meta data of the returned RES entry includes a unique ID for each entry that is removed from the container. These entry IDs can then be used to take the same entries at the residual replica containers (using a key-based coordinator).

If errors occur during the replication process (e.g. because a Space is not reachable), the Plugin has to react accordingly after a timeout and restore a consistent state for all active replicas. Using the Peer Model, such recovery services can be triggered via the internal timeout mechanisms. If the TTL of individual entries or an entire flow expires (e.g. because not enough RES entries have arrived to satisfy the service logic in W3), the corresponding entries are garbage collected and replaced by an exception entry that includes their data. These entries can then be wired like regular entries to start a recovery service.

The creation of new containers via CCR entries can be modeled similarly to container access by using a three-stage approach. At first the Data Management Peer is queried to return the list of available Spaces where replicas can be placed. Then, CCR requests are sent to a subset of these locations to initialize the replicated containers and finally the Data Management Peer is triggered again to update its replica directory and to initialize the meta data for the new container.

The Plugin also has to interact with the framework's Replication Worker. For RIR entries, the replica locations are queried from the Data Management

Peer using RDQ entries. Then, the availability of replicas is checked using simple read requests and the results are returned to the Replication Worker. Adding new replicas for existing containers via CRR entries is more complex. After querying available spaces and current replica locations, the container content needs to be retrieved. Read requests to an active replica are used to extract the entries, while queries to the Data Management Peer yield the corresponding container meta data. Then, the new replicas are initialized on not yet used spaces via CCR requests and filled with content using ACR requests. Finally, the replica directory is updated via the Data Management Peer.

Sections 4.2 and 4.3 describe two variants for realizing the Data Management Peer, thus providing a fully functional replication mechanism.

4.2   Hazelcast Replication

As shown in Fig. 4, the Hazelcast version of the Data Management Peer uses a proxy peer to integrate the DHT implementation Hazelcast into the replication framework. Any request (e.g. an RDQ entry) is forwarded to this proxy peer as a *Hazelcast Command (HCC)* entry. The proxy peer consumes any of these entries and internally invokes its Hazelcast instance to manage the replication meta data. The return value is then wrapped into a *Hazelcast Result (HCR)* entry and routed back to the Data Management Peer, whose second wiring transforms the result into the correct type expected by the Plugin. The *Query Data (QD)* entry is necessary to properly correlate requests and responses via their flow identifiers.

Location and container meta data is stored in distributed maps that are replicated by Hazelcast to several other cluster members. If a new member of the Hazelcast cluster starts up, it looks for already existing members in the network neighborhood. If such a member is found, the new member will connect to and share the meta data with the cluster. The Data Management Peer uses the distributed locking mechanism of Hazelcast where a lock can be acquired that is identified via the corresponding container name. Hazelcast applies a simple heartbeat approach to discover dead members, which avoids that a container is locked by a dead process and therefore unavailable for the rest of the cluster.

4.3   Native Replication

The native version of the Data Management Peer (Fig. 5) does not use an additional framework for the communication between the cluster members, but only the built-in XVSM functionality. Thus, the already available Spaces that hold the replicated data are also used to manage the associated meta data via ACR (and CCR) requests that are targeted at special containers. It is assumed that for each Data Management Peer there is also a local Space.

On start-up, the peer initializes the list of available replication locations in the local ReplicationLocationLookupContainer (RLLC) with known neighbors. For each location, the process reads all entries from the remote Replication-LookupContainers (RLC) and initializes the replica lists in its local RLC, which

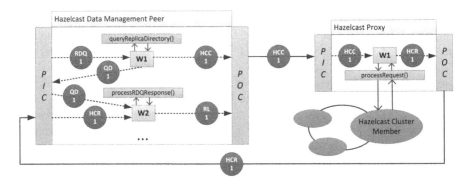

Fig. 4. Hazelcast Data Management Peer.

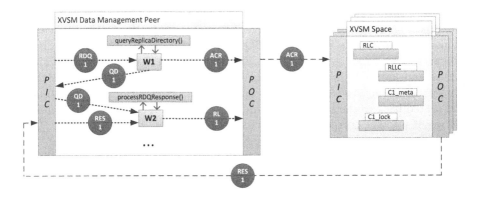

Fig. 5. XVSM Data Management Peer.

contains the mapping of containers to their replica locations. Furthermore, the peer adds the location of its local space to the RLLC of the remote sites. For storing the container meta data, a meta container is created for each replicated container. This meta container itself is then replicated to every replica location of the associated container.

To implement its own distributed locking mechanism, a special lock container is created for each replicated container and registered in the corresponding meta containers via its URI. If an update is performed on a replica, a lock is acquired on the lock container using XVSM transactions. Because every replica of a specific container uses the same lock container, concurrent modifications can be avoided. After the update has been performed, the lock is released. If a node crashes while holding a lock, transaction timeouts ensure that the container will eventually be unlocked. If the node holding the lock container crashes, it has to be recreated at a different site.

5   Evaluation

The presented generic framework provides a flexible way of defining replication mechanisms for space-based middleware via loosely coupled components that can be exchanged easily. The plugins themselves may contain nested components, which enables the construction of complex replication patterns consisting of simpler building blocks that can be developed independently. The Peer Model design approach facilitates the high composability of coordination patterns and the flexible integration of new logic into distributed applications like the XVSM replication framework. Even within individual peers, business logic can be modified easily as wirings may support different kind of policies implemented by different services. Services themselves are loosely coupled as they only communicate with each other in an asynchronous way via space containers. The wiring mechanism also enables the dynamic reconfiguration of connections and the exchange of peers at run-time.

The bootstrapping of the Peer Model via XVSM containers for PIC and POC adds additional features to the architecture. The replication mechanism profits from the persistency features of XVSM, which enables the recovery of replicas after a crash. Another relevant feature is a security mechanism that allows the definition of fine-grained access control rules for containers [6]. In the scope of the replication framework, direct access to spaces may be restricted to prevent any user from bypassing the Replication Plugin when accessing replicated containers, which could lead to inconsistent replicas. Additionally, access to PICs and POCs may be limited so that only trusted users or components are allowed to inject entries and reconfigure wirings. Another advantage of this architecture is that the peers can be physically distributed among many hosts without affecting their implementation. The individual components of the framework may be located on different hosts, which improves scalability. In this case, only the guard and action links on the wirings have to be reconfigured to point to different containers, which are addressed via simple URIs. Even multiple peer instances can compete for the same type of requests and thus share the load. Finally, the system can be easily monitored as the current state is accessible via containers.

Compared to direct invocation of components via method calls, the decoupled peer-based approach naturally causes an additional performance overhead. The framework architecture is, however, superior if flexibility is required, e.g. in testbed scenarios or when different replication mechanisms should be activated based on dynamic properties like the current load. As there is always a trade-off between performance and consistency when regarding replication and different use case scenarios require different QoS guarantees, a fixed replication mechanism is not the best solution.

In P2P traffic management scenarios, a suitable architecture must provide traffic information to vehicles in near-time while replicating data among nodes in a robust way to ensure fault tolerance. Asynchronous multi-master replication as provided by the presented plugins ensures that no node acts as single point of failure and that replication occurs in the background, thus preventing delays when interacting with vehicles that are only in range for a short time span. The generic pattern outlined in this paper is not yet a complete solution for fully consistent and highly scalable replication, but it shows how complex strategies can be designed efficiently. Using the framework, researchers may evaluate and fine-tune further plugins that are adjusted to the specific use case.

The basic framework and the presented plugins were previously implemented on top of the Java version of XVSM[1], without using the advanced decoupling features provided by the Peer Model runtime. Still, several benchmark results [7] could be obtained that prove the feasibility of the framework as a testbed. The comparison of the plugins has shown that the XVSM-based approach for meta data management scales better than the Hazelcast approach, mainly due to the additional overhead of invoking a DHT with high consistency guarantees. We have also noticed that the loose consistency model scales much better than the strict model, which is expected due to the added constraints. Further tests with additional, more sophisticated replication algorithms will provide us with a set of suitable container replication strategies for several P2P scenarios with different requirements.

6   Conclusions

In this paper, we have presented a flexible and highly customizable replication framework for space-based middleware that supports different replication strategies via exchangeable plugins. This way, the best replication plugin for the given use case can be chosen. A peer-based design methodology for plugin development supports the composition of complex replication patterns from simpler components. As a proof-of-concept for the flexibility of the framework, two plugins were designed that perform multi-master replication on space containers. While one plugin manages meta data via distributed hash tables, the other one uses the space-based middleware itself for this task. Both variants share the same general strategy, which is realized as a separate generic component that can be easily adapted to specific requirements.

Future work includes the integration of the framework prototype with a Peer Model runtime implementation, the design and evaluation of additional, more sophisticated replication mechanisms for practical use case scenarios, and a detailed investigation of security and privacy concerns for replication.

Acknowledgements. The work is partially funded by the Austrian Federal Ministry for Transport, Innovation and Technology (bmvit) under the program FFG BRIDGE, project no. 834162 LOPONODE Middleware.

---

[1] http://www.mozartspaces.org

References

1. Bernstein, P., Hadzilacos, V., Goodman, N.: Concurrency Control and Recovery in Database Systems. Addison-Wesley, Reading (1987)
2. Bessani, A., Alchieri, E., Correia, M., da Silva Fraga, J.: DepSpace: a byzantine fault-tolerant coordination service. ACM SIGOPS Oper. Syst. Rev. **42**, 163–176 (2008)
3. Byers, J., Considine, J., Mitzenmacher, M.: Simple load balancing for distributed hash tables. In: Kaashoek, M.F., Stoica, I. (eds.) IPTPS 2003. LNCS, vol. 2735, pp. 80–87. Springer, Heidelberg (2003)
4. Cabri, G., Leonardi, L., Zambonelli, F.: MARS: a programmable coordination architecture for mobile agents. IEEE Internet Comput. **4**(4), 26–35 (2000)
5. Cecchet, E., Candea, G., Ailamaki, A.: Middleware-based database replication: the gaps between theory and practice. In: ACM SIGMOD International Conference on Management of Data, pp. 739–752. ACM (2008)
6. Craß, S., Dönz, T., Joskowicz, G., Kühn, E., Marek, A.: Securing a space-based service architecture with coordination-driven access control. J. Wirel. Mob. Netw. Ubiquit. Comput. Dependable Appl. (JoWUA) **4**(1), 76–97 (2013)
7. Craß, S., Hirsch, J., Kühn, E., Sesum-Cavic, V.: An adaptive and flexible replication mechanism for space-based computing. In: 8th International Joint Conference on Software Technologies (ICSOFT), pp. 599–606. SciTePress (2013)
8. Craß, S., Kühn, E., Salzer, G.: Algebraic foundation of a data model for an extensible space-based collaboration protocol. In: 13th International Database Engineering & Applications Symposium, (IDEAS). pp. 301–306. ACM (2009)
9. Gelernter, D.: Generative communication in Linda. ACM Trans. Program. Lang. Syst. **7**(1), 80–112 (1985)
10. Gilbert, S., Lynch, N.: Brewer's conjecture and the feasibility of consistent, available, partition-tolerant web services. SIGACT News **33**, 51–59 (2002)
11. Haerder, T., Reuter, A.: Principles of transaction-oriented database recovery. ACM Comput. Surv. **15**, 287–317 (1983)
12. Hazelcast: Hazelcast - in-memory data grid (2012). http://www.hazelcast.com
13. Jiménez-Peris, R., Patiño Martínez, M., Alonso, G., Kemme, B.: Are quorums an alternative for data replication? ACM Trans. Database Syst. **28**, 257–294 (2003)
14. Kühn, E.: Fault-tolerance for communicating multidatabase transactions. In: 27th Hawaii International Conference on System Sciences (HICSS), vol. 2, pp. 323–332. IEEE (1994)
15. Kühn, E., Craß, S., Joskowicz, G., Marek, A., Scheller, T.: Peer-based programming model for coordination patterns. In: De Nicola, R., Julien, C. (eds.) COORDINATION 2013. LNCS, vol. 7890, pp. 121–135. Springer, Heidelberg (2013)
16. Kühn, E., Marek, A., Scheller, T., Sesum-Cavic, V., Vögler, M., Craß, S.: A space-based generic pattern for self-initiative load clustering agents. In: Sirjani, M. (ed.) COORDINATION 2012. LNCS, vol. 7274, pp. 230–244. Springer, Heidelberg (2012)
17. Kühn, E., Sesum-Cavic, V.: A space-based generic pattern for self-initiative load balancing agents. In: Aldewereld, H., Dignum, V., Picard, G. (eds.) ESAW 2009. LNCS, vol. 5881, pp. 17–32. Springer, Heidelberg (2009)
18. Mordinyi, R., Kühn, E., Schatten, A.: Space-based architectures as abstraction layer for distributed business applications. In: 4th International Conference on Complex, Intelligent and Software Intensive Systems (CISIS), pp. 47–53. IEEE (2010)

19. Murphy, A.L., Picco, G.P.: Using LIME to support replication for availability in mobile Ad Hoc networks. In: Ciancarini, P., Wiklicky, H. (eds.) COORDINATION 2006. LNCS, vol. 4038, pp. 194–211. Springer, Heidelberg (2006)
20. Pritchett, D.: BASE: an acid alternative. Queue **6**, 48–55 (2008)
21. Russello, G., Chaudron, M.R.V., van Steen, M.: Dynamically adapting tuple replication for managing availability in a shared data space. In: Jacquet, J.-M., Picco, G.P. (eds.) COORDINATION 2005. LNCS, vol. 3454, pp. 109–124. Springer, Heidelberg (2005)

Realizable, Connector-Driven Software Architectures for Practising Engineers

Mert Ozkaya$^{(\boxtimes)}$ and Christos Kloukinas

School of Informatics, City University London, London EC1V 0HB, UK
{mert.ozkaya.1,c.kloukinas}@city.ac.uk

Abstract. Despite being a widely-used language for specifying software systems, UML remains less than ideal for software architectures. Architecture description languages (ADLs) were developed to provide more comprehensive support. However, so far the application of ADLs in practice has been impeded by at least one of the following problems: (i) advanced formal notations requiring a steep learning curve, (ii) lack of support for user-defined, complex connectors, and (iii) potentially unrealizable architectural designs.

This paper proposes XCD, a new ADL that aims at supporting user-defined, complex connectors to help increase architectural modularity. It also aims to help increase the degree of reusability, as now components need not specify interaction protocols, as these can be specified independently by connectors (which increases protocol reusability too).

Connector support requires to ensure that architectural designs are always realizable, as it is currently extremely easy to obtain unrealizable ones. XCD eliminates potentially unrealizable constructs in connector specifications.

Finally, XCD employs a notation and notions from Design-by-Contract (DbC) for specifying software architecture behaviour. While DbC promotes a formal and precise way of specifying system behaviours, it is not as challenging for practising developers as process algebras that are usually employed by ADLs.

Keywords: Component based software engineering · Software architecture · Modular specifications · Connector realizability · Separation of functional and interaction behaviours · Design-by-contract

1 Introduction

A number of specialized architecture description languages (ADLs) have been proposed for specifying software architectures [20], since the early work on software architectures [12,23]. Currently UML has become a de facto design language for specifying and designing software systems – more practitioners use it than all other languages (e.g., AADL, ArchiMate, etc.) combined [19], even though it is less than ideal [16]. This is despite its lack of support for formal architectural analysis, unlike many ADLs that have formally defined semantics. In our view,

© Springer-Verlag Berlin Heidelberg 2014
J. Cordeiro and M. van Sinderen (Eds.): ICSOFT 2013, CCIS 457, pp. 273–289, 2014.
DOI: 10.1007/978-3-662-44920-2_17

there are three main problems that ADLs suffer from: (i) formal notations for behaviour specifications that require a steep learning curve, (ii) lack of support for complex connectors (i.e., interaction protocols), and (iii) potential for producing unrealizable designs. Indeed, to the best of our knowledge, there is no ADL that is easy to learn, treats connectors as first-class elements and ensures that architecture specifications are realizable.

While condition (i) has been identified by practitioners as being a serious impediment to their adoption of current ADLs [19], condition (ii) is not an issue that they consider as crucial, as does a number of researchers since many ADLs do not support complex connectors. Nevertheless, we believe that it can substantially help in developing concise designs, as it increases modularity and reusability by allowing designers to reuse not only components but interaction protocols as well, thus facilitating architectural exploration and avoiding reuse-by-copy. Condition (iii) is in fact something that has not been identified at all so far to the best of our knowledge but we believe that it is crucial to identify and resolve, if a connector-centric ADL is to succeed among practitioners. Below we briefly examine each of these issues.

Formal Notations. Many ADLs (e.g., Wright [1], LEDA [6], SOFA [24], CON-NECT [15], etc.) adopt formal notations, e.g., process algebras [4], for specifying the behaviours of architectural elements. They do so in order to enable the architectural analysis of systems, which is extremely important in uncovering serious system design errors early on in the lifetime of a project. Indeed, if such an analysis is not possible, then there is no point in using a specialized language for software architectures – even simple drawings suffice. However, ADLs employ notations that practitioners view (with reason) as having a steep learning curve [19]. Thus, practitioners end up avoiding them and use instead simpler languages, even if that means that they lose the ability to properly describe and analyse their systems – better an informal description of a system that everybody understands than a formal description of a system that people struggle understanding.

Limited Support for Complex Connectors. Another problem with many ADLs (e.g., Darwin [18], Rapide [17], LEDA [6], and AADL [10]) is that they provide limited or no support for complex connectors, treating them instead as simple connections. This is unfortunate because connectors represent the interaction patterns between components, i.e., the interaction *protocols* that are employed to achieve the system goals using the system components, such as reliability. By instead offering support only for components, architects end up with two alternatives. One is to ignore protocols, which inhibits the analysis of crucial system properties, such as deadlock-freedom, and also can lead to architectural mismatch [11], i.e., the inability to compose seemingly compatible components due to wrong assumptions these make about their interaction. The other is to incorporate the protocol behaviour inside the components themselves, which leads to complicated component behaviour that is neither easy to understand nor to analyse and makes it difficult to reuse components with different protocols,

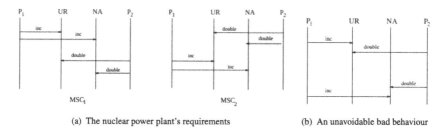

(a) The nuclear power plant's requirements   (b) An unavoidable bad behaviour

Fig. 1. A nuclear power plant [2].

connector Plant_Connector =
role P_1 = ur→na→P_1.
role P_2 = ur→na→P_2.
role NA = increment→ NA ⊓ double→NA.
role UR = increment→ UR ⊓ double→UR.
glue =P_1.ur→UR.increment→P_1.na→NA.increment
        →P_2.ur→UR.double→P_2.na→NA.double→ **glue**
   □P_2.ur→UR.double→P_2.na→NA.double→P_1.ur
        →UR.increment→P_1.na→NA.increment → **glue**.

Fig. 2. Wright's *(unrealizable)* connector for Alur's nuclear power plant.

as well as to find errors in specific protocol instances. Incorporating protocol behaviour inside components is essentially following a reuse-by-copy approach, whereby each component has its own copy of the protocol constraints. On the other hand, support for protocols through first-class connectors promotes a reuse-by-call approach. There is only one instance of the protocol constraints and these are simply called wherever they are needed, making it easier to keep them correct and to replace them with those of another protocol if needed.

Potentially Unrealizable Designs. The third problem of existing ADLs is that when they do support user-defined, complex connectors, they do so in a way that can lead to unrealizable designs. All ADLs in this category follow the approach initiated by Wright [1] and require connectors to include a glue element. In Wright [1], a connector role specifies the *"obligations of [a] component participating in the interaction"* and a glue specifies *"how the activities of the [...] roles are coordinated."* – a connector glue is supposed to be more than simple definition/use relationships. The fact that the glue can introduce inter-role interaction constraints is deeply problematic because these constraints cannot always be implemented in a decentralized manner by the components that assume the connector roles, as these can only observe their local state [27,28]. In fact, it has been shown that the general problem of deciding whether a glue is realizable is undecidable [2,3,27,28], so there is no general algorithm that can be implemented to warn architects that the glue they are specifying is not realizable by the existing roles. The only easy solution to realize a protocol then

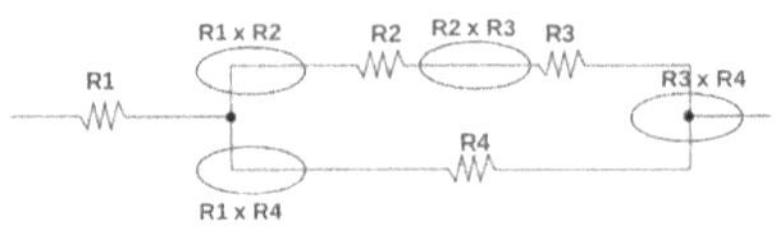

(a) Simple connectors, i.e., wires   (b) Complex connectors

Fig. 3. Connectors in circuits.

is to introduce yet another component that will assume the role of the glue, thus transforming all protocols into centralized ones and potentially invalidating architectural analyses concerning scalability, performance, reliability, information flows, etc.

An example of such an unrealizable protocol is the simplified nuclear power plant [2], shown in Fig. 1a. The interaction therein involves two client roles (P_1 and P_2) updating the amounts of the Uranium fuel (UR) and Nitric Acid (NA) server processes in a nuclear reactor. After the update operations, the amounts of UR and NA must be equal to avoid nuclear accidents, for which reason we wish to allow only the sequences shown in Fig. 1a. The interaction of the two clients with the NA and UR variables, can easily be specified in Wright as in Fig. 2. Note that this glue specification does two things. First it establishes bindings between clients and servers (e.g., P_1.ur → UR.increment). Then it constraints interactions by requiring that we only allow UR.increment → NA.increment or UR.double → NA.double. This specification is however unrealizable [2] because it is impossible to implement it in a decentralized manner in a way that avoids behaviours excluded by the glue, e.g., the one depicted in Fig. 1b. The only way to achieve the desired behaviour is to introduce another role, for a centralized controller G. Roles P_1 and P_2 then need to inform G when they wish to interact with UR and NA and have G perform the interactions with UR and NA in their place.

2   Our Approach

The ADL we are developing, called XCD, tries to overcome the problems identified in the previous section and offer: *(i)* first-class support for user-defined, complex connectors; *(ii)* realizable software architectures by construction; and *(iii)* a simple to understand, yet formal, language for specifying behaviour, based on design-by-contract (DbC).

2.1   Support for Complex Connectors

XCD grants connectors in software architectures first-class status, allowing designers to specify both simple interaction mechanisms and complex protocols. These can then be instantiated as many times as needed, allowing architects to simplify the specifications of their components and easily reuse the specification of complex protocols.

To illustrate how important this is for both architectural understandability and also analysis, we will use a simple example from electrical engineering. Let us consider k concrete electrical resistors, $r_1, \cdots, r_k$, i.e., our system components. When using a sequential connector ($\rightarrow$), the overall resistance is computed as $R^{\rightarrow}(N, \{R_i\}_{i=1}^{N}) = \sum_{i=1}^{N} R_i$, where N, R_i are variables (R_i correspond to connector roles), to be assigned eventually some concrete values k, r_j. If using a parallel connector ($\|$) instead, it is computed as $R^{\|}(N, \{R_i\}_{i=1}^{N}) = 1/\sum_{i=1}^{N} 1/R_i$. So the interaction protocol (connector) used is the one that gives us the formula we need to use to analyse it – if it does not do so, then we are probably using the wrong connector abstraction. The components (r_j) are simply providing some numerical values to use in the formula, while the system configuration tells us which specific value (k, r_j) we should assign to each variable (N, R_i) of the connector-derived formula. By simply enumerating the wires/connections between resistors/components, we miss the forest for the trees. This leads to architectural designs at a very low level that is not easy to communicate and develop – as [8] found the case to be with AADL.

Figure 3a shows the number of simple connectors (identified with ellipses) that are needed in our system. It is easy to see that there are many of them and it is not so easy to identify the protocol logic, especially as the system size increases – this is the equivalent of spaghetti code. By making interaction protocols implicit in designs, analysis also becomes difficult and architectural errors can go undetected until later development phases. Indeed, we are essentially forced to reverse-engineer the architect's intent in order to analyse our system – after all, the architect did not select the specific wire connections by chance but because they form a specific complex connector. When complex connectors are employed instead as in Fig. 3b then the number of connectors to be considered is reduced substantially. This makes it much easier to understand the system and to analyse its overall resistance by taking advantage of the connector properties as:

$$R_{\rightarrow(r_1, \|(\rightarrow(r_2, r_3), r_4))} = r_1 + R_{\|(\rightarrow(r_2, r_3), r_4)} = r_1 + \frac{1}{\frac{1}{R_{\rightarrow(r_2, r_3)}} + \frac{1}{r_4}} = r_1 + \frac{1}{\frac{1}{r_2 + r_3} + \frac{1}{r_4}}$$

The use of connectors allows us to separate interaction patterns/protocols from components and renders components independent from these – resistors do not need to know if they will be connected in series or in parallel. Both modularity and reuse (for both components and protocols) are increased. Unlike physical systems, where configuration patterns are enough to specify connectors as interaction in them is governed by known physical laws, software systems connectors also need to specify role interaction.

2.2   Realizable Software Architectures

Connectors in our ADL are not specified with glue-like elements. Instead, we consider connectors as a simple composition of roles, which represent the

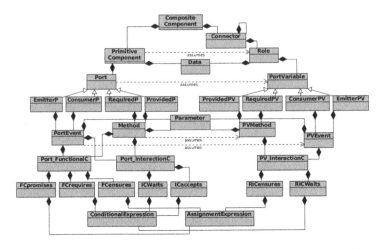

Fig. 4. Meta-model of XCD.

interaction behaviour of participating components, and built-in sub-connectors (i.e., links) that allow actions of one role to reach another. Coordination is now the responsibility of roles alone. If a particular property is desired then it must be shown that the roles satisfy it. But this is a problem that is decidable for finite state systems – model-checking. Thus an architect can easily specify a protocol and be sure that it has the required properties. Designers can also feel reassured that the architectural protocols are indeed realizable in principle, without the need to transform them into centralized ones, which might invalidate architectural analyses concerning scalability, performance, reliability, information flows, etc., as aforementioned.

So in the case of Fig. 1a, the architect should quickly realize that the desired property is not satisfied by the roles and opt for a centralized protocol instead, by adding a centralized controller. Thus, surprises are avoided – it becomes clear early on whether something can be made to work in a decentralized manner or not, as it is tested by the more experienced architect. The less experienced designers do not have to waste their time trying to achieve the impossible or take the easy (and dangerous) way out and turn a decentralized protocol into a centralized one. We essentially turn the glue from constraints to be imposed, to a property that needs to be verified, thus turning an undecidable problem that the less experienced designers have to deal with, into a decidable one for them (and pushing the responsibility to resolve the issue to the more experienced architect).

2.3 Design-by-Contract for Architecture Specifications

The Java Modelling Language (JML) [7] seems to be gaining popularity among developers, as they use it for "test-driven development" and even for static analysis in some instances. XCD attempts to follow this trend so as to maximize

```
1 component user(){
2   int data:=0;
3   required port puser_r {
4     @Functional{
5       ensures: data := \result; }
6     int get();
7   }
8   emitter port puser_e {
9     @Functional{
10      promises: data_arg := 7; }
11     set(int data_arg);
12   }
13 }
14
15 component memory(int numOfUsers) {
16   bool initialized_m := false;
17   int sh_data := 0;
18   provided port pmem_p[numOfUsers] {
19     @Interaction{
20       accepts: initialized_m; }
21     @Functional{
22       ensures: \result := sh_data; }
23     int get();
24   }
25   consumer port pmem_c[numOfUsers] {
26     @Functional{
27       ensures: intialised_m := true;
28                sh_data := data_arg; }
29     set(int data_arg);
30   }
31 }
```

```
1 connector memory2user(
2               userRole{pvuser_r,
3                        pvuser_e},
4            memoryRole{pvmem_p,
5                       pvmem_c}) {
6   role userRole {
7     required port pvuser_r {
8       int get();
9     }
10    emitter port pvuser_e {
11      set(int data_arg);
12    }
13  }
14  role memoryRole {
15    bool initialized := false;
16    provided port pvmem_p {
17      @Interaction{ waits: initialized; }
18      int get();
19    }
20    consumer port pvmem_c {
21      @Interaction{
22        ensures: initialized := true; }
23      set(int data_arg);
24    }
25  }
26  channel async
27  user2memory_m(userRole{pvuser_r},
28                memoryRole{pvmem_p});
29  channel async
30  user2memory_e(userRole{pvuser_e},
31                memoryRole{pvmem_c});
32 };
33
34 component sharedData() {// Composite
35   component user user1();
36   component user user2();
37   component memory mem(2);
38   connector memory2user
39     x1(user1{puser_r,puser_e},
40        mem{pmem_p[0],pmem_c[0]});
41   connector memory2user
42     x2(user2{puser_r,puser_e},
43        mem{pmem_p[1],pmem_c[1]});
44 }
```

Fig. 5. Shared-data access in the XCD ADL.

adoption by practitioners. Thus, it departs from the ADLs that adopt process algebras, and instead follows a Design by Contract (DbC) [21] approach like JML, specifying behavioural aspects of systems through simple *pairs of method pre-/post-conditions*, in a syntax reminiscent of JML. DbC allows for a formal specification of systems, as it is based on Hoare's logic [13] and VDM's [5] rely-guarantee specification approach. DbC has so far been mainly considered for programming languages (e.g., Java through JML), which is why contracts have been restricted to provided services (i.e., class methods).

There are very few ADLs that employ DbC. The work of Schreiner et al. [26] along with the TrustME ADL [25] are some of the very few examples applying DbC at the level of software architecture. Schreiner et al.'s work transforms connectors into components themselves, which we believe loses many of the

connector benefits, as these are needed to essentially drive the component interactions. Doing so through wrapper-like components [26] makes it difficult to
control component required ports, i.e., the ones initiating calls. This is because
a wrapper-like explicit connector can delay a call request, while a proper connector can ensure that it never gets triggered at all. TrustME does not provide
support for user-specified, complex connectors at all, as it essentially follows the
approach of Darwin [18], enriching it with contracts.

Our approach attempts to apply DbC in a more comprehensive manner,
covering component methods and events. As we view connectors as first-class
elements, we use DbC to specify their behaviour as well. XCD further extends
DbC by structuring component port action contracts into separate functional
and interaction parts.

3   DbC-based Specifications with XCD

Figure 4 gives the meta-model of the XCD language. There are two main elements
for specifying software architectures with XCD: components (primitive and composite ones), used to specify abstractions of computational units in a system, and
connectors, that specify the complex interaction protocols of components.

We use the shared-data case study [1] to facilitate the presentation of the
XCD language. In this system, user components retrieve and update some shared
data stored in a memory component. The memory component accepts requests
for data retrieval only if the data has been initialized – otherwise, it rejects the
request and commences a chaotic behaviour.

The XCD specification of the shared-data access is given in Fig. 5. Two
primitive component types are specified, user in lines 1–13 and memory in lines
15–31. Both the user and the memory comprise data-variables (line 2 and line 16
respectively) representing their states and ports that are the points of interaction
with their environment. There is also a connector type memory2user specified
(lines 1–32 at the right side), which represents the interaction between a memory
and a user. Connector memory2user uses some other connectors (here built-in
ones) to establish the communication links between its role ports (lines 26–31).
Its roles (userRole at line 6 and memoryRole at line 14) constrain the behaviour
of the components that assume them. Finally, we specify a composite component
type sharedData (lines 34–44 at the right side), which includes component and
connector instances and represents their configuration.

Primitive Component Types. Component user has a required port puser_r (lines
3–7) through which it makes method calls to its environment (i.e., the memory) to retrieve the value of some data. Port puser_r has a single method get,
whose functional contract ensures post-assignment clause (lines 4–5) assigns
the method's result to the component data – it has no pre-condition (i.e., a
requires clause). Component user also has an emitter port puser_e (lines 8–
12) to emit events. Port puser_e declares a single event set, whose functional
contract promises clause assigns its parameter to 7 – the event has no pre-
condition (i.e., a requires clause) or post-assignment (i.e., an ensures clause).

It should be noted here that while method and event **requires** clauses are conditions, method and event **promises** and **ensures** clauses are assignment sequences, not conditions. A **requires** clause specifies the functional requirements for a method call (or event) to be acceptable, while an **ensures** clause states how the state should be modified by the call. Finally, a **promises** clause states what values the parameters of a call request will have.

Component **memory** has an array of provided ports **pmem_p** (lines 18–24). It uses each of these ports to provide method **get** to a different **user** component instance. Unlike the contracts of component **user**, the contract of these ports have an additional **@Interaction** part (lines 19–20). This states that a **pmem_p** port will accept a **get** method-call only if the component data **initialized_m** is true. Otherwise, the call is rejected and the component starts behaving in a chaotic manner. If a call is accepted, then the functional contract (lines 21–22) is considered, which sets the result of the method call to be the value of the component **sh_data** variable. The array of consumer ports **pmem_c** (lines 25–30) serves to receive **set** events. Reception of such an event modifies the component state.

Complex Connector Types. Connector type **memory2user** (lines 1–32 at the right of Fig. 5) specifies the protocol used in the system between the memory and the users. It serves to ensure that the memory will not behave chaotically. The connector has two roles, **userRole** (lines 6–13) and *memoryRole* (lines 14–25). Role **userRole** has a required port-variable **pvuser_r** (lines 7–8), reflecting port **puser_r** of component **user**, and an emitter port-variable **pvuser_e** (lines 10–11), reflecting port **puser_e**. These port-variables do not impose any interaction constraints on the role.

Role **memoryRole** has a provided port-variable **pvmem_p** (lines 16–19) reflecting port **pmem_p** of component **memory**. Unlike the port-variables of **userRole**, this port-variable introduces extra interaction constraints on the behaviour of its methods. It requires that calls to method **get** are considered only when the role's **initialized** data is true, thus delaying them while this condition is not satisfied.

The role's consumer port-variable **pvmem_c** (lines 20–24) reflects port **pmem_c** of component **memory**. It uses its interaction contract to note that the memory has been set, through its **ensures** clause. The combination of the contracts of the two ports means that the memory cannot start behaving chaotically, as requests at non-accepting states are delayed until they are safe.

Composite Component Types. The **sharedData** component type (lines 34–44 at the right of Fig. 5) includes two instances of the **user** component and a single instance of the **memory** component. The component instances are passed as arguments to the two connector instances, in lines 38–43, to bind them together and constrain their interactions.

XCD *Notation and Expressiveness.* As can be seen by Fig. 5, the notation used for DbC in the XCD ADL follows a JML-like syntax, which should prove much easier for practitioners to understand and use effectively than formal languages such as process algebras. Indeed, we would expect one to be able to use XCD with minimal training. At the same time, XCD introduces connector constructs that are essentially (decentralized) algorithms (i.e., protocols) – configuration patterns of component variables, on which we have imposed additional interaction constraints. Apart from π calculus' ability to send channels as messages, which XCD does not support, the XCD ADL should allow architects to express the static architectures that one can express now with ADLs based on process algebras. However, XCD does not support dynamic architectures currently.

4   XCD Semantics

Figure 6 shows the general behaviour of a (primitive) component described using Dijkstra's guarded command language [9]. Each instance is a concurrent process, that initializes its data and then enters a loop, executing the actions of its ports (lines 6–12) or performing a skip action (line 14). The behaviour of port actions is shown in Fig. 7 for the four different port types.

Provided and required ports (Fig. 7(d) and (b)) employ a pair of channels (`request` and `response`) to realize the method call interaction protocol, while emitter and consumer ports (Fig. 7(c) and (a)) employ a single channel (`stream`). Channels are essentially (finite) buffers of messages and a `send` action adds another message into them. A `read` action retrieves some message from a channel (in a non-deterministic order). Finally, a `readCond` action retrieves a message in a non-deterministic order, with the additional constraint that its parameters satisfy a predicate, which is passed as the fourth parameter of the action (see lines 1–2 of Fig. 7(d)).

As can be seen from Fig. 7, all port actions correspond to a single atomic block of guarded actions, apart from required port method requests that correspond to two atomic blocks of guarded actions (separated by a single blank line at line 9). Event and method guarded action patterns have been aligned vertically so as to make it easier to establish their similarities and differences.

An emitter port event (Fig. 7(a)) attempts to assign the event parameters in a way that satisfies its own and its roles' interaction constraints. If successful, it assigns the component and role data and sends the event over the port event stream channel. If the parameter values do not satisfy the interaction constraints then it simply passes control back to the component (possibly retrying). The role interaction constraints RICs(p, e) are the delaying constraints imposed by the port-variables assumed by the event's port and associated with this event, as shown in Fig. 6(b).

A required port method (Fig. 7(b)) is enabled if no method request is currently active on the port, in which case it assigns the parameters of this method request and verifies that they satisfy the method's interaction constraints. If they do, it notes that the method is currently active on this port and emits the method request over the channel p.request. A second atomic block is enabled when there is a response for this method. So, if the functional constract precondition (`requires` clause) is satisfied, then, it assigns the component data

```
1 FORALL c ∈ Model.Components
2 process c ... {
3 // initialization of data
4 Start:
5 do
6   FORALL p ∈ c.EmitterPorts
7     FORALL e ∈ p.Events
8       // see Fig. 7(a)
9   FORALL p ∈ c.RequiredPorts
10    FORALL m ∈ p.Methods
11      // see Fig. 7(b)
12  FORALL p ∈ c.ConsumerPorts
13    FORALL e ∈ p.Events
14      // see Fig. 7(c)
15  FORALL p ∈ c.ProvidedPorts
16    FORALL m ∈ p.Methods
17      // see Fig. 7(d)
18  [] true → skip; // do nothing
19 od
20 }
```

```
1 // all associated
2 // Role Interaction Constraints
3 RICs(port p, action a) {
4   pvs = p.associatedPortVariables;
5   return ∪_{pv∈pvs} pv.a.RICs;
6 }
```

(a) Component

(b) RICs for action a of a port p

Fig. 6. Semantics of components.

```
1 [] true →
2   assign_params(e.FCPromises);
3   if
4   [] e.ICWaits
5     ∧ ∧_{re∈RICs(p,e)} re.RICWaits→skip
6   [] else → goto Start
7   fi;
8
9
10
11
12  assign_data(e.FCensures);
13  FORALL re ∈ RICs(p, e)
14    assign_data(re.RICensures);
15  send(p.stream, e, e.params);
```

(a) Emitter port p's event e

```
1 [] p.activeM = NULL →
2   assign_params(m.FCPromises);
3   if
4   [] m.ICWaits
5     ∧ ∧_{rm∈RICs(p,m)} rm.RICWaits→skip
6   [] else → goto Start
7   fi; p.activeM := m;
8   send(p.request, m, m.params);
9
10 [] readCond(p.response, m, m.result,
11    p.activeM = m) →
12   if
13   []m.FCrequires→
14    assign_data(m.FCensures);
15    FORALL rm ∈ RICs(p, m)
16     assign_data(rm.RICensures);
17    p.activeM := NULL;
18   fi
```

(b) Required port p's method m

```
1 [] readCond(p.stream, e,e.params,
2    e.ICWaits ∧∧_{re∈RICs(p,e)} re.RICWaits)
3 → if
4   [] e.ICaccepts ∧ e.FCrequires →
5     assign_data(e.FCensures);
6     FORALL re ∈ RICs(p, e)
7      assign_data(re.RICensures);
8   // [] ! e.ICaccepts → chaos
9   fi
```

(c) Consumer port p's event e

```
1 [] readCond(p.request, m, m.params,
2    m.ICWaits ∧∧_{rm∈RICs(p,m)} rm.RICWaits)
3 → if
4   [] m.ICaccepts ∧ m.FCrequires →
5     assign_data(m.FCensures);
6     FORALL rm ∈ RICs(p, m)
7      assign_data(rm.RICensures);
8     send(p.response, m, m.result);
9   // [] ! m.ICaccepts → chaos
10  fi
```

(d) Provided port p's method m

Fig. 7. Semantics of a port p's actions.

according to the **ensures** clause of the method functional contract (and similarly for its roles).

Consumer events and provided methods are the dual of these, with the difference that a provided method is a single atomic block instead of two. Another difference is that, unlike the former actions, these latter port actions can cause the component to exhibit chaotic behaviour, as seen in lines 9 of Fig. 7(c) and (d). This occurs when the action's delaying interaction constraints (in line 2) imposed by its associated roles are satisfied but the component interaction constraints at line 4 are not satisfied.

Race Conditions. Being atomic blocks of actions, emitter/consumer port events and producer port methods do not suffer from race conditions. Required port methods on the other hand are by necessity modelled as a pair of states – one initiating a method call and another receiving the method response. The post-assignments (**ensures** clause) at the latter can suffer from two types of race-conditions. First, an assignment may attempt to use the value of some data at the pre-state, i.e., when the request was being made. If another port has modified this value, then we have a *write-read* kind of race-condition. If an assignment tries to update the value of some data that has been updated in the meantime by another port, then we have a *write-write* kind of race-condition. In our semantics we employ extra variables (not shown in the presented semantics) to identify these conflicts and notify architects about them.

4.1 Data Assignments in Contracts

XCD contracts use *assignments* to establish values for action parameters and to update the data after these actions. This is done so as to render the resulting formal models more tractable. So XCD does not accept post-conditions like "**ensures:** $0 \leq x + y + z \leq 25$;". In order to ensure that variables x, y, z receive values that meet such a condition we would need to consider all possible combinations of their values in the range $[0, 25]$, i.e., consider $26^3 = 17576$ cases. Instead, XCD requires that the specification is transformed to a sequence of assignments, such as "**ensures:** $x \in [0, 25]; y \in [0, 25 - x]; z \in [0, 25 - x - y]$;". Through the use of a generalized form of assignment that also supports ranges as here, XCD permits non-deterministic choices but it requires that these choices are done sequentially and only depend on constants and variables that have been assigned already. So in this case, there would be at most $26 * 3 = 78$ cases to consider, which is a substantial reduction.

Assignments are treated differently for action parameters (**assign_params**) and data updates (**assign_data**), e.g., as seen in lines 2 and 12 of Fig. 7(a). This is because missing parameter assignments are added implicitly by assigning unconstrained parameters some values from their domain. This is not however done for missing data updates. It is instead assumed that these data should not be updated and retain whatever value they have at that point. The other difference between assigning parameters and data has to do with how the well-definedness of an assignment sequence is done in each case.

Well-Definedness of Assignment Sequences. Let us consider an assignment sequence $v_i := e_i$, where $1 \leq i \leq n$ and v_i and e_i are a variable and an expression respectively. For `assign_params`, an assignment expression sequence as a whole is well-defined *iff* the left hand side is a parameter and the right hand side e_i of each assignment expression is an expression constructed according to the following rules:

Expression: 1. a Formula f
2. a range, i.e., $[min, max]$, where min and max are Formulas and $min \leq max$.

Formula: 1. a Formula f (e.g., $+, -, /, *$) of formulas $f_1, \cdots, f_n$.
2. a Term t

Term: 1. a constant, e.g., some Boolean or integer value.
2. a (known) variable, i.e., one of:
   (a) a v_j, where $j < i$
   (b) a (pre-state) value of some data d_k

As aforementioned, if the set of v_i is a strict subset of the set of parameters used in the respective action, then the other parameters are assigned values in their domain in a non-deterministic manner.

For `assign_data`, an assignment expression sequence as a whole is well-defined *iff* the left hand side is a component or role data variable and the right hand side e_i of each assignment expression is constructed according to the same rules as previously. In this case though all parameters are variables with known values, so a term can also be a parameter p_m.

Unlike `assign_params` that assigns all parameters some value by choosing some non-deterministic value from their domain if not constrained otherwise, `assign_data` does not modify data variables that have not been assigned explicitly in the model.

4.2   XCD and Architecture Realizability

All constraints in XCD are *local*, expressed on local component/role data and parameters. Indeed, components do not even synchronize on message emission – asynchronous channels are used to ensure that they are completely decoupled and independent.

Non-local interaction constraints, like those imposed by the glue in Fig. 2, cannot be expressed in XCD. This ensures that XCD connectors are always realizable in a way that respects the architecture, i.e., without transforming decentralized designs to centralized ones. When non-local interaction constraints are desired, they can be verified as properties of some connector or configuration.

Data themselves are encapsulated either by components or connector roles, so there are no aliasing problems, and concurrency is controlled through component ports. Each port is a concurrent unit (a monitor), thus ensuring that actions of a port are mutually exclusive to each other. As event emission/consumption and

Table 1. Verification results.

Model Size	State-vector (in Bytes)	States		Memory (in MB)	Time (in sec)
		Stored	Matched		
1 user	140	1954	1511	128	0.00
2 users	220	364691	575897	195	0.95
3 users	312	27327216	68152656	7024†	97.80
4 users	392	21466341	69412168	7024†	69.60

Spin (v 6.2.4) and gcc (v 4.7.2) commands used, for up to 7024MB of RAM and a search depth of 500:
```
spin -a model.pml
gcc -DMEMLIM=7024 -O2 -DXUSAFE -DSAFETY -DNOCLAIM -w -o pan pan.c
./pan -m500 -c1
```
Column "States Stored" refers to the number of unique global system states stored in the state-space, while column "States Matched" refers to the number of states that were revisited during the search - see: spinroot.com/spin/Man/Pan.html#L10

method servicing (at provided ports) are atomic, architects need only guarantee (and verify) that method calling (at required ports) will not lead to data race conditions.

5   Formal Verification Analysis

The semantics of XCD described in Sect. 4 are used to automatically transform XCD architectures into corresponding ProMeLa models, which can be analysed by the Spin model-checker [14]. Each component instance of an architecture becomes a ProMeLa process. Instances of primitive component types follow the patterns described in Figs. 6 and 7. For composite component instances we produce again ProMeLa processes that initiate the processes of their sub-components and establish the channels that these should be using. The transformation to ProMeLa models is done through a tool that is available from the XCD web page [22], along with other case studies and information about the XCD language.

We easily transformed the shared data specification in Sect. 3 into Promela and analysed the Promela codes using the model checker. The verification results are given in Table 1. Its verification allowed us to quickly evaluate whether the system components behave compatibly without deadlocking. Although in some cases, the memory may go beyond the required amount for a full verification (indicated with a † in Table 1), designers can still obtain useful information about their system models and increase their confidence in their correctness.

In the rest of this section, we discuss some of the issues that we identified through the formal verification.

5.1   Avoiding Chaotic Behaviour Through Connector Protocols

The `memory` component is specified in Listing 3 with an `accepts` guard stating that it will enter chaotic behaviour if it receives a call for method `get` when

```
1  role userRole {                    1  role userRole {
2   required port pvuser_r {          2   bool initialized := false;
3    int get();                       3   required port pvuser_r {
4   }                                 4   @Interaction{ waits: initialized; }
5   emitter port pvuser_e {           5    int get();
6    set(int data_arg);               6   }
7   }                                 7   emitter port pvuser_e {
8  }                                  8    @Interaction{
                                      9     ensures: initialized := true; }
                                     10    set(int data_arg);
                                     11   }
                                     12  }

        (a) Original user role              (b) Constrained user role
```

Fig. 8. Constraining role user of connector memory2user specified in Fig. 5.

Table 2. Verification results for the constrained user role of Fig. 8.

Model Size	State-vector (in Bytes)	States		Memory (in MB)	Time (in sec)
		Stored	Matched		
1 user	148	1744	1374	128	0.00
2 users	236	286735	479528	182	0.95
3 users	336	1998023	5594597	662	5.92
4 users	424	20477758	70199771	7024†	81.10

the data is not yet initialized. This is avoided through the `memory2user` connector that constrains memory such that it does not receive requests for method `get` before the event `set` that initializes its data. Indeed, when we remove this constraint from the memory role of the connector and re-run our verification, an assertion violation error occurs identifying that the memory component has entered a chaotic behaviour.

5.2   Reducing the State Space

When the number of user components in the system configuration becomes more than 2, the state space of the formal model increases and hinders a full verification. Therefore, design errors may be left uncaught. The state space can be reduced by further constraining the possible behaviour of components. To do so, we introduce further interaction constraints on user components via the user role of the `memory2user` connector. When the user role is modified as shown in Fig. 8, user components cannot make requests for method `get` before they emit event `set`. When we re-run the verification the state space is reduced as shown in Table 2, enabling us to fully verify a system with three users.

6   Conclusions

The XCD ADL supports user-defined, complex connectors, that can recursively use other connectors to model protocols and sub-protocols, in the same way as components can have sub-components. Complex connectors allow architects to increase the modularity of their specifications, and produce component specifications that are agnostic to their usage contexts. This increases the re-usability of component specifications and can help CBSE by permitting the development of general component specifications. It also helps with the reuse of protocol specifications as these can be specified independently of specific usage instances. Finally, it aids architectural exploration, since architects can easily replace protocols and components without having to rewrite their specifications.

Many ADLs have supported connectors so far, with Wright [1] being the first one to provide formal support for them. Unfortunately, the connector structure proposed by Wright, and all those inspired from Wright ever since, permits the specification of unrealizable architectures. We showed how this can occur and presented XCD's approach for avoiding this issue and guaranteeing that connectors will always be realizable.

The paper also presented how XCD uses and extends Design-by-Contract so as to hopefully make it easier for practitioners to use it for specifying the architectures of their systems and for communicating these architectures to others. The transformation of the XCD language constructs was shown with the use of patterns of Dijkstra's guarded commands that can be easily modelled with the Spin model-checker's language ProMeLa.

Preliminary verification results showed promise, though the current tool support needs to be improved. In the future we plan to apply a number of patterns to reduce the state space of the models produced and explore ways to perform other optimizations, e.g., to reduce the state size itself.

References

1. Allen, R., Garlan, D.: A formal basis for architectural connection. ACM Trans. Softw. Eng. Methodol. **6**(3), 213–249 (1997)
2. Alur, R., Etessami, K., Yannakakis, M.: Inference of message sequence charts. IEEE Trans. Softw. Eng. **29**(7), 623–633 (2003)
3. Alur, R., Etessami, K., Yannakakis, M.: Realizability and verification of MSC graphs. Theor. Comput. Sci. **331**(1), 97–114 (2005)
4. Bergstra, J.A., Ponse, A., Smolka, S.A. (eds.): Handbook of Process Algebra. Elsevier, Amsterdam (2001)
5. Bjørner, D., Jones, C.B. (eds.): The Vienna Development Method: The Meta-Language. LNCS, vol. 61. Springer, Heidelberg (1978)
6. Canal, C., Pimentel, E., Troya, J.M., Canal, C., Pimentel, E., Troya, J.M.: Specification and refinement of dynamic software architectures. In: Donohoe, P. (ed.) WICSA. IFIP Conference Proceedings, vol. 140, pp. 107–126. Kluwer, Dordrecht (1999)
7. Chalin, P., Kiniry, J.R., Leavens, G.T., Poll, E.: Beyond assertions: advanced specification and verification with JML and ESC/Java2. In: de Boer, F.S., Bonsangue, M.M., Graf, S., de Roever, W.-P. (eds.) FMCO 2005. LNCS, vol. 4111, pp. 342–363. Springer, Heidelberg (2006)
8. Delanote, D., Baelen, S. V., Joosen, W., Berbers, Y.: Using AADL to model a protocol stack. In: ICECCS, pp. 277–281. IEEE Computer Society (2008)
9. Dijkstra, E.W.: Guarded commands, nondeterminacy and formal derivation of programs. Commun. ACM **18**(8), 453–457 (1975)

10. Feiler, P.H., Gluch, D.P., Hudak, J.J.: The Architecture Analysis & Design Language (AADL): An Introduction. Technical report, Software Engineering Institute (2006)
11. Garlan, D., Allen, R., Ockerbloom, J.: Architectural mismatch or why it's hard to build systems out of existing parts. In: ICSE, pp. 179–185 (1995)
12. Garlan, D., Shaw, M.: An introduction to software architecture. In: Ambriola, V., Tortora, G. (eds.) Advances in Software Engineering and Knowledge Engineering, pp. 1–39. World Scientific Publishing Company, Singapore (1993). Also appears as SCS and SEI technical reports: CMU-CS-94-166, CMU/SEI-94-TR-21, ESC-TR-94-021
13. Hoare, C.A.R.: An axiomatic basis for computer programming. Commun. ACM **12**(10), 576–580 (1969)
14. Holzmann, G.J.: The SPIN Model Checker - Primer and Reference Manual. Addison-Wesley, Reading (2004)
15. Issarny, V., Bennaceur, A., Bromberg, Y.-D.: Middleware-layer connector synthesis: beyond state of the art in middleware interoperability. In: Bernardo, M., Issarny, V. (eds.) SFM 2011. LNCS, vol. 6659, pp. 217–255. Springer, Heidelberg (2011)
16. Ivers, J., Clements, P., Garlan, D., Nord, R., Schmerl, B., Silva, J.R.O.: Documenting component and connector views with UML 2.0. Technical report CMU/SEI-2004-TR-008, Software Engineering Institute (Carnegie Mellon University) (2004)
17. Luckham, D.C.: Rapide: a language and toolset for simulation of distributed systems by partial orderings of events. Technical report, Stanford University, Stanford, CA, USA (1996)
18. Magee, J., Kramer, J.: Dynamic structure in software architectures. In: SIGSOFT FSE, pp. 3–14 (1996)
19. Malavolta, I., Lago, P., Muccini, H., Pelliccione, P., Tang, A.: What industry needs from architectural languages: a survey. IEEE Trans. Softw. Eng. **39**(6), 869–891 (2013)
20. Medvidovic, N., Taylor, R.N.: A classification and comparison framework for software architecture description languages. IEEE Trans. Softw. Eng. **26**(1), 70–93 (2000)
21. Meyer, B.: Applying "design by contract". IEEE Comput. **25**(10), 40–51 (1992)
22. Ozkaya, M.: XCD website (2013). http://www.soi.city.ac.uk/abdz276/xcd.html
23. Perry, D.E., Wolf, A.L.: Foundations for the study of software architecture. SIGSOFT Softw. Eng. Notes **17**(4), 40–52 (1992)
24. Plasil, F., Visnovsky, S.: Behavior protocols for software components. IEEE Trans. Softw. Eng. **28**(11), 1056–1076 (2002)
25. Schmidt, H., Poernomo, I., Reussner, R.: Trust-by-contract: modelling, analysing and predicting behaviour of software architectures. J. Integr. Des. Process Sci. **5**(3), 25–51 (2001)
26. Schreiner, D., Göschka, K.M.: Explicit connectors in component based software engineering for distributed embedded systems. In: van Leeuwen, J., Italiano, G.F., van der Hoek, W., Meinel, C., Sack, H., Plášil, F. (eds.) SOFSEM 2007. LNCS, vol. 4362, pp. 923–934. Springer, Heidelberg (2007)
27. Tripakis, S.: Undecidable problems of decentralized observation and control. In: Proceedings of the 40th IEEE Conference on Decision and Control, Orlando, FL, USA, vol. 5, pp. 4104–4109. IEEE, December 2001
28. Tripakis, S.: Undecidable problems of decentralized observation and control on regular languages. Inf. Process. Lett. **90**(1), 21–28 (2004)

Improving Recommender Systems with Simplification Logic to Manage Implications with Grades

J. L. Leiva[1], M. Enciso[1(✉)], C. Rossi[1], P. Cordero[2], Á. Mora[2], and A. Guevara[1]

[1] Department of Languages and Computer Science,
University of Málaga, Málaga, Spain
{jlo,enciso,rossi,guevara}@uma.es
[2] Department of Applied Mathematics, University of Málaga, Málaga, Spain
{pcordero,amora}@uma.es

Abstract. Recommender systems are considered powerful tools to suggest items to users according to their interests. The main problem in this process is the big amount of items to be managed. In this work we take advantage of the user context information to prune the original set of items stored in the data set. By providing a smaller set of data to be managed, we will improve the efficiency of the recommender system. We use fuzzy relations and implications with grades to specify the context and Simplification Logic to develop a linear pre-filtering process. Finally, we show the benefits of our approach with an illustrative example on the tourism sector.

Keywords: Recommender systems · Fuzzy logic · Context · Formal concept analysis

1 Introduction

In recent years, the use of recommender systems has become popular in many different applications to offer a personalized selection of products. The big amount of items to be recommended causes that in many cases users feel overwhelmed because they have to select from a wide range of alternatives. In this work we focus on tourism recommender systems, that should implement filtering mechanisms to provide a set of points of interest (POIs) which are accurately adjusted to the real needs of the tourist. This type of system is necessary in tourist destinations [1], because this way, tourists can easily and quickly find products that best adapt to their preferences among the extensive list of POIs that destination websites usually offer.

In [2], the authors presented a classification of the types of most commonly used recommender systems:

- Collaborative: it provides results obtained from the qualifications made by users. The user will be recommended items that people with similar tastes and preferences liked in the past.

© Springer-Verlag Berlin Heidelberg 2014
J. Cordeiro and M. van Sinderen (Eds.): ICSOFT 2013, CCIS 457, pp. 290–305, 2014.
DOI: 10.1007/978-3-662-44920-2_18

- Content-based: it categorizes items and suggests products that have similar characteristics to those requested by the user or to those that he evaluated positively in the past [3].
- Demographic: it classifies users by different personal parameters, and recommendations are made taking into account the demographic group to which the user belongs.
- Knowledge-based: it has information about how an item satisfies a user, and establishes a relationship between need and recommendation.
- Utility-based: it recommends those items that maximize an utility function.
- Case-based: it uses information about resolving problems (cases) previous to the resolution of the present case. They can be viewed as a subtype of the knowledge-based and utility-based recommender systems.

In a detailed description of content-based recommender systems, they can be classified into two groups:

- With memory: in this case, it is common to have information about user preferences and take into account items previously selected by the user, as well as how he or she evaluated them. The main problem with recommendation systems based on content with memory is that they should manage information on previous recommendations and/or user profiles.
- Without memory: it is not necessary that the user has evaluated items nor knowledge about user preferences. In these systems, the users must explicitly specify their current preferences. Therefore, the users must indicate some characteristics that the products should have and that the system will recommend.

In order to be used in tourism systems, a significant problem detected in previous models is not using context attributes [4]. The context is a multi-faceted concept that has been studied in different disciplines, including Computer Science (mainly in Artificial Intelligence), Cognitive Science, Linguistics, Psychology and Organizational Science [5]. In order to improve the quality of recommendations, the system should not only use the qualifications and characteristics of different POIs, or tourist preferences. Systems need to handle information of different nature such as weather, company, schedules, location, time, etc. [6]. Some authors include the user's emotional status and expand the definition to any information that can be characterized and that is relevant to the interaction between an user and an application [7].

The types of recommender systems (described above) that only consider items and users are called recommender systems in two dimensions [4].

Therefore, in order to improve the recommendations, we have to take into account the contextual information available as additional categories of data [2]. In [6] the authors affirm that the recommender system should take into consideration three dimensions (users, items and context). They propose different paradigms of context-aware recommender systems:

- Contextual pre-filtering (or contextualization of recommendation input): contextual information drives data selection or data construction for that specific context. The selected data will be the input of a 2D recommender system.

– Contextual post-filtering (or contextualization of recommendation output): the ratings are predicted using any traditional 2D recommender system on the entire data. Afterwards, the resulting set of recommendations is adjusted (contextualized) for each user using the contextual information.
– Contextual modeling (or contextualization of recommendation functions). In this recommendation paradigm, contextual information is used directly in the modeling technique as part of rating estimation.

In our opinion, a recommender system for a consolidated tourist destination (probably with thousands of POIs) should apply the contextual pre-filtering paradigm. Thus, the recommender system works with a reduced number of POIs, decreasing the execution time. Another important advantage of this approach is that it can be combined with any existing 2D recommendation technique.

The recommender system proposed in this paper uses a content-based contextual pre-filtering, based on contextual attributes and desirable characteristics of the POIs. Therefore, it is not necessary to have information about previous visits or qualifications of other tourists, i.e., we apply a content-based recommendation without memory.

Some authors [8] propose the use of fuzzy logic as a formal basis for recommender systems. Nevertheless we are looking for a new approach which allows us to also cover another question proposed in [9]: incorporation of diverse contextual information into the recommendation process. In this paper we tackle this issue by means of the Formal Concept Analysis (FCA).

From the point of view of Philosophy, a *concept* is a general idea that corresponds to some kind of entity and that may be characterized by some essential features of the class. When B. Ganter and R. Wille [10,11] conceive a framework inside the lattice theory to *formalize concepts*, they probably do not guess the wide diffusion of their original work.

Nowadays, FCA has become an useful framework both in the theoretical and in the applied areas. The works related to FCA cover from data analysis, information retrieval, knowledge representation, etc. It is considered an outstanding tool in emergent environments like data mining, semantic web, etc.

The main goal of Formal Concept Analysis (FCA) is to identify in a binary table the relationships between set of objects and set of attributes. These relationships establish a Gallois Connection which allows us to identify the concepts using a formal framework inside the lattice theory. Apart from building the concept lattice itself, one of the key problems is to extract the set of attribute implications which hold in the concept lattice. Implications constitute important information that is extracted in a separate stage from data and constitute a dual representation of the lattice itself. One of the most important advantages in the use of implications is that they may be managed using Functional Dependencies Logics [12].

Another novelty in this work is the integration of the context into the FCA method by means of set of implications. We propose the generation of a set of fuzzy implications which corresponds with a given context. Thus, when the user identifies his/her context (company, weather, etc.), the system enriches the

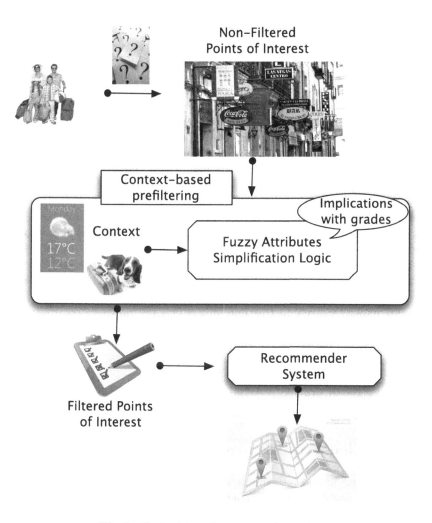

Fig. 1. Context-based recommender system.

specification by adding a set of new implications which corresponds with this context. The new information is treated with our fuzzy logic to automatically reduce the specification by removing redundancy. The reduction in the set of implications allows a more efficient validation process which prune the original set of POIs, and therefore the content-based 2D recommender works with a smaller set of POIs. In Fig. 1 the system architecture of our proposal is depicted.

The paper is organized as follows: in the next section we analyze some related works. Section 3 introduces the theoretical background of our work and describes an executable logic to manage fuzzy implications, named FASL. It will be used in Sect. 4 to introduce a context-aware recommender system with a solid base. Finally some conclusions and future works are presented.

2   Related Works

In [8] fuzzy logic is presented as a proper framework for tourist recommenders, addressing the problems described in [9]. Particularly, their approach uses features of items as background data and users feedback such as ratings of items as input. That paper provides a solid and well-founded method to incorporate the subjectiveness, imprecision and vagueness that usually appear in items features and users feedback. One outstanding result of the paper is that, despite of the flexible and enriched language to specify user interest and item features, they develop a method to infer recommendations which shows an improvement in precision without loss of recall.

Some authors have used FCA methods as an interesting approach in recommender systems. In [13] the authors propose FCA as an approach to group items and users into concepts. That work may be considered a collaborative recommender system and it shows how FCA may be used to find neighbours in a efficient and accurate way. A similar and recent approach to the same problem with similar results may be found in [14]. These works shows that FCA may be successfully used in collaborative recommenders.

In this paper we work in this line and enrich the previous results in some points. First, we aim to add a more flexible specification by considering fuzzy relations in FCA. This extension was first introduced in [15]. The problems that arise are related with the development of new methods to infer the concepts and manage implications in fuzzy relations. We apply our previous theoretical results presented in [16] to provide a sound and complete fuzzy logic for functional dependencies as a framework for the efficient management of implications.

3   Implications with Grades

As we mentioned in the introduction, we propose the specification and management of the context to enrich content-based recommendation systems. Our main goal is to design a uniform way to incorporate user interests and context knowledge in form of constraints that provide a pruning of the items. Thus, the reduction in the number of items will render a faster execution of content-based recommenders.

Our approach is focused on the use of implications with grades (or fuzzy implications), which has been very well stablished in the area of Formal Concept Analysis [11]. They are formulas of the form

$$A \stackrel{x}{\Rightarrow} B, x \in [0,1] \tag{1}$$

such as

$$\left\{ {}^{0.2}/y_1, y_2 \right\} \stackrel{0.7}{\Rightarrow} \left\{ {}^{0.8}/y_3 \right\}. \tag{2}$$

Formulas of the form (1) have an interpretation given by object-attribute data with grades in which (2) means: every object that has attribute y_1 to degree

at least 0.2 and attribute y_2 to degree 1, has (with a truthfulness threshold of
0.7) attribute y_3 to degree at least 0.8.

This interpretation extends the attribute implications in binary data saying
that presence of certain attributes implies presence of other attributes. The
incorporation of fuzzy sets in the attributes and a degree in the dependency
itself provide the maximum level of uncertainty specification in the implications.

Nevertheless, as we shall see later, the high expressive power of this fuzzy
implications may be managed in an equivalent and simpler way by assuming the
fuzzy value of the implication inside its right-hand side. Thus, we get a higher
expressive power in the specification and a simpler language for the automated
processing.

The implications may be then transformed into formulas of the form

$$A \Rightarrow B \tag{3}$$

The implications (or rules) used in this paper serve several purposes. From
the point of view of knowledge acquisition, the rules represent important if-
then patterns that can be derived from data and are capable of representing
various if-then dependencies that are present in the data. For instance, [17] shows
that each object-attribute data table representing ordinal (graded) dependencies
between objects and their attributes (features) can be characterized by a base
of rules like (1). Thus, bases of this type of rules are concise representations of
knowledge inferred from data. In order to gain more knowledge from a base, one
has to come up with an efficient inference system. In Sect. 3.2 we summarize the
FASL axiomatic system for implications and an automated method to reason
about dependencies in data involving grades. An automated process is used to
reduce the original set of implication so that an efficiency improvement of the
recommender system is produced.

3.1   FASL Logic

In this paper we will make use of a logic for dependencies in data with grades
named FASL. It was presented in [16] and also an efficient automated reasoning
method based on its axiomatization was provided.

We assume that the set of degrees, such as 0.2 or 0.8 in (2), is partially ordered
and equipped with particular aggregation operations. Such structures are known
from fuzzy logic [18–21], aggregation theory [22], and have been used in various
models for combination of ordinal information [23]. In particular, we denote
the set of degrees by L and assume that it forms an algebraic structure $\mathbf{L} = \langle L, \wedge, \vee, \otimes, \rightarrow, \seardot, ^*, 0, 1 \rangle$ such that $\langle L, \wedge, \vee, 0, 1 \rangle$ is a complete lattice, $\langle L, \otimes, 1 \rangle$ is
a commutative monoid, and the following conditions are fulfilled:

- $\otimes$ and $\rightarrow$ satisfy the following adjointness property:
  for all $a, b, c \in L$, $a \otimes b \leq c$ if and only if $a \leq b \rightarrow c$;
- $\diagdown$ and $\vee$ satisfy the following adjointness property:
  for all $a, b, c \in L$, $a \diagdown b \leq c$ if and only if $a \leq b \vee c$;

– * is a unary operation (so-called hedge) satisfying: for all $a, b \in L$,
   $1^* = 1$, $a^* \leq a$, $(a \to b)^* \leq a^* \to b^*$, and $a^{**} = a^*$.

We recall that the above conditions mean that $\langle L, \wedge, \vee, \otimes, \to, 0, 1 \rangle$ forms a complete residuated lattice [19,21] and $\langle L, \wedge, \vee, \diagdown, 1 \rangle$ is a Brouwerian algebra (or equivalently, its dual $\langle L, \vee, \wedge, \diagdown, 0 \rangle$ is a Heyting algebra, which implies that the lattice is distributive). $\otimes$ and $\to$ are interpreted as a many-valued conjunction and implication; $\diagdown$ as a many-valued non-implication (used for set difference); and * as an intensifying hedge such as "very true", see [24].

The most commonly used set L is the real unit interval $L = [0, 1]$ (or its finite subchains), in which case $\wedge$ and $\vee$ are the minimum and the maximum, $\otimes$ and $\to$ a left-continuous t-norm and its residuum, respectively, and $\diagdown$ is given by

$$x \diagdown y = \begin{cases} x & \text{if } x > y, \\ 0 & \text{otherwise.} \end{cases} \tag{4}$$

Two important, boundary cases of hedges are identity and so-called globalization (i.e. $1^* = 1$ and $x^* = 0$ for all $1 \neq x \in L$). We use the usual notions of **L**-sets, graded subsethood, and define if-then formulas like (2) and their interpretation in a general way (cf. early approaches like [25]), see [17] for details.

A fuzzy set in a universal set U is a mapping $A \colon U \to [0, 1]$ and the set operations are defined pointwise as follows: for $A, B \colon U \to [0, 1]$, for all $u \in U$, $(A \cup B)(u) = A(u) \vee B(u)$, $(A \cap B)(u) = A(u) \wedge B(u)$, $(A \otimes B)(u) = A(u) \otimes B(u)$, $(A \to B)(u) = A(u) \to B(u)$, $(A \diagdown B)(u) = A(u) \diagdown B(u)$, and $A^*(u) = (A(u))^*$. Moreover, $\varnothing$ and U are the fuzzy sets in which, for all $u \in U$, $\varnothing(u) = 0$ and $U(u) = 1$.

The set inclusion can be extended as follows: for $A, B \colon U \to [0, 1]$, the grade in which A is a subset of B is

$$S(A, B) = \bigwedge_{u \in U} (A(u) \to B(u))$$

Particularly, if $S(A, B) = 1$ we write $A \subseteq B$ and, in this case, $A(u) \leq B(u)$ for all $u \in U$.

We are going to work with finite fuzzy sets, that is, fuzzy sets in which at most a finite number of elements has non-zero values. In the notation that we are going to use, zero-valued elements does not appear and grade 1 is omitted. So, for example, $A = \{b/_{0.4}, d/_{0.1}, f\}$ denotes that $A(b) = 0.4$, $A(d) = 0.1$, $A(f) = 1$ and $A(x) = 0$ otherwise.

As we have presented before, we will organize the information of the recommender system using the fuzzy extension of Formal Concept Analysis (FCA) introduced in [15] that may be consider the most current trend in this area.

The starting point in fuzzy FCA is the fuzzy relation[1] that captures the degree in which a given attribute holds on an object. Specifically, given a finite

---

[1] In FCA literature, this fuzzy relation is usually called "context" but we omit this denomination to avoid confusion with the term context used in recommender systems.

set of objects X and a finite set of attributes Y, fuzzy FCA extracts knowledge from a fuzzy relation $I\colon X \times Y \to [0,1]$ where $I(x,y) = \vartheta$ means that ϑ is the degree in which the object x has the attribute y. Usually, the fuzzy relation I is showed in a table in which rows represents objects, columns corresponds to attributes and in position (x,y) on the table appears the degree $I(x,y)$.

An important information that can be extracted from the fuzzy relation is given in terms of attribute implications.

They are formulas of the form $A \Rightarrow B$ where A and B are fuzzy sets of attributes. The grade in which this attribute implication is satisfied by a fuzzy relation I is given by

$$||A \Rightarrow B||_I = \bigwedge_{x \in X} (S(A, I_x)^* \to S(B, I_x))$$

where I_x denotes the fuzzy set in which $I_x(y) = I(x,y)$ for all $y \in Y$. So, for example,

$$\{b/_{0.2}, d\} \Rightarrow \{c/_{0.8}\} \tag{5}$$

means that every object that has attribute b to degree at least 0.2 and attribute d to degree 1, has attribute c to degree at least 0.8.

Observe that the left and right hand side of the implications (the A and B sets) may be empty. If B if the empty set, the implication captures an information which always valid and it has not to be considered in the inference process. Nevertheless, if the A set is empty the implication provides a relevant information, particularly in the application we are working with. For instance, the implication $\varnothing \Rightarrow \{c/_{0.8}\}$ is interpreted as follows: the c attribute must have a degree at least 0.8.

As we have previously mentioned, user context specification will be a set of formulas where a grade is added to the implications. The grade represents a threshold of truthfulness of the implication. Given a fuzzy relation I, $A \overset{\vartheta}{\Longrightarrow} B$ denotes that the implication $A \Rightarrow B$ holds to degree at least ϑ.

The following theorem, introduced in [17], leads to an equivalent representation of implications with grades:

Theorem 1. *Let $A, B \in L^Y, \vartheta \in L$ and $\mathcal{I}$ be a fuzzy relation*

$$\vartheta \le ||A \Rightarrow B||_{\mathcal{I}} \text{ if and only if } ||A \Rightarrow \vartheta \otimes B||_{\mathcal{I}} = 1$$

This theorem allows us a reduction in the complexity of the original language, so that implications with grades will be reduced to equivalent implications where the grades are translated to the right-hand side of the dependency using the t-norm. We use $\vartheta \otimes B$ to denote so-called ϑ-multiple of B which is a fuzzy set such that $(\vartheta \otimes B)(y) = \vartheta \otimes B(y)$ for all $y \in Y$. Thus, for instance $\{y_1,^{0.8}/y_2\} \overset{0.9}{\Rightarrow} \{^{0.6}/y_3\}$ is equivalent to $\{y_1,^{0.8}/y_2\} \Rightarrow \{^{0.9 \otimes 0.6}/y_3\}$. The above result eases the management of implications.

Now, we introduce FASL axiomatization, which was proven to be complete in [16]. The axiomatization forms a theoretical base for the automated prover and it provides the following benefit over the Armstrong-like [12] axiomatizations from [17,26]: the rules can always be applied to all formulas, meaning there is no restriction on the form of the formulas that appear in the input part of the inference rules. This property makes the rules suitable for sequential execution by an automated prover.

3.2 FASL Axiomatic System

In [26], the authors presented an axiomatic system for reasoning with formulas (1) that is syntactico-semantically complete w.r.t. the two kinds of semantics described in the previous section. The system consists of three deduction rules,

$$[\text{Ax}] \ \vdash AB \Rightarrow A \qquad\qquad\qquad\qquad\qquad\qquad\qquad (\text{Axiom})$$
$$[\text{Cut}] \ A \Rightarrow B, \ BC \Rightarrow D \vdash AC \Rightarrow D \qquad\qquad\qquad (\text{Cut})$$
$$[\text{Mul}] \ A \Rightarrow B \vdash c^*{\otimes}A \Rightarrow c^*{\otimes}B \qquad\qquad (\text{Multiplication})$$

where $A, B, C, D \in L^Y$ and $c \in L$. In [Ax] and [Cut], we use the convention of writing BC instead of $B \cup C$, etc., and in [Mul], we use $a{\otimes}B$ to denote so-called a-multiple of $B \in L^Y$ which is an **L**-set such that $(a{\otimes}B)(y) = a \otimes B(y)$ for all $y \in Y$ (i.e., the degrees to which $y \in Y$ belongs to B is multiplied by a constant degree $a \in L$).

If $\mathcal{R}$ is an axiomatic system (like that containing the rules [Ax], [Cut], and [Mul]), a formula $A \Rightarrow B$ is said to be provable from a theory T by using $\mathcal{R}$, denoted by $T \vdash_\mathcal{R} A \Rightarrow B$ in the usual way.

The results in [26] have shown among other things that $\mathcal{R}$ consisting of [Ax], [Cut], and [Mul] is complete in the following sense:

Theorem 2. *Let* **L** *and* Y *be finite. Then for every set* T *of formulas,* $T \vdash_\mathcal{R} A \Rightarrow B$ *if and only if* $T \models A \Rightarrow B$. $\qquad\qquad\qquad\qquad\square$

The rule [Cut] is powerful but it is not directly suitable for automated deduction. We now present a new syntactico-semantically complete axiomatic system which overcomes this drawback by replacing [Cut] by a new rule, called rule of simplification (denoted [Sim]). The new system consists of the following rules:

$$[\text{Ax}] \ \vdash AB \Rightarrow A$$
$$[\text{Sim}] \ A \Rightarrow B, \ C \Rightarrow D \vdash A(C - B) \Rightarrow D$$
$$[\text{Mul}] \ A \Rightarrow B \vdash c^*{\otimes}A \Rightarrow c^*{\otimes}B$$

where $A, B, C, D \in L^Y$ and $c \in L$. The new system is called FASL (Fuzzy Attribute Simplification Logic). The main motivation for introducing a new axiomatic system is to obtain a system that may be used for an efficient system of automated reasoning with formulas (1). Unlike [Cut], the new simplification rule [Sim] can be applied to any pair of formulas which makes it more suitable for automated provers. In [16], we prove completeness of FASL axiomatic system.

Recall that a deduction rule is called derivable in a given axiomatic system if the output formula of the rule is provable from the input formulas of the rule. The following assertion shows important derivable rules:

Lemma 1. *The following deduction rules are derivable in FASL: Let $A, B, C, D \in L^Y$. Then,*

[Dec] $\{A \Rightarrow BC\} \vdash A \Rightarrow B$;   (Decomposition)

[Com] $\{A \Rightarrow B, C \Rightarrow D\} \vdash AC \Rightarrow BD$.   (Composition)

Using [Dec] and [Com], we can obtain observations how certain formulas can be equivalently replaced by other formulas while retaining the semantic entailment. We call theories T_1 and T_2 equivalent, denoted by $T_1 \equiv T_2$, if the set of derivable formulas from both theories coincide. Using Lemma 1, we get the following observation.

Theorem 3. *Let $A, B, C, D \in L^Y$. The following equivalences can be obtained from* [Ax] + [Sim].

   (**DeEq**) *Decomposition Equivalence:* $\{A \Rightarrow B\} \equiv \{A \Rightarrow B - A\}$;

   (**UnEq**) *Union Equivalence:* $\{A \Rightarrow B, A \Rightarrow C\} \equiv \{A \Rightarrow BC\}$;

   (**SiEq**) *Simplification Equivalence: If $A \subseteq C$ then*
        $\{A \Rightarrow B, C \Rightarrow D\} \equiv \{A \Rightarrow B, A(C - B) \Rightarrow D - B\}$.

The previous equivalences, read from left to right, enable us to remove redundant information in the formulas. Namely, the sets on the right-hand sides can be seen as equivalent simplifications of the sets on the left-hand sides (simplified either in terms of the number of formulas as in case of (**UnEq**) or in terms of the number of elements in formulas (as in case of the other equivalences).

In the automated deduction method we will make use of three depurated generalized equivalence proved with the FASL axiomatic system. We start by remarking that for any crisp theory T, the fact $T \vdash A \Rightarrow B$ can equivalently be expressed by provability using formulas with empty antecedents derived from $A \Rightarrow B$, i.e., formulas of the form $\emptyset \Rightarrow C$ where $C \in L^Y$.

Theorem 4. *If T is a crisp theory, then for any $A \Rightarrow B$, we have $T \vdash A \Rightarrow B$ iff $T \cup \{\emptyset \Rightarrow A\} \vdash \emptyset \Rightarrow B$.*   □

We can extend Theorem 4 from crisp theories to arbitrary theories (**L**-sets of formulas) (see [16] for technical details). This result allows us to introduce the following three equivalences which constitute the core of the simplification procedure described below.

Theorem 5. *The following equivalence can be obtained from FASL rules:*

   (**gSiEq**) *Generalized Simplification Equivalence:*
        $\{\emptyset \Rightarrow A, U \Rightarrow V\} \equiv \{\emptyset \Rightarrow A', U - A' \Rightarrow V - A'\}$,
   (**gSiUnEq**) *If $U - A' = \varnothing$ then* $\{\emptyset \Rightarrow A, U \Rightarrow V\} \equiv \{\emptyset \Rightarrow A'V\}$;
   (**gSiAxEq**) *if $V - A' = \varnothing$ then* $\{\emptyset \Rightarrow A, U \Rightarrow V\} \equiv \{\emptyset \Rightarrow A'\}$,

where $A, U, V \in L^Y$ and $A' = A \cup (S(U, A)^* \otimes V)$.   □

These three generalized equivalences may be applied to simplify an input set of formulas: we exhaustively use each implication to simplify (by using **gSiEq**, **gSiUnEq** or **gSiAxEq**) the others implications in the set with a quadratic cost (see Example 4).

4   Application of FASL to a Context Recommender System

Up to now, we have presented all the theoretical foundations that we combine to incorporate the context into a recommender system. Our proposal is based on fuzzy attribute implications. Fuzzy Logic and fuzzy multivalued FCA have been shown to be sound formalisms to specify and reasoning with uncertainty.

We propose a unified combination of context-based reasoning inside a content-based recommendation framework. In our approach, the recommendation model follows the next steps:

Each object that can be recommended, will be associated and defined by their characteristics.

a. Definition of a set of implications from contextual attributes: tourism experts design different rules called context segment, where each of them has associated a set of fuzzy implications defined on the items characteristics.
b. Identification of the user context: in this phase the system should extract user information about different contextual attributes. Some of these attributes may be obtained explicitly, such as the company, and other attributes may be obtained implicitly, such as the weather. Based on the contextual attributes that the user presents, the system retrieves different fuzzy implications for the corresponding context segments.
c. Context simplification: our reasoning methods depurate the set of all associated implications with grades to get an equivalent and simpler set of implications.
d. Validation process (Contextual pre-filtering phase): The final set of implications is used to validate the items to be recommended. for each point of interest that can be recommended, the system performs a process to determine if the POI does not meet any of the implications. If a POI is not valid in an implication, it is removed and cannot participate in the next phase. Thus, the original set of items is pre-filtered and only a subset of them will be the input of the recommender system.

Now, we detail how context information is represented by means of fuzzy implications. POIs are represented by a set of attributes which describes its features (it is cheap or expensive, its atmosphere is romantic or cheerful, etc.). Real world data are often complex and difficult to be labelled with a binary domain without loss of information. For instance a restaurant may have a very beautiful garden with some tables where children may enjoy and also an intimate hall with quiet music for a romantic dinner. We propose to store these items features by using a fuzzy relation, as Example 1 shows. Thus, each row corresponds with an object and each column with an attribute.

Example 1. We consider a group of POIs of a tourism destination with some attributes to describe them (Design, Atmosphere, Price and Facilities). Each attribute has a set of finite possible values and let us suppose that a destination

Table 1. FCA representation of POIs.

		Standard Restaur.	Michelin Star	Burger	Tapas Bar	Pizzeria	Beach Fresh Fish
Design	Open space	0.3	0.1	0.3	0.3	0.1	0.9
	Closed space	0.8	0.8	0.8	0.8	0.9	0.2
Atmosphere	Quiet	0.8	0.9	0.3	0.2	0.3	0.3
	Lively	0.5	0.2	0.8	0.8	0.8	0.8
	Picturesque	0.2	0.1	0.1	0.9	0.7	0.8
Price	Inexpensive	0.7	0	0.9	0.9	0.9	0.5
	Moderate	0.3	0.1	0.3	0.5	0.5	0.7
	Expensive	0.3	0.9	0.1	0.1	0.3	0.8
Facilities	Air Cond.	0.3	0.9	0.8	0.5	0.8	0.3
	Views	0.3	0.5	0.1	0.1	0.3	0.9
	Terrace	0.3	0.1	0.4	0.1	0.5	0.9

expert manages the system by giving a degree to each value in the domain. Thus, we get a table of objects with grades by flattening the information to obtain a fuzzy relation (see Table 1).

The context of the system is represented by a set of discrete domains $C = \{C_1, \ldots, C_n\}$. Each domain is associated with a dimension of the context (for instance weather, company, time of the day, etc.) and it has a finite set of values: $C_i = \{v_1^i, \ldots, v_n^i\}$. We define the user context, named *state*, as a n-tuple of pairs *(value of the domain, degree)*.

Example 2. Let Weather, Company and Time of the day be three context dimensions with the following domains: Weather = {hot, warn, cloudy, rainy}, Company = {alone, friends, couple, family, large group} and Time = {morning, afternoon, evening, night}. A user may specify his context by means of the state: [(hot, 0.8), (afternoon, 0.8), (family, 0.7)].

We define a context segment to be an specific value of a domain and its associated degree. We provide a framework where each context segment is associated with a set of fuzzy implications. As we presented in Sect. 3, implications may be labelled with a degree to express the truthfulness of the implication itself. Thus, the degree of the context segment is inherited by all its implications.

Example 3. The implications associated with each context segment are introduced as follows (observe that the degree of the context is transferred to the implication):

- Context segment: Hot/$_{0.8}$. Implications:

  Expensive/$_{0.8}$, ClosedSpace/$_{0.8}$ $\overset{0.8}{\Rightarrow}$ Air Cond./$_{0.8}$, Views/$_{0.9}$, Picturesque/$_{0.2}$

  OpenSpace/$_{0.8}$ $\overset{0.8}{\Rightarrow}$ Inexpensive/$_{0.7}$

- Context segment: Afternoon/$_{0.8}$. Implications:

  OpenSpace/$_{0.8}$ $\overset{0.8}{\Rightarrow}$ Terrace/$_{0.6}$, Inexpensive/$_{0.9}$
- Context segment: Family/$_{0.7}$. Implications:

  $\emptyset \overset{0.7}{\Rightarrow}$ Inexpensive/$_{0.6}$

  ClosedSpace/$_{0.8}$ $\overset{0.7}{\Rightarrow}$ Air Cond./$_{0.9}$

As we introduce in previous Subsect. 3.1 (see page 8), the graded implication $\emptyset \overset{0.7}{\Rightarrow}$ Inexpensive/$_{0.6}$ in the last context segment indicates that if the user is accompanied by his family with degree 0.7 then the restaurant need to be inexpensive with a degree greater than 0.6.

When a system manages a certain amount of information, we have to provide an automatic way to analyze and extract the important information to reduce the computation cost. In our approach we propose to use the automatic methods developed over FASL to depurate the specification of the context and obtain a canonical set of implications. There is a lot of works related with the search of basis in FCA. An up to date and complete work is [27] where the authors identify a set of properties that may be cover by different basis definitions (minimal, direct, canonical, etc.). These characteristics may be combined providing a different notion of basis. The work of Bertet and Monjardet is focussed on crisp FCA and it is still an open problem the definition of suitable definitions for fuzzy implications basis for fuzzy FCA.

Nevertheless, as Example 4 shows, it is possible to illustrate the benefits of using FASL to get an equivalent and simpler set of implications.

Example 4. From the specification of the above example, if we have that the context provided by the user is {Hot/$_{0.8}$, Afternoon/$_{0.8}$, Family/$_{0.7}$} then the set of implication is built by adding all the above implication in a unified set:

  {Expensive/$_{0.8}$, ClosedSpace/$_{0.8}$ $\overset{0.8}{\Rightarrow}$ Air Cond./$_{0.8}$, Views/$_{0.9}$, Picturesque/$_{0.2}$;

  OpenSpace/$_{0.8}$ $\overset{0.8}{\Rightarrow}$ Inexpensive/$_{0.7}$;

  OpenSpace/$_{0.8}$ $\overset{0.8}{\Rightarrow}$ Terrace/$_{0.6}$, Inexpensive/$_{0.9}$;

  $\emptyset \overset{0.7}{\Rightarrow}$ Inexpensive/$_{0.6}$;

  ClosedSpace/$_{0.8}$ $\overset{0.7}{\Rightarrow}$ Air Cond./$_{0.9}$}

Using the equivalences of FASL presented in Theorem 5 we remove redundant information and we obtain the following equivalent and simpler set of implications:
{expensive/$_{0.8}$, ClosedSpace/$_{0.8}$ $\overset{0.8}{\Rightarrow}$ Views/$_{0.9}$, Picturesque/$_{0.2}$;

  OpenSpace/$_{0.8}$ $\overset{0.8}{\Rightarrow}$ Terrace/$_{0.6}$; $\emptyset \overset{0.7}{\Rightarrow}$ Inexpensive/$_{0.6}$;

  ClosedSpace/$_{0.8}$ $\overset{0.7}{\Rightarrow}$ Air Cond./$_{0.9}$}

It should be noted that the redundancy removal algorithm has a quadratic complexity with respect to the number of implications. This number is much lower than the number of POIs (usually several thousands) in any touristic destination. Finally, our system make use of the information associated with the user context, provided by the unified and depurated set of implications, to stretch the set of POIs to be recommended to the user. For each POI in the FCA table, we validate the set of implications, removing all the POIS that does not satisfied them. The complexity of this last step is $O(n)$ where n is the number of POIs. This way, we have designed a linear contextual pre-filtering process.

Example 5. As in Example 4, if the user context is the afternoon of a hot day, traveling with his family, our contextual pre-filtering process reduces the list of restaurants of Table 1 to Burger and Pizzeria, since:

- Michelin star does not satisfy Expensive/$_{0.8}$, ClosedSpace/$_{0.8}$ $\overset{0.8}{\Rightarrow}$ Views/$_{0.9}$, Picturesque/$_{0.2}$
- Beach Fresh Fish does not satisfy $\emptyset \overset{0.7}{\Rightarrow}$ Inexpensive/$_{0.6}$
- Standard restaurant and Tapas bar do not satisfy ClosedSpace/$_{0.8}$ $\overset{0.7}{\Rightarrow}$ Air Cond./$_{0.9}$

This way, the set of POIs to be managed by the content-based recommender is significatively reduced.

5   Conclusions and Future Works

Content-based recommender systems may be significatively improved by including contextual information. To achieve this goal, we use fuzzy logic and formal concept analysis as a solid framework to combine context information and content-based recommenders. More specifically, we use Simplification Logic to develop an intelligent and linear pre-filtering process. This process generates a set of implications which captures the context information and that it is used to validate the items to be recommended. The method is applied in two steps: in the first one we translate the context information provided by a user as an *state*, i.e. a simplified set of fuzzy implications, and in the second step, the implications are used to filter the items which fulfills them.

This work may be extended by considering two future works related with the two steps of the pre-filtering process. First, the implications induced by the context may be enriched with implications automatically extracted from the user interests stored in the content. We propose to use formal concept analysis to extract this information. As a second trend, we propose to substitute the recommender algorithms by formal concept analysis techniques.

References

1. Lymberopoulos, D., Zhao, P., König, A.C., Berberich, K., Liu, J.: Location-aware click prediction in mobile local search. In: CIKM, pp. 413–422 (2011)
2. Leiva, J.L., Guevara, A., Rossi, C.: Sistemas de recomendación para realidad aumentada en un sistema integral de gestión de destinos. Revista de Análisis Turístico **14**, 69–81 (2012)

3. Bezerra, B.L.D., de Carvalho, F.A.T.: A symbolic approach for content-based information filtering. Inf. Process. Lett. **92**(1), 45–52 (2004)
4. Adomavicius, G., Tuzhilin, A., Berkovsky, S., Luca, E.W.D., Said, A.: Context-awareness in recommender systems: research workshop and movie recommendation challenge. In: RecSys, pp. 385–386 (2010)
5. Bazire, M., Brézillon, P.: Understanding context before using it. In: Dey, A.K., Kokinov, B., Leake, D.B., Turner, R. (eds.) CONTEXT 2005. LNCS (LNAI), vol. 3554, pp. 29–40. Springer, Heidelberg (2005)
6. Adomavicius, G., Tuzhilin, A.: Context-aware recommender systems. In: Ricci, F., Rokach, L., Shapira, B., Kantor, P.B. (eds.) Recommender Systems Handbook, pp. 217–253. Springer, New York (2011)
7. Dey, A., Abowd, G.D., Salber, D.: A conceptual framework and a toolkit for supporting the rapid prototyping of context-aware applications. Hum.-Comput. Interact. **16**(2), 97–166 (2001)
8. Zenebe, A., Norcio, A.F.: Representation, similarity measures and aggregation methods using fuzzy sets for content-based recommender systems. Fuzzy Sets Syst. **160**, 76–94 (2009)
9. Adomavicius, G., Tuzhilin, A.: Towards the next generation of recommender systems: a survey of the state of the art and possible extensions. IEEE Trans. Knowl. Data Eng. Arch. **17**(6), 734–749 (2005)
10. Wille, R.: Restructuring lattice theory: an approach based on hierarchies of concepts. In: Rival, I. (ed.) Ordered Sets, pp. 445–470. Reidel, Dordrecht (1982)
11. Ganter, B., Wille, R.: Formal Concept Analysis. Mathematical Foundations. Springer, New York (1999)
12. Armstrong, W.W.: Dependency structures of data base relationships. In: IFIP Congress, pp. 580–583 (1974)
13. du Boucher-Ryan, P., Bridge, D.: Collaborative recommending using formal concept analysis. Knowl.-Based Syst. **19**, 309–315 (2006)
14. Li, X., Murata, T.: A knowledge-based recommendation model utilizing formal concept analysis and association. In: 2nd International Conference on Computer and Automation Engineering (ICCAE), vol. 4, pp. 221–226 (2010)
15. Belohlavek, R.: Fuzzy Galois connections. Math. Logic Q. **45**(4), 497–504 (1999)
16. Belohlavek, R., Cordero, P., Enciso, M., Mora, A., Vychodil, V.: An efficient reasoning method for dependencies over similarity and ordinal data. In: Torra, V., Narukawa, Y., López, B., Villaret, M. (eds.) MDAI 2012. LNCS, vol. 7647, pp. 408–419. Springer, Heidelberg (2012)
17. Bělohlávek, R., Vychodil, V.: Attribute implications in a fuzzy setting. In: Missaoui, R., Schmidt, J. (eds.) ICFCA 2006. LNCS (LNAI), vol. 3874, pp. 45–60. Springer, Heidelberg (2006)
18. Goguen, J.A.: The logic of inexact concepts. Synthese **19**(3–4), 325–373 (1969)
19. Gottwald, S.: A Treatise on Many-Valued Logics. Studies in Logic and Computation, vol. 9. Research Studies Press, Baldock (2000)
20. Gottwald, S.: Mathematical fuzzy logics. Bull. Symbolic Logic **14**(2), 210–244 (2008)
21. Hájek, P.: Metamathematics of Fuzzy Logic. Kluwer Academic Publishers, Dordrecht (1998)
22. Grabisch, M., Marichal, J.L., Mesiar, R., Pap, E.: Aggregation Functions. Cambridge University Press, Cambridge (2009)
23. Fagin, R.: Combining fuzzy information: an overview. SIGMOD Rec. **31**(2), 109–118 (2002)

24. Hájek, P.: On very true. Fuzzy Sets Syst. **124**(3), 329–333 (2001)
25. Raju, K.V.S.V.N., Majumdar, A.K.: Fuzzy functional dependencies and lossless join decomposition of fuzzy relational database systems. ACM Trans. Database Syst. (TODS) **13**, 129–166 (1988)
26. Belohlavek, R., Vychodil, V.: Axiomatizations of fuzzy attribute logic. In: IICAI'05, pp. 2178–2193 (2005)
27. Bertet, K., Monjardet, B.: The multiple facets of the canonical direct unit implicational basis. Theor. Comput. Sci. **411**(22–24), 2155–2166 (2010)

Task Oriented Context Models
for Social Life Networks

Maneesh Mathai[✉] and Athula Ginige

School of Computing, Engineering and Mathematics, University of Western Sydney,
Locked Bag 1797, Penrith, NSW 2751, Australia
{m.mathai,a.ginige}@uws.edu.au
http://www.sln4mop.org/

Abstract. Better decisions can be made in the profession of the users
if they can easily access and filter out the relevant information from all
available information sources. The mass availability of the mobile devices
has enabled the users to quickly access timely information from any location. We have developed a novel approach to provide timely information
in context by capturing contextual information. We developed a model to
identify the context of the user by identifying the task being performed.
The system through the domain experts, is aware of the information
need and the information source for each task of the user and the relevant information is filtered from the information source, by using the
users context. The context model was designed and tested for the farming
domain, to support the livelihood activities of the farmer, by extending
the concepts of social life networks.

Keywords: Context modelling · Content aggregation · Social life
networks · Mobile based information system

1 Introduction

In Sri Lanka over production of vegetables is a regular problem due to many
farmers growing the same crop without being aware of what others are cultivat-
ing [1,2]. Neither the farmers nor government agencies are able to make necessary
adjustments for lack of timely information on what farmers plan to cultivate, or
have cultivated. Reference [3] have shown that farmers can make an informed
decision on what crop to grow if they have access to a mobile phone based
information system to inquire what others in that region are growing. The information system can provide this information only if most farmers use this system
and indicate what crop they plan to grow. Aggregating the information provided
by the farmers the information system can also inform the government agencies
monitoring and managing agriculture sector, fertilizer and pesticide suppliers
and potential buyers what has already been grown for better management of
the overall crop production.

Mobile phone usage in the world has grown rapidly including among people
in developing countries. At present, 90 % of the world population is covered by

© Springer-Verlag Berlin Heidelberg 2014
J. Cordeiro and M. van Sinderen (Eds.): ICSOFT 2013, CCIS 457, pp. 306–321, 2014.
DOI: 10.1007/978-3-662-44920-2_19

a mobile signal, 128 % of the world population has a mobile subscription and in developing countries the subscription rate is 89 % [4]. Further, smartphone prices are rapidly decreasing and now are comparable to a cost of a basic mobile phone few years ago. A smartphone can be considered as a sensor in the hands of a human capable of capturing user input as text, voice or gestures and other environmental parameters using build in sensors such as GPS, camera etc. It is also capable of communicating with the user using range of media types; text, images, video, and audio. A smartphone is now easily accessible to farmers in Sri-Lanka.

An International Collaborative research project [5] was started to develop a Social Life Network (SLN); a mobile based information system to support livelihood activities of people in developing countries. Social Life Networks (SLN) [6] tries to extend the capabilities of current social networks by combining them with the technological advances now found in smartphones that include myriad of sensors. In order to get a deeper insight into research challenges and to investigate possible solutions a specific real world problem was selected. The first SLN was developed for farmers in Sri-Lanka to address the over production problem mentioned above. A high-level knowledge framework proposed by [7] is implemented which enables the farmers to make an informed decision, the solution is based on Social Life Network concept where farmers using a Mobile Based Information System (MBIS) will report the extent of their crop cultivation. This information is then aggregated based on location, time and crop type to derive current production levels for different crops in real time. The aggregated information is made available to farmers who are about to decide what crop to grow. The underlying expectation is that this will enable them to make an informed decision resulting in minimizing the over production situations that are experienced by farmers at present. In the due course of the project, it was also identified that farmers need additional static and dynamic information to make informed decisions [3].

2   Background

2.1   Components for SLN

Social Life Networks (SLN) tries to extend the capabilities of current social networks by combining them with the technological advances now found in Smartphones that include myriad of sensors. Reference [6] proposed that there are a few basic components for realizing the vision of social life networks. Data coming from multiple users and heterogeneous devices needs to be wrapped into a common format and made accessible to the system. Logically the data needs to be translated from localized sensor/human input to higher level situational abstractions. There is also an encompassing issue of user engagement. Both intrinsic and extrinsic factors matter, but enhanced feedback and user motivation are key aspects of it. The biggest catalyst for the adoption of the traditional Web was the presence of search engines which routed users to their desired resources (static web pages). A situation analysis performs a similar role in the dynamic social life networks i.e. routing the users to the appropriate resources based on situation detected. In this paper we propose that to carry out the situation analysis, it is vital to identify the context and using the contextual information will result in a more personalized set of results for the user.

2.2   Context

During the past two decades, researchers have developed techniques that enable systems to adapt to their users in many different ways [8]. One of the major research directions for human computer interaction (HCI) and Information Retrieval (IR) has been exploring the novel forms of interaction that can be achieved by integrating computer technology with the everyday physical world in which we live and work. Ubiquitous or pervasive computing represents a powerful shift in computation, where people live, work and play in a seamless computer-enabled environment and people are surrounded by computing devices and a computing infrastructure that supports us in everything we do [9]. Ability to accurately represent user context is very important to make optimum use of these smart environments. For this we need to model the context by acquiring the physical data to provide meaningful abstractions with respect to the application domain and the needs of the users interacting with the application. A qualified definition of context is given by [10]. In this work the term context is defined as follows: *Context as any information that can be used to characterize the situation of an entity. An entity is a person, place, or object that is considered relevant to the interaction between a user and an application, including the user and applications themselves.*

In this paper, we describe the design of the task oriented context models that provide context-specific information and knowledge to farmers. It further discusses the design and implementation of the first version of a mobile application for farmers. The remainder of the paper is organized as follows. Section 4 describes the high level architecture. Section 5 presents the first version of the mobile application. Finally, Sect. 6 concludes the paper.

3   Task Oriented Context Model

Activity is a set of tasks performed by a user. A sequence of activity is performed within any domain to accomplish a goal. The tasks and activities are driven by the final goal or objectives of the user and for each of these tasks to be completed the appropriate information needs to be acquired by the user. To provide relevant information to a user we need to determine the context of the user. In task oriented context, the contextual information is used to determine the context of the user performing a task; the context models that helps to identify the context of the user has been proposed in this section and the different knowledge which shapes the context is identified. This sections also contains scenarios from the farming domain that is used to explain how the task oriented context model uses the contextual information of the farmer to provide the relevant information.

3.1   Need for Context Analysis in Farming Domain

Many researchers have identified lack of information as a major reason preventing farmers from making better decisions [11, 12]. Researchers have highlighted the inefficacy of the existing information dissemination methods such as face to face communication with agriculture officers, websites and other communication methods such as use of mass media. Information needed by farmers include market prices, current production levels, seasonal weather, best cultivars and seeds, fertilizers and pesticides, information on pest and diseases and their control methods, harvesting and post harvesting methods, and details relating to farming machinery and practices.

Information must be relevant and meaningful to farmers, in addition to being packaged and delivered in a way preferred by them [13] cited in [14]. Context-specific information could have a greater impact on the adoption of technologies and increase farm productivity for marginal and small agricultural landholders [15] cited in [14]. Despite the additional cost and time associated with generating localized content, this content could be more relevant and useful in meeting farmers information needs [16] cited in [14]. Reference [14] discuss clearly the importance of contextualized information and knowledge for the farmers in India. They further explain how effective this knowledge can improve their productivity and income since this information is more relevant to their farm enterprises and better reflects needs of the farmers. They therefore recommend that the existence of context-specific and relevant information should be considered when developing approaches for farmers.

The information need of farmers varies mainly depending on the stage of the farming life cycle [3, 11, 17]. For example, in the selection phase of farming, the features of a crop (e.g. color, size, shape, flavor, and hardiness), farm condition, environmental conditions, available resources, and market demand are key determinants for a decision in this phase. In the post-harvesting stage of farming, the information required by the farmer includes post harvesting issues and management, packaging, grading, storing, standardization, transportation, and value added products [17].

Some of this information is available from government websites, leaflets, and mass media in several different formats; text, audio, video. Sometimes different terminologies to express the same concept have been used. This knowledge is not reaching the farmers due to the use of unstructured and different formats, lack of appropriate delivery methods and the general nature of the information. Using a task oriented context model can help in providing these knowledge to farmers.

3.2   External or Domain Knowledge

External or domain knowledge is the sum total knowledge about the domain, it is the collective knowledge, and it includes both the tacit and explicit knowledge. Most of the knowledge of a domain is captured in the written form.

The knowledge about a domain can be organized in many ways. The organization would be influenced by the higher level of concepts in the domain. For example, knowledge can be structured using ontology, explicit formal specifications of the terms in the domain and relations among them [18]. The ontology can be created by capturing the explicit information from written sources such as books, journals and research papers and the tacit knowledge can be captured by interacting with experts in the field. Thus, ontology is a process to organize the external knowledge, based on the important concepts of the domain. Better organization of knowledge in domain allows more flexibility in accessing information. Information can be obtained at macro level, or as a large list or as small bit of information depending on the level of organization of the information in the domain knowledge source.

Identifying Higher Level Concept in Farming Domain. Deeper information need analysis revealed that the farmers need two types of information; dynamic information such as current extent of crop cultivation, market prices etc. and more stable static information such as crop types, cultivars, suitable pesticides, fertilizer, previous market prices etc. [3, 17]. The dynamic information can be obtained in structured manner in the form of web services and the static information can be expressed using ontology. Reference [19] created a knowledge repository of agricultural information to respond to user queries taking into account the context in which the information is needed and because of the complex nature of the relationships among various concepts, an ontological approach was selected that supports first order logic to create the knowledge repository. The agriculture domain knowledge obtained from [17], suggests that farm environment, types of farmers, farmers preferences and farming stages are the important factors that needs to be considered for structuring static information. This structuring of the knowledge is required for easy filtering of relevant information, as it helps us to identify the higher level concepts on which the farming domain is structured.

3.3 Task Knowledge

The structured knowledge does not have any relation to the task being performed, but deals with how the information is partitioned in a domain. The task knowledge contains all the activities that the user needs to perform to accomplish his goals. For each activity a number of tasks need to be accomplished. To perform a specific task, we take a subset of knowledge from the domain knowledge which matches the information requirement of the task being performed. The collection of all the activities along with the information requirement of each task of the activity is known as the task knowledge. Task knowledge can be captured by looking at the decision made by users, the information required to make this decision and the tasks that they perform [20].

Identifying Task knowledge in Farming Domain. The activities, task and decision points in farming domain can be identified by analyzing the decisions made by the farmers at various stages of farming. By analyzing, the information need analysis and information flow model for farmers based on the work of other researchers working in the farming domain, helps us to identify the task knowledge for the farming domain.

Information Need Analysis of Farmers. In a study done by interviewing farmers in four countries; Bangladesh, India, Sri Lanka and Thailand; [11] have identified 26 different types of information needs across 6 stages of farming as shown in Fig. 1. This report sheds light on the information and knowledge needs in low-income smallholder farms and agricultural micro-enterprises in Bangladesh, India, Sri Lanka and Thailand. The micro-enterprises in the study included traders, collectors and small retailers that sell agricultural produce. The report also explores the use of Information and Communication Technologies (ICTs) and especially mobile phones amongst these micro-enterprises.

Information Flow Model for Farmers. Reference [3] has identified that farmers in Sri-Lanka need specific information rather than generic information. For instance, farmers need agricultural information relevant to their situation such as the location of their farmland, their economic condition, their interest and belief, need and available equipments etc. [3] carried out a causal analysis to determine the factors that influence farmers decision making at various stages of the farming life-cycle and in that process they identified what specific information is required in each stage. The causal analysis was carried out through a series of surveys. In this process, they also looked at the various information sources currently available for farmers following which [3] determined how the information needs to flow to the farmers. Reference [3] identified crop choosing, growing and selling stages as the key phases that create a direct impact on the farmer revenue. In view of farming domain, revenue is determined by the selling price of the harvest. There are three main price determinants for a specific crop yield. Yield quality, supply and demand. These factors create a huge impact on price fluctuations at the market level, where market is the place where both buyers (demanders) and sellers (suppliers) come together to cater for each others needs.

The flow model [3] identified that the yield quality is determined by weather, pest, diseases, fertilizer, usage of new farming mechanisms and seed quality. Thus, by knowing these factors beforehand would also help the farmer to maintain the quality of the yield. For example, having prior knowledge with regard to seed quality would help farmers to maintain the expected quality of yield at the market level. It thus creates a competitive market in deciding the price of a particular crop. The analysis work done by [3] highlighted many important issues. The selection of what crop to grow depends on many factors, not only on the current production levels as it appeared on the surface. Farmers are looking at range of factors including issues related to growing the crop as well as selling the crop. They wanted information to support all stages of the farming life-cycle. To make meaningful use of the information, [3] postulated that the information should be made available to farmers in context and one of the important aspect of that is the stage in the farming cycle.

	Information Needs of farmers by stages	
	Current market prices for a specific crop(s) in the specific market that I sell at	Deciding
	Current market prices for a specific crop(s) in market(s) other than what I sell at	
	Expected future market prices for a specific crop(s) around the time when your crops will be ready for harvesting	
	Information on finance (formal and informal sources, the cost involved etc)	
	Information on govt. schemes (including subsidies and minimum support prices) and policies on agriculture (current as well as changes)	
	Information on higher yield crops	Seeding
	Information on best farming practices including how to grow a particular crop	
	Information on crop diseases and how to solve them	
	Information on input availability and associated costs	
	Information on labour availability and associated costs	
	Information on land availability and associated costs	Preparing and planting
	Information on farming machinery/equipment and associated costs	
	Information on electricity timings	
	Information on water availability	
	Information on weather	
	Input supply (who is selling, what they are selling, where and costs	Growing
	Variety and type of seeds as well on pros and cons of different seeds and varieties	
	Finance (formal and informal sources, the cost involved) to purchase seeds	
	Best farming practices including how to prepare seeds	
	Finance (formal and informal sources, the cost involved) to help with preparing land	
	Information on fertilizers (types, sources and costs)	Harvesting, packing and storing
	Information on pesticides/herbicides (types, sources and costs)	
	Information on transportation (types, sources and costs)	
	Information on packing materials (types, sources and costs)	
	Information on warehouses and/or cold storage (source and cost)	Selling
	Information on buyers/collectors/traders	

Fig. 1. Information needs of farmers.

Thus, it can be seen from the work of [3,11] that the tasks and information need of the tasks, i.e. the task knowledge is highly influenced by the different stages of farming. By modeling the task knowledge based on the farming stages helps us to better organize the flow of information to the farmer.

3.4   Procedural Knowledge

Now, from all the information required by the task knowledge, we require only a smaller subset of information to fulfill an individual task, and the knowledge required to filter out this information is known as the procedural knowledge. The procedural knowledge is responsible for identifying the source of information and the higher level concepts used to structure the information in that information source which is relevant to the current task being performed. The procedural knowledge includes the query that needs to be generated and the query parameters which are used to obtain the relevant information from the information source. The mapping required to convert the query parameters to match the higher level concepts of the information source also forms the part of the procedure knowledge.

3.5   Application Domain Knowledge

The application domain knowledge is the specific information that is relevant to the domain in which the application is being developed. This knowledge is captured in the form of a software requirements specification, which is a complete description of the behavior of the application and the interactions the user will have with the application. The application domain knowledge is independent of the task knowledge, but the application domain knowledge determines the attributes and relationships that need to be captured which is used by the procedural knowledge as query parameters to filter out information from different information source.

For example, in the farming domain, the application domain is independent of the farming practice, but relies on the way farming is being carried out. The location in which the task is being performed is one of the key factors that influence the filtering of the relevant information from the information source and the farming domain is a specific domain in which the user can have multiple locations, in the form of different farms, associated with them and the application domain knowledge helps us to capture this specific knowledge that is only applicable to the farming application.

3.6   Context Models

The physical context attributes are the raw environmental parameters which are captured in real time using sensors or pre-stored in the system. The physical context is designed based on the analysis obtained from the application domain knowledge. Thus, the application domain knowledge specifies the structure and attributes of physical context. Each user of the application will have different physical values according to their settings. The different parameters that need to be captured is obtained using the generic model of physical context [21].

The task context is the current activity that is being performed by the user. The task context would be one of the task that has been defined as part of the task knowledge. Every task would have its own domain based logical interpretation of the stored physical data. The system needs to map the physical context to higher level concepts of the domain knowledge to get relevant information based on task being performed.

The procedural context is generated by combining the task context with the physical context. The procedural knowledge is used to identify the attributes of the physical context that needs to be mapped into higher level concepts used in the domain knowledge. After the mapping, the higher level concepts is used as the parameters of the query to filter out relevant information from the information source. Thus, the different contextual knowledge is used to match the information organized in the domain context to the users context to filter out relevant information. An appropriate organization of knowledge in the domain is required to provide information to users based on task. The Fig. 2 captures the different context models that are used to retrieve the relevant data from the information source.

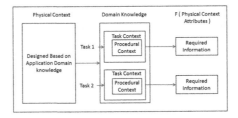

Fig. 2. Context model to retrieve required information.

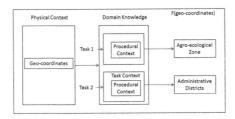

Fig. 3. Procedural context used to retrieve information from information.

Context Models in Farming Domain. The physical context of the farmer is identified by making the farmer select his farms through a series of interfaces where the map of Sri-lanka is used. The different farming stages associated with its corresponding tasks is displayed through the user interface. When a farmer selects one of these stages, a farmers task context is identified. The farm location as geo-cordinates is captured by the system and can be interpreted in many possible ways like agro-ecological zones or administrative districts based on the concepts in the domain (Fig. 3).

If the objective of the task knowledge is to determine the environmental attributes of the region then the procedural context can map the geo-coordinates into agro ecological zones otherwise if the objective of the task context is to obtain the market price of the region, then the procedural context can determine under which administrative district the given geo-coordinates belong and then query the appropriate information source to get the relevant data. Thus the task context is combined with the user's physical context to create the procedural context and then the procedural context is used to filter out the relevant subset of information from the domain knowledge.

Thus, it can be seen that the same physical context attribute can be mapped into different domain knowledge attribute according to the information requirements of each of the task being performed. So, one of the important capabilities of the context expanding application would be to facilitate this conversion of raw physical data to match the required higher level concepts in the domain knowledge. Different task context uses the procedural context to have space-time-user related information and activities represented different ways which would allow procedural context to identify and querying different information sources static or dynamic, based on the requirements.

4   Architecture of SLN Application

Social life network (SLN) application is a mobile based information system that aims to provide relevant information about the task being performed by the user,

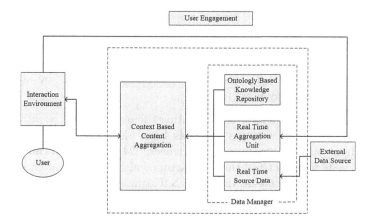

Fig. 4. Architecture of SLN application.

to help the user make better decision in their profession. The key features of an SLN application is that it needs to have an interaction environment suitable to the needs of the users, a context based module to provide relevant information from different sources, a data manager to manage the static and dynamic information and a user engagement module to motivate and encourage users to contribute. The Fig. 4 represents the modules in a SLN application.

Interaction Environment. For the SLN4Farmers application, the interaction environment was designed by [22], through the investigation of ways to develop a suitable user interface for a Social Life Network application. They used scenario based approach of [23] to develop the interface for farmers in Sri Lanka and created some typical personas and interaction scenarios based on earlier survey findings [22] and these scenarios were analysed to determine the user interfaces.

Context based Content Aggregation. An appropriate infrastructure for social life networks should support most of the tasks required to identify the context. The context based content aggregation module, the main contribution of this work for SLN, needs to focus on a scalable context management. It has the task knowledge, which defines the tasks to be performed and the information requirement for those tasks. The task context is captured when the application is running and it then uses the user's physical context and the procedural knowledge to filter out the relevant information. The users physical context is responsible for keeping the context state updated for each individual user of the application. The context characterizing properties that change with spatial and temporal attributes is captured by the users physical context model.

Data Manager. Data manager is responsible for reasoning and concept representation. Conceptually the data manager can be grouped into three, ontology based knowledge repository for static information, real time aggregation module for dynamically aggregated information and the real time source data available as web-services from external sources. Reference [17] has shown how ontology can be used to find a response to queries within a specified context in the domain of agriculture. This structured view is essential to facilitate knowledge sharing, knowledge aggregation, information retrieval, and question answering. The real time source data provides dynamic information such as market price or weather information from external source while the real time aggregation module is used to obtain dynamic knowledge about the prevailing conditions by aggregating micro-information sent by users.

User Engagement. The issue of motivating the users to engage with and contribute to the common resource pool has been identified as one of the most important issue and frequently cited bottlenecks [24,25] in social (life) networks [6]. Reference [6] has identified that the factors which can motivate users to contribute to social life networks. In the SLN4Farming application, the farmer is motivated to engage with the application. Once the farmer has made a decision on a particular crop, the farmer is given the option of entering his expected produce into the application. The information gathered from different farmers are aggregated by the real time aggregation module to give an indication of current production, where a colour coding scheme is used to visually represent the current production level of the crops. Specific colours (Green, Yellow, Red) were used to represent different thresholds and when it reaches a specific threshold farmers were warned of the danger (high-lighted using Red) of selecting the same crop as it may create an oversupply at the market level. The colors were chosen based on the work done by [22] on user interface. The farmers providing the information about the crop being grown meant that the system now understood which crop was grown by the farmer in his individual farms and thus this information helps the system to create a context about the farmer. Now when the farmer uses the application again, the system would be able to provide additional information required by the farmer for growing the selected crop. This acts as a motivation for farmers to provide the production information.

Flow of Information. The task and procedural knowledge is captured and used to design the Context Based Content Aggregation module. The task knowledge dictates the interface design of the interaction environment. The procedural knowledge identifies the information source for each task in the task knowledge. When a task is selected, the information is passed on from the interface environment to the Context Based Content Aggregation module through a web-service. The information required for the task is captured from the static or dynamic information source by the Context Based Content Aggregation module, which queries the relevant information source. The dynamic source might also include the output from real time aggregation module depending on the procedural knowledge. The data from the information source is passed on to the Context Based Content Aggregation module as web-services and this information is aggregated and then passed on as web-service to the interaction environment.

5   First Version Mobile Prototype

The architecture specified in Sect. 4 was implemented as a mobile application for Android phone connected to a back-end server through api. The initial version of the application based on the preliminary studies focused on the crop choosing stage of the farming life cycle. This initial prototype was evaluated with a sample of farmers to check the usefulness of provided information and usability of the application in order to support their day to day decision making process. The prototype included a basic login facility to identify the farmer and Fig. 5(a) shows the interface which allows the system to capture the context of the user. The farmers geo-coordinates is identified by associating the farmer with his farm and then identifying the farm in the Sri-Lanka map. A farmer can have the option of associating his profile with multiple farms, and information would be made available according to the selected farm. Figure 5(b) shows the interface where the 6 main stages of the farming life cycle is included and the capturing of the task context by identifying the farming stage in which the information is needed.

The prototype targeted mainly the crop choosing stage. Thus, only the crop planning functionalities were available in the initial version used for the

(a) Farm Selection   (b) Farming Stages   (c) Crop Selection

(d) Colour scheme   (e) Characteristics   (f) Production Quantity

Fig. 5. Screenshots of first version of the mobile prototype (color figure online).

evaluation. Crop planner function directed the user to the next screen, illustrated in Fig. 5(c). It included 3 main categories namely vegetables, fruits and other. These categories were identified based on the preliminary field trials carried out by [3]. Suitable vegetables and varieties were listed based on the region and the season.

A colour coding scheme was used to visually represent the current production level of a crop as shown in Fig. 5(d). Specific colours were used to represent different thresholds and when it reaches a specific threshold farmers were warned of the danger (highlighted using Red) of selecting the same crop as it may create an oversupply at the market level. Once the farmer selects a specific crop variety it shows the variety specific special characteristics such as yield colour, weight, length/size etc. Moreover, it also illustrates special statistics (refer Fig. 5(e)) such as current production and last year production to make farmers aware of the current as well as the last year situation. The system has the ability to capture new information from user as illustrated in Fig. 5(f), where the quantity of production of the farmer is captured. Another special feature included in this prototype is the comparison facility of two or more crops. In the future versions, the system will have the ability to capture new information such as crop disease, pesticide information, information on finance and soon. This new information can be aggregated and can be used by other users such as farmers, agriculture experts, micro bankers and suppliers of pesticides. Thus an interconnected network of information and users can be established.

6   Evaluation

The evaluation study activities were designed and done by the SLN research group members, with the objective of determining the effectiveness of context models in providing relevant information. The initial prototype along with a set of questionnaire were used in this evaluation study. The questionnaire included both multiple choice questions and open ended questions to encourage and capture wide range of answers based on the participant's knowledge. The participant were asked to perform the task of selecting a crop to grow. In order to measure their performance, the starting and the end time were recorded during each task. After performing the tasks questionnaire was given to get their feedback on the initial prototype. The questionnaire was used to assess the issues in relation to the information provided for the crop choosing stage of the farming life cycle and to identify new functionalities that are needed. The results of this evaluation has been published [26].

In total 63 % of the farmers agreed that the initial prototype has covered the basic information needs at the crop choosing stage. Rest expected more information related to crop variety and seeds. They also agreed that this information is essential knowledge during this stage of farming life cycle which they lack in current practices.

7   Conclusions

To understand the research challenges and to derive possible solutions to provide context based information in Social Life Networks, we have taken a concrete example in the form of an application for farmers that could meet the information needs within the farmers context. To represent information in context, we have developed an approach to model context. The context module interacts with a ontology [17] developed specifically to meet the needs of the farmer to obtain the static information and the dynamic information is obtained from external sources through web-services. The new information in the form of production level is captured by the context module through the mobile interface and aggregated to derive current production level for different crops in real time. This information is then made available to farmers who are about to decide what crop to grow through the mobile interface.

The solution described in this paper have been tested by creating a mobile application which has allowed us to prove that the solution is feasible and meets the information needs of farmers in Sri Lanka. The current application is a specific instance of the SLN project and we plan to create a generalized architecture that would be useful in creating many application for SLN.

References

1. Hettiarachchi, S.: Leeks cultivators desperate as price drops to record low. Sunday Times, Sri Lanka (2011)
2. Hettiarachchi, S.: N'eliya carrot farmers in the dumps: bumper harvest, but prices low. The Sunday Times Sri Lanka (2012)
3. De Silva, L.N., Goonetillake, J.S., Wikramanayake, G.N.: Towards using ICT to enhance flow of information to aid farmer sustainability in Sri Lanka. In: Proceedings of the 23rd Australasian Conference on Information Systems 2012, ACIS, pp. 1–10 (2012)
4. International Telecommunication Union: The world in 2013: Ict facts and figures (2013)
5. Ginige, A., Ginige, T., Richards, D.: Architecture for social life network to empower people at the middle of the pyramid. In: Kop, C. (ed.) UNISON 2012. LNBIP, vol. 137, pp. 108–119. Springer, Heidelberg (2013)
6. Jain, R., Sing, V., Gao, M.: Social life networks for middle of the pyramid. In: 2011 International Conference on Advances in ICT for Emerging Regions (ICTer), p. 1. IEEE (2011)
7. Ginige, T., Richards, D.: A model for enhancing empowerment in farmers using mobile based information system. In: ACIS 2012: Proceedings of the 23rd Australasian Conference on Information Systems 2012, ACIS, pp. 1–10 (2012)
8. Seher, I., Ginige, A., Shahrestani, S.: A personalized query expansion approach using context. In: 3rd IET International Conference on Intelligent Environments, IE 07, pp. 383–390. IET (2007)
9. Poslad, S.: Ubiquitous Computing: Smart Devices, Environments and Interactions. Wiley, Chichester (2011)
10. Dey, A.K.: Understanding and using context. Pers. Biquitous Comput. 5, 4–7 (2001)
11. Lokanathan, S., Kapugama, N.: Smallholders and micro-enterprises in agriculture: information needs and communication patterns. LIRNE asia, Colombo, Sri Lanka, pp. 1–48 (2012)
12. Punchihewa, D.J., Wimalaratne, P.: Towards an ICT enabled farming community. E-Governance in Practice, India, pp. 201–207 (2010)
13. Diekmann, F., Loibl, C., Batte, M.T.: The economics of agricultural information: factors affecting commercial farmers information strategies in ohio. Appl. Econ. Perspect. Policy 31, 853–872 (2009)
14. Babu, S.C., Glendenning, C.J., Okyere, K.A., Govindarajan, S.K.: Farmers' information needs and search behaviors: case study in Tamil Nadu, India. In: 2012 Conference International Association of Agricultural Economists, Foz do Iguacu, Brazil, 18–24 August 2012
15. Samaddar, A.: Traditional and posttraditional: a study of agricultural rituals in relation to technological complexity among rice producers in two zones of west bengal, india. Cult. Agric. 28, 108–121 (2006)

16. Cecchini, S., Scott, C.: Can information and communications technology applications contribute to poverty reduction? lessons from rural india. Inf. Technol. Dev. **10**, 73–84 (2003)
17. Walisadeera, A.I., Wikramanayake, G.N., Ginige, A.: An ontological approach to meet information needs of farmers in Sri Lanka. In: Murgante, B., Misra, S., Carlini, M., Torre, C.M., Nguyen, H.-Q., Taniar, D., Apduhan, B.O., Gervasi, O. (eds.) ICCSA 2013, Part I. LNCS, vol. 7971, pp. 228–240. Springer, Heidelberg (2013)
18. Gruber, T.R., et al.: A translation approach to portable ontology specifications. Knowl. Acquisition **5**, 199–220 (1993)
19. Walisadeera, A., Wikramanayake, G., Ginige, A.: Designing a farmer centred ontology for social life network. In: International Conference on Data Technologies and Applications. Springer (2013)
20. Johnson, P., Johnson, H., Waddington, R., Shouls, A.: Task-related knowledge structures: analysis, modelling and application. In: BCS HCI, pp. 35–62. Citeseer (1988)
21. Mathai, M., Ginige, A.: Context based content aggregation for social life networks. In: 8th International Joint Conference on Software Technologies, pp. 570–577 (2013)
22. Di Giovanni, P., Romano, M., Sebillo, M., Tortora, G., Vitiello, G., Ginige, T., De Silva, L., Goonethilaka, J., Wikramanayake, G., Ginige, A.: User centered scenario based approach for developing mobile interfaces for social life networks. In: 2012 First International Workshop on Usability and Accessibility Focused Requirements Engineering (UsARE), pp. 18–24. IEEE (2012)
23. Sears, A., Jacko, J.A.: The Human-computer Interaction Handbook: Fundamentals, Evolving Technologies and Emerging Applications. CRC Press, Boca Raton (2007)
24. Maia, M., Almeida, J., Almeida, V.: Identifying user behavior in online social networks. In: Proceedings of the 1st Workshop on Social Network Systems, pp. 1–6. ACM (2008)
25. Nov, O., Naaman, M., Ye, C.: Motivational, structural and tenure factors that impact online community photo sharing. In: ICWSM (2009)
26. De Silva, L.N.C., Goonetillake, J.S., Wikramanayake, G.N., Ginige, A.: Farmer response towards the initial agriculture information dissemination mobile prototype. In: Murgante, B., Misra, S., Carlini, M., Torre, C.M., Nguyen, H.-Q., Taniar, D., Apduhan, B.O., Gervasi, O. (eds.) ICCSA 2013, Part I. LNCS, vol. 7971, pp. 264–278. Springer, Heidelberg (2013)

Author Index